New Swan Shakespeare

GENERAL EDITOR

ADVANCED SERIES

Bernard Lott M.A. Ph.D.

Hamlet

WILLIAM SHAKESPEARE

Hamlet

Edited by Bernard Lott M.A., Ph.D.

Longman

Longman Group Ltd, London
Associated Companies, branches and representatives throughout the world.

This edition © Longman Group Ltd. (formerly Longmans Green
& Co Ltd.) 1968; 1970

First published 1968
New edition 1970
New impression 1971

ISBN 0 582 527422

Phototypeset by Oliver Burridge Filmsetting Ltd, Crawley, Sussex
Printed in Great Britain
by Butler and Tanner Ltd.

Contents

Acknowledgements We are grateful to the following for permission to reproduce copyright material:

Geoffrey Bles Ltd. for an extract from 'Hamlet: The Prince or the Poem' by C. S. Lewis from the collection *They Asked for a Paper*; Faber & Faber Ltd. and Harcourt, Brace & World Inc. for an extract from 'Hamlet and his Problems' from *Selected Essays*, (New Edition) by T. S. Eliot, copyright 1932, 1936, 1950 by Harcourt, Brace & World Inc., copyright 1960, 1964 by T. S. Eliot; The Hogarth Press Ltd. and Mrs. Katharine Jones for an extract from 'Hamlet & Oedipus' from *Essays in Applied Psycoanalysis* by Ernest Jones; Macmillan & Co. Ltd., Martin's Press Inc., and the Macmillan Company of Canada Ltd. for an extract from *Shakespearean Tragedy* by A. C. Bradley; and Methuen & Co. Ltd. for an extract from 'The Embassy of Death: an Essay on Hamlet' from *The Wheel of Fire* by Wilson Knight.

The illustrations are reproduced by courtesy of the following:
The Raymond Mander and Joe Mitchenson Theatre Collection pages xi a to e, and xiv: The Rank Organisation page xi: The Mansell Collection page xv: The National Museum, Copenhagen page xx: The Harry R. Beard Theatre Collection page xxii: The University Library, Utrecht page xxv.

GENERAL EDITOR'S Foreword

THE AIM of the edition of *Hamlet* in the *New Swan Shakespeare Advanced Series* is to ensure that the reader fully understands and appreciates the play itself. To this end it goes into exceptional detail in explanation of the actual wording of the text. A large number of points that other editions take for granted or touch upon inconclusively are here treated at length, and besides dealing with such matters as archaic language and allusions to bygone customs, the notes explain briefly certain rare words still current in English which happen to occur in the play (e.g. *bodkin*, *blazon*). Help is also given with complicated syntactical constructions and with patterns of imagery which may not be obvious at first sight. The content of the play, its historical, social, and philosophical bases, and the conventions implied in the way characters react to one another may be strange to many readers; these matters are treated in detail too. Nevertheless the bulk of the notes on the left-hand pages is not very great. There are two reasons why they are comparatively short and yet comprehensive. First, the explanations are simple in language. Many notes on Shakespeare are more complicated than the text they refer to, either because the editors feel more at home using long words and technicalities, or because they want to bring out very fine shades of meaning in the text. Second, much space has frequently been given in other editions to alternative readings of the text and to various conjectural explanations of difficult passages. It often seems that the more trivial the point in the play, the longer the note. This edition omits nearly all speculation of this kind. Where the meaning is doubtful, numerous alternative explanations are not given; instead, the editor has chosen the one which seems to fit the context most satisfactorily; if *one* possible alternative really serves to make the meaning clearer, this is added. Reference is made to variant readings of the original text (the Folios, the Quartos) only where a more helpful explanation of the passage will result. The text of this edition is taken from the New Variorum Edition of *Hamlet*, itself derived from a conflation of the Second Quarto (1604) and the First Folio (1623). For further discussion of the texts see pp. xlvi–xlvii.

Some background knowledge is essential to a full understanding of the play. Certain passages can be explained only in the light of some aspect or other of the 'world view' of Shakespeare's day, or by some piece of information about the region and period in which the action supposedly takes place. Some of these things will be unknown to many readers, especially those who are not very familiar with the British background to Shakespeare's plays. This information is given briefly so as to clarify the meaning of the passage in question, although there is no attempt at a far-reaching account of the whole subject. Readers who are completely familiar with the British background will occasionally be able to ignore notes of this type, but others may find them useful, since they will remove difficulties rooted not in the use of the language but in the general Shakespearian ethos.

At the back of the book there is an index which glosses and gives the location of all the difficult or unusual words in the text. By reference to the location in the text the student will find a note which will in most instances expand the brief equivalent given in the glossary. The index will also help him to trace passages in the play: if he remembers a key word likely to be treated in the index, he can look it up and find there a line reference to the text. In this way the glossarial index is also an index to the notes.

The only way to full enjoyment of the play is full understanding of what it means. All the help offered, in the form of notes, glosses, and introduction has only this end in view. No attempt has been made to give elaborate criticism of the play, but sources of good criticism are indicated in the bibliography. A study of these sources, however, can wait until the play is thoroughly known and appreciated for its own sake.

Part One of the Introduction which follows is a general essay on *Hamlet*. Part Two contains a series of articles which give more detailed information on certain subjects, as listed on page xl; these are not essential to an understanding of the play, but include matter which the student of the play may like to have in order to widen his knowledge. The section contains also some extracts from the great critics of *Hamlet*.

Introduction

PART ONE

The significance of Hamlet today

Hamlet must be the best known of all characters in the theatre of the world. Interest in him and in Shakespeare's play about him is as strong today as it ever was, books continue to be written about him, and interpretations of his character on the stage are unending in number and variety.

Like a few other great characters in world literature, Hamlet lives and is significant today primarily because his experience, as presented in the play, stirs the awareness of similar experiences in ourselves. This is not to say that any of us is ever likely to have to avenge his father's death or curse a loved one, nor does it imply that our own experiences are likely to be patterned in an orderly plot like the plot of the play. It does mean, however, that Hamlet, placed in his own peculiar predicament, is shown responding to it in ways which are totally familiar to our own deepest natures. It has been said that no one comes fresh to *Hamlet*. This is true in two senses: everyone who reads English knows his name and is likely to have some idea of what he did; also, Hamlet's deliberation and his passion are familiar, since placed in similar predicaments we ourselves deliberate and feel in similar ways.

Hamlet is so placed that urgent forces compel him in two directions at once. In the first part of the play he seeks and finds sufficient proof that his uncle murdered his father in order to become King himself. The Queen, his mother, has married his uncle. The experience is devastating, and his slow progress from some awareness of these wrongs to irrefutable proof of his uncle's guilt changes his whole view of life. He is thoughtful and human, and finds at first the greatest difficulty in accepting the new situation and understanding its implications. Testing the validity of the Ghost's evidence is deliberately prolonged so that with it can go an acclimatization to the new situation. Far from taking action, he allows his uncle to get back the initiative and banish him from the country. In the second part of the play he returns to Denmark, and, furious at the suicide of Ophelia, the woman he once loved, he takes the only action he can, killing the King and proclaiming the Norwegian prince successor to the throne of Denmark. But by this time he is himself dying, as his antagonist in the fatal duel is too, and the Queen is dead already.

With just the bare bones of the plot set out in this way, it is not easy to see

ix

why *Hamlet* has any significance for the modern reader. Heads of state are still assassinated occasionally, but not as a result of dynastic quarrels or with the same far-reaching consequences to the state. On the surface, then, it looks as if Hamlet's experience can have little bearing on life today and can retain only historical interest. Yet the perennial popularity of the play suggests strongly that this is not so and it may be enlightening to discover why.

The play continues to command interest because it is among the very few plays in the world in which character and plot are co-ordinated to almost everyone's satisfaction. A plot is an ordering of life, and a perfectly shaped plot has a perfect ordering of events: an original situation is changed by a measured sequence of events which in turn resolve, with no loose ends, in conclusions by which the new situation is achieved. The dramatist rides above the action, bringing system into the ordinary unpatterned going-on of life. *Hamlet* does this and more; to the achievement of the plot is added that of character development. Instead of being rigidly confined to a pattern of events, the characters develop in Shakespeare's hands, taking over the plot by themselves changing as it progresses. And since the play is about people, it is they who capture our interest. A poorer play would have fitted puppets into the various incidents, and shown them acting according to the dramatist's self-imposed demands when the plot was laid down. Character and plot are interwoven with a deftness and a mastery beyond all except the greatest of the world's plays.

But if this were the major part of what could be said in praise of *Hamlet*, there might be little justification for spending time studying it today. It does not pretend to be accurate history, since events are subordinated to the organic structure of the plot. In any case the setting is a time remote from our own. Despite all this, the play's appeal remains universal. The principal reason for this must be that the audience at any competent performance has a sense of living through a profound experience not restricted to the world of the characters and the plot. The exact nature of this experience and of the qualities in the play which produce it remains something of a mystery, yet the mystery is worth exploring if the exploration will lead to a deeper understanding of the play.

One factor must naturally be the generalizing tendency of all art, its way of taking us behind and beyond the present towards a universal set of values. *Hamlet* is not simply a play on generalized themes, e.g. about right and wrong. Prince Hamlet is placed in a situation where snap judgements as to the rightness or otherwise of a course of action cannot be made. It is true that the forces of life, as symbolized by the vigour of Claudius, are evil, and revenge leading to death seems to be the correct course to take, yet the onset of this wild justice is terrifyingly slow. There are other, more particularized forces at work.

a

Mr KEAN as HAMLET.

d

*Hamlet
as portrayed by*

a) *David Garrick
   1754.*

d) *Edmund Kean
   1814.*

b

e

b) *John Henderson
   1777.*

e) *Henry Irving
   1874.*

c

f

c) *John Phillip
   Kemble 1783.*

f) *Laurence Olivier
   1948.*

There is Hamlet's own nature. Noble of mind in an evil world, he alternates as any human being does between reason and emotion. His soliloquies are the fruits of reason; in them we find him relying on deliberation to settle for him the right course of action to follow. But they contain also impassioned outbursts, sometimes immediately recognizable as such, but at other times veiled by the 'antic disposition' he puts on.

Then there is the Ghost of old Hamlet. Even in death the late king wants a hand in the continued structuring of the future. Prince Hamlet finds himself driven by impulses emanating from his father's Ghost – or from whatever ancestral force it may represent – without the power to question the rationality of those impulses.

And then there is Fate, or whatever we must call the most powerful force of all. Like ourselves, Hamlet sees that men are not what they think they are; their potentialities are far from limitless. They can cope with what is around, with their physical environment, and the greatest of them can confront what is within, but time and accident frustrate both reason and emotion. As the Player King says:

> Our wills and fates do so contrary run
> That our devices still are overthrown.
>
> (III.ii.199, 200)

And Hamlet himself:

> If it be now, 'tis not to come; if it be not to come, it will be now; if it be not now, yet it will come. The readiness is all.
>
> (v.ii.203–5)

This conception of man pitted against a supreme power places *Hamlet* at a culmination of world drama. For the Greeks, tragedy portrayed bewildered man in relation to some supreme, unknowable power, a background before which his own littleness is emphasized. In a later development drama in this tragic mould became religious, the power being seen as a Godhead. Something of the significance of *Hamlet* today may spring from this, but development has moved further: Hamlet is not a mere pawn moved here and there by a supreme power. He is an agent of the divine authority, bringing justice and retribution, and as such he is a part of the supreme power; and at the same time, as victim, he is an opponent of that power. The puppet controlled by the whim of Fate has become the man at the centre of the conflict of predestination and free will, a contest as vitally interesting in our own day as in Shakespeare's. Hamlet is now on one side, now on the other. It has fallen upon him, he says, to be both 'scourge and minister,' i.e. he who commits the crime and must suffer for it and he who without guilty involvement brings punishment to others; charged with revenge, he brings vengeance on himself; he forgives Laertes, yet he kills him; he is Hyperion and the satyr in one, the god-man and the animal-man, and cannot achieve his purpose of punishment without becoming involved in the crime. A fairly simple pattern of events is thus overwhelmed by complications beyond human range, and the hero submits to Providence (or 'Heaven', as it is often called in the play),

> so that with [this dual role, Hamlet] also accepts, though he does not comprehend, himself and his own plot, so mysteriously composed of good and evil, in that universal design which 'shapes our ends'.*

The patterning of events which is the plot is itself an image of 'Heaven' shaping and ordering what close up appears chaotic and arbitrary, a surrender to the powers of darkness. Shakespeare's age was an age of violence; the world his audiences lived in had many of the features of a battlefield on which the forces of evil (insurrection, disease, for instance) were for ever set to disrupt the primeval order, the 'Heaven' or 'Providence'. Much in the physical world was misunderstood and remained unexplained; much learning so-called was nothing but folklore; much in men's actions (especially when they were prompted by passion) seemed unaccountable. Forces for good were thought of in the first place as ordering this bewildering situation, just as in some ways a strict routine for children spells safety and security for them.

The Elizabethans and Hamlet

We can now turn to a more detailed account of the historical settings of the play. Two earlier periods have to be considered, viz. the last years of the reign of Queen Elizabeth I (1558–1603), and the actual historical period to which the story of the play refers. The second of these is the less important, and will be touched on in connection with the sources of the play (p. xix). The first is important because it affords further significance to the play, this time with reference to the age which produced it. Shakespeare's audience did not demand that a play should present them with accurate history established by methods involving the critical study of documents and other sources. Such an attitude was hardly possible, since historical studies as we now know them were only beginning: such illusions as the calculated age of the world, 6,000 years or so, and the belief that British history was in ancient times the history of free men, were hardly questioned. The crude outline of history as seen by Shakespeare's contemporaries had its advantages, however: for instance, a simple, almost childlike view tended to remove complications and leave the lines of the story clear for the writer to work on. The dramatist was committed

....

*   Harold Jenkins, in *Shakespeare Survey*, 18, p. 45

to his story, not to the presentation with verisimilitude of some period in the remote past. The same applies to location; the play is about a Danish prince but the audience who first saw it were Londoners who probably knew little and cared less about Denmark and its people.

At that time, London was not the vast, sprawling mass it is today. Houses, shops and churches were almost entirely confined within the old defensive wall of the Roman city, and places such as Westminster were in the country. Within the old city, dwellings were densely packed, and the ordinary people lived there in close contact with one another. Life itself was precarious, not just because of infection from virulent diseases but because the various agents of government could be harsh and vindictive: arrest and death were only around the corner. The violent deaths in *Hamlet* were much more a reality of everyday life at that time than they are now. Again, although the Queen's reign had brought immense prestige for the country in the eyes of all, with pride at home and envy abroad, the various threats to her power were always present, and increased in intensity as she grew older. Her prerogative as absolute ruler of her realm was frequently challenged in the struggles for political power. The grievances occasioning or serving as pretext for one uprising or another were many and complex, but the Earl of Essex, who led the most famous of the rebellions, had a large following of common people who could hardly have pretended to a very percipient view of affairs, and represented a genuine threat to the Queen's person and her government. Like the others, his rebellion was crushed, but events of this sort supplanted for ever the buoyant displays of national solidarity and enthusiasm which began her reign and led Britain to victory against the threat of the Catholic empire of Spain.

This contrast between the political climate of the early part of Elizabeth's reign and that of its closing years is one of the many brought about by the transition which moved European culture from the medieval into the modern world. The play of *Hamlet* was born of such transitions, and many of the contrasts in the play can be discussed usefully in political terms. Medieval society in Britain was, at least in principle, feudal: feudal lords had rights over all ranks in society below them, down to the peasant class which had few or no rights of its own and little protection from oppression. These feudal lords guarded jealously what they conceived to be their rights, and constantly felt the need to assert them so as to avert encroachment by the sovereign or by those whose power sprang directly from him. Barons' wars and dynastic quarrels characterize the medieval history of western nations. One by-product of this way of life was a chivalric code perpetuated by oral traditions which laid down courses of action in war and love. Members of the chivalric orders were compelled to follow these courses of action. The code had to do with duty and honour, with the guarding of reputations and the proper conduct of

A view of London in the early 17th century showing St. Paul's Cathedral and the theatres on the South Bank (from an engraving by Visscher 1616).

warlike affairs. And some vague notion of a set of dictates on which a man's honour depends lasted in peoples' minds long after knightly combat with lances and swords was reduced to brawls, duels, and drunken squabbles between hot-blooded young men. In the churches up and down England one can see monuments commemorating Elizabethan gentlemen with stone effigies showing knights in armour, although in few cases would the man remembered have been in battle, least of all battle where that type of armour would have been of any use. What remained was a romantic idealization of lost chivalry. But all was not lost: honour, duty, the correct behaviour of the well-to-do in society – such ideas remained important, and had to be reconciled somehow with the tendency of the sovereign to take on central authority and responsibility for the affairs of the nation. We know that Queen Elizabeth I saw herself as the centre of responsibility, carrying willingly and with full realization the burdens of the state on her own shoulders. Duty, as conceived in the feudal code, demanded violent action by the individual in answer to any wrong he had suffered; the new world would look to a bureaucratic authority for redress. A Hamlet of the old world would have seen only material impediments to the goal of vengeance; not so a Hamlet of the new world.

The centralizing state was to achieve an almost moral significance (it is now 'wrong' to cheat the government of the income-tax which is its due), and because of this sharing of authority at the centre life has slowly become more humane, more considerate of the ordinary man. Of course there was no sudden, detectable change in men's thinking; only the pace of the change was accelerated. The Renaissance world, founded on a reverent study of the Greek and Roman classics, encouraged men to think of the sources of their actions in the light of philosophy and morality, and the new influences mark a watershed between the two worlds. Hamlet talks of conscience, which is a Renaissance concept, and one part of him is checked and balanced in the struggles of conscience. Now the impediments in the way of vengeance are conscientious objections; the concept of duty to avenge is blurred by morality. The sudden assumption of total authority in accordance with a code is inhibited by considerations of religion and ethics.

Such political and ethical abstractions were in the air, and men read and talked about them. But abstractions do not make popular drama. The history of ideas has to be animated with actualities before a play is born. *Hamlet* sprang fittingly from such a context. and its appeal struck home from the first performance. It dealt, in lively incidents and wise and beautiful language, with a current abstraction, and gave it a location and a special form of reality. No one imagines that the ordinary playgoer would recognize himself in this outline of opinion, since movements of thought remain largely unconscious, to be seen and atomized later as factors in history. But some such awareness there undoubtedly was.

To this mixture of increasing state responsibility and individual conscience Shakespeare has added another ingredient. It is as if he is asking, 'What if the power of the new state is also corrupt?' Time and again in the play, the audience is aware of hidden corruption beyond the individual viciousness of Claudius. The rottenness is in the state of Denmark, not solely in Claudius himself; a centralized authority is dragging people down to its own level. The argument is not pursued except in that the deaths at the end cleanse some of the corruption, and a new (though distinctly feudal) ruler from Norway is declared successor. The problem of detecting this corruption is also touched upon: there are references in the play to diseases; these typify the corruption of the state. And sometimes a man dies, dies of an 'imposthume' which 'shows no cause without' (IV.iv.27, 28). Here again there is everyday significance: we are reminded of Kafka's much more recent description of the state machine which the ordinary man totally fails to penetrate and spends his time guessing over. *Hamlet* is a play about not knowing for sure; the Ghost's testimony has to be substantiated before the Prince is wound up for action, since scruples over its validity are an unbearable addition to scruples about the nature of the action to be taken. For the thinker as well as the doer the dilemma is inscrutable, and 'resolution Is sicklied o'er with the pale cast of thought' (III.i.84, 85).

The Revenge Tragedy

Shakespeare used his folk-tale material to lend substance to current political and ethical problems and did it so skilfully that the play seems to spring like a natural growth from its time. But Shakespeare, as a man of the theatre, knew too how to adopt and adapt dramatic traditions to his own ends. One particular tradition calls for special attention here, that of the Revenge Tragedy. Revenge is the individual taking the law into his own hands, whereas one of the duties which has accrued to the nation-state of today is the righting of wrongs done to individuals. This matter of vengeance for wrongs done is only one instance of the puzzlement, in the period of transition, over where authority rested, yet is nevertheless a problem of importance in the history of the drama in Europe. The theme of the earlier tragedies of revenge was the punishment of an evil-doer through someone who had suffered because of him. Plainly the story-source on which *Hamlet* was based had a dominating revenge theme; Shakespeare must have known, and perhaps even acted in, earlier plays of this type and could easily see how the Hamlet theme might be treated in the way of these older plays. (An older, 'original' Hamlet play, now lost, is known to have existed; what is recorded of it suggests that it may have been written by Thomas Kyd, the writer of *The Spanish Tragedy*.) It is impossible to say why that particular aspect of human behaviour came to predominate in a particular style of drama; but one can venture the guess that the revenge theme was recognized as appropriate to ranting and the display of passion, followed by violent action, and in the early days of the secular theatre these would have more immediate appeal than, say, the actions of characters in a more static series of situations at a lower emotional pitch; the trivialities of life are unlikely to stir people to a pitch of retaliation approaching revenge. Certainly revenge as a theme needed exciting plots to convey it, and such plots were in the tradition of the Revenge Tragedy.

This style of tragedy is especially associated with the Roman playwright Lucius Seneca (c. 4 B.C. – A.D. 65). Seneca was a learned man, a statesman and philosopher, well read in Greek literature; his nine tragedies treat incidents from Greek mythology, but instead of exercising the restraint of classical Greek tragedy he brought out the tragic effect by horrific incidents, bloody action, and ranting speeches. *Hercules Furens* ('Raging Hercules') is an example, its title sufficiently indicative of the thematic treatment. A stock element of the revenge situation came to be the ghost, a manifestation of a spirit left restless through waiting for vengeance against the person who had inflicted suffering; its role is to urge the avenger to action, and vengeance is then sought and taken in a series of sensational episodes. *Hamlet* has clear affinities with this type of revenge tragedy, even though the actual works of Seneca may have exercised an influence only indirectly, e.g. through the poetry of Ovid, whose *Metamorphoses* deals with similar legends, and by a continuing tradition of classical themes on the English medieval stage. And *Hamlet* is not the first or only play in English to show the connection. The early years of the reign of Elizabeth I saw an intellectual revival of interest in the Greek and Latin classics of literature, and the drama found there things that it could profitably imitate, the revenge tragedy being one. Playwrights reflected the highlights of Senecan drama, not only in the matter of the bloody action and the ranting but also in the larger-than-life stage figures, and the madness brought on by desperation. Among the English antecedents of *Hamlet* in this style the most famous is Kyd's *The Spanish Tragedy* (1587); here a father, Hieronimo, avenges the murder of his son. The son has been done to death by a Portuguese prince, who is his rival in the wooing of a high-born lady, Belimperia, and a young Spanish nobleman. The father delays, often lamenting his lot in passionate outbursts akin to madness (the subtitle of the play is *Hieronimo is mad again*), and he and Belimperia get their victims in a 'play-within-the-play', not as in *Hamlet* by using it to indicate awareness of the guilty person, but by doing in earnest what appears to be make-believe. The play is not as crude as it sounds: Hieronimo, the father, is a character followed through with great psychological insight. The anonymous *Locrine* (1595) is another example, dealing this time with revenge of a brother for a brother.

This too has a ghost which shrieks for vengeance. But in all these plays material considerations prevent fulfilment, whereas in *Hamlet* the impediment is conscience. Shakespeare chose a theme which deals with a duty higher than the others, a son's revenge for the murder of his father. There is, too, much psychological refinement, even upon Kyd's fine play, since conscience has taken over from physical impediment as the deterrent, and the play therefore moves in a higher plane of significance, through the reflections of the hero and through his relationship with the outside world. The crudity of the violence is proportionately damped down, partly by means of the poetry but also through the psychological penetration which so stirs the spectator.

Sources of the Play

Shakespeare, familiar with the Senecan style (he had already written *Titus Andronicus*, which is a clear example), and visualizing its potentialities as raw material capable of further refinement, must have cast around for a suitable plot on which to develop his approach. He found it in the Hamlet story, then current in the form of a play (now lost) and a version in French (still extant). The story is found in the folk literature of Iceland, Ireland, and Denmark. The Danish historian Saxo Grammaticus ('Saxo the Literate', the man who could read and write) put it into its first literary form. The legend of Hamlet (called Amleth in Saxo) appears in the third and fourth books of the *Historia Danica* ('Danish History'), a work finished probably early in the thirteenth century, but not printed until 1514. Later in the sixteenth century the story from Saxo was translated into French by Francis de Belleforest as an item in his collection *Histoires tragiques* ('Tragic stories'), Volume 5 (1570). Some of the stories in this collection were translated from French into English during the sixteenth century, but no translation of the Hamlet story is known to have existed before 1608. It appeared after the latest possible date for the production of Shakespeare's *Hamlet*, and cannot therefore have been one of Shakespeare's sources. And since it is very doubtful whether any earlier translation existed, we must assume that Shakespeare got his story either from the original French or from the lost earlier play of *Hamlet*, which was itself based on the French version of the story.

Shakespeare does not follow Saxo's story closely. For instance, he changes the names of all the characters in it. Yet there is a king in Saxo's history who is murdered by his brother; the brother ascends the throne and marries the dead king's widow. (Her name in Saxo is Gerutha). Her son, Amleth, plans to take revenge on his uncle, and to protect himself pretends to be raving mad. The king is suspicious, and tries to find out whether the madness is genuine. It is arranged that Amleth should be spied on by a beautiful girl. He is also

The Fortress of Kronborg in Helsingør (Elsinore) c. 1580.
This is the earliest known picture of Hamlet's castle.

spied on as he talks to his mother, and finds the spy (a court adviser, 'fuller of assurance than wisdom') hidden in the straw which lies in the room; he kills him and brutally dismembers the body. He then tells his mother he will pretend to be mad so as to get his revenge and in this his mother promises to help him. Amleth is sent in exile to England, but by changing the letters he carries to the King of England (they are carved on wood), he manages to get his two companions killed in his place. After being away for a year, he returns in disguise, makes the courtiers drunk at a funeral feast intended to celebrate his death, sets fire to the palace, and kills his uncle with the sword. He succeeds to the throne and after warlike activity dies in battle.

It will be seen from this summary that Shakespeare undoubtedly got his main ideas from this source. But the source itself is crude in style and content. In one place, for instance, Amleth pretends to be a cock and comes into the room flapping his arms as if they were wings. The court adviser, the original of Polonius, is killed and dismembered, and the sections of his body are boiled and fed to pigs. Shakespeare's refinements change the whole nature of the story.

There is some evidence that the legend is based on historical fact, but proof is lacking. The early history of the European peoples as we now have it seems to be a mixture of history and legend. The story of Hamlet is set vaguely in some century before the Norman Conquest of Britain (1066). The fact that Claudius is able to send orders to the King of England suggests a time when the Danes held considerable power in the British Isles. For centuries before this, the Danes had been the pirates of the North, a race of ruthless seafarers, but it was not till the reign of Sweyn I (died 1014) that any systematic attempt was made to dominate England. Sweyn's son, Canute, made himself King of England, after his father's death and a struggle over the succession, in 1016. It may be said, then, that the action takes place at some indeterminate period in the tenth century.

The Theatre of Shakespeare's day

Shakespeare moulded this material into dramatic form to suit and exploit the resources of a stage very different from what we are used to seeing today. The modern theatre normally consists of a stage with a proscenium arch above it which acts as a division or barrier between it and the audience. Watching a play is like looking into a huge picture-frame with living, moving people as the figures in the picture. The public theatre of Shakespeare's day was arranged very differently. It was round or octagonal, the shape deriving from the 'pits' or arenas used for holding cock-fights or bear-baiting. In these the spectators stood all round the pit and watched the sports from close at

The Globe Theatre, redrawn in 1830 from Visscher 1616.

hand. The public theatres were, however, larger, and in this they show another influence in construction, that of the inn-yard. The more imposing and elaborate type of Elizabethan inn consisted of a road front with an archway in it. This archway led into a courtyard enclosed on all four sides, with galleries round at the levels of the upper floors; the doors to the rooms were reached by these galleries. Travelling troupes of players were sometimes permitted to set up movable stages in these inn-yards, and people could watch the plays either from the galleries or from the ground-level in the inn-yard. We must assume that as this arrangement became common the archway was sealed off for the duration of the play, and people were admitted only if they paid either for standing-room at ground-level or for admission to the galleries. When *Hamlet* was written, there were at least four such theatres in London. All were used by the company of players which Shakespeare was associated with, but in 1599 their headquarters became the *Globe*, a new theatre on the south side of the River Thames. The construction of the Globe conformed, as far as we can tell, to previous patterns. It is not impossible that the arena of the Globe was used for bear-baiting and cock-fighting in the same way as the inn-yards from which it had evolved. Only the galleries and the stage itself were roofed over. The central area was open to the sky, and, since plays were generally presented in the afternoon, no artificial lighting was necessary.

Today, the ordinary stage with its 'picture frame' effect presents the action taking place at a distance from the audience and for the most part behind the proscenium arch. The Elizabethan stage projected far out into the place where the audience sat or stood; spectators were on three sides of it, and therefore in very close contact with the players. This 'outer stage,' as it was called, had no curtains, but was partly covered by a projecting roof. There was a trap-door in the floor of the stage, through which ghosts and devils could appear and disappear, and at the back, if we can judge accurately from the few extant sketches of Elizabethan theatres, were two doors, set obliquely, through which the actors passed on and off the stage. Between them was an 'inner stage', a recess covered with a curtain which could be used to reveal some action going on in a setting remote from the rest. Above the recess was a balcony or *terras* for use as a small upper stage, or possibly little more than standing-room for a few actors. Beside it were the actors' dressing-rooms, reached by stairs from the doors in the main stage. There is some evidence to suggest that in the Globe, for instance, there were bay windows on either side of the balcony through which actors could be seen at a distance. Action which called for remoteness from the main course of the play could be staged in one or other of these bay windows.

In the sketch of the Swan theatre on page xxv, the projecting roof looks as if it covered only the inner stage, the rest being open to the sky. In some other theatres the roof was probably a more important feature: it projected farther out and was sometimes painted with a dark blue sky and representations of the moon and the stars. This was called 'the heavens'. In some theatres there was even a trap device in 'the heavens' for letting actors down on to the stage for special effects, and for picking them up off the stage to 'disappear' in the roof. Right at the top, above 'the heavens', was a room with a thatched roof where a trumpeter stood and played flourishes on his trumpet to attract people's attention to the theatre. From the roof of this room a flag flew during performances.

Although some points of detail about the Elizabethan theatre are in doubt, the important effects of the stage arrangement are clear. First, the visual impression was three-dimensional: there was plenty of scope for actors to move far away from the audience, or right up among them, virtually mingling with the spectators standing around the stage. The balcony made it possible for players to appear well above the stage as a matter of course, not just as a specially contrived spectacle. Second, in the early records of the theatre there is almost no mention of scenery, but *properties* (i.e. easily movable objects for use in plays) are often referred to. In an extant list of properties, the 'golden sceptre' would have been used to symbolize a king, the 'bay tree' a garden, and so on. Scenes may possibly have been identified by signboards hung up on the stage, but if this device was in fact used it has had little effect on the plays. Shakespeare wrote without assuming any scenic effects to reinforce the visions evoked by his verse. The opening lines of his scenes often tell the audience something about the setting, not necessarily through straight description but at least by some hint which, in the movement of the play, is all that is needed:

> The air bites shrewdly; it is very cold
>
> (I.iv.1)

– which clearly refers to a situation out of doors.

> Is she to be buried in Christian burial . . .?
>
> I tell thee she is; and therefore make her grave straight.
>
> (v.i.1, 3)

– which places the scene in a graveyard. The absence of scenery is the cause of much fine poetry. Later dramatists might, for instance, have put Ophelia's death on the stage for all to see. Shakespeare, knowing there could be no scenery to particularize the setting, lets the Queen recount it, in the beautiful lines beginning:

> There is a willow grows aslant a brook,
> That shows his hoar leaves in the glassy stream; . . .
>
> (IV.vii.167–8)

Shakespeare was a poet, and would have written poetry whatever the nature of the stage he employed. But at least the scene-setting poetry in the plays was not extraneous to dramatic performances in his day.

The inner stage was used for scenes set away from the main action of the play or placed for some reason differently from the main action. In *Hamlet* it is likely that the Queen's private chamber (*closet*) was represented in this way. The curtains which could be drawn to conceal this inner stage indicated tapestried hangings round a room of state, hung to keep out the chill of the stone walls. Behind these Polonius hides himself when he spies on Hamlet and the Queen. Perhaps the inner stage was used also to indicate a different location without any implication of a small closed space: Polonius talking to his servant at home (II.i) could thus be distinguished from the action on the castle battlements (the main stage and the balcony) which has preceded it.

If Shakespeare exploited the contemporary stage and wrote plays with its special character and facilities in mind, he also used the theatre and its stage as a source for imagery, thus constantly reminding his audience that the physical paraphernalia they saw around them were to convey much more than the mere parts of a building or pieces of stage furniture. Often the indications are direct and unambiguous; Scene II.ii, for instance, has many. With the Swan illustration in mind, it is easy to imagine Hamlet at one of the

The interior of the Swan Theatre as seen in 1596
(from a sketch by van Buchell after De Witt).

columns springing from its plinth at mid-stage. Indicating the open sky, Polonius asks:

> Will you walk out of the air, my lord?

Hamlet, with method in his madness, replies:

> Into my grave?

(II.ii.206–7)

(referring to the trap and the wide space beneath the wooden boards of the stage), which Polonius agrees *is* out of the air, although not what he was asking; for the conditions of the stage make the '*room in the castle*' look like a loggia, a room partly open to the air, and Polonius was thinking of an inner room – 'indoors', he meant. Polonius leaves as Rosencrantz and Guildenstern enter. Polonius officiously shows them where Hamlet is, but one can see some reality in this gesture if one recalls the size of the stage and the interchange of positions which was possible on it: Hamlet turns again to his reading and his courtier acquaintances surprise him at it. He gives a cordial and very informal greeting to them both. It soon transpires that they were sent for, and we see the cross-motivations (secrecy and feigned madness) worked out in asides which, on the Elizabethan stage, could be addressed very pointedly at the audience. Hamlet tells Rosencrantz and Guildenstern how he has lost his good humour and his joy in the works of nature:

> this goodly frame, the earth, seems to me a sterile promontory; this
> most excellent canopy, the air, look you, this brave o'erchanging firma-
> ment, this majestical roof fretted with golden fire – why, it appears no
> other thing to me than a foul and pestilent congregation of vapours.

(II.ii.291–96)

The demonstratives, *this* – , *this* – add point to the theatrical setting: the building-frame of the theatre symbolized the earth, the stage thrust out into the audience area was a 'sterile promontory', the open air a 'canopy' like that over part of the stage, fretted with the rays of the sun like the gilded canopy of the heavens. Again, when the players arrive there was space enough to accommodate their movement in relation to Polonius and the other courtiers. At the end of this scene Hamlet again touches upon the question of the Ghost's credentials as the spirit of his dead father.

> The spirit that I have seen
> May be the devil.

(II.ii.573–4)

This recalls the movement underground which so baffled him and Horatio and Marcellus at the end of Act I, the ceremony of swearing. At this point the

Ghost acted like a devil and shifting about below ground infected the spot it was beneath. And if it is a fiend it can be treated derisively, not with the respect due to a father:

> You hear this fellow in the cellarage

(i.v.151)

– a very homely theatrical symbol for the depths of hell, where the spirit receives such appelations as 'old Mole'.

No women acted on the English stage from Tudor times until the Restoration of the Monarchy, 1660. Women's parts were played by boys, suitably dressed. It requires a great effort of the imagination to visualize Gertrude's part, or Ophelia's, being played by boys among grown men, but so it was. A glimpse of current theatrical controversies is given in the scene with Hamlet and the players. Hamlet recognizes a boy in the troupe and wonders whether his voice has broken – for if it has, the players will need another boy to take on the female parts:

> What, my young lady and mistress! By'r lady, your ladyship is nearer to heaven than when I saw you last by the altitude of a chopine [high-heeled shoes]. Pray God, your voice, like a piece of uncurrent gold, be not cracked within the ring.

(ii.ii.403–6)

The association of children with the theatre had become an important issue by the time *Hamlet* was written. Shakespeare's own company was feeling the competition of child players at the Blackfriars theatre; they

> cry out on the top of question, and are most tyrannically clapped for 't. These are now the fashion, and so berattle the common stages – so they call them – that many wearing rapiers are afraid of goose-quills, and dare scarce come thither.

(ii.ii.327–31)

This increase in public esteem of the groups of child players is symptomatic of a change in the world of the theatre. Shakespeare took the theatre as he found it, a traditional source of entertainment for the common people: his genius is well displayed in the way he utilized this tradition for his own ends. But the 'Children of the Revels', who played at the Blackfriars theatre, and similar troupes (sometimes made up from singers in the cathedral and royal chapels in London) set a new fashion, a style of theatre which was distinctly upper-class and even courtly in its aims. Masques (expensive and elaborate stage entertainments) were given privately by these children in the palaces and houses of lords.

A parliamentary ordinance at the beginning of the Civil War (1642) brought the closure of all public theatres in London. Dramatists were by that time becoming increasingly attached to the party supporting the King and opposing the Parliament and playhouse audiences were therefore officially looked upon as potentially dangerous meetings. When theatres were re-opened or established after the Restoration (1660), influences from overseas, especially France and Italy, changed the nature of public performances in many ways.

The Language of the Play

Just as *Hamlet* grew in Shakespeare's mind as a play for the stage he knew, so was it born of the language of his time. Drama is essentially spoken language and *Hamlet* has its tap-roots down in the speech of the people. Yet even a glance at the text of the play shows that the English used is in some ways very different from the ordinary language of today.

Much of it is noticeably intense in a way quite unfamiliar to us. For instance, in the two lines:

> As harbingers preceding still the fates,
> And prologue to the omen coming on

> (I.i.122–3)

there is a rush of heavily-charged words (*harbingers, preceding, fates, prologue, omen*). Such words were not especially common in Shakespeare's time any more than they are today. They are there to add a dramatic intensity to the unfolding of the plot, and any genuine appreciation of the play must spring from due attention to these 'difficult' words and to the ways in which they are arranged for dramatic effect. A few lines of modern verse, picked at random from *Penguin Modern Poets, I*, will indicate how different are the poetic modes of today.

> Last night they came across the river and
> Entered the city. Women were awake
> With lights and food.

> (Elizabeth Jennings: *The Enemies*, 1–3)

There are lines in Shakespeare which display something of the same moving simplicity of language, but *Hamlet* contains no obvious examples. (*King Lear* and *Macbeth*, by contrast, have passages in which the dramatic effect is dependent mainly upon simplicity of diction.) The reader of *Hamlet*, then, must be ready to spend some time thinking over the exact meanings and the implications of a number of 'difficult' words, and must try to see their cumulative effect in the play. The strangeness of much of the diction (the words and phrases) and some of the syntax (sentence construction) in the play undoubtedly makes it difficult to study. The reader will have to come to terms with many words and phrases which are totally unfamiliar and have no place in modern English. Some were once current and have now passed out of ordinary usage; some were simply coined by Shakespeare himself on the pattern of words already in existence; some appear to have existed in the language but have never had wide currency. Shakespeare's imagination and his immense knowledge and experience of the language made it possible for him to write like this. Yet despite the strangeness of much of the language as it appears on the printed page, it sounds more or less normal when spoken on the stage (which was of course what it was written for). The movement and interest of the plot usually cancel out any peculiarities about the language. Even the involutions of Hamlet's own speeches seem straightened out, the evident complications of phraseology and syntax remaining to serve as a reflection of the inner turmoil in his soul.

Those who read or study *Hamlet* from the printed page may like some advice on how this very real language difficulty may be overcome.

The general meaning of an utterance in the play is more important than the literal meanings of the individual words. For instance, Hamlet, about to leave for England, is sure that Rosencrantz and Guildenstern are involved in a plot against him; he is determined that they themselves will suffer from it, and the prospect pleases him:

> 'tis the sport to have the enginer
> Hoist with his own petar.

> > > (III.iv.207–8)

The essential meaning here is, 'It is good fun to see people suffer from the very things they have contrived to make others suffer.' The precise meanings of the obsolete words (*hoist*: blown into the air; *petar*: bomb) are less important; they are, of course, recorded in the notes in this edition, but, as on the stage, the real message of the lines bypasses, as it were, the literal meanings of the words and gets at once to the real significance in the context. Learning the literal meanings of many strange words is an unrewarding task and it may even be a misleading one, since it may tempt some readers, especially those for whom English is a foreign language, to think that *petar* is a 'better' word than *bomb*, or *hoist* than *blown up*, or *reechy* (III.iv.185) than *filthy*. It is the significant meaning in the play which must be grasped. The rest is of secondary importance.

The value attached to a syllable is important, always so in verse and sometimes in prose also. The basic pattern of Shakespeare's lines is of five iambic feet, i.e. of five groups of two syllables each, the first lightly stressed, the second more heavily:

To be|forestal|led ere|we come|to fall,|

Or par|doned be|ing down?|Then I'll|look up;|

(III.iii.49–50)

Here each foot is divided from the next by a vertical stroke (|); weak stresses are marked ˘ and strong ones ´. The basic arrangement is therefore:

˘ ´|˘ ´|˘ ´|˘ ´|˘ ´|

Hamlet contains a large number of lines which conform closely to this pattern:

Ă litt|le ere|the might|iĕst Jul|iŭs fell|

(I.i.114)

So ex|cellent|a king,|that was|to this,|

(I.ii.139)

Ĭ shall|th' effect|ŏf this|good les|son keep|

(I.iii.45)

The last example shows a type of slight adjustment to the spelling which has to be introduced to make the rhythm clear: in *th'effect*, the letter *e* of *the* has been omitted to show that the phrase *th'effect* has the value of two syllables, not three.

In some places in the play there are lines which do not at first appear to fit into this basic pattern. There are two possible reasons for this: either they include words which in Shakespeare's time were not stressed as they are today; or, for reasons of dramatic significance or variety, the pattern is deliberately violated. Here is an example of the first type:

A couch for luxury and damned incest

(I.v.84)

The word *incest* is, in modern English, stressed on the first syllable (*íncest*), but in Shakespeare's day it was very probably frequently stressed on the second (*incést*). If this fact is borne in mind, the line can be scanned without difficulty.

Ă couch|for lux|ŭ ry|and damned incest|

Another example of this unexpected incidence of word-stress is at I.ii.87, which includes *commendable*:

'Tis sweet and commendable in your nature, Hamlet

In this text of the play, unexpected stresses have been marked, to give the reader guidance in speaking the verse lines.

The second type of irregularity is introduced to achieve some special dramatic effect, or to avoid general monotony by varying the rhythm of the lines. A full metrical analysis of all the variations on the basic rhythmic pattern of the iambic pentameter (line of five feet, each containing two syllables, with the stronger stress on the second) as they occur in *Hamlet* would be out of place in this edition. But here is an example.

Sometimes weakly-stressed syllables are added to the basic pattern; these are spoken quickly, without special emphasis, so that the general rhythmic flow of the lines is maintained:

'Tĭs swéet│aňd cóm│mĕndáb│lĕ in your ná│tŭre, Hámlĕt

In this line the syllables

– lĕ in your –

are to be passed over lightly, so that the time taken to say the syllables in each foot (the space between each bar) remains about the same, and the rhythm of the line is unbroken. It will be noticed that the last foot has one extra syllable:

– tŭre Hámlĕt –

this contains a final weak stress on -*let*. This line illustrates the shifting of word-stress which has already been touched upon (*commendable*).

The play is not, of course, appreciated more readily by means of detailed metrical analysis, but the ground-swell of the verse rhythms is a fact which all readers should be aware of. The verse itself is there to give the words a special measured motion as they are spoken. The rhythmic movement is sufficiently controlled to show some regularity, but at the same time not so slavishly followed that it would be reduced to a monotonous beat. In some ways the speeches are like careful conversation; each word is chosen to give the fullest possible effect, yet the rhythm of the lines which keeps up the swinging movement of the words when spoken ensures that heaviness is avoided.

It is natural to ask at this point why Shakespeare wrote a large part of his plays in verse, mostly blank (unrhyming) verse, and why the audience he wrote for expected them to be written like this. Apart from the feeling for measured conversation, the main reason is the historical one. Up to Shakespeare's time, it had been traditional to write plays in verse; the earliest English drama is closely associated with the rituals of the Christian Church, and is written almost entirely in metre. One advantage of this arrangement was that the lines were easily remembered. In fact a large part of *all* the early literature of England is in verse because it grew from a tradition of oral literature; the handing-down of folk stories was made easier if they were told in the regular beat of a verse scheme. In his earlier plays, Shakespeare adopted this convention; there is no prose in the first part of *Henry VI* (1591–2), whereas *Hamlet* (1600–1) has a good deal.

Shakespeare recognized that verse lines are more memorable than prose, but the blank verse line he chose as the vehicle for the speeches in his plays brings with it other advantages. In his hands it is moulded into the forms of careful speech. No one expects a play to be exactly like life; such a work would be too flat and slow moving to hold the interest of an audience. It is a concentrated rendering of life, a reasoned and deliberate selection of certain aspects of a life-like position. The aspects finally selected are then shaped to fit organically into the sequence of events which make up the plot. The plot is communicated in a clear and orderly way to the spectators. But the essentials of this plot are not enough; a summary of the action would be as boring as an account with every detail filled in. Here again the dramatist selects; he transmits with the plot just enough of the finer details of character and action to create those impressions of the events being revealed which he wishes to convey to his audience. The writing of a play such as *Hamlet* is therefore very different from the writing of a novel. The novelist can, if he wishes, use a huge number of words with which to create and build upon and exploit the scenes, the actions and the characters he is inventing. When the playwright is at work he must have in mind the brevity of his contact with the audience. Even *Hamlet*, the longest by far of Shakespeare's plays, takes less than three hours to perform. Shakespeare fulfilled the demands of brevity and point by embracing the rigid dictates of the verse-form. In his hands the iambic pentameter reached a height of perfection in English which it hardly attained again. It gained in fluency and flexibility without losing neatness and precision. Verse-forms, then, were the vehicle Shakespeare chose to give point and immediacy to the speech he put into the mouths of his characters.

It is usually easy to see the reasons for some parts of *Hamlet* being not in verse but in prose. Verse was chosen as a vehicle for setting forth the subject-matter with point and precision. Logically, when situations occur which are not on a high pitch of intensity, there is less need for verse. In *Hamlet*, the scenes and incidents in which emotion is on a comparatively low level are mostly in prose. Prose is used by Hamlet when he instructs the players in what he wants them to do, and what little they have to say in reply is also in prose (II.ii and III.ii); Hamlet and the gravediggers naturally talk in prose, this being the only truly comic exchange in the play (V.i); Hamlet's conversation with Osric, a caricature of a courtier, is also comic in intent, and is in prose. Prose, too, is a social marker; the servants never speak lines in verse.

A unique feature in *Hamlet* is the use of prose for one special purpose regardless of the pattern just observed: whenever Hamlet is feigning madness he talks in prose, as if even here the poise and control of blank verse, reflecting those same qualities in the mind, are temporarily abandoned, and the emotional release, even though only pretence, is effected naturally in prose. If there is emotional intensity here, it is of a different order from the soliloquies or the breathless, frightened exchanges at the appearances of the Ghost of the late King. It is at the second level, that of poignant tragedy; yet the poignancy is acted out, and it is not intrinsic.

The contrastive uses of verse and prose can be clearly seen for instance in II.ii. The scene begins quietly with the King and Queen welcoming Rosencrantz and Guildenstern (royal personages and courtiers – verse); Polonius has something to say about his daughter, but insists on the King first seeing the ambassadors from Norway (still on a courtly level – verse); when Hamlet enters, he quickly falls into conversation with Polonius, and, to make the old man appear ridiculous, gives certain answers which appear to be nonsense – but Polonius says of them:

> Though this be madness, yet there is method in't
>
> (II.ii.205)

(Hamlet is feigning – prose); after that, Hamlet meets his old schoolfellows, and in this very informal setting the talk is breezy and at a low emotional pitch (prose); there is a further exchange with Polonius, this time about the players, in which Polonius is made to look ridiculous again, and falls into exaggerated styles of speech to justify himself (prose; verse would have made the exchange sound too serious); Hamlet's second conversation with the players is in prose, suiting their social status, but when Hamlet and the First Player recall a speech from a play, this turns out to be in an old-fashioned, highly wrought style, on a classical subject (the lines are nearly always end-stopped and the diction is heavy with 'poetic' words – see the notes to this passage, pp. 84ff, for more detailed observations). Polonius and Hamlet have a further exchange (prose); and, at the end of the scene, Hamlet delivers one of his greatest and most stirring soliloquies; there is no feigning of madness here, and the mood of profound self-criticism is deeply felt:

> O, what a rogue and peasant slave am I!
>
> (II.ii.523)

(verse). A fact not illustrated in this scene should also be noticed: Hamlet everywhere seems to feel closer in spirit to Horatio than to anyone else in his circle; they speak together entirely in verse.

Blank verse adds depth, control, poise, balance to speech. It is not in *Hamlet* a scheme of steady unbroken beats, but an instrument giving just that control which marks it off from everyday conversation.

Rhyme is not much used, except in the songs and jingles sung by Hamlet, Ophelia, and the Gravediggers. There are some examples of an arrangement by which scenes, or long speeches within scenes, are finished off with a rhyming couplet. The end of the scene (II.ii) already examined for the prose/verse contrasts is an instance:

> More relative than this. – The play's the thing
> Wherein I'll catch the conscience of the king.
>
> (II.ii.579–80)

The rhyme gives a note of finality, as do the final rhyming couplets of Shakespeare's sonnets, rounding off what has gone before. These rhyming couplets could also have been an indication to the stage-hands that the end of a sequence had been reached.

There are quite a number of phrases in *Hamlet* which sound to us as if they come from the general store-house of the English language, but turn out to be almost certainly Shakespeare's own inventions. Because of the extreme popularity of the play these phrases have passed into the language and are now universally used by speakers of English, most of whom are unaware of their origin. Here are some examples:

. . . the mind's eye	(I.i.112)
In my mind's eye	(I.ii.184)
. . . . to the manner born	(I.iv.15)
Something is rotten (in the state of Denmark)	(I.iv.90)
. . . caviare to the general	(II.ii.413)
it out-herods Herod	(III.ii.13)
To be, or not to be	(III.i.56)
. . . a sea of troubles	(III.i.59)
. . . there's the rub	(III.i.65)
. . . a bare bodkin	(III.i.76)
Hoist with his own petar	(III.iv.208)
. . . dog will have his day	(v.i.273)

These phrases are not intrinsically of great importance, but they are together perhaps the best illustration in English of the way in which collocations can be absorbed into a language from a favourite and very widely known work of literature. One or two of them are now everyday expressions, e.g. *the mind's eye*. A part of Shakespeare's genius is the faculty he had for sparking out telling phrases which carry in small space and in a kind of natural harmony a great deal of feeling and significance.

Hamlet was written more than 350 years ago. It is not therefore surprising that some of the words and constructions used in the play are archaic and do not occur in modern English. The word *clepe*, meaning 'call, name', in

> They clepe us drunkards   (I.iv.19)

is one example of an obsolete word which has left no trace in modern English. Similarly, words still in use today may appear in constructions which are quite unfamiliar. An example is:

> His virtues else   (I.iv.33)

meaning 'his other virtues; the rest of his virtues'; today the word *else* is not used in this position with ordinary nouns, although the construction survives with pronouns: *something else, anyone else*, etc.

These uncommon and archaic words and constructions seem to occur rather frequently in *Hamlet*. The word *clepe*, already quoted, is found in Shakespeare only here and in a parody of the old pedantic style in the character of Holofernes (*Love's Labour's Lost*). Some other words of this type are in Shakespeare unique to *Hamlet*. There can be little doubt that Shakespeare brought them in deliberately for special effects, perhaps to give a somewhat formal and old-world tone to the dialogue.

One special value of poetry in plays lies in the added significance of 'poetic language' as a language with symbolic meanings. Prose normally says one thing at one time. It communicates directly, and without ambiguity. Poetry, on the other hand, moves both backwards and forwards in the sense that words and phrases can have more than one meaning at one time, and the full meaning or implication of what has gone before may be illuminated only by what comes after. The same consideration applies to ideas or incidents: they too are often ambiguous in bearing one interpretation at one time but taking on other interpretations in the light of what follows. To read a poem effectively is to read it whole and appreciate its unity; the various ambiguities make more than one level of meaning or implication. It has been suggested that the nature of verse-lines is to emphasize this 'going back' to a fixed pattern of rhythm with increasing enlightenment as the poem proceeds. As for the play, the reader or the audience are positively encouraged to watch the levels at which the verse moves, and to keep their minds open to references and patterns of imagery which will not be immediately obvious, but whose presence marks certain passages as especially powerful and profound, and gives a meaning beyond what is plainly the everyday content-matter of the lines.

In addition to acting out the actual events of the story, the actors in the play are given other material (words, actions) which illuminates what they are saying and doing but is not obviously essential to the simple recounting of the story itself. Yet on closer study and reflection these other related subjects are seen to add new light to the play, and deepen one's understanding of it and of the arrangement of its events. Such matter additional to the main course of the plain events is called *imagery*. Poetry facilitates such understanding of events, since statements of analogy can often be bolder in poetry than in prose; for instance, the line

> That I must be their scourge and minister
>
> (III.iv.176)

does not need to say, 'I must act like a whip, and administer these punishments;' the plain prose statement momentarily makes us think of Hamlet as a whip to scourge the royal couple for their misdeeds. The poetic line can use the metaphor (Hamlet *is* a whip), and has no need to use the more explicit style of simile (Hamlet is, in some respects, *like* a whip). In fact, by this time *scourge* had come to take on the additional meaning of a wicked man who punished wickedness in others by indulging in the use of the whip (see note to this line, p. 144). There are, of course, instances of simile in verse just as there are metaphors in prose. Indeed, the dividing line between plain statement and the use of imagery to widen and deepen the significance of that statement is sometimes impossible to define. For instance, Hamlet tells his mother to explain his feigned madness to the king when they are fondling one another as husband and wife. Hamlet says

> . . . let him . . .
> Make you to ravel all this matter out
>
> (III.iv.185, 187)

using *ravel out* to mean 'untangle' – *ravel* is used normally of threads becoming entangled or knotted, and needing to be *unravelled*. It is impossible to know how far on the way to a purely figurative meaning the word *ravel* had reached when Shakespeare wrote. It was almost certainly closer to its literal meaning than it is now; today people would not normally think of threads when someone talked to them about 'unravelling' a problem, any more than they would think of a river when they heard the word *rival* (which comes from a Latin word meaning, literally, 'on the same stream').

It is not particularly interesting or helpful to enquire into the nature of a great number of images in *Hamlet*, though critics have done this a number of times, and have pointed out, for instance, a somewhat high frequency of references to diseases. This reflects one facet of the story, and was naturally a suitable range of reference for Shakespeare to use in portraying the rottenness of Denmark. But there are patterns of meaning which carry much wider significance. Here is a detailed investigation of one of them.

Hamlet has a large number of contexts which bring in the word *nature*. On the face of it this may not be surprising, since the word is in common, every-day use today. But the word *nature* had not the same meanings in Shake-speare's day as it has now; its significance was both more wide-ranging and more precise. The passages in which the word *nature* occurs may therefore be taken to merit close attention, and this study will lead to a fuller perception of the word as Shakespeare used it. Other passages, where the concept of nature but not the word itself is dealt with, will also need to be considered, since the first concern of the reader must be with ideas, not words. The ordering of the resultant images is full of meaning.

The basic reference is to nature as the 'natural' order of things, essential and beneficial to humankind, but all too prone to disturbance and disarray. When Hamlet begins to meditate in earnest on the enormity of his mother's second marriage, he calls the world

> an unweeded garden
> That grows to seed; things rank and gross in nature
> Possess it merely

(I.ii.135–7)

Nature, true nature, is balanced, the good with the bad, the fresh with the rank, the delicate with the gross. The unweeded garden shows the bad in nature beginning to outweigh the good. When the King calls him *cousin*, Hamlet says to himself:

> A little more than kin, and less than kind

(I.ii.65)

– where *kind* is a concept closely associated with nature: *kind* and nature are linked in philosophy, and etymologically too a person is *kind* if he acts according to his true, i.e. worthy and most honourable, nature. Hamlet is in fact punning on *kin* and *kind*, which are related words, one's kin being those of one's own sort or race or family, one's own *kind*. Hamlet says in effect that his relationship with his step-father is somewhat closer than ordinary kinship (as the word *father* indicates), yet it is not *kind*, i.e. natural, according to the best or what was looked upon as normal in nature. Yet nature is all too vulner-able, despite the essentially optimistic world-view shown in the word *kind*. At birth men can have

> some vicious mole of nature in them

(I.iv.24)

which is, put in different terms, what is lacking in Horatio's system of ideas relating to the nature and general scheme of the universe:

> There are more things in heaven and earth, Horatio,
> Than are dreamt of in your philosophy.

(I.v.166–7)

There seems, indeed, no reason why *philosophy* here should not be taken to mean, very precisely, 'natural science,' i.e. knowledge of the universe arrived at by 'natural' reason. But whether this is true or not, the blemishes in nature,

> the stamp of one defect,
> Being nature's livery, or fortune's star
>
> (I.iv.31–2)

are always present. The play is about this natural streak of evil in the 'nature' of the royal house of Denmark, which, tainting everything which was good, brings it to ruin. The plainest manifestation of this 'against-nature' theme is Hamlet's feigned madness,

> Grating so harshly all his days of quiet
> With turbulent and dangerous lunacy
>
> (III.i.3–4)

And so the play moves on to innumerable images of nature uncontrolled, of the times being out of joint. Act III scene iv is full of such images. Hamlet, showing his mother a picture of her second husband, says he is

> like a mildewed ear,
> Blasting his wholesome brother.
>
> (III.iv.65–6)

(The reference is to an ear of corn, decayed and spreading the decay throughout the rest of the grain.) If there is any hope for this tainted nature, it must lie in constant discipline: a rigorous control will bring results which come more and more easily as this control becomes more and more 'natural':

> For use almost can change the stamp of nature
>
> (III.iv.169)

But the chances of this happening to the Queen are remote. The natural functions of her senses must be impeded or she would not have fallen to the blandishments of her second husband. Hamlet says it must have been a devil, an evil in nature, which has so affected her senses:

> Eyes without feeling, feeling without sight,
> Ears without hands or eyes, smelling sans all,
> Or but a sickly part of one true sense
> Could not so mope.
>
> (III.iv.79–82)

When Hamlet determines on the final onslaught, he calls the King

> this canker of our nature
>
> (v.ii.69)

and concludes that it would be a fault in himself to allow the King to go on living.

This account does not exhaust the occurrences and meanings of the word *nature* in *Hamlet*. It is meant to show through a number of quotations how the effect of the imagery does not depend primarily upon the recurrence of particular words or very limited references to objects and actions related to the story of the play. It depends on the frequent recourse made to a particular pattern of thought: nature is primarily good, but can all too easily become blemished. This pattern of thought represents one level of meaning which the play takes on, one which exists as a factor in the full significance of the play. *Hamlet* does not just tell a story; it brings some kind of logical order and significance into the recounting of a historical or quasi-historical event. These associated levels of meaning cannot strictly be called literary imagery. They are rather the results of the calling-in of a large number and wide variety of images, which, added together, give a totality of revelation to the play, and are therefore infinitely more important than any individual simile or metaphor, or purely verbal repetition.

There is a third cause of difficulty in reading the text: at some places the words as we have them are almost certainly not what Shakespeare wrote but a faulty version resulting from incorrect copying, mis-hearing, misunderstanding, or bad printing. In one or two places Shakespeare's words appear to be completely lost. Such points of difficulty (known technically as *cruces*, singular *a crux*) are not frequent, but because they have given rise to a great deal of speculation they are often treated in great detail by editors, to an extent out of all proportion to their importance in the play. The most famous crux in *Hamlet* is at I.iv.36. The reading of the earliest extant version of *Hamlet* at this point is

> The dram of eale
> Doth all the noble substance of a doubt
> To his own scandal.*

The safest and fairest way of treating such passages is to admit that they make no sense, and to try to gauge from the context of the passages what they are intended to mean. In the lines quoted above, *eale* and *scandal* (at least) are evidently incorrect renderings of other words which we cannot identify.

....

* As elsewhere in this edition, the spelling of the words is modernized.

PART TWO

This part gives more detailed information than that in Part One on the following subjects:

(i) Language difficulties

Very little space is devoted to textual cruces in this edition. Where they occur, the notes suggest the general meaning of the passage, taking into consideration the context and the possible meanings of the doubtful words. Derivations of words are not normally given, since these are likely to distract the reader from the study of the play as drama and literature. When derivations are mentioned, this is done to help the reader remember the meaning of a word which best suits the context. For example, here are three lines containing words which have something in common, the letter *d-* at the beginning; two of these words are likely to be quite unfamiliar to the reader.

> Then up he rose, and *donned* his clothes
> And *dupped* the chamber door

> (IV.v.51–2)

> But that this folly *douts* me

> (IV.vii.192)

The word *donned*, 'put on', may be familiar to most readers; *dupped* and *douts* not so. It is useful to know, therefore, that, just as *don* comes from *do on*, so *dupped* is formed from *do up*, and *douts* from *do out* – 'put out, extinguish'. Here is another instance: *aught*, 'anything', is not used in ordinary modern English, and may seem entirely strange. But its opposite, *nought*, 'nothing, zero', is quite familiar, and the association of *aught* with *naught* makes the meaning of the first word easy to remember. Again, *amazement* means not, as in modern English, 'great surprise' but 'bewilderment', such as one would experience in a *maze*. At least, this is the meaning in III.iv.113, although at III.ii.306, the meaning of *amazement* is somewhat nearer to that in modern

English. In fact it may be considered as in transition, since Hamlet gets some fun out of the phrase in which it appears:

ROSENCRANTZ . . . your behaviour hath struck her into amazement and
    admiration.
HAMLET O wonderful son, that can so astonish a mother

(III.ii.305–7)

The glossarial index at the end of the book gives the meanings of all the rare and strange words in the text. It also gives line references to each of the words listed. The references are meant to encourage the student not to learn the words and their meanings in isolation but to use the index as a way of access to the relevant passage so that the words may be read in context and studied as they actually occur in the play. As we have seen, their history and general associations are less important than the sense they are used in in the play and the general implications they bring to the passage. The index is a useful means of revision, too, since it can lead to passages of particular difficulty through the tracing of individual words.

There is below a short list of words which are seldom used today as Shakespeare used them, but which occur frequently in the play. They have either changed their meanings since Shakespeare's day, or have completely fallen out of use in current English, or are shortened forms which Shakespeare used for some special effect, e.g. so that they would fit into the metrical pattern of the lines.

an: 'if'; this is a clipped form of *and*, which itself often appears for 'if' in the
    earliest editions of Shakespeare.
anon: 'at once'.
ay: 'yes'; or 'ah! alas!', as in *ay me*!
do: – This and its derived forms are often used as an auxiliary verb without
    any separate meaning, whereas in modern English it would give special
    emphasis to the main verb:

The serpent that did sting thy father's life
Now wears his crown.

(I.v.39–40)

where *did sting* = 'stung'. Conversely, *do* and its derived forms are sometimes not used in positions where we would expect them in modern English, e.g. with questions and negative commands:

If thou hast nature in thee, bear it not

(I.v.81)

where *bear it not* = 'do not bear it'.

ere, ever, e'er: 'before'; in Hamlet this word is used along with *or*, e.g.

> ... or e'er those shoes were old ...
>
> (I.ii.147)

> Or ever I had seen that day, Horatio!
>
> (I.ii.183)

fain: 'glad, gladly, pleased', especially as an adverb with *would*, e.g.

> I would fain prove so
>
> (II.ii.131)

= 'I would willingly prove to be so', i.e. 'It is my earnest desire to be so.'
mark: 'notice, watch, attend to'.
marry: '(By the Virgin) Mary!' an oath
methinks: 'it seems to me (that)', merging into 'I think'.
perchance: 'by chance, perhaps'.
presently: 'immediately, at once, at the present moment'.
't: 'it'; this clipped form occurs frequently where the rhythmic pattern of the
line does not demand a full syllable:

> If it be so, as so 'tis put on me
>
> (I.iii.94)

-th – This is frequently the ending of verbs associated with *he, she, it* and
singular nouns, where *-s* regularly occurs in modern English; e.g.

> he hath very oft of late
> Given private time to you,
>
> (I.iii.91–2)

thou, thee, thy, thine: 'you, your, yours.' There is some discrimination in the
use of these forms. *Thou* and the forms derived from it are used among
members of a family and in cases where someone who considers himself
socially superior talks to an inferior. In fact, a good deal of the relationship existing between acquaintances in the play can be gauged from
their use of these second person pronouns; in general the *you*-forms are
cold, formal and respectful, whereas the *thou*-forms are warm, friendly,
or commanding. But even in Shakespeare's day the finer distinctions
were wearing thin, and there are some usages in *Hamlet* which can
hardly be explained by reference to this pattern. Yet *thou*, etc. are
consistently retained for the grand style of poetry, and, of course, in
prayers. Here is an example of the contrastive use of *you*, etc. and *thou*,
etc.: Hamlet and his mother are talking together; she wishes to appear
kind and understanding towards him, but he cannot find it in himself
to be like that with her. She addresses him *thou*, but he addresses her
you.

> QUEEN Let not thy mother lose her prayers, Hamlet.
>   I pray thee, stay with us; go not to Wittenberg.
>
> HAMLET I shall in all my best obey you, madam.
>
> (I.ii.118–20)

The verb associated with *thou* ends in *(e)st*; e.g.

> Thou canst not then be false
>
> (I.iii.80)

The verb *to be* – *thou art* – and one or two others are irregular in this respect:

> What art thou, that usurp'st this time of night
>
> (I.i.46)

we, us, our – These are normally used instead of *I*, etc. by the King when he refers to himself. They were probably thought to sound grander than the forms for the singular, though originally they may have indicated simply that the sovereign was speaking of himself and his subjects, as the body of the state. A proof that their significance is singular is contained in the sentence, spoken by the King:

> Be as ourself in Denmark

– not *ourselves*; we may call this usage the 'royal *we*'.

> (I.ii.122)

yet: 'still'.

(ii) The provenance of Hamlet: the extant texts

Some of the problems in interpreting the play arise from serious uncertainty as to what exactly Shakespeare wrote and intended should be spoken on the stage. To understand the reasons for this we must know something of the way playwrights worked in his day. We can be quite certain that Shakespeare did not write his plays, get them printed, and then give his actors copies of the book, while other copies circulated freely among ordinary readers outside the theatre. Quite the contrary; there is no evidence to suggest that Shakespeare cared what happened to his manuscripts after they had been copied into parts for his actors. The demand for plays was very great, since the total number of theatre-goers in the population was small by today's standards, and there was therefore a constant demand for new entertainment. This compulsion to work quickly (and Shakespeare had his own company of players to cater for) must be a reason for the great number and diversity of the plays he wrote during his busiest years (1591–1611) as well as for the many places where the texts seem to be imperfect.

The stage history of *Hamlet* begins with a play referred to in 1589 in a way which suggests that it was already well known. No copies of this old play now exist, but references to it indicate that it was a 'tragedy of revenge'; as we have already seen, it may be the work of Kyd, who wrote *The Spanish Tragedy* (1587). The early *Hamlet* must have had a Ghost which cried 'Hamlet, revenge'; this catch-phrase is echoed in writings as late as 1618.

Shakespeare's play was first printed in 1603, in a 'Quarto' version (*quarto* means folded twice, i.e. having pages made from sheets of paper folded to give four leaves) which is now known as the First Quarto (Q1). It is much shorter than the version we now use. It reads in places like a simplified form of the play, with many of the more philosophical speeches cut down in length, and the movement of the lines more abrupt. Although it might be an earlier draft of the play it is more likely that the First Quarto is a 'pirated' version, that is to say one taken down without permission at a stage performance. The copyist who prepared this text for publication could have used a kind of shorthand, and would of course have been helped in his work by a general idea of the plot. He may also have seen some sheets on which individual actors' parts were written out, and stage promptbooks (copies used by the prompter who helped the actors with their words). He evidently had a vivid memory of the lines associated with the action, but a much vaguer idea of the philosophical speeches. In these he seems to have remembered key words here and there together with the general drift of some lines, but he often gives an over-all meaning quite at variance with that in the fuller versions of the play. Here are a few lines from the counterpart of Hamlet's soliloquy beginning 'To be, or not to be' (III.i.56):

> To be, or not to be; ay, there's the point
> To die, to sleep, is that all? Ay, all;
> No, to sleep, to dream. Ay, marry, there it goes,
> For in that dream of death, when we awake
> And borne before an everlasting judge
> From whence no passenger ever returned
> The undiscovered country, at whose sight
> The happy smile, and the accursed damned.*

Later the speech refers to

> a hope of something after death

....

*   spelling modernized.

THE
Tragicall Hiſtorie of
HAMLET
Prince of Denmarke

By William Shake-ſpeare.

As it hath beene diuerſe times acted by his Highneſſe ſer-
uants in the Cittie of London : as alſo in the two V-
niuerſities of Cambridge and Oxford, and elſe-where

At London printed for N.L. and Iohn Trundell.
1603.

The title-page of the First Quarto of Hamlet (1603).

where the later versions read *a dread* . . ., which completely changes the meaning. The appearance of the word *borne* is worked into a context quite different from the one we are familiar with:

> The undiscovered country from whose bourn
> No traveller returns.   (III.i.79–80)

– here *bourn* is a different word. But the problem of Q1 is complicated by the fact that many lines in it are very similar to the later versions; this suggests that where the copyist remembered well we are near to the original version of Shakespeare's play. But we can be certain that Shakespeare did not authorize publication of this version. Modern texts of the play are not based on it, and only very rarely does it give useful readings. Even the names of the characters are different in some cases from the familiar ones.

The First Quarto of the play, although dated 1603 on the title page, was registered in the Stationers' Company during the previous year. (This London Company or 'guild' maintained a register of all published books for the purposes of ensuring copyright.) The play must therefore have been written before this date. It is unlikely that the play was written before 1598. In that year, in a book by Francis Meres called *Palladis Tamia*, there appeared a list of Shakespeare's plays. Twelve of them are noted, but *Hamlet* is not among them. Since the play became very popular, it is unlikely that Meres would have overlooked it. His book is a survey of English literature from Chaucer to his own day, with plentiful quotations; and he is not likely to have passed over so significant a piece. These observations fix the date of the play between 1598 and 1602. Between these years, the year 1601 is a probable date for the first production. Late in 1600 a group of boy actors began staging plays at the Blackfriars theatre in London. They quickly became popular, and apparently they drew audiences away from Shakespeare's company, playing at the Globe theatre. The Globe company went on tour in the autumn of 1601, to get audiences, it seems, from the provinces. It is probably this event which is referred to in the long exchange between Hamlet, Rosencrantz and Guildenstern II.ii.326–345. Q1 has a different reading, which includes the lines (about the players from Wittenberg):

> For the principal public audience that
> Came to them, are turned to private plays,
> And to the humour of children.

This passage may have been inserted to explain to provincial audiences why London's most famous group of actors was on tour. The year 1601 is therefore a likely date for the first production of the play.

Q1 is not, then, a good basis for a study of the play. A new version appeared a year later (Q2, 1604), most probably in order to suppress the earlier Q1.

Q2 was in all probability published with Shakespeare's approval. As the title-page says, it is 'enlarged to almost as much again as it was, according to the true and perfect copy'. Q2 forms the basis of the accepted text of *Hamlet*. It is indeed nearly twice as long as Q1; the philosophical passages especially are printed more fully, and the whole play is generally coherent, unlike the Q1 version. This tends to confirm the suggestion that Q1 is a rough version from shorthand notes, while Q2 is in fact, as the title-page says, taken from the written version of the play. Three more quartos appeared during Shakespeare's lifetime, but the differences between Q2 and Q3 are so slight that the latter may be taken as a reprint of the former. Together these make the best sources of our knowledge of the play. Where the meaning is doubtful, Q2 usually gives the most likely suggestions.

After Shakespeare's death (1616), two of his associates prepared a large collection of his plays which became known as the First Folio (published 1623). This can be taken as the memorial volume to Shakespeare, assembled from manuscripts at least very close to the actors' versions of the plays. Many of the plays in this collection (unlike *Hamlet*) are unknown elsewhere, and the compilers must have had a formidable task getting the papers into some order and having so many plays printed in one collection. The printing itself is not well done; in places the printer seems to have set up his type without knowing what the passage meant, and the type-face is sometimes un-clear. But the First Folio forms the most complete collection of Shakespeare's plays and many would have been irrecoverably lost if they had not been saved for it. F1, then, is the second key source for *Hamlet*; it omits some of the philosophical passages in Q2 (suggesting that F1 is close to an acting version, whereas Q2 was meant more for reading) and has a few lines which do not appear in Q2. These lines are unimportant and in some cases appear to have been omitted from Q2 because they might have been taken to refer to current affairs; for instance, the lines about the child actors (already mentioned in connection with dating the play) do not appear in Q2, perhaps because at the time that edition appeared the Blackfriars company had become 'The Children of the Queen's Revels', and any disparaging reference to them would have been offensive to the Court.

(iii) The principal characters in Hamlet

HAMLET carries in himself the plot of the play. One way of formalizing the progress of the plot is to see Hamlet, already placed in a potentially tragic situation, seizing devices which at once corroborate the evidence of Claudius's guilt and provide reasons for delaying the taking of revenge. People and incidents impinge upon him, pass in and out of his sphere, but he remains fixed at the centre of the story as it proceeds and leads to its tragic conclusion.

It has become almost customary for critics to refer to the 'problem' of Hamlet, i.e. the reasons which lie behind his actions and his inaction. This adhesion to the problematic aspects of his nature has brought its own rewards: intensive studies of Hamlet's psychological condition, as it might be deduced from what he says and does in the play, have illuminated matters which had up till then been obscure, or (more likely) overlooked in the onrush of the narrative. Today, despite continuous critical writing on this subject, we would be well advised to play down the problematic sides of his character, since there is less of the sharp disagreement over it which was evident some decades ago. Critics now go about looking for facts which cast new light on the various facets of his character rather than openly saying they are baffled by him or the play in general. And this change of emphasis is surely to the good, since the play continues to give powerful intellectual enjoyment, whether or not we are able to give a scientific account of Hamlet's personality or the actions which he undertakes. What follows in this character-sketch will be found generally acceptable today, even though there may be shifts of emphasis over the relative importance of various incidents (e.g. Laertes' surprising expedition back to Denmark to challenge the King) and certain characters (e.g. Fortinbras).

Many people have been puzzled by Hamlet's delay. He is constantly resolving to take action to avenge his father's death, but he never really comes to it. And when he does kill Claudius, he is avenging his own murder, not that of his father. But there is really nothing surprising about this. It is in the nature of all human beings, one would guess, to put off a searching task or an impelling duty involving something disagreeable or worse. A man who has to write a difficult letter will turn to trivial matters such as getting his desk in order or looking out of the window before he begins. When death is near to a member of one's family, any delay is welcomed, even though the conclusion is inevitable and we know in our hearts that the postponement cannot make any real difference to the conclusion. So with Hamlet; the delay is simple, not complex, and can be matched with a similar inclination in us all. (Many critics, from Hazlitt to C S Lewis, have made much of this point; some think that the enduring power of the play lies in this human touch.) And this argument may be taken further: far from adding puzzlement to the old history of Hamlet, Shakespeare has humanized it. The original story was ideally suited to treatment as a revenge play, in which the prince would merely await a good opportunity to take his revenge. The interest of the play lies in waiting for circumstances to present an opening for desperate action. Once this happens, the hero has no compunctions over exploiting it. The evidence in the play suggests that Hamlet is really delaying action because it is human to do so; only his purpose remains firm; as Coleridge said of him, he 'loses the power of action in the energy of resolve' (See also p. lxiv).

One ground for this inaction is revulsion from a horrible deed, and that is human enough. But in *Hamlet* there is another set of pressures which argue against action and are readily used by Hamlet himself. How much they are objectively considered, and how much they are embraced to subserve the human instinct for delay it is hard to say. The two factors are best considered as inseparable, since the action of the play is compounded of the two. The arguments against action frequently refer to the danger of accepting appearances as reality. From the Ghost's first showing, its *appearance* is not in doubt. But its significance is suspect, most of all to Hamlet himself, who could be most strongly influenced by an evil spirit taking on the likeness of his father. The same applies to all the events closing in upon Hamlet and Claudius in turn: the stage presents them objectively, but Hamlet's problem is that of interpretation: what are the true nature and implications of these events? Where will they lead? What is to be done in the face of them? Hamlet's human resources of passion and reason contend in answering these questions. His 'blood' and 'judgement', as he calls them, are often at variance, and the play takes life and meaning from this tragic conflict. Action based on sure foundations presupposes an ability to know reality. This challenge baffles Hamlet and urges him to seek corroborative evidence which will leave no doubt whatever that the King is guilty, so that his reason is satisfied. Only then can passion properly come into its own.

Some very deep and sensuous attachment to his mother is supposed by some to prevent him from doing anything which may conceivably hurt her. Certainly he never talks to her in the style of half-crazed raillery he uses for the King and most of his friends as his passion increases. She evidently entered willingly into marriage with her first husband's brother, despite the late king's saintly memory, and she must have reckoned with the possibility of her second husband being somehow implicated in her first husband's death. Yet with her Hamlet is solicitous, and his treatment of her compares strangely with the crudity of what he says to his beloved, Ophelia. With his mother he is gently persuasive:

> But go not to my uncle's bed;
> Assume a virtue, if you have it not . . .
> Refrain tonight;
> And that shall lend a kind of easiness
> To the next abstinence;

(III.iv.160–1, 166–168)

Some critics and psychologists have read a good deal into this more gentle treatment which Hamlet gives his mother. There is a short, key extract from the most famous exposition of this view (E. Jones: 'Hamlet Psychoanalysed') on p. lxix. A strong countercriticism of this view is on the grounds that there is insufficient evidence for assuming that Hamlet's relationship with his mother is an example of a general trait, itself insufficiently evidenced, that men have a powerful attraction to their mothers which is not filial. Shakespeare may be doing no more than showing that a family tie from mother to son is hard to snap, and allowances will be made on either side.

We know of Hamlet that at the time of the play he is no longer a young man (this is made clear in the gravediggers' scene, v.i) but that he has only recently left his university in Germany. These facts point to what proves to be true, that his inclinations are towards the quiet life of study and friendship with compatible people. Among all his friends only Horatio pleases him entirely, and Horatio is one whom the changes of fortune do not trouble overmuch. Hamlet is naturally shrewd and sensitive to outside influences; the company he is with has noticeable effects on his behaviour. He is adept in some courtly pursuits, fencing for instance, and warm and sociable with those who are in sympathy with him. His diction is often so involved, sometimes to the point of obscurity, that he clearly cares for expression and thought, and is what we would now call an intellectual. And in ordinary terms he cannot be called a man of action. His career has been no parallel to that of the warlike Fortinbras, who is his counterpart in Norway. Even the rowdiness of the Danish court, which he has been born into, he finds unpleasant. He is more the scholar than the soldier. Yet there is another side to his nature: unlike the prototype scholar, he is not cool and thoughtful or calculating when under the stress of affairs. On the contrary, he is emotional, and his pretended madness is in part an outlet for his pent-up emotion. He is compounded of both blood and judgement. When he does act, he acts precipitately, on the spur of the moment, as with the players; or he can fight with fierce determination, as against the pirates after he puts out on the voyage to England. He sends his acquaintances Rosencrantz and Guildenstern to their death without compunction. Again, one explanation of this diversity of character can be discovered if we look into ourselves. Human beings in real life are compounded of just such diversities and apparent contradictions, so that Hamlet's behaviour need not wholly surprise us. Like many thinkers he is a 'good' man who finds the world round him uncongenial. Yet because the very action he needs to take is the one he cannot bring himself to, lacking confirmation and assurances, he is in fact a failure, and the ruin that was begun by other people he brings to finality. He knows that this is the inevitable, the 'natural' outcome of his true nature, and the world therefore disgusts him. Womankind, too, disgusts him, since women are so deeply involved in the start of this downward trend. His disgust is vented on the woman whom he says he once loved, but it is kept from his mother.

He lays elaborate plans for his assumed madness, warning his associates that they are not to divulge its true nature by any word or gesture, even if strongly tempted to do so (end of I.v). He does, as he planned, act in feigned madness before the court and especially to his beloved, and the news of this goes out to the common people. The first gravedigger calls him

> young Hamlet . . . he that is mad, and sent into England.
>
> (v.i.133–4)

Yet nothing comes of all this and it serves no useful purpose, since all that he does to avenge his father's death could perfectly easily have been without the pretence of madness. At best it provides a cloak for a watcher and a justification for delay. He is looking for proof of Claudius's guilt and for an opportunity to exact the penalty he wants. People will be less on their guard if they think they are dealing with a man whose mind is unsound. Those passages where the pretended madness is evident are often moving and full of meaning dramatically. Perhaps even more so are the places where he is on the borderline, unable to decide whether or not the 'antic disposition' is to be brought into play. The end of the play-within-the-play, with his nonsense-rhyme, his somewhat wayward words with Horatio, and his subsequent encounter with the two courtiers (III.ii), is strongly emotive. Now we hear the feverish outcries of a man who is marked for tragedy. Yet the carefully laid plan, and the oath of secrecy about it, come to little. It is possible that the best explanation is an historical one. Revenge plays are extant in which the hero uses madness effectively to gain his ends. His irresponsible actions are allowed for, and he is able to carry out his revenge under the cover of activities which he is not called upon to explain. Such may have been the case in the earlier versions of Hamlet. The ghost of Hamlet's father seems to assume that the pretended madness will be an essential part of the action to be taken. It repeats Hamlet's solemn request that his friends should not reveal his secret, for from the depths the Ghost calls out 'Swear!' after Hamlet, and when the oath has been administered the spirit is told to be at rest. Here we may have a vestige of an earlier *Hamlet*, left in because the ordinary run of the audience expected it to be there. Shakespeare has humanized the drama, however, and the vestigial device is lost in the subtler and more essentially real patterning of action and delay which follows.

CLAUDIUS, like the concept of Hamlet's madness, seems to be close to an earlier play. Unlike Hamlet himself, Claudius seems somewhat crude and inconsistent in his action. Yet Hamlet treats him, as he should do, with utter contempt for what he has done and also for his ingratiating manner when he attempts to wheedle himself into Hamlet's favour.

The first impression he creates of himself is the true one. In the second scene of the play he gives a very businesslike account of how he has managed to get where he is, and having done that turns equally efficiently to questions of state (relations with Norway) and court affairs (Laertes' appeal that he should be allowed to go back to Paris). Then there is the question of Hamlet's melancholy to be attended to. Here he does nearly all the talking, and Hamlet is clearly not persuaded: the sadness at his father's death and at his mother's second marriage is too firmly fixed in his soul to be uprooted by a few diplomatic words from the villain. But behind this smoothness he is always ready to catch Hamlet out, and unhesitatingly accedes to Polonius's suggestion that they should both spy on Hamlet (II.ii.164). Before this can take place the King reveals in an aside, sparked off by a short moral speech from Polonius, that he has a conscience of a kind which is causing him some remorse:

> How smart a lash that speech doth give my conscience! . . .
> O heavy burden!
>
> (III.i.50, 54)

When the meeting takes place, as arranged, the King and Polonius spy on Hamlet, and the King's appraisal is obviously the right one; Polonius's harping on love-madness is silly. True to type, the King quickly determines a way of getting Hamlet out of the court – he will send him to England on a pretext connected with the payment of tribute by the English king. Rosencrantz and Guildenstern are his agents in this undertaking, so to them he talks freely and intimately. But again, when he is left alone, strong remorse returns, and he prays on his knees for divine comfort. In this posture Hamlet comes upon him but fails to take advantage of his defenceless position. When Hamlet shows his mother the miniatures of his father and Claudius (III.iv. 55ff.), there is something in the features of Claudius which marks him as a poor counterpart of his brother. Hamlet speaks with utter revulsion of him and Gertrude living as husband and wife.

Claudius has the schemer's facility for quickly adjusting his plans to the current circumstances, and using good advice to this end. As soon as Polonius's body is disposed of, he takes quick action to inform his friends at court about his plans:

> So, haply, slander –
> . . . may miss our name,
> And hit the woundless air.
>
> (IV.i.40, 43)

He looks coolly at the possibility of gossip arising from Hamlet's unexpected departure, and at the plot he has laid by means of letters to the English king that Hamlet should be killed while he is there.

When the tragic incidents close in on him, he is not insensitive. He shows little of Macbeth's spirit for fighting to the last ditch. Seeing Ophelia in her unbalanced state, he thinks of her condition as one among a number of troubles which, like a gun with many shots, are all aimed to kill him:

> O my dear Gertrude, this,
> Like to a murdering-piece, in many places
> Gives me superfluous death.

(IV.v.90–2)

And with inexorable speed and fitness Laertes' mercenary force bursts in. The King skilfully quietens Laertes, and leads him to the plot by which Laertes will be the instrument of Hamlet's death, as the King so much desires. Much time is devoted to the persuasion, which goes forward step by step until Laertes' mind is made up for him: he is determined to kill Hamlet. At the end of the scene in the graveyard, the King remains in a position of control. He reminds Laertes of his resolution and tells him the fencing-match will take place without delay. In the castle hall the King, seemingly patient and unruffled, goes over the conditions of the match, and he watches without show of passion as Hamlet and Laertes fight to the death. He reveals no emotion when his wife is poisoned, and makes no effort to save her. Even when he himself is killed, he tries to make little of it.

POLONIUS always raises a laugh in any performance of *Hamlet*, but perhaps our view of him is coloured by Hamlet's own. And we have seen that Hamlet's judgement of others is not always a good one. Polonius is in his dotage, but had at one time been a useful, high-ranking state officer, much respected by the late king. His post as Lord Chamberlain leads us to believe that he has worked his way up through a lifetime of service to the court, culminating in duties which involved the management of the royal household. There is a hint here and there that he transferred his devotion to Claudius in a way which gratified the new king. Claudius tells Laertes:

> The head is not more native to the heart,
> The hand more instrumental to the mouth,
> Than is the throne of Denmark to thy father.

(I.ii.47–9)

Much fun has been made of Polonius's moralizing for his son's benefit (I.iii). But in an age more compassionate than Shakespeare's one cannot avoid the feeling that a different man giving the same precepts would be treated with greater respect. Doubtless what he says is to be taken as a summary of some pious book of moral precepts, but it is apposite, full of sound common sense – it is, all in all, a plea for moderation – and turns out to be exactly what Laertes needs by way of guidance in behaviour. The tragedy of the killings at the end of the play might have been averted if he had put into action what his father told him. The culmination of his father's speech, in the famous lines beginning

> This above all: to thine own self be true,
>
> (I.iii.78)

and the blessing which follows, can hardly be taken as objects of fun. What is wrong, or 'false', here, is the inaccessibility of the advice. What *is* one's own self? The problem is everyone's, but Hamlet's in particular, since he is in himself a battle ground for reason and passion. The scene ends with more advice, this time for Ophelia. Again Polonius is sensible: Hamlet the prince would be less restrained in his love-making than ordinary people, and Ophelia must therefore be on her guard.

Perhaps Polonius's fatal blemish is his love of words, his pleasure in subordinating everything he says to a turn of phrase, even if what he wants to say is valuable and worthy of his status as a senior courtier and counsellor. In a rather touching way he is himself aware of this flaw. When he plays on Ophelia's word *tenders*:

> [Hamlet] hath . . . made many tenders
> Of his affection to me,
>
> (I.iii.99–100)

he is aware that he has indulged in some out-of-breath chasing after childish word-play, which inevitably makes the subject appear less serious than it really is:

> Tender yourself more dearly
> Or – not to crack the wind of the poor phrase,
> Running it thus – you'll tender me a fool.
>
> (I.iii.107–9)

This reduces the efficacy of advice which would otherwise have been good; he even advises 'in plain terms' at the end of the scene.

When we next see Polonius, he is giving his servant Reynaldo some long-winded instructions about spying on Laertes in Paris. Again, Polonius cannot prevent himself from enjoying the words of his directions as words: he repeats phrases which he thinks are effective. This interview is a calm opening to the impassioned account given by Ophelia of Hamlet's evident madness. It is never quite clear whether Polonius really believes that this madness arises from the melancholy of desperate love, or whether that is simply what he hopes to be the truth. His talk with the King and Queen about this has to be postponed while the Norwegian ambassadors are given an audience. When they have gone, Polonius tries to persuade the King and Queen that Hamlet is suffering from love madness. He presents his case badly; the Queen asks for 'More matter, with less art'. When he reads Hamlet's love letter, it is a stage tradition that he makes an embarrassed pause after

'In her excellent white bosom', these &c . . .

(II.ii.113)

as if something more intimate follows which he does not wish to read aloud. This action reduces his stature to the level of broad comedy. Having arranged for his son to be spied on in Paris, he now plots to watch in secret how Hamlet and Ophelia behave when they are alone together. Before this can take place there is a brief encounter between him and Hamlet. Hamlet makes outrageous fun of the old man, which Polonius partly understands:

Though this be madness, yet there is method in 't.

(II.ii.205)

When the players arrive, Hamlet continues to make Polonius a comedy figure: he is a bringer of stale news, and he seems not to be able to go farther than the actual words in his appreciation of the speeches rendered by Hamlet and the player. Before the play takes place, the King and Polonius are able to observe Hamlet and Ophelia together. Polonius foolishly persists in believing (or making believe) that Hamlet's supposed madness has its origin in love. The King knows better. Polonius, although through his office the master of ceremonies at the play, takes little part in the presentation. Just as Hamlet is intent on watching the King, so Polonius is intent on watching Hamlet and Ophelia together. But his part is nearly over. He appears especially foolish when, having delivered the Queen's summons to Hamlet, he is made to change his mind more than once over the images that the cloud-shapes they can see suggest to him. Polonius hides behind an arras in the Queen's closet, and when she is frightened of Hamlet's behaviour she calls for help. Polonius answers from behind the arras, and Hamlet runs his sword through the curtain and what lies behind. He wonders whether the spy he has killed is the King. When he discovers who he has murdered, he says:

Thou wretched, rash, intruding fool, farewell!
I took thee for thy better.

(III.iv.32–3)

Hamlet is so little moved that he continues to arraign his mother, and does not mention Polonius again until the end of this long scene. Polonius's death serves as a motive for his son's return, and brings affairs to a head between Hamlet and the King.

Polonius is much more than the comic figure he is often made out to be. He is at the centre of affairs and respected by the royal couple despite his garrulity, but his unsubtle view of life, his persistence in his opinions, and his ever-readiness to intrude in the affairs of others bring about his downfall.

HORATIO has a special place in Hamlet's heart:

> Since my dear soul was mistress of her choice,
> And could of men distinguish, her election
> Hath sealed thee for herself.

(III.ii.59–61)

Whereas Hamlet is sometimes quickly moved to unpremeditated action, and yet holds back when the most searching demands are made of him, Horatio adheres to a golden mean of thought and action. Hamlet tells him,

> For thou hast been
> As one, in suffering all, that suffers nothing;
> A man that fortune's buffets and rewards
> Has ta'en with equal thanks. And blest are those
> Whose blood and judgement are so well commingled
> That they are not a pipe for Fortune's finger
> To sound what stop she please. Give me that man
> That is not passion's slave, and I will wear him
> In my heart's core, ay, in my heart of heart,
> As I do thee.

(III.ii.61–70)

This passage is the best comment on Horatio's character and leaves virtually nothing to add. Out of this character springs a contrast with Rosencrantz and Guildenstern, and indeed all the other courtiers and officers that Hamlet has dealings with. As Horatio is, in many ways, a counterpart of Hamlet, so Hamlet is set against all the scheming and false flattery of the rest of the court.

Horatio is sceptical of the appearance of the Ghost, but, when he is convinced, it is he who is persuaded to speak to it, evidently because he is thoughtful and well educated. It is he who gives a quick, dramatic summary of the events which have taken place before the play opens, a summary that sets the action against its historical background. A further attempt to play down the Ghost is thwarted by a second appearance. Then Horatio, who has not seen Hamlet since they were at Wittenberg together, gives an account of what he has encountered. Hamlet is impressed as he would not have been if the news had come from someone else. When they are together on the battlements, it is Horatio who tries to prevent Hamlet from going apart with the Ghost. But Hamlet goes, and when they are together again Horatio can only express his amazement. Hamlet says

> There are more things in heaven and earth, Horatio,
> Than are dreamt of in your philosophy.

(I.v.166–7)

Horatio is ready to swear silence over the whole affair, and, being what he is, he will surely keep his promise.

Hamlet tells him about the mousetrap play, and together they arrange to watch the King's reactions. When the King gives himself away, it is with Horatio that Hamlet exults. He reports to the Queen on Ophelia's condition (IV.v beginning). Fittingly Hamlet writes to him in some detail about his voyage and his escape. Hamlet sees Horatio immediately after his return, and together they wander by the graveyard. Here with the gravediggers he is something of a foil to Hamlet, little more than a means to show that Hamlet can with him be relaxed, normal and lively. The last scene of the play begins unpretentiously with further exchanges between them. To Horatio Hamlet gives an account of his voyage and the plot to kill Rosencrantz and Guildenstern, and Horatio continues to be Hamlet's interlocutor when Osric comes, and so on up to the time of the fencing-match. This he finds very suspect:

> If your mind dislike anything [about the arrangements for the match], obey it: I will forestall their repair hither, and say you are not fit.
>
> (v.ii.200–1)

Their devotion to each other is such that Hamlet before he dies entrusts Horatio with the task of reporting correctly the course of his life and death; Horatio wants to take his own life now that his close friend is dying, but Hamlet restrains him:

> Absent thee from felicity awhile,
> And in this harsh world draw thy breath in pain,
> To tell my story.
>
> (v.ii.329–31)

Horatio indicates that he accepts this duty, and is in control of the situation to the end. He attends to the English ambassadors and orders that the bodies are to be displayed to the world as evidence of what has taken place. The play ends in triumph for Horatio, the intellectual, who can remain master of his passions when others give way.

LAERTES. Whereas Hamlet and Horatio are in some aspects complementary in character, Laertes is a complete contrast to Hamlet. It may not be too fanciful to see in the relationship between these three a triangle of forces, with each character exerting strong stresses on the others.

Laertes is a man of action; unlike Hamlet, he has no scruples and needs no corroborative evidence to support his courses of action. His readiness to believe Hamlet's ultimate responsibility for all the tragic events in the court during his absence, and his willingness to go farther than the King to ensure that Hamlet will be killed in the fencing, are witness to this. Against that, he too has suffered bitter sorrow at the loss of his father and his sister, and any impetuous man would do as he does to redress his grievances.

Before he leaves for France, Laertes bids an affectionate farewell to his

sister Ophelia. Like his father, he is able and ready to give advice which, on
the face of it, is valuable and sensible. He certainly shows himself to be a man
of the world, and his sister sees him as such, as she shows when she neatly
turns the tables on him by asking him to watch his own morals (I.iii.46–51).

On his return to Denmark, Laertes is quickly in front of the King, accusing
him of the death of Polonius. He wants quick action and is determined to take
revenge. The King begins to work on him, but is interrupted by the entry of
Ophelia. Laertes is overwhelmed at her condition. But his impetuosity is
somewhat stayed by the King's careful, controlled manner, and he is taken
away by the King for further discussion. Laertes, despite the smouldering
passion in him, is in full command of his senses. Why, he asks, did the King
not take action against Hamlet, if Hamlet's guilt is so certain? But like his
father he lacks insight into the working of more subtle minds, and it is not
hard for the King to make him a cat's-paw in the murder of Hamlet. Laertes
even begs to be the instrument of Hamlet's death. If he is unsubtle, he is not
without conscience: the duel is contrary to his father's advice against giving

> any unproportioned thought his act
>
> (I.iii.60)

but in the end, as he admits his own guilt and proclaims that of the King
(v.ii.295–302), he shows his natural honesty, and perhaps also the belated
effect of his father's advice:

> . . . to thine own self be true.
>
> (I.iii.78)

THE QUEEN, Gertrude, has little personality to set against the strong indivi-
duality of the men. She rarely takes any positive action. She is carried along
by events which concern her closely but which she cannot hope to control
or affect in any significant way. It is therefore easy to imagine her readily
succumbing to the persuasive wooing of Claudius which quickly followed the
the death of King Hamlet.

When we first see her she is, characteristically, echoing the prayers of her
husband that Hamlet should not return to the university. Here and throughout the play, Hamlet treats her with deference, because she is his mother, and
because she can hardly be held responsible for the events she is caught up in.
Yet her mind is clear; not all the explanations and excuses put up for Hamlet's
strange behaviour can cloud the issue in her eyes:

> KING   He [Polonius] tells me, my dear Gertrude, he hath found
>   The head and source of all your son's distemper.
> QUEEN   I doubt it is no other but the main:
>   His father's death, and our o'erhasty marriage.
>
> (II.ii.54–7)

She is not convinced when, later in the same scene, Polonius makes every effort to prove that Hamlet is suffering from love-madness:

> It may be, very likely , , ,
>
> (II.ii.152)

she says, unconvinced, in answer to a question from the King. Later she expresses, neatly and succinctly, her hope that Ophelia is the cause of Hamlet's disturbance of mind; yet she carefully avoids saying she thinks it is so (III.i.38ff). Her comment on the play-within-the-play is famous for its shrewdness; she says of the Player Queen

> The lady doth protest too much, methinks.
>
> (III.ii.218)

meaning that the Player Queen asserts her faithfulness to her husband so extravagantly that one is compelled to suspect it.

The Queen's most important appearance is in III.iv, when she and her son talk together in her closet, with Polonius hidden behind the arras. Hamlet takes care not to reprove his mother openly, for although it is her he talks to, his barbs are for the King. To her he is polite, not satirical. He pleads, reveals the situation as he sees it, but does not openly arraign her for the part she has played in the falling-off. This implies that, just as she has had power enough to win Claudius's love when her first husband, King Hamlet, was still alive, so she is now able to continue some kind of motherly understanding for her son, who himself retains a genuine devotion for her. She is, in turn, devoted to him, and also to her husband; when Laertes and his rebel Danes burst in upon them, she tries desperately to restrain Laertes from falling on the King in his fury.

But this blind and colourless devotion remains, as we should expect, ineffectual. She has known Ophelia well from a child, and has seen her drowning, yet at the funeral she reacts conventionally:

> I hoped thou shouldst have been my Hamlet's wife;
> I thought thy bride-bed to have decked, sweet maid,
> And not have strewed thy grave.
>
> (v.i.225–27)

When she comes to assert herself, saying she will drink the wine, and then drinks it although her husband has told her not to, she takes the poisoned cup and quickly dies. Her last words are a warning to her son.

OPHELIA has hardly more will of her own that the Queen has. As Hamlet dominates the play, so he overshadows nearly all the characters in it, and especially the woman he professes to love. She has been brought up in complete submission to her father, and is still ready to obey him blindly. Her

particular kind of devotion is transferred to her lover. She shows a submission to these men which is hardly impressive, but since the play is about
the struggles of Hamlet within himself, a more forceful type of loved-one
would be a distraction. It should therefore not be taken as an inadequacy on
Shakespeare's part that Ophelia is no more than she is. For wit, common
sense, and homely nobility, she cannot compete with Shakespeare's great
heroines, but she was not intended to do so. And any lack of verve and resolution in her personality as revealed in the first part of the play is fully com-
pensated for when her mind becomes deranged and she speaks in her madness, revealing her inmost thoughts, in a kind of crazy logic.

The submissiveness of her being is plain when she first appears. Laertes,
her brother, tells her that Hamlet's apparent love for her is lust, and she
should guard against it. She readily agrees to do so, but when he has gone and
her father takes up the same theme, she is less sure. Her father asks her about
it and she wants his opinion:

> POLONIUS: Do you believe his tenders, as you call them?
> OPHELIA: I do not know, my lord, what I should think
>
> (I.iii.103–4)

She makes a fitful effort to justify her feelings for Hamlet, but when her father
expressly forbids her to see him again she yields without a struggle.

Ophelia's great dramatic moment is her appearance in dishevelled clothing
with garlands of flowers about her (IV.v). Her mind is distracted. The pathos
of her condition is conveyed in the snatches of rhymes she sings. Their theme
is of a girl forsaken by her lover, through either unfaithfulness or death. Her
thoughts run on to the death of her murdered father, and she thinks for a
moment of what her brother might do to bring about revenge. She leaves, and
when she appears again later in the same scene she brings with her flowers
which she distributes in kinds according to the language of flowers which
she remembers from folklore. She leaves with a prayer for all Christian souls,
and is not seen again.

The horror of the fight between Hamlet and Laertes in her grave recalls the
attention to Hamlet's love for her. She certainly loved him and, weak and
clinging as she is, she looked to him as a support for herself in married life.
And to this love she has become a martyr. Hamlet never seems to see her as
more than an example of womankind, and his bitter attacks addressed to her
in particular are really directed in general. Yet we are to assume that he has
loved her devotedly with a love which flickers and bursts into flame again
when he sees her dead body. Seen in this way, his assertions and challenges
to Laertes are not extravagant, even though they obviously parody Laertes'
style. But before this, his preoccupations with revenge on his uncle and with
his mother's lack of fidelity to her first husband prevent him from playing

the part one v ould expect of a lover who was a prince, an educated person, and a publi idol.

THE GHOST has been shown to represent an important part of the stage tradition of the revenge play; the physical features of the contemporary stage itself made possible the appearance of supernatural characters above or from beneath the stage through a trapdoor.

The Ghost is that of Hamlet's father. Almost everyone in Shakespeare's day believed in the possibility of dead men's spirits,

> Doomed for a certain term to walk the night,
> (I.v.10)

taking on the appearance of those bodies they inhabited on earth. The appearance of the Ghost in Hamlet is extremely effective: it comes very soon after the beginning of the play and it is seen clearly by three men, none of whom is directly connected with Hamlet's personal trial. Horatio, the scholar, is invited to arrest its progress and speak to it (I.i). The sceptic, who first thinks the Ghost will not appear, is in this way quickly won over to acknowledging its objective reality. Horatio is the man to make representations about it to Hamlet. The Ghost motions as if to speak, but in the end does not do so. Now Hamlet determines to talk to it himself but it is something malevolent, or appears to be, and that is reason enough for strict secrecy about it.

When it next appears, it beckons Hamlet apart in a further effort to maintain strict secrecy in communication, and then it speaks at length. Being a spirit within the tradition of the time, it has full knowledge of the death of the body it was once attached to. Hamlet listens intently to each point in the account of his father King Hamlet's death, and to each injunction which follows. The 'purpose' of the Ghost filling in a precise history of the events leading up to Claudius's accession is to corroborate previous hints, and confirm Hamlet's determination to avenge his father's death:

> thy commandment all alone shall live
> Within the book and volume of my brain.
> (I.v.102–3)

And from then on, Hamlet puts on the 'antic disposition' when he wants to.

The behaviour of the Ghost in relation to its surroundings is conventional and follows the fashion of the traditional folklore of Shakespeare's audience. The Ghost is a spirit which cannot rest in the other world because certain evil deeds done during its time on earth remain unexpiated. By day it suffers in the torments of the nether regions; by night it is condemned, for a certain period, to walk the earth, symbolically seeking comfort and expiation for the past wrongdoing. The disturbed spirit is not necessarily the evil-doer but Hamlet cannot be entirely certain of its role: is it benevolent, a true configuration of his father, or is it an evil spirit which has assumed the likeness of the old king so as to trick Hamlet and bring him to destruction? Hamlet tries it out on these lines by varying his modes of address, from the formal to the familiar and back again. In this case, the Ghost cannot rest until the wrongs it has suffered are avenged. The crowing of the cock, a signal that dawn is near, is a warning that spirits must leave the earth. As it goes it calls out from below, touching again on the need for secrecy in the purpose Hamlet has taken upon himself. He gives it the assurance it needs:

> Rest, rest, perturbéd spirit.   (I.v.182)

The only other appearance it makes is at the climax of the play (III.iv) when Hamlet sees the Queen in her closet, after the play-within-the-play. The Queen cannot see the Ghost, and thinks Hamlet is mad when he seems to address the air. The Ghost has come, it tells Hamlet,

> to whet thy almost blunted purpose   (III.iv.112)

– but the Queen remains unconvinced. The Ghost can do no more.

(iv) Shakespeare's Life

Little is known of Shakespeare's life, and that little is seldom of much use in enhancing the enjoyment of his plays. He was a person without special advantage in the way of birth or education. His plays, therefore, do not represent either a leisurely pursuit after perfection or the results of hard study or studious application. They are, rather, the spontaneous outpourings of a superlatively intelligent and imaginative mind, working as the occasion demanded and learning the trade as the opportunity arose. The plays have been arranged in the order in which they are thought to have written, and in this way show a movement from gifted apprenticeship to supreme competence.

William Shakespeare was born in 1564 in the market town of Stratford-upon-Avon, in Warwickshire, which lies in the middle of the land-mass of England and Wales. (The county town, Warwick, is known as the centre of England.) The country around is pleasant and unspectacular, and there are still in the town a number of buildings, houses and the church, for instance, which were there in Shakespeare's day. His father was a wealthy trader, and held office as mayor of the borough; his mother came from a well-to-do county family. It is assumed that he went as a boy to the local grammar school, where he would have had a good education on classical lines. All the teaching would have been in Latin, and most of the school hours would have been devoted to the study of the Latin classics. Some Greek was also taught. Such schooling would have been quite sufficient to give Shakespeare the sort of knowledge of Roman history and mythology which is evident in his plays, and it is not impossible that through his facility in reading Latin he became quickly competent in reading French and Italian. He was undoubtedly a great reader, and would have read some literature in English as well. To generalize, he seems to have got the source material for his plots from foreign works, but his skill in utilizing the resources of the language derives from the study of earlier English literature and a keen ear for the dialects of the English midlands where he lived. He married, at the early age of 18, a farmer's daughter, and they had children. But nothing more is known for certain about Shakespeare until he appears as an actor in London in 1592. His name occurs in lists of actors for two plays by Ben Jonson. (There is a tradition recorded by John Aubrey, a biographer of the following century, that Shakespeare took the part of the Ghost in his own *Hamlet*.) His father fell from affluence to comparative poverty during his boyhood. The Queen's company of actors visited Stratford in 1587. These two events may have been among the reasons which induced Shakespeare to leave home. By 1592 he was so well known as a playwright that another dramatist, Robert Greene, made an attack on him, the outcome of intense jealousy at his successes; Greene called him 'an upstart Crow beautified with our feathers', evidently because Shakespeare had not been to a university whereas Greene was leader of a group of dramatists who called themselves the 'University Wits'. Shakespeare published two long poems during the following two years, and by 1595 had fully established himself as an actor and playwright. He played for the Queen, and *Richard III*, *A Midsummer Night's Dream*, and *Romeo and Juliet* are among the plays written during this period. He became rich, redeeming the family reputation by buying one of the best houses in his native town.

During the period 1595 to 1601 he consolidated his reputation by writing his successful and much-loved history plays and comedies, including the two parts of *Henry IV*, *The Merchant of Venice*, *As You Like It* and *Twelfth Night*. In 1599 he acquired a financial share in the newly-built Globe theatre in London, and his plays were regularly staged there.

At the turn of the century Shakespeare seems to have passed to a more sombre cast of mind, since the great tragedies, *Hamlet*, *Othello*, *King Lear* and *Macbeth*, and the 'bitter comedies', *All's Well that Ends Well* and *Measure for Measure*, date from this time. This period in English history is characterized in many respects by a pervading air of disillusion, a turn away from the joyous youthfulness and buoyancy of the early Elizabethan age to a grimmer view of life associated with the Jacobean age; this may be reflected in the plays. When King James I came to the throne (1603) he took the Globe company into his direct patronage. This action did something to remove Shakespeare and his fellow actors from close touch with ordinary people, and from 1608 onwards there is much in his work (e.g. *Cymbeline*, *The Tempest* and the history play *Henry VIII*), which is withdrawn and romantic instead of directly confronting the essences of life as these are normally understood. The Globe theatre was burnt down in 1613 during a performance of *Henry VIII*, probably through an accident when the artillery was shot off in the play (I.iv). But by this time Shakespeare seems to have retired to Stratford, where he died in 1616, and where lies buried.

(v) A few passages of literary criticism relating to Hamlet

More must have been written about *Hamlet* than about any other single work of literature in the history of the world. Here are reproduced a few famous passages from this immense corpus. They are, clearly, literary criticism in the best sense; their aim is to increase the reader's enjoyment of the play through an added awareness of its significances and its beauties.

(a) *Coleridge* saw *Hamlet* as a psychological study of a man who could not bring about a balance between his inward thoughts and the external world.

> I believe the character of Hamlet may be traced to Shakespeare's deep and accurate science in mental philosophy. Indeed, that this character must have some connection with the common fundamental laws of our nature may be assumed from the fact that Hamlet has been the darling of every country in which the literature of England has been fostered. In order to understand him, it is essential that we should reflect on the constitution of our own minds. Man is distinguished from the brute animals in proportion as thought prevails over sense; but in the healthy processes of the mind, a balance is constantly maintained between the impressions from outward objects and the inward operations of the intellect; for if there be an overbalance in the contemplative faculty, man thereby becomes the creature of mere meditation, and loses his natural power of action. Now, one of Shakespeare's modes of creating characters is to conceive any one intellectual or moral faculty in morbid excess, and then to place himself, Shakespeare, thus mutilated or diseased, under given circumstances. In Hamlet he seems to have wished to exemplify the moral necessity of a due balance between our attention to the objects of our senses and our meditation on the working of our minds, – an *equilibrium* between the real and the imaginary worlds. In Hamlet this balance is disturbed; his thoughts and the images of his fancy are far more vivid than his actual perceptions, and his very perceptions, instantly passing through the *medium* of his contemplations, acquire, as they pass, a form and a colour not naturally their own. Hence we see a great, an almost enormous, intellectual activity, and a

proportionate aversion to real action consequent upon it, with all its symptoms and accompanying qualities. This character Shakespeare places in circumstances under which it is obliged to act on the spur of the moment: Hamlet is brave and careless of death; but he vacillates from sensibility, and procrastinates from thought, and loses the power of action in the energy of resolve. Thus it is that this tragedy presents a direct contrast to that of *Macbeth*: the one proceeds with the utmost slowness, the other with a crowded and breathless rapidity.

Coleridge describes Hamlet the introvert:

The first question we should ask ourselves is: What did Shakespeare mean when he drew the character of Hamlet? He never wrote anything without design, and what was his design when he sat down to produce this tragedy? My belief is, that he always regarded his story before he began to write much in the same light as a painter regards his canvas before he begins to paint: as a mere vehicle for his thoughts, as a ground upon which he was to work. What, then, was the point to which Shakespeare directed himself in *Hamlet*? He intended to portray a person in whose view the external world and all its incidents and objects were comparatively dim and of no interest in themselves, and which began to interest only when they were reflected in the mirror of his mind. Hamlet beheld external things in the same way that a man of vivid imagination, who shuts his eyes, sees what has previously made an impression on his organs. The poet places him in the most stimulating circumstances that a human being can be placed in. He is the heir-apparent of a throne: his father dies suspiciously; his mother excludes her son from his throne by marrying his uncle. This is not enough; but the Ghost of the murdered father is introduced to assure the son that he was put to death by his own brother. What is the effect upon the son? – instant action and pursuit of revenge? No: endless reasoning and hesitating, constant urging and solicitation of the mind to act, and as constant an escape from action; ceaseless reproaches of himself for sloth and negligence, while the whole energy of his resolution evaporates in these reproaches. This, too, not from cowardice, for he is drawn as one of the bravest of his time, – not from want of forethought or slowness of apprehension, for he sees through the very souls of all who surround him, but merely from that aversion to action which prevails among such as have a world in themselves . . .

S T Coleridge: *Notes and Lectures upon Shakespeare, 1808.*

(b) *Andrew Cecil Bradley* was Professor of Poetry at Oxford when he wrote the book from which the next extract is taken. He attributes Hamlet's failure to take action to a state of deep melancholy amounting almost to a disease of the mind, but not to be confused with insanity.

Is it possible to conceive an experience more desolating to a man such as we have seen Hamlet to be; and is its result anything but perfectly natural? It brings bewildered horror, then loathing, then despair of human nature. His whole mind is poisoned. He can never see Ophelia in the same light again: she is a woman, and his mother is a woman: if she mentions the word 'brief' to him, the answer drops from his lips like venom, 'as woman's love.' The last words of the soliloquy, which is *wholly* concerned with this subject, are,

> But break, my heart, for I must hold my tongue!

He can do nothing. He must lock in his heart, not any suspicion of his uncle that moves obscurely there, but that horror and loathing; and if his heart ever found relief, it was when those feelings, mingled with the love that never died out in him, poured themselves forth in a flood as he stood in his mother's chamber beside his father's marriage-bed.

If we still wonder, and ask why the effect of this shock should be so tremendous, let us observe that *now* the conditions have arisen under which Hamlet's highest endowments, his moral sensibility and his genius, become his enemies. A nature morally blunter would have felt even so dreadful a revelation less keenly. A slower and more limited and positive mind might not have extended so widely through its world the disgust and disbelief that have entered it. . . . But Hamlet has the imagination which, for evil as well as good, feels and sees all things in one. Thought is the element of his life, and his thought is infected. He cannot prevent himself from probing and lacerating the wound in his soul. One idea, full of peril, holds him fast, and he cries out in agony at it, but is impotent to free himself ('Must I remember?' 'Let me not think on't'). And when, with the fading of his passion, the vividness of this idea abates, it does so only to leave behind a boundless weariness and a sick longing for death.

And this is the time which his fate chooses. In this hour of uttermost weakness, this sinking of his whole being towards annihilation, there comes on him, bursting the bounds of the natural world with a shock of astonishment and terror, the revelation of his mother's adultery and his father's murder, and, with this, the demand on him, in the name of everything dearest and most sacred, to arise and act. And for a moment, though his brain reels and totters, his soul leaps up in passion to answer this demand. But it comes too late. It does but strike home the last rivet in the melancholy which holds him bound.

> The time is out of joint! O cursed spite
> That ever I was born to set it right, –

so he mutters within an hour of the moment when he vowed to give his life to the duty of revenge; and the rest of the story exhibits his vain efforts to fulfil this duty, his unconscious self-excuses and unavailing self-reproaches, and the tragic results of his delay.

'Melancholy,' I said, not dejection, nor yet insanity. That Hamlet was not far from insanity is very probable. His adoption of the pretence of madness may well have been due in part to fear of the reality; to an instinct of self-preservation, a fore-feeling that the pretence would enable him to give some utterance to the load that pressed on his heart and brain, and a fear that he would be unable altogether to repress such utterance. And if the pathologist calls his state melancholia, and even proceeds to determine its species, I see nothing to object to in that; I am grateful to him for emphasising the fact that Hamlet's melancholy was no mere common depression of spirits; and I have no doubt that many readers of the play would understand it better if they read an account of melancholia in a work on mental diseases. If we like to use the word 'disease' loosely, Hamlet's condition may truly be called diseased. No exertion of will could have dispelled it. Even if he had been able at once to do the bidding of the Ghost he would doubtless have still remained for some time under the cloud. It would be absurdly unjust to call *Hamlet* a study of melancholy, but it contains such a study.

But this melancholy is something very different from insanity, in anything like the usual meaning of that word. No doubt it might develop into insanity. The longing for death might become an irresistible impulse to self-destruction; the disorder of feeling and will might extend to sense and intellect; delusions might arise; and the man might become, as we say, incapable and irresponsible. But Hamlet's melancholy is some way from this condition. It is a totally different thing from the madness which he feigns; and he never, when alone or in company with Horatio alone, exhibits the signs of that madness. Nor is the dramatic use of this melancholy, again, open to the objections which would justly be made to the portrayal of an insanity which brought the hero to a tragic end. The man who suffers as Hamlet suffers – and thousands go about their business suffering thus in greater or less degree – is considered irresponsible neither by other people nor by himself: he is only too keenly conscious of his responsibility. He is therefore, so far, quite capable of being a tragic agent, which an insane person, at any rate according to Shakespeare's practice, is not. And finally, Hamlet's state is not one which a healthy mind is unable sufficiently to imagine. It is probably not further from average experience, nor more difficult to realise, than the great tragic passions of Othello, Antony or Macbeth.

A. C. Bradley, *Shakespearean Tragedy, 1904*

(c) *Ernest Jones* published in 1910 a paper in which he psychoanalysed Hamlet according to the system laid down by Freud. He found that, according to this theory, Hamlet's delay in taking action against Claudius springs from a cause he cannot discover; it was left to the psychologists to say what this cause was. Jones's argument is too close-packed to represent adequately in a short extract. Here, however, are some key passages taken from the book he finally wrote on the subject.

We are compelled then to take the position that there is some cause for Hamlet's vacillation which has not yet been fathomed. If this lies neither in his incapacity for action in general, nor in the inordinate difficulty of the particular task in question, then it must of necessity lie in the third possibility – namely, in some special feature of the task that renders it repugnant to him. This conclusion, that Hamlet at heart does not want to carry out the task, seems so obvious that it is hard to see how any open-minded reader of the play could avoid making it . . .

For some deep-seated reason, which is to him unacceptable, Hamlet is plunged into anguish at the thought of his father being replaced in his mother's affections by someone else. It is as if his devotion to his mother had made him so jealous for her affection that he had found it hard enough to share this even with his father and could not endure to share it with still another man. Against this thought, however, suggestive as it is, may be urged three objections. First, if it were in itself a full statement of the matter, Hamlet would have been aware of the jealousy, whereas we have concluded that the mental process we are seeking is hidden from him. Secondly, we see in it no evidence of the arousing of an old and forgotten memory. And, thirdly, Hamlet is being deprived by Claudius of no greater share in the Queen's affection than he had been by his own father, for the two brothers made exactly similar claims in this respect – namely, those of a loved husband. The last-named objection, however, leads us to the heart of the situation. How if, in fact, Hamlet had in years gone by, as a child, bitterly resented having had to share his mother's affection even with his own father, had regarded him as a rival, and had secretly wished him out of the way so that he might enjoy undisputed and undisturbed the monopoly of that affection. If such thoughts had been present in his mind in childhood days they evidently would have been 'repressed', and all traces of them obliterated, by filial piety and other educative influences. The actual realization of his early wish in the death of his father at the hands of a jealous rival would then have stimulated into activity these 'repressed' memories, which would have produced, in the form of depression and other suffering, an obscure aftermath of his childhood's conflict. This is at all events the mechanism that is actually found in the real Hamlets who are investigated psychologically.

The explanation, therefore, of the delay and self-frustration exhibited in the endeavour to fulfil his father's demand for vengeance is that to Hamlet the thought of incest and parricide combined is too intolerable to be borne. One part of him tries to carry out the task, the other flinches inexorably from the thought of it. How fain would he blot it out in that 'bestial oblivion' which unfortunately for him his conscience condemns. He is torn and tortured in an insoluble inner conflict . . .

Ernest Jones: *Hamlet and Oedipus*, 1949

H. J. Eysenck, in *Sense and Nonsense in Psychology* (1957), attempts a complete refutation of Jones's theory.

(d) *T. S. Eliot*, in a famous essay dated 1919, wrote on the inadequacy of *Hamlet* as a work of art. He later retracted from this extreme position, but what he said then about the relationship between Hamlet and his mother remains valid and helpful.

The grounds of *Hamlet's* failure [as a work of art] are not immediately obvious. Mr Robertson [J. M. Robertson, an American critic] is undoubtedly correct in concluding that the essential emotion of the play is the feeling of a son towards a guilty mother:

'[Hamlet's] tone is that of one who has suffered tortures on the score of his mother's degradation . . . The guilt of a mother is an almost intolerable motive for drama, but it had to be maintained and emphasized to supply a psychological solution, or rather a hint of one'.
This, however, is by no means the whole story. It is not merely the 'guilt of a mother' that cannot be handled as Shakespeare handled the suspicion of Othello, the infatuation of Antony, or the pride of Coriolanus. The subject might conceivably have expanded into a tragedy like these, intelligible, self-complete, in the sunlight. *Hamlet*, like the sonnets is full of some stuff that the writer could not drag to light, contemplate, or manipulate into art. And when we search for this feeling, we find it, as in the sonnets, very difficult to localize. You cannot point to it in the speeches; indeed, if you examine the two famous soliloquies you see the versification of Shakespeare, but a content which might be claimed by another, perhaps by the author of the *Revenge of Bussy d'Ambois*, Act v.Sc.i. We find Shakespeare's *Hamlet* not in the action, not in any quotations that we might select, so much as in an unmistakable tone which is unmistakably not in the earlier play.
The only way of expressing emotion in the form of art is by finding an

'objective correlative'; in other words, a set of objects, a situation, a chain of events which shall be the formula of that *particular* emotion; such that when the external facts, which must terminate in sensory experience, are given, the emotion is immediately evoked. If you examine any of Shakespeare's more successful tragedies, you will find this exact equivalence; you will find that the state of mind of Lady Macbeth walking in her sleep has been communicated to you by a skilful accumulation of imagined sensory impressions; the words of Macbeth on hearing of his wife's death strike us as if, given the sequence of events, these words were automatically released by the last event in the series. The artistic 'inevitability' lies in this complete adequacy of the external to the emotion; and this is precisely what is deficient in *Hamlet*. Hamlet (the man) is dominated by an emotion which is inexpressible, because it is in *excess* of the facts as they appear. And the supposed identity of Hamlet with his author is genuine to this point: that Hamlet's bafflement at the absence of objective equivalent to his feelings is a prolongation of the bafflement of his creator in the face of his artistic problem. Hamlet is up against the difficulty that his disgust is occasioned by his mother, but that his mother is not an adequate equivalent for it; his disgust envelops and exceeds her. It is thus a feeling which he cannot understand; he cannot objectify it, and it therefore remains to poison life and obstruct action. None of the possible actions can satisfy it; and nothing that Shakespeare can do with the plot can express Hamlet for him. And it must be noticed that the very nature of the *données* [fundamental ideas] of the problem precludes objective equivalence. To have heightened the criminality of Gertrude would have been to provide the formula for a totally different emotion in Hamlet; it is just *because* her character is so negative and insignificant that she arouses in Hamlet the feeling which she is incapable of representing.

The 'madness' of Hamlet lay to Shakespeare's hand; in the earlier play a simple ruse, and to the end, we may presume, understood as a ruse by the audience. For Shakespeare it is less than madness and more than feigned. The levity of Hamlet, his repetition of phrase, his puns, are not part of a deliberate plan of dissimulation, but a form of emotional relief. In the character Hamlet it is the buffoonery of an emotion which can find no outlet in action; in the dramatist it is the buffoonery of an emotion which he cannot express in art. The intense feeling, ecstatic or terrible, without an object or exceeding its object, is something which every person of sensibility has known; it is doubtless a subject of study for pathologists. It often occurs in adolescence: the ordinary person puts these feelings to sleep, or trims down his feelings to fit the business world; the artist keeps them alive by his ability to intensify the world to his emotions.

T. S. Eliot: 'Hamlet', in *Selected Essays*, 1932

(e) *Wilson Knight* finds Hamlet the man almost supernaturally shrewd; he has 'seen through humanity', and the essential rightness of his view makes the world a sad and disillusioning place for those around him.

Claudius' virtues . . . are manifest. So are his faults – his original crime, his skill in the less admirable kind of policy, treachery, and intrigue. But I would point clearly that, in the movement of the play, his faults are forced on him, and he is distinguished by creative and wise action, a sense of purpose, benevolence, a faith in himself and those around him, by love of his Queen:

> . . . and for myself –
> My virtue or my plague, be it either which –
> She's so conjunctive to my life and soul,
> That, as the star moves not but in his sphere,
> I could not but by her.
>
> (IV.vii.12–16)

In short he is very human. Now these are the very qualities Hamlet lacks. Hamlet is inhuman. He has seen through humanity. And this inhuman cynicism, however justifiable in this case on the plane of causality and individual responsibility, is a deadly and venomous thing. Instinctively the creatures of earth, Laertes, Polonius, Ophelia, Rosencrantz and Guildenstern, league themselves with Claudius: they are of his kind. They sever themselves from Hamlet. Laertes sternly warns Ophelia against her intimacy with Hamlet, so does Polonius. They are, in fact, all leagued against him, they are puzzled by him or fear him: he has no friend except Horatio, and Horatio, after the Ghost scenes, becomes a queer shadowy character who rarely gets beyond 'E'en so, my lord', 'My lord ——', and such-like phrases. The other persons are firmly drawn, in the round, creatures of flesh and blood. But Hamlet is not of flesh and blood he is a spirit of penetrating intellect and cynicism and misery, without faith in himself or anyone else, murdering his love of Ophelia, on the brink of insanity, taking delight in cruelty, torturing Claudius, wringing his mother's heart, a poison in the midst of the healthy bustle of the court. He is a superman among men. And he is a superman because he has walked and held converse with death, and his consciousness works in terms of death and the negation of cynicism. He has seen the truth, not alone of Denmark, but of humanity, of the universe: and the truth is evil. Thus Hamlet is an element of evil in the state of Denmark. The poison of his mental existence spreads outwards among things of flesh and blood, like acid eating into metal. They are helpless before his very inactivity and fall one after the other, like victims of an infectious disease. They are strong with the strength of health – but the demon of Hamlet's mind is a stronger thing than they. Futilely they try to get him out of their country; anything to get rid of him, he is not safe. But he goes with a cynical smile, and is no sooner gone than he is back again in their midst, meditating in graveyards, at home with death. Not till it has slain all, is the demon that grips Hamlet satisfied. And last it slays Hamlet himself:

> The spirit that I have seen
> May be the devil . . .
>
> (II.ii.573–74)

It was.
It was the devil of the knowledge of death, which possesses Hamlet and drives him from misery and pain to increasing bitterness, cynicism, murder, and madness. He has indeed bought converse with his father's spirit at the price of enduring and spreading Hell on earth. But however much we may sympathize with Ophelia, with Polonius, Rosencrantz, Guildenstern, the Queen, and Claudius, there is one reservation to be made. It is Hamlet who is right. What he says and thinks of them is true, and there is no fault in his logic. His own mother is indeed faithless, and the prettiness of Ophelia does in truth enclose a spirit as fragile and untrustworthy as her earthly beauty; Polonius is 'a foolish prating knave'; Rosencrantz and Guildenstern are time-servers and flatterers; Claudius, whose benevolence hides the guilt of murder, is, by virtue of that fact, 'a damned smiling villain'. In the same way the demon of cynicism which is in the mind of the poet and expresses itself in the figures of this play, has always this characteristic: it is right. One cannot argue with the cynic. It is unwise to offer him battle. For in the warfare of logic it will be found that he has all the guns.

> G. Wilson Knight – 'The Embassy of Death: An Essay on *Hamlet*',
> in *The Wheel of Fire*, 1930, 1949.

(f) *C. S. Lewis* said, in 1942:
I believe that we read Hamlet's speeches with interest chiefly because they describe so well a certain spiritual region through which most of us have passed and anyone in his circumstances might be expected to pass, rather than because of our concern to understand how and why this particular man entered it. I foresee an objection on the ground that I am thus really admitting his 'character' in the only sense that matters and that all characters whatever could be equally well talked away by

the method I have adopted. But I do really find a distinction. . . . In Shakespeare himself I find Beatrice to be a character who could not be thus dissolved. We are interested not in some vision seen through her eyes, but precisely in the wonder of her being the girl she is. A comparison of the sayings we remember from her part with those we remember from Hamlet's brings out the contrast. On the one hand, 'I wonder that you will still be talking, Signior Benedick', 'There was a star danced and under that I was born', 'Kill Claudio'; on the other, 'The undiscovered country, from whose bourne no traveller returns', 'Use every man after his desert, and who should 'scape whipping?', 'The rest is silence.' Particularly noticeable is the passage where Hamlet professes to be describing his own character. 'I am myself indifferent honest, but yet I could accuse me of such things that it were better my mother had not borne me; I am very proud, revengeful, ambitious'. It is, of course, possible to devise some theory which explains these self-accusations in terms of character. But long before we have done so the real significance of the lines has taken possession of our imagination for ever. 'Such fellows as I' does not mean 'such fellows as Goethe's Hamlet, or Coleridge's Hamlet, or any Hamlet': it means *men* – creatures shapen in sin and conceived in iniquity – and the vast, empty visions of them 'crawling between earth and heaven' is what really counts and really carries the burden of the play.

It is often cast in the teeth of the great critics that each in painting *Hamlet* has drawn a portrait of himself. How if they were right? I would go a long way to meet Beatrice or Falstaff or Mr Jonathan Oldbuck or Disraeli's Lord Monmouth. I would not cross the room to meet Hamlet. It would never be necessary. He is always where I am. The method of the whole play is much nearer to Mr Eliot's own method in poetry than Mr Eliot suspects. Its true hero is man – haunted man – man with his mind on the frontier of two worlds, man unable to either quite to reject or quite to admit the supernatural, man struggling to get something done as man has struggled from the beginning, yet incapable of achievement because of his inability to understand either himself or his fellows or the real quality of the universe which has produced him. To be sure, some hints of more particular motives for Hamlet's delay are every now and then fadged up to silence our questions, just as some show of motives is offered for the Duke's temporary abdication in *Measure for Measure*. In both cases it is only scaffolding or machinery. To mistake these mere *succedanea* [substitutions] for the real play and to try to work them up into a coherent psychology is the great error. I once had a whole batch of School Certificate answers on the 'Nun's Priest's Tale' by boys whose form-master was apparently a breeder of poultry. Everything that Chaucer had said in describing Chauntecleer and Pertelote was treated by them simply and solely as evidence about the precise breed of these two birds. And, I must admit, the result was very interesting. They proved beyond doubt that Chauntecleer was very different from our modern specialized strains and much closer to the Old English 'barn-door fowl'. But I couldn't help feeling that they had missed something. I believe our attention to Hamlet's 'character' in the usual sense misses almost as much.

Perhaps I should rather say that it *would* miss as much if our behaviour when we are actually reading were not wiser that our criticism in cold blood. The critics, or most of them, have at any rate kept constantly before us the knowledge that in this play there is greatness and mystery. They were never entirely wrong. Their error, in my view, was to put the mystery in the wrong place – in Hamlet's motives rather than in that darkness which enwraps Hamlet and the whole tragedy and all who read or watch it. It is a mysterious play in the sense of being a play about mystery. Mr Eliot suggests that 'more people have thought *Hamlet* a work of art because they found it interesting, than have found it interesting because it is a work of art'. When he wrote that sentence he must have been very near to what I believe to be the truth. The play is, above all else, *interesting*. But artistic failure is not in itself interesting, nor often interesting in any way: artistic success always is. To interest is the first duty of art; no other excellences will even begin to compensate for failure in this, and very serious faults will be covered by this, as by charity. The hypothesis that this play interests by being good and not by being bad has therefore the first claim on our consideration. The burden of proof rests on the other side. Is not the fascinated interest of the critics most naturally explained by supposing that this is the precise effect the play was written to produce? They may be finding the mystery in the wrong place; but the fact that they can never leave *Hamlet* alone, the continual groping, the sense, unextinguished by over a century of failures, that we have here something of inestimable importance, is surely the best evidence that the real and lasting mystery of our human situation has been greatly depicted.

C. S. Lewis: *Hamlet: The Prince or the Poem*, 1942

(vi) Bibliography

(See also the sources quoted in the foregoing section of this Introduction).

(1) General Criticism and helps to the study of Shakespeare, with special reference to *Hamlet*:

Bradley, A. C.: *Shakespearean Tragedy: Lectures on 'Hamlet', 'Othello', 'King Lear', and 'Macbeth'*, Macmillan, 1904. Subjective, philosophical studies of the characters in the tragedies.

Gittings, R. (ed.): *The Living Shakespeare*, 1960. Transcriptions of a lively series of BBC talks.

Granville-Barker, H.: *Prefaces to Shakespeare*, 1927–48. Volume I (newly issued in 1958) contains the preface on *Hamlet*. A valuable account of the views of an actor-producer.

Halliday, F. E.: *Shakespeare and his Critics*, 1958. A survey of trends in Shakespeare criticism.

Halliday, F. E.: *A Shakespeare Companion: 1550–1950*, 1952.

Knight, G. Wilson: *The Wheel of Fire*, 1930, 1949.

Leech, C.: *Shakespeare's Tragedies and Other Studies in Seventeenth Century Drama*, 1950.

Raleigh, W.: *Shakespeare*, 1907. An excellent general introduction to the plays.

Ridler, A. (ed.): *Shakespeare Criticism 1919–35*, Oxford, 1936.

Shakespeare Survey 9, Cambridge, 1956. This number is devoted to *Hamlet*.

Smith, D. N.: *Shakespeare Criticism: Heminge and Condell to Carlyle*, Oxford, 1916.

Spencer, H.: *The Art and Life of William Shakespeare*, New York, 1940.

(2) Shakespeare's Language and Imagery.

Hulme, H. M.: *Explorations in Shakespeare's Language*, 1962.

Onions, C. T.: *A Shakespeare Glossary*, Oxford, 1953 (latest edition with new addenda). Comprehensive and not difficult to use.

Spurgeon, C. F. E.: *Shakespeare's Imagery and what it tells us*, Cambridge, 1935.

(3) Sources.

Muir, K.: *Shakespeare's Sources*, Vol. 1, 1957. The sources of *Hamlet* are discussed at pp. 110ff.

(4)   The texts of the play.

Duthie, G. I.: *The 'Bad' Quarto of 'Hamlet': A Critical Study*, Cambridge, 1841. A specialized study; for general information on Quartos and Folios, see a 'companion' in list (1) above.

(5)   The Age of Shakespeare.

Craig, H.: *The Enchanted Glass: The Elizabethan Mind in Literature*, New York, 1936, Oxford, 1950.
Ford, B. (ed.): *The Age of Shakespeare. A Pelican Guide to English Literature*, Vol. 2. 1955. A volume of essays suitable for advanced students on many aspects of Shakespeare's age.
Lee, S. and Onions, C. T. (editors): *Shakespeare's England: An Account of the Life and Manners of his Age*, Oxford, 2 vols., 1916.
Tillyard, E. M. W.: *The Elizabethan World Picture*, Chatto & Windus, 1943.

(6)   The Theatre of Shakespeare's day.

Adams, J. C.: *The Globe Playhouse: its Design and Equipment*, Cambridge, U.S.A., 1942.
Bradbrook, M. C.: *Elizabethan Stage Conditions: a Study of their Place in the Interpretation of Shakespeare's Plays*, Cambridge, 1932.
Hodges, C. W.: *The Globe Restored: A Study of the Elizabethan Theatre*, Benn, 1953, Oxford 1968.
Mander, R., and Mitchenson, J.: *Hamlet through the Ages: a Pictorial Survey from 1709*, 1952.
Shakespeare Survey 12, Cambridge, 1959.

(7)   Shakespeare's Life.

Williams, C.: *A Short Life of Shakespeare*, 1933.

Hamlet PRINCE OF DENMARK

Dramatis personae

CLAUDIUS, *King of Denmark*
HAMLET, *son of the late king, and nephew of the present king*
POLONIUS, *the Lord Chamberlain*
HORATIO, *a friend of Hamlet's*
LAERTES, *Polonius' son*
VOLTIMAND,
CORNELIUS,
ROSENCRANTZ, } *courtiers*
GUILDENSTERN,
OSRIC
A GENTLEMAN,
A PRIEST.
MARCELLUS, } *officers*
BERNARDO,
FRANCISCO, *a soldier*
REYNALDO, *Polonius' servant*
PLAYERS.
TWO CLOWNS, *grave-diggers*
FORTINBRAS, *Prince of Norway*
A CAPTAIN.
ENGLISH AMBASSADORS.
GERTRUDE, *Queen of Denmark, Hamlet's mother*
OPHELIA, *Polonius' daughter*
LORDS, LADIES, OFFICERS, SOLDIERS, SAILORS, MESSENGERS, *and
other* ATTENDANTS
GHOST *of Hamlet's father, King Hamlet*

SCENE – *Denmark*

I. i.   The play begins with the changing of the guard on a cold winter's night at the castle of Elsinore. The men talk about a ghost they think they have seen looking exactly like the dead King of Denmark. The fact that his spirit is not at rest must forebode some great misfortune – perhaps, they think, an invasion from Norway. The ghost appears a second time and, without speaking, fades as the cock crows. The men believe it will speak to young Hamlet, the dead King's son.

    In this scene are brought together both dramatic interest (the change of guard, the nervous, worried exchanges of the men, the appearances of the ghost) and some initial information on the political situation in Denmark (a king recently dead, turmoil at the threat of an invasion). Thus a long exposition is avoided; the drama begins at once, without long explanations. The play is about a ghost and the message it brings. It is certainly an appearance which stands for some reality, but the nature of that reality is as yet unclear. Horatio and Bernardo are in fact wrong to link it with the threatened invasion but it means that trouble of some sort is coming. The Ghost first appears as an intruder, usurping the night. At the second appearance it is majestic, the ruler against whom violence would be wrong. The cock crows at the approach of dawn, and natural conditions return.

*   *Elsinore:* is a large castle with towers and courtyards on the east coast of the island of Zealand in Denmark. The *platform* is a level place within the castle used for mounting guns.

2   *Stand . . . yourself:* Stop and identify yourself. – Bernardo is the *relief* at the change of guard.

6   *upon your hour:* at the exact time (for the changing of the guard).

13   *rivals of my watch:* companions on guard with me.

15   *ground:* country.

15   *liegemen . . . Dane:* men who are loyal servants of the Danish King.

16   *Give . . . night:* (May God) give you a good night.

19   *A piece of him* – Perhaps he means that he has not yet woken up fully to the surroundings and has left part of himself downstairs in the warmth. Horatio is not in sympathy with all the tension that the others feel.

21   *this thing* – i.e. the ghost. When they have changed guard, they begin almost at once to talk about *this thing*, but do not immediately refer to it by name; this heightens the suspense and sets the drama moving quickly. Up to now, all have spoken in short strained phrases, showing that some deep-set fear is oppressing them.

23   *fantasy:* imagination.

24   *let belief . . . Touching:* allow himself to believe anything about.

25   *of us:* by us.

Hamlet ACT I scene i

Elsinore. A platform in front of the castle.*

FRANCISCO *at his post.*
BERNARDO *enters and goes up to him.*

BERNARDO	Who's there?	
FRANCISCO	Nay, answer me. Stand, and unfold yourself.*	
BERNARDO	Long live the king!	
FRANCISCO	Bernardo?	
BERNARDO	He.	5
FRANCISCO	You come most carefully upon your hour.*	
BERNARDO	'Tis now struck twelve; get thee to bed, Francisco.	
FRANCISCO	For this relief much thanks. 'Tis bitter cold,	
	And I am sick at heart.	
BERNARDO	Have you had quiet guard?	
FRANCISCO	Not a mouse stirring.	10
BERNARDO	Well, good night.	
	If you do meet Horatio and Marcellus,	
	The rivals of my watch,* bid them make haste.	
FRANCISCO	I think I hear them. – Stand, ho! Who is there?	

Enter HORATIO *and* MARCELLUS.

HORATIO	Friends to this ground.*	
MARCELLUS	And liegemen to the Dane.*	15
FRANCISCO	Give you good night.*	
MARCELLUS	O, farewell, honest soldier.	
	Who hath relieved you?	
FRANCISCO	Bernardo has my place.	
	Give you good night.	[*Exit*
MARCELLUS	Holla! Bernardo!	
BERNARDO	Say –	
	What, is Horatio there?	
HORATIO	A piece of him.*	
BERNARDO	Welcome, Horatio. Welcome, good Marcellus.	20
MARCELLUS	What, has this thing* appeared again tonight?	
BERNARDO	I have seen nothing.	
MARCELLUS	Horatio says 'tis but our fantasy,*	
	And will not let belief* take hold of him	
	Touching this dreaded sight twice seen of us.*	25

1

29   *approve our eyes:* confirm what we have seen. – Horatio is sceptical of what he has been
        told about a ghost.
30   *Tush* – an exclamation of contempt: 'Nonsense!'
31   *assail your ears:* attack your hearing (with), i.e. tell you forcibly. – The image of an army
        attacking (*assail*) is continued with *fortified* in the following line.
33   *sit we:* let us sit. – Horatio says this with an air of resignation.
35   *Last night of all:* Only last night.
36   *yon same star:* that very star over there. – It is probably a star in the constellation of the
        Great Bear, which swings around the Pole Star. The point Bernardo wishes to
        make is that it is *exactly* the same time, as shown by the stars; the apparition
        may then be very near.
37   *his:* its. – The form *its* occurs in some places in Shakespeare, but *his* is much more common
        for inanimate objects as well as human beings.
37   *t'illume:* to light up.
41   *the same . . . dead:* the same form, just like the dead king.
42   They have brought Horatio against his will to see the ghost, and now they want him to
        speak to it, because, as they say, he is a scholar, not just a common soldier.
        Perhaps they think he will speak in Latin, since Latin was considered to be an
        effective language for exorcizing spirits.
44   *harrows me:* tears into me – like the sharp teeth of a harrow cutting through the earth.
        The word *harrow* is still used in modern English in this sense, but the force
        of the metaphor is lost.
45   *It would . . . to:* It wants to be spoken to.
46   *usurp'st:* intrude upon. – The spirit has intruded upon the night, when all should be
        quiet, to walk about, and has wrongfully taken on the appearance of the dead
        King of Denmark (the *majesty of buried Denmark* in line 48), whose body
        should be at rest.
49   *charge:* order. – But the ghost will not be ordered, and walks away in anger. It also seems
        to be offended because it has been accused of usurping.
54   *fantasy:* Marcellus (in line 23) reported that Horatio called it *fantasy*.
55   *on't:* of it.
56   *Before my God . . . eyes* (line 58): I swear before my God, I could not bring myself to believe
        this if it were not for the undeniable proof (*true avouch*) of my senses (*sensible*),
        my own eyes.

Therefore I have entreated him along
With us to watch the minutes of this night,
That, if again this apparition come,
He may approve our eyes,* and speak to it.

HORATIO Tush,* tush, 'twill not appear.

BERNARDO   Sit down awhile,   30
And let us once again assail your ears,*
That are so fortified against our story,
What we two nights have seen.

HORATIO   Well, sit we* down,
And let us hear Bernardo speak of this.

BERNARDO Last night of all,*   35
When yon same star* that's westward from the pole
Had made his* course t'illume* that part of heaven
Where now it burns, Marcellus and myself,
The bell then beating one –

MARCELLUS Peace, break thee off; look, where it comes again!   40

Enter GHOST.

BERNARDO In the same figure,* like the king that's dead.
MARCELLUS Thou art a scholar;* speak to it, Horatio.
BERNARDO Looks it not like the king? Mark it, Horatio.
HORATIO Most like – It harrows me* with fear and wonder.
BERNARDO It would be spoke to.*
MARCELLUS   Question it, Horatio.   45
HORATIO What art thou, that usurp'st* this time of night,
Together with that fair and warlike form
In which the majesty of buried Denmark
Did sometimes march? By heaven I charge* thee, speak!
MARCELLUS It is offended.
BERNARDO   See, it stalks away!   50
HORATIO Stay! speak, speak! I charge thee, speak!

                              [*Exit* GHOST

MARCELLUS 'Tis gone, and will not answer.
BERNARDO How now, Horatio! You tremble and look pale.
Is not this something more than fantasy?*
What think you on 't?*   55
HORATIO Before my God,* I might not this believe
Without the sensible and true avouch
Of mine own eyes.
MARCELLUS   Is it not like the king?

61 *Norway*, i.e. the King of Norway.
62 *parle:* conference, which became heated and led to fighting.
63 *He smote . . . ice:* he beat the Poles in sledges (*sledded*) on the ice. – This must refer to some
       skirmish fought between the Danes and Poles on a frozen river or lake.
65 *jump:* exactly.
66 *martial stalk:* proud military walk.
67 *In what . . . not:* I do not know precisely what one should think and plan to do (*to work*)
       (about this).
68 *in the gross . . . opinion:* my general impression is that – He thinks that the apparition may
       signify bad fortune (*bodes some strange eruption* in the following line) for
       Denmark. An upheaval of the state he calls an *eruption*, as the earth has erupted
       a spirit from the dead.
            But nothing more can be known for certain, since the ghost refused to
       speak. They sit down again, after having leapt up when the ghost appeared,
       and Marcellus turns to another subject; he asks why this special watch has
       been posted in Elsinore. The question is an opportunity for the current
       political position of Denmark to be explained.
70 *Good now:* Well – as an interjection which makes a fresh start to the conversation.
72 *So nightly . . . land:* makes the people (*subject*) of the country work every night in this way.
73 *why:* why there is.
73 *cast:* casting; *brazen:* brass.
74 *foreign mart:* marketing abroad.
75 *impress:* forced labour.
75 *sore:* heavy.
76 *Does not divide . . .* – i.e. they are forced to work building ships on Sundays as well as
       week-days.
77 *might be toward:* can be under way, on hand.
78 *joint-labourer:* a worker together. – The workers are being forced to work at night as
       well as during the day-time. Shakespeare combines the ideas of work and time
       by making Marcellus talk of the night and the day themselves as labourers.
80 *whisper:* rumour, what is whispered among the people. Horatio is given the opportunity
       to speak about the political situation of Denmark, and, as a scholar, he rises
       to the occasion admirably. Shakespeare has thus made it possible for his
       audience to learn something of the recent history of Denmark, of events which
       took place before the action of the play begins.
81 *even but now:* only just now.
83 *Thereto . . . pride:* urged on to it (*Thereto*) by his (Fortinbras's) great pride and ambition;
       pricked suggests 'spurred on' as a horse is spurred; *emulate* implies that he
       wanted to be like the King of Denmark in power and glory.
84 *the combat:* fight (between two people).
84 *Hamlet* – not the hero of the play but his father, the dead King.
85 *so* – i.e. as valiant.
85 *this side . . . world* – i.e. everyone in this part of the world, 'all of us'.
86 *a sealed . . . heraldry:* a certified agreement made fully binding by civil law and the
       formalities of chivalry. – In medieval times, *heraldry*, the science of coats of
       arms, formed a part of the code of chivalry, a series of unwritten rules by which
       contestants fought in battles. Knights and other officers displayed devices on
       their shields (coats of arms), primarily so that people could recognize them
       when they were cased up in armour, and they were bound to fight according
       to an elaborate set of rules which the bearing of such coats of arms committed
       them to. The word *compact* is to be stressed on the second syllable.
89 *stood seized of:* had in his possession (*seize* is used in a technical, legal sense here).
90 *Against the which:* on the other hand.
90 *a moiety competent:* an equally large (*competent*) share (*moiety*) of land. – Legal phrases in
       English sometimes take the form of a noun followed by an adjective, the
       reverse of the usual arrangement, as in *court martial*. Horatio uses other
       phrases of this type, e.g. *article designed* (line 94) and *terms compulsatory*
       (line 103) in this speech.
91 *gaged:* pledged.
91 *which had returned . . . Hamlet* (line 95): which would have been made part of (*returned To*)
       the possessions (*inheritance*) of Fortinbras, if he had been the conqueror
       (*vanquisher*), as, by the same agreement (*covenant*) and terms (*carriage*) of the

HORATIO As thou art to thyself.
     Such was the very armour he had on   60
     When he the ambitious Norway* combated;
     So frowned he once, when, in an angry parle,*
     He smote the sledded Polacks on the ice. —*
     'Tis strange.

MARCELLUS Thus twice before, and jump* at this dead hour, 65
     With martial stalk* hath he gone by our watch.

HORATIO In what particular thought to work I know not;*
     But, in the gross* and scope of my opinion,
     This bodes some strange eruption to our state.

MARCELLUS Good now,* sit down, and tell me, he that knows, 70
     Why this same strict and most observant watch
     So nightly* toils the subject of the land,
     And why* such daily cast* of brazen cannon,
     And foreign mart* for implements of war.
     Why such impress* of shipwrights, whose sore* task 75
     Does not divide* the Sunday from the week?
     What might be toward,* that this sweaty haste
     Doth make the night joint-labourer* with the day?
     Who is 't that can inform me?

HORATIO   That can I;
     At least, the whisper* goes so: our last king, 80
     Whose image even but now* appeared to us,
     Was, as you know, by Fortinbras of Norway,
     Thereto* pricked on by a most emulate pride,
     Dared to the combat;* in which our valiant Hamlet* —
     For so* this side* of our known world esteemed him — 85
     Did slay this Fortinbras; who, by a sealed* compact,
     Well ratified by law and heraldry,
     Did forfeit, with his life, all those his lands
     Which he stood seized of* to the conqueror;
     Against the which,* a moiety competent* 90
     Was gaged* by our king, which had returned*

---

91 (*cont'd*) relevant clause (*article designed*), Fortinbras's (piece of land) went to King
      Hamlet. – Horatio the student talks about legal affairs in the involved language
      of law itself. In case the attention of his listener is flagging he takes steps to
      engage it again with *Now, sir* in the next sentence.

95   *young Fortinbras* – i.e. the son of the dead King of Norway, who was given his father's name, just as the hero of the play was given the name of King Hamlet his father.

96   *Of inapprovéd . . . full:* hot-spirited and full of untried (*inapprovéd*) courage. – Some early editions of the play have *unimproved*, 'not (yet) usefully employed' for *inapproved.*

97   *skirts:* outlying regions – where men would be less under the firm control of a central government.

98   *Sharked . . . diet, to:* picked up indiscriminately (as a *shark* picks up food) a company (*list*) of unruly adventurers (*resolutes*) who will, for nothing but regular meals (*food and diet*), take on.

100   *hath a stomach in't:* gives an opportunity for courage. – In Shakespeare's day many people thought that the 'seat', or place of origin, of courage in a person was the stomach; *stomach*, therefore, came to mean 'courage'. Here there is probably a play on the idea of *food* and *diet* in the line before.

101   *doth well . . . state:* is very clearly evident to our rulers.

102   *of:* from.

103   *compulsatory:* that cannot be avoided, compelling.

103   *foresaid:* mentioned before – yet another legal term.

106   *source of:* origin of, reason for. – The image is of the *source* or spring of a river; it is extended by *head*, i.e. fountain-head, at the end of the line.

107   *post-haste:* moving about with great speed.

107   *romage:* turmoil.

109   *Well may it sort:* It may very well fit in (with this explanation). – As we shall see, this is not the reason for the appearance of the ghost, but we are to believe that as yet no one in the court suspects that King Hamlet was murdered. (Some have thought that *sort* means 'turn out' here, as it sometimes does elsewhere; the meaning of the phrase would then be, 'I pray that things may turn out well.')

111   *That was . . . question:* who has been and now is the cause (*question*).

112   *A mote . . .* – Horatio is no longer disposed to underestimate the importance of the apparition. In itself it is as trifling as a speck of dust (a *mote*), but when the speck gets into the eye it causes great trouble. This and the phrase *the mind's eye* (i.e. one's imagination) make vivid imagery. Horatio goes on to give a learned account of spirits which have played a part in Roman history.

113   *most high . . . Rome:* the commonwealth (*state*) of Rome at its highest and most glorious (*palmy*, since the palm was an emblem of glory and victory).

114   *the mightiest Julius:* the most mighty Julius (Caesar). – In Shakespeare's play *Julius Caesar* (written shortly before *Hamlet*), it is Cassius who speaks of spirits as instruments of fear and warning (I.ii.70–1). In the same play, Caesar's wife Calpurnia speaks of those who say they have seen terrible happenings. It is the night before Caesar's death:

> graves have yawned, and yielded up their dead   (II.ii.18)

The theme of this passage in *Hamlet* is that spirits have appeared at other times, when everything seemed to be going well, to warn people of disasters to come.

115   *tenantless* – i.e. empty, unoccupied by the dead.

115   *sheeted:* in winding sheets – the usual clothing for the dead in Shakespeare's day.

117   *As, stars . . .* – It is difficult to see how this line and the three following are connected with what has gone before. The passage makes good sense if (as J. Dover Wilson has suggested) it is moved so as to follow line 125. The drift of the passage is then (from line 121). 'Similar spirits have appeared as a warning to us in our own country, and in the heavens as well as on earth; there have, for example (line 117), been comets, sun-spots and eclipses of the moon'. People in Shakespeare's day believed that all such manifestations in the sky were evil omens.

117   *dews of blood* – Comets were believed to be the cause of 'red dew', drops of red liquid seen on the ground in the early morning. (Scientists now think that red dew is caused by drops of red liquid falling from chrysalises when the butterflies cased in them break their way out.)

118   *Disasters* – The use of this word and of *influence* in the next line is very appropriate, since both relate to astrology, the study of the ways in which stars are supposed to influence human life on the earth. *Disaster* comes from Latin *dis astre*, meaning 'unfavourable star', and its present-day meaning, 'calamity', arises from this.

To the inheritance of Fortinbras,
Had he been vanquisher, as, by the same covenant
And carriage of the article designed,
His fell to Hamlet. Now, sir, young Fortinbras,*   95
Of inapproved* mettle hot and full,
Hath in the skirts* of Norway, here and there,
Sharked up* a list of lawless resolutes,
For food and diet, to some enterprise
That hath a stomach in 't;* which is no other —   100
As it doth well appear unto our state* —
But to recover of* us, by strong hand
And terms compulsatory,* those foresaid* lands
So by his father lost. And this, I take it,
Is the main motive of our preparations,   105
The source of* this our watch, and the chief head
Of this post-haste* and romage* in the land.
BERNARDO I think it be no other but e'en so.
Well may it sort* that this portentous figure
Comes arméd through our watch, so like the king   110
That was and is the question* of these wars.
HORATIO A mote* it is to trouble the mind's eye.
In the most high* and palmy state of Rome,
A little ere the mightiest Julius* fell,
The graves stood tenantless,* and the sheeted* dead   115
Did squeak and gibber in the Roman streets:
As, stars* with trains of fire, and dews of blood,*
Disasters* in the sun; and the moist star,*
Upon whose influence Neptune's empire stands,

---

118 (cont'd) *the moist star:* the moon. — Shakespeare often thinks of the moon as moist or watery,
because it controls the tides of the Earth's oceans. (The oceans are spoken of as
Neptune's empire in the following line; Neptune was god of the sea in Roman
mythology.)

120 *sick almost to doomsday* – i.e. extremely pale, giving very little light because it was eclipsed. The Bible prophesies that when Christ comes again, 'Immediately . . . shall the sun be darkened, and the moon shall not give her light' (*Matthew* 24 : 29), and Horatio associates this with doomsday, the day on which God will judge the earth. In general, eclipses were thought to be very bad omens.

121 *the like precurse:* similar omens.

122 *harbingers:* heralds.

122 *still:* always.

122 *the fates:* goddesses of destiny – hence 'disasters'.

125 *climatures:* regions.

127 *I'll cross . . . me:* I will cross its path, even if it destroys me with its curse (*blast*). – It was thought that anyone who crossed the path of a ghost fell under its evil influence. Horatio now breaks up the measured flow of his speech, and in his excitement calls out in lines of various lengths.

131 *do ease:* give comfort.

133 *art privy to:* have secret knowledge of.

134 *Which happily . . . avoid:* which, if it becomes known beforehand, your country may perhaps (*happily*) be able to avoid. – This line is an example of how Shakespeare is able to dispense with ordinary signals of grammar, and packs a great deal of meaning into a small space.

137 *Extorted:* taken by force.

137 *womb:* stomach. – Horatio has heard that spirits were sometimes said to walk on the earth because they had secretly buried treasure, and could not rest until they had told a living being where it was hidden.

*   *Cock crows* – The crowing of the cock is taken as a sign that the dawn is breaking; the ghost must go because spirits walk only at night.

140 *partisan:* battle-axe.

141 *stand:* stop. – They think they engage it, but it disappears.

143 *being so majestical:* since it is so majestic in its bearing.

144 *the show of:* a display of.

146 *our vain . . . mockery:* our blows aimed at it are fruitless (*vain*), a laughable imitation of enmity (*malicious mockery*). – Marcellus tried to stop it by hitting out at it, but it went nevertheless.

148 *started:* jumped.

148 *a guilty . . . summons:* a guilty person in terror when called (to answer a charge).

150 *the trumpet to the morn* – i.e. the cock 'wakes up' the morning as an army trumpeter sounds his trumpet to wake up the soldiers.

153 *sea . . . air* – This is a way of enumerating the four 'elements', which, so it was believed, were the basis of all creation. The line therefore means 'absolutely everywhere'.

154 *Th' extravagant . . . confine:* the wandering, straying spirit hurries (*hies*) away to its place of confinement. – The words *extravagant* and *erring* both mean 'wandering away from the proper path' but *extra-* suggests also 'beyond its proper limits'. In this line *his* means *its*; the ghost is everywhere referred to as *it*, and the possessive form *its* is rarely used in Shakespeare (see note to line 37 above).

156 *made probation:* gave proof.

Was sick almost to doomsday* with eclipse.   120
And even the like precurse* of fierce events –
As harbingers* preceding still* the fates,*
And prologue to the omen coming on –
Have heaven and earth together demonstrated
Unto our climatures* and countrymen. –   125
But, soft, behold! Lo, where it comes again!
Enter GHOST *again.*
I'll cross it,* though it blast me. – [*To the* GHOST] Stay,
illusion!
If thou hast any sound or use of voice,
Speak to me.
If there be any good thing to be done,   130
That may to thee do ease* and grace to me,
Speak to me.
If thou art privy to* thy country's fate,
Which happily* foreknowing may avoid,
O, speak!   135
Or if thou hast uphoarded in thy life
Extorted* treasure in the womb* of earth,
For which, they say, you spirits oft walk in death,
                                                [Cock crows
Speak of it. – Stay, and speak! – Stop it, Marcellus.
MARCELLUS Shall I strike it with my partisan?*   140
HORATIO Do, if it will not stand.*
BERNARDO   'Tis here!
HORATIO   'Tis here!
MARCELLUS 'Tis gone!   [*Exit* GHOST
We do it wrong, being so majestical,*
To offer it the show of* violence,
For it is as the air, invulnerable,   145
And our vain blows malicious mockery.*
BERNARDO It was about to speak when the cock crew.
HORATIO And then it started* like a guilty thing*
Upon a fearful summons. I have heard,
The cock, that is the trumpet to the morn,*   150
Doth with his lofty and shrill-sounding throat
Awake the god of day, and at his warning,
Whether in sea or fire, in earth or air,*
Th'extravagant* and erring spirit hies
To his confine. And of the truth herein   155
This present object made probation.*

158   *ever 'gainst . . . Wherein:* always when the time approaches at which.
159   *our Saviour's birth* – i.e. the birthday of Jesus Christ; the season referred to is Christmas,
          the time of year when his birth is celebrated.
160   *The bird of dawning* – i.e. the cock.
161   *abroad:* away from its proper resting-place.
162   *wholesome:* pure – free from spirits.
162   *strike:* exert evil influence.
163   *takes:* strikes (creatures down) with disease.
166   *in russet mantle clad:* dressed (*clad*) in a mantle of rust-coloured cloth. – The image is of
          the red dawn walking like a man over the eastern skyline.
168   *Break we . . . up:* Let us disperse our guard.
170   *young Hamlet* is the hero of the play, introduced here so easily and casually; we are to see
          him in the next scene, and this passage serves to herald his appearance.
170   *upon my life* – He swears 'upon his life' that what he says will come true.
173   *needful . . . loves:* required of us by reason of our love (for him as prince).
175   *convenient,* for *conveniently.*

The general mood of the play is now established: in the dark, cold, silent night men who
are bewildered at what they feel and see around them, who are 'sick at heart' with some
undefined terror, have created an air of tension which promises tragedy. They have tried
to link their fears with the military preparations under way; but it is Horatio, the scholar
and thinker, who is sceptical of the evidence, and he who determines to speak to Hamlet
and establish the real cause of the turmoil. The suspense now created makes us want to
see Hamlet himself.

I. ii.   The setting changes from tense apprehension under the open sky at night to the pomp
and ceremony of the King's Council Chamber. The King deals with the state business: he
announces his marriage to the widow of the dead king, his brother; he sends letters to the
old King of Norway about Fortinbras's invasion; Laertes gets permission to return to
France. The King then turns to Hamlet, dressed in black, with his eyes to the ground. He
and his Queen try to persuade Hamlet to shake off his depression and reconsider the wish
he has expressed to go back to his university in Germany.

Alone, Hamlet is so rapt in his thoughts that he does not immediately recognize his old
friend Horatio when the men on guard come to tell him about the Ghost. Hamlet is
determined to see it and discover what evil prevents it from resting.

In contrast to the nervous exchanges of the first scene, relieved only by the approach of
dawn, here is the courtly worldliness of the new King's life within the castle; uncertainty
is changed to order. His smooth contrived speeches show how ready he is to win Hamlet's
favour if he can. Hamlet finds these efforts ingratiating, and is especially revolted by the
King exploiting their family relationship. Gertrude comments on the melancholy which
seems to hang over him; but to him it is not just an appearance. It is reality, real disgust
at his mother's actions. The King wants to keep a watch over him (he lets Laertes go away,
but not Hamlet) and displays his royal power with the image of the cannon reverberating
in the heavens. Hamlet, left alone, turns to thoughts of desperate action against himself,
but memories of his father's goodness take his mind to nobler things in humanity.

A kind of climax has already been reached: the King is a man with a past; the initiative
has passed to Hamlet, whose action and passion are now at the centre of the play.

*   *Enter the* KING, *etc.* – This entry would be in a splendid procession which moved into the
          richly decorated state room in the castle. Very little scenery was used in the
          theatres of Shakespeare's time, but the actors wore splendid, gaily-coloured
          clothes.
1   *Hamlet . . . death:* the death of Hamlet, my dear brother, i.e. the former king. – The King
          refers to himself as *we, us, our,* (the 'royal *we*') in the formal fashion of the
          speech of a ruler at that time. His speech here suggests an official pronounce-
          ment.
2   *green* – i.e. fresh, not dead.
2   *that it us befitted:* though it was right and proper for me.
3   *and our . . . woe:* and (it also *befitted*) my entire kingdom to be drawn together (*contracted*
          in a frown) in one sad forehead (*brow of woe*). – The image is of everybody in
          the kingdom wearing the same look of sorrow; the foreheads of all are clouded.

MARCELLUS It faded on the crowing of the cock.
Some say that ever 'gainst* that season comes
Wherein our Saviour's birth⁴ is celebrated,
The bird of dawning* singeth all night long;   160
And then, they say, no spirit dare walk abroad.*
The nights are wholesome;* then no planets strike,*
No fairy takes,* nor witch hath power to charm –
So hallowed and so gracious is the time.

HORATIO So have I heard, and do in part believe it.   165
But, look, the morn, in russet mantle clad,*
Walks o'er the dew of yon high eastern hill.
Break we our watch up;* and, by my advice,
Let us impart what we have seen tonight
Unto young Hamlet;* for, upon my life,*   170
This spirit, dumb to us, will speak to him.
Do you consent we shall acquaint him with it,
As needful in our loves,* fitting our duty?

MARCELLUS Let's do 't, I pray; and I this morning know
Where we shall find him most convenient.*   175

[Exeunt

scene ii

A room of state in the castle.

Enter the KING,* QUEEN, HAMLET, POLONIUS, LAERTES,
VOLTIMAND, CORNELIUS, LORDS, *and* ATTENDANTS.

KING Though yet of Hamlet* our dear brother's death
The memory be green,* and that it us befitted*
To bear our hearts in grief, and our* whole kingdom
To be contracted in one brow of woe,
Yet so far hath discretion fought with nature   5
That we with wisest* sorrow think on him,

----

6   *wisest* – This word is emphasized; although nature makes the King mourn the loss of his
       brother, discretion mixes this sorrow with some attention to his own well-
       being.

8	*sometime:* former. – Gertrude, who was his sister-in-law (*sister*), is now his wife.
9	*jointress:* widow who holds a jointure, i.e. the whole estate of her husband, for life.
10	*a defeated joy* – The King now uses a number of figures of speech in which two opposing ideas are brought closely together: *defeated* ('spoilt') and *joy*; *mirth* and *funeral*; *dirge* and *marriage*. He does this partly to make his long, formal speech sound impressive and fitting for a king. But he also uses these elaborate figures as a way of covering up his guilt. To marry his sister-in-law so soon after his brother's death was an evil thing, and by using fine phrases he hopes to make it sound less evil than it really is.
11	*auspicious . . . dropping* – One eye shows happiness, the other droops, i.e. looks sad.
12	*dirge* – a sad song sung at the time of a person's death.
13	*dole:* sorrow. – This word alliterates with *delight*, adding a further touch or decoration to the speech. The amount of *dole* balances the amount of *delight* (*In equal scale weighing*).
14	*Taken to wife:* taken as my wife; married.
14	*Nor have . . . wisdoms:* And in this (*herein*) I have not rejected (*barred*) your superior advice (*better wisdoms*). – His councillors have given him support, and he is at pains to point this out so that people will not think that he has acted alone.
15	*which have freely . . . along:* (you) who have supported (*gone . . . along* with) this affair freely, without being compelled to do so.
17	*that you know:* what you already know.
18	*Holding . . . worth:* having a poor opinion (*supposal*) of my strength – i.e. military strength.
20	*Our state . . . frame:* that my kingdom is disorganized (*disjoint*, for *disjointed*) and out of order.
21	*Colleaguéd:* linked. – He dreams of his own profit as linked with the supposed disorganization of Denmark, which he hoped to take advantage of.
22	*message,* for *messages.*
·23	*Importing:* relating to.
24	*bands of law:* all the binding formalities of the law. – Horatio has also emphasized this point (I.i.86–7).
27	*writ,* for *written.*
28	*Norway* means, as before, the King of Norway.
29	*bed-rid,* for *bed-ridden.*
30	*to suppress . . . herein:* to stop him from going (*gait*) further with it (his *purpose*).
31	*in that . . . subject* (line 33): since the troops (*levies*), the lists of forces, and the whole establishment of the army (*full proportions*) consist entirely of his subjects (*subject*). – Since they are all Norwegians, and therefore the King of Norway's subjects, it is reasonable for me King of Denmark to ask the King of Norway to stop them from taking part in young Fortinbras's venture.
33	*dispatch:* send. – Cornelius and Voltimand are sent as the King's messengers.
35	*For:* as.
37	*business:* do business, negotiate.
37	*more,* here, is strictly unnecessary since the idea is covered by *further* in the previous line.
38	*delated:* clearly stated. – The two are not to act as ambassadors, but simply to convey the King's message.
39	*commend your duty:* give proof of your sense of duty (to me).
41	*We doubt it nothing:* I have no doubt at all about it.
43	*suit:* request – such as would be asked of an important person.
44	*reason:* what is reasonable.
44	*the Dane* – i.e. the King of Denmark.
45	*lose your voice:* waste your breath. – He will listen to any reasonable request, and no one speaks to him in vain.
45	*thou* – The King now changes from the formal *you* to the informal *thou* when he speaks to Laertes. He is trying to seem very friendly, but he still speaks in formal phrases which suggest that everything he says has been carefully planned beforehand, e.g. the following line.
46	*my offer . . . asking:* what I offer readily, not what you ask. – There can be nothing Laertes wants, he means, which he will not grant of his own free will, and not because Laertes asks for it.

Together with remembrance of ourselves.
Therefore our sometime* sister, now our queen,
Th' imperial jointress* of this warlike state,
Have we, as 'twere with a defeated joy* –   10
With one auspicious,* and one dropping eye,
With mirth in funeral, and with dirge* in marriage,
In equal scale weighing delight and dole* –
Taken to wife.* Nor* have we herein barred
Your better wisdoms, which have freely* gone   15
With this affair along. – For all, our thanks.
Now follows that* you know: young Fortinbras,
Holding* a weak supposal of our worth,
Or thinking by our late dear brother's death
Our state* to be disjoint and out of frame,   20
Colleaguéd* with the dream of his advantage –
He hath not failed to pester us with message,*
Importing* the surrender of those lands
Lost by his father, with all bands* of law,
To our most valiant brother. So much for him. –   25
Now for ourself, and for this time of meeting.
Thus much the business is: we have here writ*
To Norway,* uncle of young Fortinbras –
Who, impotent and bed-rid,* scarcely hears
Of this his nephew's purpose – to suppress*   30
His further gait herein, in that* the levies,
The lists, and full proportions, are all made
Out of his subject. – And we here dispatch*
You, good Cornelius, and you, Voltimand,
For* bearers of this greeting to old Norway,   35
Giving to you no further personal power
To business* with the king, more* than the scope
Of these delated* articles allow.
Farewell, and let your haste commend* your duty.

CORNELIUS &   In that and all things will we show our duty.   40
VOLTIMAND

KING   We doubt it nothing;* heartily farewell.
                        [*Exeunt* VOLTIMAND *and* CORNELIUS
And now, Laertes, what's the news with you?
You told us of some suit;* what is 't, Laertes?
You cannot speak of reason* to the Dane*
And lose' your voice. What would'st thou* beg, Laertes,   45
That shall not be my offer,* not thy asking?

47	*native to:* closely related to. – The head reasons out and puts into practice what the heart wishes.
48	*instrumental to:* acting as a tool of. – The hand is the *instrument* by which the requests of the mouth are carried out. The *head* and *hand* symbolize the *throne*, i.e. the King, who puts into effect the wishes and requests of Polonius.
50	*Dread my lord:* My revered lord. – He is *dread* because his power makes people fear him.
54	*that duty done:* since I have fulfilled that duty.
55	*bend* – This image, of Laertes' wishes 'bending' abroad again, is illuminated by *bow* in the following line. Laertes bows low to the King as he makes his request.
58	*slow* – i.e. slowly obtained, obtained with difficulty.
59	*laboursome:* laborious.
60	*Upon his will . . . consent:* I gave my hard-won (*hard*) consent to his wishes. – Polonius likes legal phrases, and he speaks of his consent as a *seal* such as is fixed on a document as a sign of approval. In the line before, *petition* also has a legal ring.
62	*Take thy fair hour* – This expression is not very clear; perhaps the King means, 'Take this time for your enjoyment', and is thinking that Laertes is still young, and ready to enjoy the gay life of Paris once more.
63	*And thy . . . will:* you have the highest character (*your best graces*); spend the time as you wish. – This seems to be a suggestion that, although Laertes is going away to enjoy himself, the King hopes that he will do so in moral ways, that he will indulge his good desires, not his bad ones.
64	*cousin* is used by Shakespeare to refer to any near relative. Hamlet is Claudius's nephew, but because Claudius has married Hamlet's mother, he calls Hamlet his *son* as well.
65	*more than . . . kind:* closer to you than a mere relative (because you are now in a sense my father), but not very kindly disposed to you. – This famous line, the first spoken by Hamlet, is a play on words, since *kin* and *kind* both come from the same root, which in Old English meant 'species', i.e. all of one sort of thing. One development of the word led to the idea 'race, people', and hence came *kinsman*, a person of the same race. Another development gave *kindly, kind*, which meant '(done) in a way which was fitting to people of one's own sort', hence 'gentle, friendly'.
66	*on:* over. – Hamlet is depressed; clouds of sadness hang over him.
67	*too much i'the sun:* too much in the sunshine of court favour – not under a cloud. But Hamlet is playing on *sun* and *son:* Claudius has called him his *son*, and that is more than Hamlet can bear.
68	*nighted colour:* black looks.
69	*Denmark* – i.e. the King.
70	*thy vailéd lids:* your eyelids lowered over your eyes. – Hamlet in his sorrow looks only at the ground.
72	*'tis common:* it (death) comes to everyone – it is *common* to all.
73	*nature:* life.
75	*particular:* uncommon, very special.
77	*not alone:* not only. – Hamlet goes on to describe his manner and appearance; the main verb, *can denote*, comes at line 83; it is not just these things which distinguish him precisely, for they are only *shows* of grief (line 82).
77	*inky:* black – the colour of mourning.
78	*customary suits:* suits which I now wear habitually.
79	*windy . . . breath:* sighs – literally, 'breathing out (*suspiration*) of sighs from forced breath'.
80	*fruitful river . . . eye:* the flowing of tears.
81	*'haviour,* for *behaviour.*
82	*moods:* dispositions (of sadness). – All these are *shows* of grief, appearances only, and Hamlet has mentioned them in response to his mother's word *seems*. But there is also the reality of his sorrow, which is different, *that within which passeth show* (line 85).
84	*play* – i.e. like an actor on the stage.

The head is not more native* to the heart,
The hand more instrumental* to the mouth,
Than is the throne of Denmark to thy father.
What wouldst thou have, Laertes?

LAERTES   Dread* my lord,   50
Your leave and favour to return to France,
From whence though willingly I came to Denmark,
To show my duty in your coronation,
Yet now, I must confess, that duty done,*
My thoughts and wishes bend* again toward France,   55
And bow them to your gracious leave and pardon.

KING   Have you your father's leave? What says Polonius?

POLONIUS   He hath, my lord, wrung from me my slow* leave
By laboursome* petition, and, at last,
Upon his will* I sealed my hard consent.   60
I do beseech you, give him leave to go.

KING   Take thy fair hour,* Laertes; time be thine,
And thy* best graces spend it at thy will! –
But now, my cousin* Hamlet, and my son –

HAMLET   [Aside] A little more than kin,* and less than kind.   65

KING   How is it that the clouds still hang on* you?

HAMLET   Not so, my lord; I am too much i' the sun.*

QUEEN   Good Hamlet, cast thy nighted* colour off,
And let thine eye look like a friend on Denmark.*
Do not for ever with thy vailéd lids*   70
Seek for thy noble father in the dust.
Thou know'st 'tis common* – all that live must die,
Passing through nature* to eternity.

HAMLET   Ay, madam, it is common.

QUEEN   If it be,
Why seems it so particular* with thee?   75

HAMLET   Seems, madam! Nay, it is; I know not 'seems'.
'Tis not alone* my inky* cloak, good mother,
Nor customary* suits of solemn black,
Nor windy* suspiration of forced breath,
No, nor the fruitful* river in the eye,   80
Nor the dejected 'haviour* of the visage,
Together with all forms, moods,* shows of grief,
That can denote me truly. These, indeed, seem,
For they are actions that a man might play.*
But I have that within which passeth show;   85
These but the trappings and the suits of woe.

90   *That father . . . his* – i.e. the father who was lost also lost *his* father.
91   *term:* period of time.
92   *To do . . . sorrow:* to behave, as expected, in the sorrowful ways of the funeral rites. – These
        are *obsequies*, hence *obsequious*; but the word includes the idea 'dutiful' as well.
93   *condolement:* sorrow. – The King now goes on to accuse Hamlet of being unmanly; a real
        man, he implies, would not be so weak as to give way to such enduring
        dejection.
94   *impious:* lacking in respect. – The King has said that the obligations of a respectful son
        (*filial obligation*, line 91) are to mourn for a certain time. After that time, such
        mourning is disrespectful (*impious*).
95   *incorrect:* not corrected. – i.e. not willing to submit.
99   *As any . . . sense:* as any of the commonest (*most vulgar*) things which our senses can
        perceive. – He is referring to death.
103   *To reason . . . fathers:* most absurd in the light of reason, which has as its most common
        subject-matter the death of fathers.
104   *still:* always, continually. – *Reason* is personified by *whose* in the preceding line, and by
        who in this one.
105   *corse:* corpse.
107   *unprevailing:* unavailing, useless.
107   *us:* me – the King is talking of himself.
109   *the most . . . throne:* the nearest in succession to the throne. – The King declares that unless
        he has a son before he dies, Hamlet, as son of the previous king, will succeed to
        the throne. There was no binding custom that kingship always descended from
        father to son.
110   *And with . . . toward you* (line 112) – Throughout this speech the King has made a great
        effort to speak forcibly. He has had to choose his words carefully, for much is
        at stake, in that Hamlet has the power to start a faction against the King if he
        wants to. In these lines the formality of the King's words seems to have got the
        better of him, for the sentence seems to change its direction. He begins as if
        to say: 'with no lower degree of love than the fondest father bears his son *do I
        love you*', but instead he uses *impart*, meaning 'make known', which makes
        with out of place and apparently needs *my love* to be supplied. (But some have
        thought that *impart* here is used without taking an object, meaning 'offer
        myself').
112   *For:* As for.
113   *Wittenberg* – a university town in Germany where Hamlet had been studying.
114   *most retrograde:* quite contrary.
115   *bend you:* incline yourself – i.e. make yourself willing.
117   *cousin:* kinsman.
118   *lose:* waste.
123   *unforced accord:* agreement offered freely. – Hamlet has not, in fact, agreed to anything
        except to obey his mother in the way he thinks best (line 120).
124   *in grace . . . earthly thunder* (line 128): and in gratitude for it (the agreement which Hamlet
        was supposed to have made), the King of Denmark will drink no merry toast
        (*jocund health*) today without (*But*) the great guns firing to tell it to the sky, and
        the sky shall echo back (*bruit again*) the noise of the King's drunken revel
        (*rouse*), re-echoing the thunder of the earth (i.e. the cannon shots). – Such noise
        and revelry are apparently true to life as it once was in the Danish court;
        cannon were fired when the King called a toast, and there was a great deal of
        heavy drinking.
            This part of the scene ends in noise and tumult. Then, in startling dramatic
        contrast, Hamlet is left alone on the stage, talking quietly to himself, lamenting
        his sad situation, and even thinking of suicide as the thing which would end it
        all for him.

ironic

KING 'Tis sweet and commendable in your nature, Hamlet,
To give these mourning duties to your father.
But you must know your father lost a father;
That father* lost, lost his; and the survivor bound   90
In filial obligation for some term*
To do* obsequious sorrow. But to persévaer
In obstinate condolement* is a course
Of impious* stubbornness; 'tis unmanly grief.
It shows a will most incorrect* to heaven,   95
A heart unfortified, a mind impatient,
An understanding simple and unschooled.
For what we know must be, and is as common
As any* the most vulgar thing to sense,
Why should we, in our peevish opposition,   100
Take it to heart? Fie! 'Tis a fault to heaven,
A fault against the dead, a fault to nature,
To reason* most absurd, whose common theme
Is death of fathers, and who still* hath cried,
From the first corse till he that died today,   105
'This must be so.' We pray you, throw to earth
This unprevailing* woe, and think of us*
As of a father. For let the world take note,
You are the most immediate* to our throne,
And with no less nobility* of love   110
Than that which dearest father bears his son
Do I impart toward you. For* your intent
In going back to school in Wittenberg,*
It is most retrograde* to our desire,
And we beseech you, bend* you to remain   115
Here, in the cheer and comfort of our eye,
Our chiefest courtier, cousin,* and our son.
QUEEN Let not thy mother lose* her prayers, Hamlet.
I pray thee, stay with us; go not to Wittenberg.
HAMLET I shall in all my best obey you, madam.   120
KING Why, 'tis a loving and a fair reply.
Be as ourself in Denmark. –
                              [To the QUEEN] Madam, come;
This gentle and unforced* accord of Hamlet
Sits smiling to my heart, in grace* whereof,
No jocund health that Denmark drinks today,   125
But the great cannon to the clouds shall tell,
And the king's rouse the heaven shall bruit again,

129   *too too solid* – This is how the First Folio reads. Other early editions, the Quartos, give the word *sallied* instead of *solid*, which in Shakespeare's English can mean 'troubled'. But *solid* contrasts with *melt*, and *dew* in the following line, and is probably the correct reading. Hamlet is speaking of the flesh of his own body.

130   *resolve:* dissolve.

131   *Or that . . . self-daughter!* – The idea of *O* . . . at the beginning of the speech is carried on to these lines: '(How I wish that) God (*the Everlasting*) had not made divine law (*canon*) against suicide!' The Bible does not, in fact, expressly forbid suicide, except in that it is a kind of murder, and therefore forbidden by the sixth of the Ten Commandments in the Old Testament.

133   *flat:* lifeless.

134   *uses of this world:* ways of ordinary life.

136   *things rank . . . merely:* it (life, the garden) is filled to the full with what is coarse and foul in nature. – Unprofitable weeds have entirely choked the garden. Here *merely* means 'wholly'.

139   *that was . . . satyr:* who was, by comparison with *this* king (*to this*) as Hyperion to a satyr. – In Greek mythology, the Titan Hyperion was the father of the sun, the moon and the dawn. Satyrs were believed to be creatures with a male human form but with the characteristics of a goat; they were said to love wine and indulge in all kinds of sensual pleasure. Such, in Hamlet's eyes, was the contrast between his father and the new king.

141   *beteem:* allow . . . to.

142   *Visit:* come to, blow on.

146   *on 't:* of it.

146   *Frailty* is personified. This sentence has become a proverbial expression. Women, he thinks, are so weak that *woman* and *frailty* are two names for the same thing.

147   *or e'er:* even before.

148   *followed* – i.e. in the funeral procession.

149   *Niobe*, in Greek mythology, was wife of a king of Thebes. She boasted to Leto of the number of children she had, and this so angered Leto's own two children, Apollo and Artemis, that they shot all Niobe's children with arrows, and killed them. Zeus, the god of gods, changed her into a rock, and the moisture which formed on this rock each summer was taken to be the tears of Niobe weeping for her children.

150   *a beast . . . reason:* even an animal, which has no faculty for reasoning – *wants:* lacks; *discourse:* the faculty of logical argument.

153   *Hercules* was a Greek hero of enormous strength. Among other tasks he met and conquered Death, and later became worshipped as a god.

154   *unrighteous* – The tears are called *unrighteous* because, apparently, they seemed sincere at the time, but could not have been so, since the queen married again so soon.

155   *Had left . . . eyes:* had stopped filling her sore (*gallèd*) eyes with tears.

156   *post . . . dexterity:* hasten with such speed. – The modern English word *post*, i.e. mail, comes from the idea of news taken at speed from one place to another.

157   *incestuous* – in the sense that religious law forbade marriage with a close kinsman, even if only kin by marriage. The Bible (*Leviticus* 18) argues that a dead wife's sister is a near kinswoman to the husband and therefore not a fit person to marry him.

        In this speech Hamlet has spoken privately of his mother's disgrace; the absence of all other characters from the stage has made it possible for him to do so. But he does not mention it to her or reprove her in public. Now others appear: Horatio and his friends come to report to Hamlet, as they said they would (I.i.169–70). Hamlet is deeply stirred by the news of the ghost and concludes that his uncle must have performed some wicked deed – a thought which does not seem to have occurred to the others.

        When Horatio greets him he gives a conventional reply, '*I am glad to see you well*', being too rapt in thought to take any notice of who is speaking to him. Then he recognizes who it is.

163   *change that name:* exchange *that* name (for 'friend'); we will call each other friend.

164   *what . . . Wittenberg:* what are you doing away from Wittenberg – Hamlet thought Horatio was still at the university there.

Re-speaking earthly thunder. Come away.

[Exeunt all but HAMLET

HAMLET   O, that this too too solid* flesh would melt,
Thaw, and resolve* itself into a dew!   130
Or that* the Everlasting had not fixed
His canon 'gainst self-slaughter! O God! God!
How weary, stale, flat,* and unprofitable
Seem to me all the uses* of this world!
Fie on 't! O, fie! 'Tis an unweeded garden   135
That grows to seed; things* rank and gross in nature
Possess it merely. That it should come to this!
But two months dead! – nay, not so much, not two.
So excellent a king, that was,* to this,
Hyperion to a satyr; so loving to my mother,   140
That he might not beteem* the winds of heaven
Visit* her face too roughly. Heaven and earth!
Must I remember? Why, she would hang on him,
As if increase of appetite had grown
By what it fed on. And yet, within a month –   145
Let me not think on 't* – Frailty,* thy name is woman! –
A little month; or e'er* those shoes were old
With which she followed* my poor father's body,
Like Niobe,* all tears – why she, even she –
O God! a beast,* that wants discourse of reason,   150
Would have mourned longer – married with my uncle,
My father's brother, but no more like my father
Than I to Hercules!* Within a month,
Ere yet the salt of most unrighteous* tears
Had left* the flushing in her gallèd eyes,   155
She married. – O, most wicked speed, to post*
With such dexterity to incestuous* sheets!
It is not nor it cannot come to good.
But break, my heart, for I must hold my tongue!

Enter HORATIO, MARCELLUS, *and* BERNARDO.

HORATIO   Hail to your lordship!
HAMLET   I am glad to see you well.   160
Horatio – or I do forget my self.
HORATIO   The same, my lord, and your poor servant ever.
HAMLET   Sir, my good friend; I'll change* that name with you
And what* make you from Wittenberg, Horatio? –
Marcellus!

168   *good my lord:* my good lord.
171   *make it truster of:* entrust it with. – Horatio has told him he had a *truant disposition*, an inclination to run away from school. But Hamlet does not want to hear Horatio give bad reports of himself.
173   *affair:* business.
174   *We'll teach you* – After his pleasant surprise at seeing his old friend Horatio has worn off, Hamlet returns to this bitterness; here he refers to the King's drinking bouts.
178   *it followed hard upon:* (the wedding) followed (the funeral) very closely.
179   *funeral baked meats* – the pastry served as refreshment at funerals. The food served hot at the funeral was served cold at the wedding.
180   *coldly furnish forth:* provide cold food for. – There may be an echo here of English phrases such as *cold comfort* – 'entertainment without food, receiving guests without giving them anything to eat'. Small villages lying near to towns in England are sometimes called *Cold Harbour*, marking a place where there was once an inn where people could stay the night but not expect to get any food. Hamlet had 'cold comfort' at his mother's wedding.
181   *Would I:* I wish that I.
181   *dearest:* most grievous. – *Dear* in this sense has a different origin from *dear* meaning 'beloved', but had already become associated with it in Shakespeare's English. The word was used to denote things which were deeply felt, whether pleasantly or unpleasantly. Hamlet means that he would rather have died, rather have met his worst enemy in heaven, than seen the day of his mother's second marriage.
182   *Or ever:* before.
183   *methinks . . . father* – It is ironic that Hamlet should say this here, because Horatio has come to say that *he* has seen the ghost of the dead king. Horatio, deeply stirred, interrupts him, only to find that Hamlet is speaking of his imagination; his phrase *'In my mind's eye'* has become an accepted phrase in the English language.
186   *He was . . . all* – The emphasis here is on *man*; considering everything, he had the essential qualities of manliness. The implication is that he had some faults also, and that Hamlet, even in his bitter grief, is not blind to them.
187   *his like:* one like him.
188   *yesternight:* last night.
190   *Season your admiration:* Moderate your astonishment (*admiration*). – *Season* is used in the sense 'add some ingredient to a dish to moderate its flavour'.
191   *attent*, for *attentive*.
191   *deliver:* recount.
196   *dead vast:* huge emptiness, still as death.
197   *thus* – i.e. 'in the way I am going to tell you about'.
198   *at point:* in readiness (for battle) – *exactly:* correct in every detail. Medieval armour consisted of many small parts, and was very complicated to put on; something is made here of the fact that each piece was exactly in its right place, as a king's armour would be.
198   *cap-a-pe:* from head to foot – this is an English form of a French phrase.
199   *Appears* – Horatio now uses the present tense to make his account as actual and vivid as possible. He doubted the account of the other gentlemen of the guard, but he has himself now seen the vision and is the one who talks most vividly about it. about it.
201   *fear-surpriséd* – Shakespeare often made compounds of this sort, with two words seldom seen together joined into one and giving a wide range of meaning: 'surprised and frightened'.
202   *distilled . . . jelly:* almost turned to jelly – which shakes about when touched, like a man shaking with fear; this is the *act*, 'action', of fear.

MARCELLUS	My good lord –

MARCELLUS My good lord –   165
HAMLET   I am very glad to see you. [*To* BERNARDO] Good even, sir. –
         But what, in faith, make you from Wittenberg?
HORATIO A truant disposition, good my lord.*
HAMLET   I would not hear your enemy say so,
         Nor shall you do mine ear that violence   170
         To make it truster* of your own report
         Against yourself. I know you are no truant.
         But what is your affair* in Elsinore?
         We'll teach* you to drink deep ere you depart.
HORATIO My lord, I came to see your father's funeral.   175
HAMLET   I pray thee, do not mock me, fellow-student;
         I think it was to see my mother's wedding.
HORATIO Indeed, my lord, it followed* hard upon.
HAMLET   Thrift, thrift, Horatio! The funeral* baked meats
         Did coldly* furnish forth the marriage tables.   180
         Would I* had met my dearest* foe in heaven
         Or ever* I had seen that day, Horatio! –
         My father – methinks* I see my father.
HORATIO O, where, my lord?
HAMLET   In my mind's eye, Horatio.
HORATIO I saw him once; he was a goodly king.   185
HAMLET   He was* a man, take him for all in all;
         I shall not look upon his like* again.
HORATIO My lord, I think I saw him yesternight.*
HAMLET   Saw? Who?
HORATIO My lord, the king your father.
HAMLET   The king my father?
HORATIO Season* your admiration for a while   190
         With an attent* ear, till I may deliver,*
         Upon the witness of these gentlemen,
         This marvel to you.
HAMLET   For God's love, let me hear.
HORATIO Two nights together had these gentlemen,
         Marcellus and Bernardo, on their watch,   195
         In the dead vast* and middle of the night,
         Been thus* encountered. A figure like your father,
         Armed at point* exactly, cap-a-pe,*
         Appears* before them, and with solemn march
         Goes slow and stately by them. Thrice he walked   200
         By their oppressed and fear-surprised* eyes,
         Within his truncheon's length, whilst they, distilled*

205   *impart they did:* they told.
207   *as they had delivered . . . good:* exactly as they had described it (*delivered*) in every detail
       (*each word made true and good*) of both time and appearance (*Form*).
210   *like* – i.e. not more like one another (than the ghost was like Hamlet's father).
214   *did address . . . speak:* prepared itself to move, as if (*like as*) it wanted to speak.
220   *writ down,* for *written down:* prescribed.
224   *Armed* – This refers to the ghost: 'Did you say it was armed?' Hamlet is now deeply
       perturbed and jumps from one subject to another. In fact, from here to the end
       of the scene is a passage of convincing reality; cf. Horatio and the others
       disagreeing as to how long the ghost remained with them (lines 236–38).
228   *his beaver up* – The front part of his helmet moved up and down to reveal or cover his face.
       This movable part was called the *beaver.*
229   *what looked he:* How did he look? What was the expression on his face?
234   *amazed* was a much more powerful word in Shakespeare's English than it is today:
       'stunned, appalled'.

Almost to jelly with the act of fear,
Stand dumb and speak not to him. This to me
In dreadful secrecy impart* they did;   205
And I with them the third night kept the watch,
Where, as they had delivered,* both in time,
Form of the thing, each word made true and good,
The apparition comes. I knew your father;
These hands are not more like.*

HAMLET   But where was this?   210
MARCELLUS My lord, upon the platform where we watched.
HAMLET Did you not speak to it?
HORATIO   My lord, I did;
But answer made it none. Yet once methought
It lifted up its head, and did address*
Itself to motion, like as it would speak;   215
But even then the morning cock crew loud,
And at the sound it shrunk in haste away,
And vanished from our sight.
HAMLET   'Tis very strange.
HORATIO As I do live, my honoured lord, 'tis true,
And we did think it writ* down in our duty   220
To let you know of it.
HAMLET Indeed, indeed, sirs, but this troubles me.
Hold you the watch tonight?
MARCELLUS &   We do, my lord.
BERNARDO
HAMLET Armed,* say you?
MARCELLUS & Armed, my lord.   225
BERNARDO
HAMLET From top to toe?
MARCELLUS &   My lord, from head to foot.
BERNARDO
HAMLET Then saw you not his face?
HORATIO O, yes, my lord; he wore his beaver* up.
HAMLET What looked he?* Frowningly?
HORATIO A countenance more in sorrow than in anger.   230
HAMLET Pale or red?
HORATIO Nay, very pale.
HAMLET   And fixed his eyes upon you?
HORATIO Most constantly.
HAMLET   I would I had been there.
HORATIO It would have much amazed* you.

235   *like:* likely.
236   *tell:* count.
238   *grizzled:* grey.
240   *a sable silvered:* deep black (*sable*) with touches of silver-grey.
243   *though hell . . . gape:* even though hell opens its wide mouth. – The place of damned souls in the after-life was often represented in medieval paintings as inside a huge mouth which was shown swallowing up the wicked. Hamlet's image is therefore doubly appropriate.
244   *hold my peace:* be quiet.
246   *Let it be . . . still:* see that you keep it to yourselves for ever – literally, 'let it be kept (*tenable*) in your silence for ever (*still*)'.
247   *hap,* for *happen.*
248   *Give it . . . tongue:* think about it, but do not speak about it.
249   *I will . . . loves:* I will reward what you do out of affection for me – i.e. 'your love, not your duty, shall be rewarded if you do what I ask'. When, in spite of this, they speak of *duty* a few lines on, Hamlet contradicts them (lines 251–2).
250   *'twixt:* between.
253   *in arms:* armed.
254   *doubt:* suspect. – Horatio and the others have said nothing to him about foul play, but the idea of his father's ghost walking, not at rest, suggests something evil. It was thought that ghosts walked when something which had happened in life disturbed them and prevented them from resting in peace. It is this idea which makes him certain that *Foul deeds will rise* (line 255), i.e. cannot remain hidden.

I. iii.   Before he leaves, Laertes warns Ophelia of the dangers in Hamlet's passionate fondness for her. She, in return, and then Polonius warn him against the vices that will tempt him in foreign lands. After Laertes has left, Polonius also warns Ophelia against Hamlet, whose motives he suspects.
           This scene completes the outline of the situation in Elsinore. There is hidden evil in the state, represented by the restless spirit of the late King (scene i); his son Hamlet is deeply troubled by his mother's precipitate marriage to the late king's brother, who is now King himself (scene ii); there is some association between Hamlet and Ophelia, the daughter of the court chamberlain Polonius. It may seem surprising that Polonius's famous advice to his son ('*This above all . . .*') is central to this scene, since Hamlet, the hero, is not personally involved. Yet this commonplace moralizing is an illustration of court conventions from which Hamlet, in his unique predicament, is becoming more and more isolated. Some commentators have gone so far as to say that the culmination of Polonius's advice:

> to thine own self be true . . . Thou canst not then
> be false to any man.

shows a complacent act of faith close to stupidity, especially since the fate of many characters in the play proves it to be wrong. But (first) the moralizing, if heard without a knowledge of the rest of the play, is generally sensible and to the point; and (second) Polonius may well have found the real problem of the play so far; what *is* one's own true self? Appearance and reality are confused, and the reality of *thine own self* remains doubtful. Fear of such confusion makes this scene essentially a series of warnings.

1   *My necessaries are embarked:* The things I need to take with me are on board.
2   *as:* whenever.
2   *give benefit:* blow advantageously (so as to drive a sailing ship from her to him).
3   *convoy is assistant:* means of transport (i.e. a ship) is available.

HAMLET	Very like,* very like. Stayed it long?
HORATIO	While one with moderate haste might tell* a hundred.
MARCELLUS & BERNARDO	Longer, longer.
HORATIO	Not when I saw't.
HAMLET	His beard was grizzled* – no?
HORATIO	It was, as I have seen it in his life,
	A sable silvered.*
HAMLET	I will watch tonight.
	Perchance 'twill walk again.
HORATIO	I warrant it will.

235

240

HAMLET   If it assume my noble father's person,
I'll speak to it, though* hell itself should gape,
And bid me hold my peace.* I pray you all,
If you have hitherto concealed this sight,   235
Let it be* tenable in your silence still;
And whatsoever else shall hap* tonight,
Give it* an understanding, but no tongue.
I will* requite your loves. So, fare you well;
Upon the platform, 'twixt* eleven and twelve,   250
I'll visit you.

ALL   Our duty to your honour.

HAMLET   Your loves, as mine to you; farewell!

> [*Exeunt all but* HAMLET

My father's spirit in arms!* All is not well;
I doubt* some foul play. Would the night were come!
Till then, sit still, my soul! Foul deeds will rise,   255
Though all the earth o'erwhelm them, to men's eyes.

> [*Exit

scene iii

A room in POLONIUS'S *house.*

Enter LAERTES *and* OPHELIA.

LAERTES   My necessaries* are embarked. Farewell.
And, sister, as* the winds give benefit,*
And convoy is assistant,* do not sleep,

5	*For:* As for.
5	*the trifling . . . favour:* that insignificant thing, his affection (for you).
6	*Hold it a fashion:* take it as a mood of the moment.
6	*a toy in blood:* a passion of no significance. – Blood was thought to be the source of passionate feelings.
7	*A violet . . . nature* – Violets are flowers which bloom in North Europe in early spring. Laertes says that Hamlet's passion must be taken as a flower in the springtime of human nature; *primy:* in its prime, in springtime.
8	*Forward:* advanced – as flowers are advanced or early for the time of year; such flowers do not last through the summer, and neither will Hamlet's love be permanent.
9	*suppliance:* pastime. – The word stress is on the second syllable here, *suppliance*. In these lyrical lines Shakespeare carries along images of sexual love (*favour, blood, youth*), of impermanence (*trifling, fashion, toy,* something which is not of lasting value, *suppliance*) and the flowers of early spring (*violet, primy, sweet, perfume*). All these images are finely woven together in a single sentence.
11	*crescent:* when it is growing.
11	*alone:* only.
12	*thews and bulk:* strength and size – *thews:* muscles, bodily strength; *bulk:* size of the body.
12	*this temple waxes:* this body grows. – The image of the body as a temple is taken from the Bible, e.g. 1 *Corinthians* 3: 16,
	Know ye not that ye are the temple of God, and that the Spirit of God dwelleth in you?
13	*The inward service . . . withal:* The internal provision (*service*) of mind and spirit broadens with it – i.e. the body and the mind grow big together. – The implications of this remark are not clear. Perhaps Laertes is hinting diplomatically that as Hamlet grows older and his power increases, his desires may make him look for love elsewhere.
15	*no soil . . . will:* no blemish (*soil*) or lack of sincerity (*cautel*) stains his virtuous intentions. – These words bring out the interplay of *mind* and *soul* two lines above, the possible trickery of the mind and the virtue of the soul's purposes.
16	*fear:* be concerned (with the fact that).
17	*His greatness weighed:* having taken his position (that of a prince) into consideration.
18	*subject to his birth:* not independent of his origins. – As a prince he has 'subjects'; but he is himself 'subject' to his own royal origins.
19	*may not:* cannot.
19	*unvalued:* of no importance.
20	*Carve for himself:* follow his own desires.
20	*choice* – i.e. his choice of a wife. When Shakespeare wrote, royal marriages were of intense interest to the people, since alliances between nations often depended on them; the prince and heir to the throne of one country marrying the princess of another would bring those countries into close alliance. The *safety and health* of a nation could very well depend on such a marriage. See also note to line 23 below.
23	*voice and yielding:* opinion and consent.
23	*that body . . . head* – i.e. the state, the 'body politic'. The desires of his own body must be subjected to the desires of that greater body, the state of which he is the head.
25	*It fits . . . believe it:* it is proper for your intellect to believe it so far.
27	*May give . . . deed:* may put his words into action.
28	*the main voice of Denmark:* the general opinion of the Danes.
29	*weigh:* consider.
30	*If with . . . songs:* if you listen (*list*) to his 'songs' (avowals of love) with an ear over-ready to believe (*too credent*).
32	*unmastered importunity:* uncontrolled and persistent requests.
34	*keep you . . . affection:* hold yourself back when love might lead you on.
35	*shot,* evidently *gun-shot*.
36	*chariest:* most modest.
36	*prodigal:* lavish. – The most modest girl is lavish enough (in showing her charms) if she reveals her beauty to the moon. The moon with its cold silvery light was taken as a symbol of chastity; showing her beauty to the chaste moon is as far as she should go.
38	*Virtue itself . . . strokes:* Not even virtue itself escapes from (*scapes*) the attacks of malicious tongues.

	But let me hear from you.	
OPHELIA	Do you doubt that?	
LAERTES	For* Hamlet, and the trifling of his favour,*	5

Hold it a fashion,* and a toy in blood,*
A violet in the youth of primy nature,*
Forward,* not permanent, sweet, not lasting,
The perfume and suppliance* of a minute –
No more.

OPHELIA   No more but so?

LAERTES   Think it no more;   10
For nature, crescent,* does not grow alone*
In thews and bulk,* but, as this temple* waxes,
The inward service* of the mind and soul
Grows wide withal. Perhaps he loves you now;
And now no soil* nor cautel doth besmirch   15
The virtue of his will. But you must fear,*
His greatness weighed,* his will is not his own,
For he himself is subject to his birth.*
He may not,* as unvalued* persons do,
Carve for himself,* for on his choice* depends   20
The safety and health of this whole state.
And therefore must his choice be circumscribed
Unto the voice* and yielding of that body*
Whereof he is the head. Then, if he says he loves you,
It fits* your wisdom so far to believe it   25
As he in his particular act and place
May give his saying deed,* which is no further
Than the main voice of Denmark* goes withal.
Then weigh* what loss your honour may sustain,
If with too credent* ear you list his songs,   30
Or lose your heart, or your chaste treasure open
To his unmastered importunity.*
Fear it, Ophelia, fear it, my dear sister,
And keep you* in the rear of your affection,
Out of the shot* and danger of desire.   35
The chariest* maid is prodigal* enough
If she unmask her beauty to the moon.
Virtue* itself scapes not calumnious strokes.

39   *The canker . . . disclosed:* The worm (*canker*) too often damages (*galls*) the young shoots in spring ('the children of the spring') before their buds (*buttons*) are opened. – The imagery is still of youth and spring.

42   *Contagious blastments:* poisonous blights – such as the canker-worms which attack young shoots. The beauty and freshness of youth and spring are repeatedly contrasted with the horror of disease and blight. The worthy and unworthy, the pure and the impure, are all aspects of Hamlet's own predicament as it develops in the play.

43   *wary:* careful.

44   *Youth . . . near:* the passions of youth will revolt (against self-restraint) even if there is no temptation near by. – The word *near* rhymes with *fear* at the end of the previous line; such rhyming couplets are often a signal in Shakespeare's plays that a long speech or a scene has come to an end.

        Laertes has spoken sincerely and passionately in the hope that his sister will seriously consider what he has so graphically expounded. But Ophelia shows in her reply, and in what she tells her father later in this scene, that she is not altogether convinced. Her love for Hamlet seems stronger than the power of her brother's words.

47   *ungracious pastors:* graceless priests. – The literal meaning of *pastor* is 'shepherd'; the priest should lead his people in the way a good shepherd leads his sheep (this image is from the Bible: the good shepherd 'putteth forth his own sheep, he goeth before them, and the sheep follow him' – *John* 10: 4). The bad shepherd, as Ophelia sees him here, shows his sheep a difficult pathway but chooses an easy one for himself.

49   *a puffed . . . libertine:* a proud and reckless man living only for his own pleasures.

50   *Himself the primrose . . . dalliance treads:* he himself (the graceless priest) walks the easy path, lined with primroses, of idle pleasure (*dalliance*). – *The primrose path* must have been a set phrase in Shakespeare's day. The porter in *Macbeth* (II.iii.22) speaks of 'the primrose way to the everlasting bonfire [i.e. hell]'. Primroses are flowers of early spring.

51   *recks not . . . rede:* does not follow his own advice (*rede*).

51   *fear me not:* do not worry about me.

53   *A double . . . leaves:* Opportunity (*occasion*) has blessed me with a second leave-taking. – It was the custom to give people a blessing when they said farewell. Polonius has evidently already blessed Laertes, and is surprised to find that he has not yet left. The *double grace* must be an echo from Ophelia's words about *ungracious pastors* in line 47 above.

55   *Yet:* Still.

56   *sits in . . . sail:* is there behind the sail of your ship – i.e. the wind is up and blowing in the right direction for the voyage.

57   *you are stayed for:* you are expected; they are waiting for you.

58   *precepts . . . character:* see that you engrave (*character*) these few precepts in your memory. – These precepts are famous. The tradition on the English stage is not to take them very seriously; they contain good advice but are delivered rather formally, and hardly in a way which a loving father, even an old man like Polonius, would normally speak to his son.

60   *Nor any unproportioned . . . act:* and do not put any ill-considered (*unproportioned*) thought into action (see note to I.i.37 for *his* = its).

61   *familiar . . . vulgar:* friendly but not equally accessible to everybody. – *Vulgar* in Shakespeare most often means 'of the common people', and is not necessarily unfavourable.

62   *and their . . . tried:* when you have tested (the friendship of) those you adopt.

63   *Grapple* – To grapple means 'to seize with a metal instrument and draw towards one'; the word was used especially with reference to enemy ships being seized with grappling irons on ropes. Polonius tells his son to bind his friends to him with *hoops of steel*.

64   *dull thy palm . . . comrade* – Here, as often elsewhere, Shakespeare has packed into a small space a great deal of meaning and imagery; it is often impossible to bring into an explanation all the many implications of an utterance of this kind. We might say, 'Do not spoil the good sense of your hospitality (*dull thy palm*) by looking after every newly-arrived and untried acquaintance'; *dull:* make blunt; *palm:* the place from which gifts are made; the comrade is likened to a

            The canker* galls the infants of the spring
            Too oft before their buttons be disclosed;   40
            And in the morn and liquid dew of youth
            Contagious blastments* are most imminent.
            Be wary,* then; best safety lies in fear.
            Youth to itself rebels,* though none else near.

OPHELIA I shall th' effect of this good lesson keep   45
            As watchman to my heart. But, good my brother,
            Do not, as some ungracious pastors* do,
            Show me the steep and thorny way to heaven,
            Whilst, like a puffed and reckless libertine,*
            Himself the primrose path* of dalliance treads,   50
            And recks* not his own rede.

LAERTES   O, fear me not.*
            I stay too long. – But here my father comes.

            Enter POLONIUS.

            A double blessing* is a double grace;
            Occasion smiles upon a second leave.

POLONIUS Yet* here, Laertes! aboard, aboard, for shame!   55
            The wind sits* in the shoulder of your sail,
            And you are stayed for.* There, my blessing with thee!
                    |*Laying his hand on* LAERTES' *head*
            And these few precepts* in thy memory
            See thou character. Give thy thoughts no tongue,
            Nor any unproportioned* thought his act.   60
            Be thou familiar,* but by no means vulgar.
            The friends thou hast, and their adoption tried,*
            Grapple* them to thy soul with hoops of steel;
            But do not dull thy palm* with entertainment
            Of each new-hatched, unfledged comrade. Beware 65
            Of entrance to a quarrel; but, being in,
            Bear 't,* that th' opposéd may beware of thee.
            Give every man* thine ear, but few thy voice.

---

64 (*cont'd*)   newly-born bird (*new-hatched*) which cannot yet fly because it has no feathers
                      (*unfledged*).
67   *Bear 't:* persist in it (so that you may win).
68   *Give every man . . . voice* – i.e. listen to everyone but speak to few people.

69   *Take . . . censure:* Consider everyone's opinion.
70   *habit:* dress. – Polonius recommends clothes which are of very good quality, but not
        showy.
74   Lines 73 and 74 are apparently incorrectly printed in all the early editions, since none of
        the three oldest versions makes good sense. In each case it looks as if the
        printers copied words in error from one line to the next. The version given in
        the text is one which is frequently adopted by modern editors (it is closest to
        that of the First Folio), and 74 can then be taken to mean: 'are very particular
        (*select*) and well-bred (*generous*), especially in this respect (that of dress)'
77   *dulls . . . husbandry:* adversely affects good household management.
81   *My blessing . . . thee:* May my blessing bring this (the advice I have given) to maturity
        (*season*) in you!
83   *tend:* are waiting.
89   *So please you:* If it pleases you (for me to say this). – This very polite and formal phrase is
        the origin of *please* as used today.
89   *touching:* concerning.
90   *Marry, well bethought:* Indeed, it is a good thing you reminded me of that – literally, 'By
        the Virgin Mary, well remembered'.
93   *your audience:* your attention. – He has heard that Ophelia has been readily and liberally
        attending to what Hamlet has been saying to her.
94   *put on:* communicated to.
97   *As it behoves . . . honour:* as my daughter and your honour must of necessity (understand).
        – He tells Ophelia, in effect, that she does not understand as well as she should
        her position (as his daughter and therefore not a royal companion for a prince)
        and the danger to her honour. It is now quite clear that neither Polonius nor
        Laertes think that Hamlet is really in love with Ophelia; they believe that he
        has only a passionate desire for her.
99   *tenders Of his affection:* offers of his love. – Polonius takes up her word *affection*, using it,
        as she does, to mean 'love'. There is no evidence that Ophelia might be using
        the word as a weaker one than *love*, like 'friendship'. He takes up her word
        tenders, too (line 103).
101   *green:* immature.
102   *Unsifted:* inexperienced.
106   *ta'en . . . for true pay:* taken these offers to be actual payment.
107   *sterling:* of true value. – It is easy to make offers but less easy to do the giving in an
        acceptable way.
107   *Tender . . . dearly:* Look after yourself more carefully. – The play on *tender* goes on, and
        lowers the pitch of intensity in this speech; it is this flippancy which reduces
        Polonius's character to something rather foolish, but his advice to his son was
        not marred in this way.
108   *not to crack . . . thus:* not to make the poor word lose its breath completely by chasing after
        it in this way. – The image is of an animal being chased in every twist and turn
        in the hunt until it is breathless and exhausted.
109   *you'll tender . . . fool* – This means either, 'you'll show yourself to be a fool in my eyes', or,
        'you'll make me look a fool (for allowing you to go with the prince)'.

Take each man's censure,* but reserve thy judgement.
Costly thy habit* as thy purse can buy,   70
But not expressed in fancy – rich, not gaudy;
For the apparel oft proclaims the man,
And they in France of the best rank and station
Are most select* and generous, chief in that.
Neither a borrower nor a lender be,   75
For loan oft loses both itself and friend,
And borrowing dulls* the edge of husbandry.
This above all: to thine own self be true;
And it must follow, as the night the day,
Thou canst not then be false to any man.   80
Farewell. My blessing season* this in thee!
LAERTES   Most humbly do I take my leave, my lord.
POLONIUS   The time invites you; go, your servants tend.*
LAERTES   Farewell, Ophelia; and remember well
What I have said to you.
OPHELIA   'Tis in my memory locked,   85
And you yourself shall keep the key of it.
LAERTES   Farewell.   [Exit
POLONIUS   What is 't, Ophelia, he hath said to you?
OPHELIA   So please you,* something touching* the Lord Hamlet.
POLONIUS   Marry, well bethought.*
'Tis told me, he hath very oft of late   90
Given private time to you, and you yourself
Have of your audience* been most free and bounteous.
If it be so, as so 'tis put on me,*
And that in way of caution, I must tell you,   95
You do not understand yourself so clearly
As it behoves* my daughter and your honour.
What is between you? Give me up the truth.
OPHELIA   He hath, my lord, of late made many tenders*
Of his affection to me.   100
POLONIUS   Affection! Pooh! You speak like a green* girl,
Unsifted* in such perilous circumstance.
Do you believe his tenders, as you call them?
OPHELIA   I do not know, my lord, what I should think.
POLONIUS   Marry, I'll teach you: think yourself a baby,   105
That you have ta'en these tenders for true pay,*
Which are not sterling.* Tender yourself* more dearly
Or – not to crack the wind* of the poor phrase,
Running it thus – you'll tender me a fool.*

112   *fashion* – another of Ophelia's words which Polonius picks up. She means 'way', but Polonius uses it in the sense 'passing fancy'; this is the meaning in line 6 of this scene.

112   *go to:* nonsense – an exclamation of derision and disbelief. But Ophelia is not dissuaded from going on with what she means to say.

113   *countenance* – perhaps both (1) 'a fair appearance' and (2) 'support'. The word *countenance* corrects the bad impression which the word *importune* in line 110 may have given.

115   *springes . . . woodcocks* – Woodcocks were easily snared and were therefore considered to be foolish. The phrase used by Polonius was proverbial; it meant 'traps to catch fools', and this is what he believes Hamlet's vows to be.

116   *prodigal:* prodigally, lavishly.

119   *Even in . . . a-making:* just as they promise to become something, as it (the fire) is being built up. – She must not confuse the sudden flashes of light (*blazes*) with a real fire. Fire and passion are frequently linked in imagery.

121   *scanter:* less liberal – the opposite of *prodigal*.

122   *Be your entreatments . . . parley:* See to it that your interviews (*entreatments*) are harder to get than (simply) by a command to speak. – Hamlet the prince can command her to talk with him.

123   *For:* As for.

125   *a larger tether:* a longer rope. – A tether is a rope by which an animal is prevented from straying; the longer the rope, the more freedom the animal has for moving about.

126   *In few:* In brief – though Polonius in fact finds it difficult to be brief when he is speaking.

127   *brokers:* go-betweens – especially in matters of love.

128   *Not of . . . suits:* not of the true colour which their outward appearance (*investments*) shows, but only (*mere*) solicitors (*implorators*) of wicked causes. – Polonius is talking about the vows of heaven which Ophelia told him of; they are 'holy' vows and yet are used for wicked ends. In the next lines they are called *sanctified* and *pious*.

130   *like . . . bonds* – (probably) '. . . vows like these', with the idea of 'marriage vows' in the background. To 'breathe' them would be to say them.

133   *slander . . . leisure:* misuse any moment's leisure – *moment* appears for *moment's* in the oldest editions.

135   *charge:* command.

135   *Come your ways:* Come away.

I. iv.   Out in the cold night, Hamlet waits with Horatio and Marcellus in the hope of seeing the Ghost. Gunfire and the noise of trumpets at the King's noisy party can be heard below.
          When the Ghost appears, Hamlet talks to it, and in silence it beckons him to follow. He obeys despite his friends' efforts to prevent him. The question of true nature is pursued again here. Hamlet reflects on the tainting of a virtuous nature by a single vice; Claudius, who earlier appeared as the skilful, calculating ruler, is known to be in drunken revelry; even the Ghost may not be heaven-sent, but a spirit from hell come to tempt Hamlet. Hamlet has the determination to overcome his own fears and his friends' opposition, and will discover the Ghost's real purpose.

1   *shrewdly:* sharply.

2   *eager:* biting.

3   *it lacks of twelve:* it is a little before midnight.

4   *it is struck* – i.e. the clock has (already) struck twelve.

OPHELIA My lord, he hath importuned me with love   110
In honourable fashion –
POLONIUS Ay, fashion* you may call 't; go to,* go to.
OPHELIA And hath given countenance* to his speech, my lord,
With almost all the holy vows of heaven.
POLONIUS Ay, springes to catch woodcocks.* I do know,   115
When the blood burns, how prodigal* the soul
Lends the tongue vows. These blazes, daughter,
Giving more light than heat – extinct in both,
Even in their promise,* as it is a-making –
You must not take for fire. From this time   120
Be somewhat scanter* of your maiden presence;
Set your entreatments* at a higher rate
Than a command to parley. For* Lord Hamlet,
Believe so much in him, that he is young,
And with a larger tether* may he walk   125
Than may be given you. In few,* Ophelia,
Do not believe his vows, for they are brokers* –
Not of that dye which their investments show,
But mere implorators of unholy suits,*
Breathing like sanctified and pious bonds,*   130
The better to beguile. This is for all:
I would not, in plain terms, from this time forth
Have you so slander any moment leisure*
As to give words or talk with the Lord Hamlet.
Look to 't, I charge* you. Come your ways.*   135
OPHELIA I shall obey, my lord.

[*Exeunt*

scene iv

The platform.

Enter HAMLET, HORATIO *and* MARCELLUS.

HAMLET The air bites shrewdly;* it is very cold.
HORATIO It is a nipping and an eager* air.
HAMLET What hour now?
HORATIO   I think it lacks of twelve.*
MARCELLUS No, it is struck.*

5   *season:* time.
6   *held . . . to walk:* usually walked.
*   *flourish:* loud noise.
8   *doth wake:* is staying up late revelling.
8   *takes his rouse:* is drinking a great deal.
9   *keeps wassail:* is feasting and making merry. – The word *wassail* referred originally to the
        drinking of toasts in wine or other strong drink; people said *Wassail*, '(Let
        there be) good health', when they raised their drink for a toast.
9   *the . . . reels:* dancing riotous dances. – It is thought that the word *upspring* refers to a wild
        dance once danced in Germany, and known to have been popular in Denmark.
10   *Rhenish* – German wine from the Rhineland.
11   *bray out . . . pledge:* sound out loudly the fulfilment ('pledging') of his toasts. – The king is
        in fact celebrating Hamlet's consent to stay in Denmark, as he said he would:
            No jocund health that Denmark drinks today,
            But the great cannon to the clouds shall tell . . .
                                                                                    (I.ii.125)
15   *to the manner born:* used to such a custom (*manner*) from my birth.
16   *More honoured . . . observance:* which would be better honoured by neglecting it than by
        observing it.
17   *east and . . . nations:* everywhere makes us criticized and censured by other races.
19   *clepe:* call.
19   *with swinish . . . addition:* dirty our reputation (*addition*, literally 'title') with words that
        suggest we are pigs (*swinish phrase*) – *swine* is another word for 'pig(s)'. Other
        nations thought the Danes behaved like pigs when they indulged in these
        drinking parties.
21   *though . . . height:* even though (they are) carried out to the utmost (of our ability).
22   *The pith . . . attribute:* the central core of our good reputation (*attribute*). – The time
        between this point and the appearance of the ghost is taken up by Hamlet
        meditating on the idea he has put forward: the Danes have this one fault,
        drunkenness, which cancels out their good reputation in other things. In
        general, one fault will ruin the good effect of many fine qualities. Hamlet's
        subsequent history illustrates this point: he tends to speculate, as here, where
        action might have been better, but his other qualities, such as honour, sincer-
        ity, integrity, are good ones, and would, in a better world, compensate for his
        failing. This, however, is the heart of tragedy.
23   *So oft it chances . . .* – The philosophical speech which follows is grammatically compli-
        cated; a full paraphrase to line 36 is therefore given: So it often happens
        (*chances*) in individual human beings, that, because of some natural blemish
        (*mole of nature*) in them which tends to vice (*vicious*), as [for instance] in their
        birth – though in this they cannot be held guilty, because life (*nature*) cannot
        choose where it will be born – by the excess (*o'ergrowth*) of one particular
        characteristic (*complexion*) often destroying the boundary (*pales*) and defences
        (*forts*) of reason, or [to give another instance] by some habit which is dispro-
        portionately mixed with (*o'erleavens*) the forms of acceptable (*plausive*)
        manners, these men carrying, as I said, the mark of one defect, which is the
        dress (*livery*) which nature gave them or the condition in which fortune placed
        them (*fortune's star*) their (*his* in the text) virtues otherwise, be they as pure as
        the grace of God, as infinite as man can experience (*may undergo*), will, in the
        opinion (*censure*) of people in general, be corrupted by that particular fault.
        Hamlet's long sentence here is complex and the grammar is imperfect, but
        there is no doubt about what he means, and this very uncertainty of grammar
        reflects the uncertainty in his mind which dogs his actions as the play proceeds.
        Two further notes need to be given on this speech:
        (i) *complexion* (line 27) means 'temperament, natural disposition', and was at
        one time closely linked in people's minds with the look on the face. This
        'nature' or natural disposition of a person was thought to be associated with
        the four principal fluids in the human body, called 'humours'; an excess of any
        one of these fluids was said to control a person's disposition and to appear in
        his face. We still talk of people being in (a) good or bad humour. The idea of
        'unhealthy excess' in this respect is emphasized in *o'ergrowth* (line 27) and
        o'er-leavens (line 29).
        (ii) *fortune's star* (line 32) recalls the belief in astrology which was universal

HORATIO   Indeed? I heard it not. Then it draws near the season*   5
          Wherein the spirit held his wont* to walk.

          [*A flourish* of trumpets, and ordnance shot off inside the castle*

          What does this mean, my lord?

HAMLET   The king doth wake* tonight, and takes his rouse,*
          Keeps wassail,* and the swaggering upspring reels.*
          And, as he drains his draughts of Rhenish* down,   10
          The kettle-drum and trumpet thus bray out*
          The triumph of his pledge.

HORATIO   Is it a custom?

HAMLET   Ay, marry, is 't;
          But to my mind – though I am native here,
          And to the manner born* – it is a custom   15
          More honoured in the breach* than the observance.
          This heavy-headed revel east and west*
          Makes us traduced and taxed of other nations.
          They clepe* us drunkards, and with swinish* phrase
          Soil our addition; and, indeed, it takes   20
          From our achievements, though performed at height,*
          The pith and marrow of our attribute.*
          So oft it chances* in particular men
          That, for some vicious mole of nature in them,
          As, in their birth – wherein they are not guilty,   25
          Since nature cannot choose his origin –
          By the o'ergrowth of some complexion,
          Oft breaking down the pales and forts of reason,
          Or by some habit that too much o'er-leavens
          The form of plausive manners, that these men,   30
          Carrying, I say, the stamp of one defect,
          Being nature's livery, or fortune's star,
          His virtues else – be they as pure as grace,
          As infinite as man may undergo –
          Shall in the general censure take corruption   35

---

23 (cont'd)   in Shakespeare's day. The arrangement of the stars in the sky at crucial times
               in one's life was taken to have a powerful influence on one's future. Here, then,
               the stars are taken as influencing man's destiny, e.g. the habits he falls into (as
               referred to in line 29), whereas *nature's livery* can carry blemishes one is born
               with (line 26).

36   *The dram . . . scandal* (line 38) – The words appearing in the text are taken from the Second
        Quarto; they do not make good sense as they are, but neither do the versions
        of these lines in the other early editions of the play. The early copyist or the
        printer, or both, have certainly made such grave mistakes in transmitting these
        lines that we now have no hope of knowing how Shakespeare wanted them.
        At least 40 possible amendments have been suggested; all that we can do here
        is to try to get at the general sense, which the context and some of the words in
        these lines suggest, as follows: 'The small element of vice often spoils the whole
        nature and brings it into disrepute.'
          After the involvements of this speech, Hamlet's manner changes as the Ghost
        appears; what he now says is, by contrast, brief, clear and to the point. Action
        from outside has helped him to be more precise in his speaking.

39   *ministers of grace:* messengers of God's grace – i.e. angels. Hamlet prays that heavenly
        beings should protect them, because he is faced with something which is not
        of this world.

40   *Be thou:* Whether you are. – Similarly *Be thy* in line 42, to which this is parallel.

40   *a spirit of health:* a spirit of well-being, a good spirit – *of health* contrasts with *damned*.

41   *Bring,* for *Bringing.*

43   *questionable shape:* shape which compels one to question (what it is). – In these lines he
        uses *thee, thou,* as the form of address, showing that he feels some kinship
        towards the apparition; otherwise he would have used *you* (see Introduction,
        p. xlii). And in fact he calls the ghost *Hamlet, King, Father.*

47   *canonized:* buried according to the rule (canon) of the Church.

47   *hearséd in death:* coffined at the time of death. – Hamlet makes much of the fact that his
        father was buried with all the rites of the Church, because, in the religious
        belief of his time, the ghost of a man might walk about if these rites had not
        been properly performed over him. Hamlet the prince makes it abundantly
        clear that this cannot be the reason for his father's spirit not yet being at rest.
        He must cast about for a different explanation.

48   *cerements:* grave-clothes.

49   *inurned:* buried.

51   *To cast . . . again:* to throw you back again (into the world). – The marble tomb (*sepulchre*)
        is likened to a mouth with *marble jaws* which has 'cast up' what it once
        swallowed.

52   *corse:* corpse, body.

52   *in complete steel* – i.e. cased in full armour made of steel, which would make the king look
        like a warrior, and therefore suggest a battle for some cause; he does not
        appear as a peaceful administrator or land-giver.

54   *and we fools . . . of our souls* (line 56): and [what can it mean—line 51] that you terrify our
        feelings (*dispositions*), making our hair stand on end (*horridly*), with thoughts
        which we, being mere foolish mortals (*fools of nature*), cannot fully contem-
        plate.

59   *impartment:* communication.

61   *removéd ground:* remote spot. – Hamlet's companions become very tense; they feel that if
        Hamlet leaves them now and follows the ghost which is gently beckoning him
        on he will be endangered by supernatural power, or led on to physical death.

64   *what . . . fear?:* what can there be to fear? – *Fear* in Shakespeare can sometimes be a noun
        meaning 'ground of, cause for fear'.

65   *set my life . . . fee:* put my life at the value of a pin. – He has no fear of physical danger
        because the message of the ghost is more important to him than life.

66   *it* – i.e. the Ghost.

69   *flood:* sea.

From that particular fault. The dram of eale*
Doth all the noble substance of a doubt
To his own scandal.

HORATIO   Look, my lord, it comes!

Enter GHOST

HAMLET Angels and ministers of grace* defend us!
Be thou* a spirit of health* or goblin damned,   40
Bring* with thee airs from heaven or blasts from hell,
Be thy intents wicked or charitable,
Thou comest in such a questionable* shape
That I will speak to thee. I'll call thee Hamlet,
King, Father, Royal Dane. O, answer me!   45
Let me not burst in ignorance; but tell
Why thy canonized* bones, hearséd in death,*
Have burst their cerements;* why the sepulchre
Wherein we saw thee quietly inurned,*
Hath oped his ponderous and marble jaws   50
To cast thee up again!* What may this mean,
That thou, dead corse,* again in cómplete steel*
Revisit'st thus the glimpses of the moon,
Making night hideous, and we fools of nature*
So horridly to shake our disposition   55
With thoughts beyond the reaches of our souls?
Say, why is this? wherefor? what should we do?
                    [GHOST *beckons* HAMLET

HORATIO It beckons you to go away with it,
As if it some impartment* did desire
To you alone.

MARCELLUS   Look, with what courteous action   60
It waves you to a more removéd ground.*
But do not go with it —

HORATIO   No, by no means.

HAMLET It will not speak; then I will follow it.

HORATIO Do not, my lord.

HAMLET   Why, what should be the fear?*
I do not set my life* at a pin's fee;   65
And for my soul, what can it* do to that,
Being a thing immortal as itself?
It waves me forth again; I'll follow it.

HORATIO What if it tempt you toward the flood,* my lord,
Or to the dreadful summit of the cliff   70

71   *beetles . . . base:* menacingly overhangs its base. – The cliffs are not only high but over-
         hanging.
73   *deprive your . . . reason:* take away (*deprive*) the sovereign power of reason in you. –
         Horatio is afraid that Hamlet will lose his mind if he is drawn away by the
         horrible vision.
75   *toys of desperation:* fanciful thoughts of self-destruction. – The most 'desperate' act was
         to take one's own life.
76   *more motive:* any other motive. – The cliffs are so high and frightening that, standing on
         the top, one thinks of jumping over without any other reason whatever.
83   *As hardy . . . nerve:* as strong as the sinews (*nerve*) of the Nemean lion. – In Greek mytho-
         logy, Hercules was compelled to carry out twelve tasks or 'labours'. The first
         was to bring back the skin of a huge lion which terrorized the valley of Nemea.
         Hercules found it so strong that his club and arrows had no effect. He therefore
         strangled it.
85   *I'll make . . . me:* I will kill anyone who hinders (*lets*) me. – The talk is all about the Ghost,
         even though it is not mentioned by name; *Hamlet's* synonym for 'kill', *make
         a ghost of* is full of irony.
87   *waxes:* becomes.
89   *Have after:* I will follow you. – Hamlet told them to go away, and, since he is a prince, they
         should have obeyed him. But fearing that he may come to some harm, they are
         determined to follow him at a distance. As earlier (lines 80–1 above), Marcellus
         acts first, while Horatio holds back.
91   *Nay:* Indeed. – Marcellus confirms what has been decided.

I. v.   At a remote spot the Ghost stops and tells Hamlet its story. It is indeed the spirit of Hamlet's
dead father. He was the victim of the worst of all crimes, a brother's murder; Claudius
killed him by pouring a deadly poison in his ear, and then had the story put about that
he had been bitten by a snake. Claudius then married Hamlet's mother. Hamlet is to
avenge this crime in the way that seems best to him but is to do nothing to harm his
mother; he swears revenge. When his friends at last discover him he is a changed man;
half serious and half mocking, he hints at the terrible discovery and makes them promise
they will say nothing of what they have seen. The Ghost persuades them to swear from
below the ground, and as they do so Hamlet, no longer afraid, talks familiarly with it.
He warns his friends not to show that they know a reason for anything strange in his
behaviour from now on.
    Hamlet now knows the truth, and his manner has changed; he seems determined to
act alone, and begins at once to alternate intense concern with off-hand humorous remarks.
People will think him odd and keep clear of him. Horatio by contrast is convinced of the
truth of the Ghost and is deeply disturbed. From now until the play scene Claudius and
Hamlet are seen making attempts to penetrate each other's disguise. And Polonius,
Rosencrantz, Guildenstern and Ophelia all in their turn try unsuccessfully to make
Hamlet account for his change of manner.

2   *My hour* – i.e. the time of dawn, cock-crow, which marks the beginning of day. The
         Ghost is condemned for a time to walk the earth during the night, and to
         suffer torment in hell (*sulphurous and tormenting flames*) in the day-time.

That beetles o'er his base* into the sea,
And there assume some other horrible form,
Which might deprive your sovereignty of reason,*
And draw you into madness? Think of it:
The very place puts toys of desperation,*   75
Without more motive,* into every brain
That looks so many fathoms to the sea,
And hears it roar beneath.

HAMLET   It waves me still.
[*To the* GHOST] Go on; I'll follow thee.

MARCELLUS You shall not go, my lord.   [*He takes hold of* HAMLET

HAMLET   Hold off your hands.   80

HORATIO Be ruled; you shall not go.

HAMLET   My fate cries out
And makes each petty artery in this body
As hardy* as the Nemean lion's nerve. [*The* GHOST *beckons*
Still am I called. Unhand me, gentlemen.
By heaven, I'll make a ghost of him that lets me.*   85
I say, away! – [*To the* GHOST] Go on; I'll follow thee.

                        [*Exeunt* GHOST *and* HAMLET

HORATIO He waxes* desperate with imagination.

MARCELLUS Let's follow; 'tis not fit thus to obey him.

HORATIO Have after.* To what issue will this come?

MARCELLUS Something is rotten in the state of Denmark.   90

HORATIO Heaven will direct it.

MARCELLUS   Nay,* let's follow him.

                                                [*Exeunt*

scene v

Another part of the platform.

Enter GHOST *and* HAMLET.

HAMLET Where wilt thou lead me? Speak; I'll go no further.

GHOST Mark me.

HAMLET   I will.

GHOST   My hour* is almost come,
When I to sulphurous and tormenting flames
Must render up myself.

HAMLET   Alas, poor ghost!

6	*bound*: ready. – But the ghost takes the word in its other meaning, 'obliged' when it says, *So art thou* [bound] *to revenge*.
11	*fast* – (apparently) suffer torment. Fire burns and also purifies what is foul.
12	*days of nature*: lifetime.
13	*But that*: If it were not [for the fact] that.
16	*harrow up thy soul* – This is a very moving image. A harrow is a heavy frame with iron teeth which is used for breaking humps of earth on ploughed land; *up* suggests doing the action thoroughly so that *harrow up* is to wound with innumerable terrible rents.
17	*start . . . spheres*: jump out of their sockets. – But *sphere* has a further meaning here, one associated with the simile of the stars. The ancients explained the movements of the heavenly bodies in the sky by assuming that each was fixed inside an invisible hollow sphere, and that these spheres all had the earth as their centre. 'Shooting stars' could not be said to keep to their proper position in their spheres, and therefore were taken to be signs of disorder or calamity to come. (The word *disaster* means, literally, 'away from the star(s)'.) Eyes starting from the head, then, are likened to stars leaving their proper courses, a sign of terrible events.
18	*knotted . . . locks*: hair smoothed down so that each hair cannot be seen separately. – Great fright is said to 'make one's hair stand on end.'
20	*the fretful porpentine*: the ill-tempered porcupine. – Porcupines were supposed to stick out their quills when angered.
21	*this eternal blazon*: this proclaiming of things to do with eternity – *eternal* is used to mean 'supernatural' in contrast with *ears of flesh and blood*.
22	*List*, another form of *listen*.
25	*unnatural* – For Shakespeare's audiences, this word was sharper in its meaning and implications than it is today. To do something 'unnatural' was to act 'against nature', i.e. to break away from the proper order of things in the universe (like stars moving out of their 'spheres'). To be 'natural' was to have 'natural' feelings of kindness and sympathy towards others, and to lack these feelings was to be 'unnatural'. In this sense the murder of a brother is supremely 'unnatural'; cf the note on *kind* (I.ii.65).
27	*in the best*: at best. – Even the best of murders is foul.
29	*Haste . . . know't*: Let me know it quickly. – This is Hamlet's first reaction to the word *murder*; the idea of his father's death by foul means must have been in his mind before, but this is the first occasion on which it is specifically stated. And Hamlet's thoughts are now turned to quick revenge.
30	*meditation*: thought. – Thought moves very quickly from object to object.
32	*duller . . . in this* (line 34): you would be duller than the gross plant (*fat weed*) that grows (*roots itself*) abundantly (*in ease*, i.e. without difficulty) on the bank of the waters of Lethe if you refused to take action (*stir*) in this matter. – It was thought that the spirits of the dead went to the river or lake of Lethe and drank the waters there; this caused complete forgetfulness of the past. The plant supposed to grow there is thought of as also bringing a state of forgetfulness and stupor: *dull(er)*, *fat*, *in ease*.
35	*orchard*: garden.
36	*serpent*: snake.
37	*by a forgéd process . . . abused*: is grossly deceived (*Rankly abused*) by a false account (*forgéd process*) of my death.
40	*prophetic* – Apparently Hamlet has already had premonitions that his father was murdered.
43	*witchcraft of his wit*: intelligence used to bewitch. – The wife of the dead King was won over by a cleverly-worked plan of seduction, and in the end was party to the schemes of the treacherous brother.

GHOST	Pity me not, but lend thy serious hearing
	To what I shall unfold.
HAMLET	Speak; I am bound* to hear.
GHOST	So art thou to revenge, when thou shalt hear.
HAMLET	What?
GHOST	I am thy father's spirit,

GHOST   Pity me not, but lend thy serious hearing   5
    To what I shall unfold.
HAMLET   Speak; I am bound* to hear.
GHOST   So art thou to revenge, when thou shalt hear.
HAMLET   What?
GHOST   I am thy father's spirit,
    Doomed for a certain term to walk the night,   10
    And for the day confined to fast* in fires
    Till the foul crimes done in my days of nature*
    Are burnt and purged away. But that* I am forbid
    To tell the secrets of my prison-house,
    I could a tale unfold, whose lightest word   15
    Would harrow up thy soul,* freeze thy young blood,
    Make thy two eyes, like stars, start from their spheres,*
    Thy knotted and combinéd locks* to part,
    And each particular hair to stand on end,
    Like quills upon the fretful porpentine.*   20
    But this eternal blazon* must not be
    To ears of flesh and blood. – List,* list, O, list! –
    If thou didst ever thy dear father love –
HAMLET   O God!
GHOST   Revenge his foul and most unnatural* murder.   25
HAMLET   Murder!
GHOST   Murder most foul, as in the best* it is;
    But this most foul, strange, and unnatural.
HAMLET   Haste me to know 't,* that I, with wings as swift
    As meditation* or the thoughts of love,   30
    May sweep to my revenge.
GHOST   I find thee apt;
    And duller* shouldst thou be than the fat weed
    That roots itself in ease on Lethe wharf,
    Wouldst thou not stir in this. Now, Hamlet, hear:
    'Tis given out that, sleeping in my orchard,*   35
    A serpent* stung me; so the whole ear of Denmark
    Is by a forgéd process* of my death
    Rankly abused. But know, thou noble youth,
    The serpent that did sting thy father's life
    Now wears his crown.
HAMLET   O my prophetic* soul!   40
    My uncle!
GHOST   Ay, that incestuous, that adulterate beast,
    With witchcraft of his wit,* with traitorous gifts –

49   *even:* in exact agreement – *hand in hand* is a pleasant phrase to use when talking of a happy marriage.
50   *to decline Upon:* to sink to the level of.
52   *To:* by comparison with.
53   *But virtue . . . garbage* (line 57) – This passage speaks of virtue, vice and other abstractions as if they were each a person characterized by that particular quality; the abstract terms are personified. 'As virtue will never be shaken, even though vice (*lewdness*) tempts it in the form of an angel (*a shape of heaven*), so lust, even though joined (in marriage) to a radiant angel, will satisfy itself in a celestial bed and (then) prey on filth'. Hamlet's father is generalizing on the way virtues and vices are unchanged by contact with one another; so the present King is unmoved and unchanged by the purity of nature formerly shown by the Queen.
58   *soft:* wait.
58   *Methinks:* It seems to me (that). – The ghost is condemned to walk at night. When day dawns, it must disappear; the first scent of the morning air persuades it to leave its moralizing and finish the message quickly.
61   *secure:* unsuspecting. – The word here means that he felt safe but was not really safe at all – the sense of security was mistaken. He was killed at a time when he felt most sure of safety, and took no care to protect himself.
62   *hebenon* – This may be either (1) henbane, a plant from which a poisonous liquor can be made; or (2) the yew tree, which was supposed to have poisonous properties. If (2) is correct, *hebenon* must be a form of *ebenus*, the Latin word for *ebony*, a very hard wood.
64   *leperous:* causing leprosy.
67   *gates and alleys* – The image of the arteries and veins of the body as roads in a city was introduced by the word *porches* (line 63) in reference to ears.
68   *posset:* curdle – like milk, which, when it turns sour, changes into thick soft lumps and a watery liquid. A *posset* was a drink made of milk curdled with some strong liquor such as beer or wine; this is the *eager droppings* of the next line. (For *eager* = 'sharp', cf. I.iv.2.) It was thought in Shakespeare's time that poison dropped into the ear would bring death very quickly.
71   *instant tetter . . . like:* immediately diseased eruptions of the skin (*tetter*), just like leprosy (*lazar-like*), covered, as bark does a tree (*barked about*) – the object is *my smooth body* (line 73). Lepers were called lazars after Lazarus, a beggar 'full of sores' about whom Christ told a story as recounted in the Bible (*Luke* 16:19–31).
75   *dispatched:* deprived.
76   *blossoms of my skin . . . unaneled* – This refers to the Christian belief of the time that a person was damned if he did not confess his sins and have them absolved by a priest shortly before he died. What the dead King's spirit feels most bitterly is that the murder took place without any opportunity for absolution, and that this was the cause of much suffering in the world to come. Hamlet takes this belief into account when he finally decides not to kill his uncle as he is kneeling in prayer: to kill him at prayer is to send his soul straight to heaven (III.iii.73ff.)
        In this passage *blossoms of my sin* means 'at the height of my sins', literally 'with my sins like flowers in full bloom'; *unhouseled* means 'not having taken the sacrament', i.e. the bread and wine of the Christian service of Holy Communion (the service was called *husl* in Old English and the word *unhouseled* comes from this); *disappointed* means 'unprepared', literally 'not properly equipped, not made ready'; and *unaneled* means 'unanointed'; to 'anoint' a person is to put oil on his body as a mark of blessing in a religious service. The whole passage, therefore, can be explained as follows: 'at the height of my sins, without having taken the sacrament, unprepared, and unanointed'. The spirit continues the same theme in the following lines; the greatest terror lay in being killed without having first gone through the required religious ceremonies.
78   *reckoning . . . account* – These words both refer to the idea that at the time of a man's death he should 'settle his account' with God, i.e. admit to his faults ('debts') and try to atone for them. The 'day of reckoning', a day when outstanding bills were settled, was looked upon as a symbol of the day of judgment when

O wicked wit and gifts, that have the power
So to seduce! — won to his shameful lust   45
The will of my most seeming-virtuous queen.
O, Hamlet, what a falling-off was there!
From me, whose love was of that dignity
That it went hand in hand even* with the vow
I made to her in marriage, and to decline*   50
Upon a wretch, whose natural gifts were poor
To* those of mine!
But virtue,* as it never will be moved,
Though lewdness court it in a shape of heaven,
So lust, though to a radiant angel linked,   55
Will sate itself in a celestial bed,
And prey on garbage.
But, soft!* Methinks* I scent the morning air;
Brief let me be. — Sleeping within my orchard,
My custom always in the afternoon,   60
Upon my secure* hour thy uncle stole,
With juice of cursed hebenon* in a vial,
And in the porches of mine ears did pour
The leperous* distilment; whose effect
Holds such an enmity with blood of man   65
That, swift as quicksilver, it courses through
The natural gates and alleys* of the body;
And, with a sudden vigour, it doth posset*
And curd, like eager droppings into milk,
The thin and wholesome blood. So did it mine;   70
And a most instant tetter* barked about,
Most lazar-like, with vile and loathsome crust
All my smooth body.
Thus was I, sleeping, by a brother's hand
Of life, of crown, of queen, at once dispatched.*   75
Cut off even in the blossoms of my sin,*
Unhouseled, disappointed, unaneled;
No reckoning* made, but sent to my account

78 (*cont'd*)   man's *account* with God was to be settled. Failure to do this was considered to
be a sin which would bring terrible consequences; the Ghost repeats the word
horrible when he speaks of it.

81   *nature* – i.e. any natural feeling.
83   *luxury:* lust.
86   *aught:* anything – the object of *contrive.*
88   *prick* and *sting* are often used in connection with conscience; Shakespeare has used
        thorns as an image for conscience – let the Queen, he said, feel only the pricking
        of her own conscience.
89   *matin:* morning. – This use of the word *matin* is unusual; it generally refers, in the plural,
        to the morning service of the Christian Church, and this may be its undertone
        here, since the ghost is deeply obsessed by religious ceremonies.
90   *'gins . . . fire:* begins to reduce the light of (*pale*) its fire, which is losing its effect (*un-
        effectual*). – The glow-worm shines brightly in the night, but as dawn breaks
        it reduces its light because it cannot compete with the brightness of the rising
        sun.
91   *Adieu:* Farewell. (The word is pronounced like *a dew* in English.)
92   *host of heaven:* army of angels.
93   *couple hell:* include hell (in the invocation).
94   *instant:* instantly – *sinews* are used as an image of bodily strength (cf. I.iii.12, *thews*).
95   *stiffly:* strongly.
97   *distracted globe* – Hamlet is referring to his head, which he touches as he says these words.
        In the philosophy of the Middle Ages, man was often thought of as resembling
        in little the world; he was called the *microcosm*, 'the little world'. Hamlet's
        brain is distracted just as the public world of Denmark is disjointed. He is
        recalling the ghost's words *remember me*, and says he will remember for as
        long as memory has any place (*seat*) in his skull.
98   *table* – a tablet (made of slate or iron) for writing on. Two 'tables' could be fixed together
        at one side with a clasp and opened up like a book; these are the *tables* Hamlet
        takes and writes on a few moments later (line 107). Here he refers to his
        memory as a 'table' on which his past education and experience have been
        written. The pattern of imagery is continued with *copied* in line 101, and *book*,
        volume, in line 103.
99   *fond:* fatuous. – The scansion of this line requires that *records* is stressed on the second
        syllable, *recórds*.
100   *saws of books:* wise sayings out of books.
100   *forms:* images.
100   *pressures past:* impressions from past experience. – The theme of Hamlet's declaration is
        that from now on he will have no dealing with borrowed or remembered
        experience (book-learning, memories) but will live with the action arising
        from his father's order always in his mind. But in a few moments he does just
        what he said he would not do, write down a 'saw', a generalized comment on
        life. This is the reaction of a man who will find it hard to live up to his promises,
        and it is symptomatic of what is to come.
105   *pernicious woman* – Hamlet's thoughts move for an instant to his mother, whom the Ghost
        has warned him not to harm, yet nowhere else has she been implicated as a
        partner to the present King in his evil deeds. She has so far only tried to
        persuade Hamlet not to remember so worrowfully and continuously the loss
        of his father (I.ii.68ff.).
107   *meet it is . . . down:* it is a proper thing (*meet*) for me to write it down. – He notes the
        maxim which he gives in the next line.
110   *word:* watchword.
113   *secure him:* keep him safe. – Hamlet's friends have been searching for him; he has been
        away from them for a long time and they are now desperate. On the stage only
        Hamlet can be seen, but the voices of the others are heard calling out from the
        back.

With all my imperfections on my head.
O, horrible! O, horrible! most horrible!   80
If thou hast nature* in thee, bear it not;
Let not the royal bed of Denmark be
A couch for luxury* and damned incest.
But, however thou pursuest this act,
Taint not thy mind, nor let thy soul contrive   85
Against thy mother aught.* Leave her to heaven
And to those thorns that in her bosom lodge
To prick* and sting her. Fare thee well at once!
The glow-worm shows the matin* to be near,
And 'gins* to pale his uneffectual fire.   90
Adieu,* adieu, adieu! remember me.   [*Exit*

HAMLET O all you host of heaven!* O earth! What else?
And shall I couple hell?* – O, fie! – Hold, hold, my heart;
And you, my sinews, grow not instant* old,
But bear me stiffly up.* – Remember thee!   95
Ay, thou poor ghost, while memory holds a seat
In this distracted globe.* Remember thee!
Yea, from the table* of my memory
I'll wipe away all trivial fond* recórds,
All saws of books,* all forms,* all pressures past,*   100
That youth and observation copied there;
And thy commandment all alone shall live
Within the book and volume of my brain,
Unmixed with baser matter. Yes, by heaven! –
O most pernicious woman!*   105
O villain, villain; smiling, damnéd villain!
My tables – meet it is I set it down,*
That one may smile, and smile, and be a villain;
At least I'm sure it may be so in Denmark.   [*Writing*
So, uncle, there you are. Now to my word;*   110
It is, 'Adieu, adieu! remember me':
I have sworn 't.

HORATIO   [*Within*] My lord, my lord –
MARCELLUS   [*Within*] Lord Hamlet! –
HORATIO   [*Within*] Heaven secure
him!*

HAMLET So be it!

115   *Illo, ho, ho:* Hallo there. – Hamlet makes a joke of this cry, calling out *Hillo* in reply, which
       was the cry of the falconer calling in his falcon; this is why he says *come, bird,
       come.*
              From this point on, Hamlet's manner is subject to frequent changes; he
       seems to be his real self in private, but in public he seems to act in many
       different ways. Here we may say that the words of the Ghost have so appalled
       him that he is beside himself. He has written down a maxim, which he said he
       would not do, and now he is playful with his friends, mocking at their concern
       for his welfare. This is one way of keeping the full knowledge of his father's
       murder to himself, and also a way of playing for time, fobbing off his friends so
       that he can as soon as possible think out quietly what he should do. Dramatic-
       ally, the lighter tone of the rest of the scene is a relief after the sombre revela-
       tions which have occurred so far. It is, too, a foretaste of the feigned madness
       which Hamlet says he will assume and which his friends are told to treat with
       surprise, as if they knew nothing about it beforehand (line 171).

121   *once:* ever.

123   *There's ne'er a villain . . . knave:* There is not a villain living in Denmark who is not an
       out-and-out (*arrant*) scoundrel. – Since *villain* and *knave* mean much the same
       thing, this remark has not even the value of a wise generalized saying of the
       sort Hamlet spoke about a few minutes back. Hamlet is uncertain what to do;
       he began by being playful, turned serious for a moment (line 121), and now
       seems to begin by wishing to confide in them what he has learnt (he sets out as
       if to say something like 'there's ne'er a villain dwelling in all Denmark who is
       more devilish than my uncle', which would have told them all they needed to
       know), but he changes his mind and reverts to a platitude which puzzles them
       profoundly.

127   *circumstance:* formality. – Yet what he then says has a formal and heartless ring, a strange
       mixture of superficiality and true feeling. This of course reflects Hamlet's
       deepest feelings and uncertainties. His companions find them *wild and
       whirling words*, and he defends them by repeating words of apology, again
       betraying his uncertainty.

136   *Saint Patrick* – Hamlet is said to swear by Saint Patrick because he is the patron saint of all
       mistakes and confusion. Hamlet now plays on the words *offend* and *offence.*
       Horatio by chance says *There's no offence* when he might have said, 'We are
       not offended'. But he could be taken to mean 'offence in general'—not
       referring to himself and Marcellus. This is how Hamlet picks up the word; the
       offence or crime is Claudius's deeds.

137   *Touching:* Concerning. – For a moment it seems that he is going to become serious again.

138   *that let me tell you:* I must tell you *that* (about it).

140   *as you may:* in any way you can.

HORATIO   [*Within*] Illo,* ho, ho, my lord!   115
HAMLET   Hillo, ho, ho, boy! come, bird, come.

Enter HORATIO *and* MARCELLUS.

MARCELLUS   How is 't, my noble lord?
HORATIO   What news, my lord?
HAMLET   O, wonderful!
HORATIO   Good my lord, tell it.
HAMLET   No; you will reveal it.
HORATIO   Not I, my lord, by heaven.
MARCELLUS   Nor I, my lord.   120
HAMLET   How say you, then? Would heart of man once* think it? –
But you'll be secret?
HORATIO *and*   Ay, by heaven, my lord.
MARCELLUS

HAMLET   There's ne'er a villain* dwelling in all Denmark –
But he's an arrant knave.
HORATIO   There needs no ghost, my lord, come from the grave   125
To tell us this.
HAMLET   Why, right; you are i' the right;
And so, without more circumstance* at all,
I hold it fit that we shake hands and part:
You, as your business and desire shall point you –
For every man hath business and desire,   130
Such as it is – and for mine own poor part,
Look you, I'll go pray.
HORATIO   These are but wild and whirling words, my lord.
HAMLET   I'm sorry they offend you, heartily;
Yes, faith, heartily.
HORATIO   There's no offence, my lord.   135
HAMLET   Yes, by Saint Patrick,* but there is, Horatio,
And much offence too. Touching* this vision here –
It is an honest ghost, that* let me tell you;
For your desire to know what is between us,
O'ermaster 't as you may.* And now, good friends,   140
As you are friends, scholars, and soldiers,
Give me one poor request.
HORATIO   What is 't, my lord? We will.
HAMLET   Never make known what you have seen tonight.
HORATIO *and*   My lord, we will not.
MARCELLUS
HAMLET   Nay, but swear 't.

146   *not I* – i.e. I will not make known what I have seen.
147   *my sword* – The handle and blade of the sword look like a cross, and to swear on the sword
      was to swear on a symbolic cross, the sacred emblem of the Christian Church.
      Hamlet insists they swear on this symbolic cross, and the voice of the Ghost is
      heard coming up from under ground insisting that they do so. When this
      happens, Hamlet seems to become distracted, shouting out to the ghost of his
      father in vulgar irreverent phrases, and shifting his ground so that he shall
      not be immediately on top of the spirit.
150   *true-penny:* honest fellow.
151   *in the cellarage:* under ground. – The voice comes from below the stage.
156   Hic et ubique? (Latin): [Are you] here and everywhere? – It is all part of Hamlet's distrac-
      tion that he should say something in Latin; the spirit come from the dead
      reminds him of the Church, and the Church's language was Latin.
162   *mole:* a small creature which burrows out tunnels in the earth.
163   *pioner:* miner. – The modern English word *pioneer*, a soldier who goes ahead of the main
      army to prepare roads, etc., is related to this word.
165   *stranger* – another piece of Hamlet's word-play: Horatio says his behaviour is 'strange';
      he seizes upon the word *strange* and asks Horatio to treat his behaviour as a
      stranger, i.e. a guest one should receive hospitably, without asking him
      questions about himself.
167   *your philosophy:* the natural science you study. – Horatio is, as we have seen, a scholar at
      heart. (It is important to notice that the word *philosophy* does not mean 'way of
      life, general belief' in this context.) Hamlet's distraction and the reappearance
      of the Ghost do not conform to scientific facts as Horatio would have known
      them; but, Hamlet says in effect, science does not explain everything. (See also
      Glossary, s.n. *philosophy*).
169   *so help you mercy* – This phrase is a variant of one used in swearing an oath: 'So help me
      God', i.e. 'as God may help me to keep this oath'; *mercy* may here be taken to
      mean 'merciful God'.
170   *How strange . . . myself:* however strangely or oddly I may behave.
172   *antic disposition:* fantastic manner. – Thus Hamlet warns them that he may act oddly (he
      will in fact pretend to be mad), but they are never to show that they understand
      why he is doing so, and what his aims may be. Perhaps at this stage Hamlet is
      himself not very clear as to why he should do this. It is a gesture of revenge,
      some action taken to avenge the death of his father.
174   *encumbered:* folded. – As he speaks he shows them the sort of gesture he has in mind.
176   *As:* such as.
176   *an if:* if. The sentence means: 'We could tell [you the reason] if we wanted to (*would*).'
177   *list:* wished.
177   *There be . . . might:* There are some [who could speak] if they were allowed to (*might*).
178   *to note:* draw attention to the fact. – This links with *shall* in line 173.
180   *So grace . . . you* – Cf. line 169 and note.

HORATIO   In faith,   145
         My lord, not I.*
MARCELLUS   Nor I, my lord, in faith.
  HAMLET   Upon my sword.*
                                  [*He takes out his sword and holds it up*
MARCELLUS   We have sworn, my lord, already.
  HAMLET   Indeed, upon my sword, indeed.
   GHOST   [*Calls out from under the stage*] Swear.
  HAMLET   Ah, ha, boy! say'st thou so? Art thou there, true-penny?* –   150
           Come on! You hear this fellow in the cellarage* –
           Consent to swear.
HORATIO   Propose the oath, my lord.
  HAMLET   Never to speak of this that you have seen,
           Swear by my sword.
   GHOST   [*Beneath*] Swear.   155
  HAMLET   *Hic et ubique?** Then we'll shift our ground. –
           Come hither, gentlemen,
                            [*They move to another part of the stage*
           And lay your hands again upon my sword;
           Never to speak of this that you have heard,
           Swear by my sword.   160
   GHOST   [*Beneath*] Swear.
  HAMLET   Well said, old mole!* Canst work i' th' earth so fast?
           A worthy pioner!* – Once more remove, good friends.
HORATIO   O day and night, but this is wondrous strange!
  HAMLET   And therefore as a stranger* give it welcome.   165
           There are more things in heaven and earth, Horatio,
           Than are dreamt of in your philosophy.*
           But come:
           Here, as before, never, so help you mercy,*
           How strange* or odd soe'er I bear myself –   170
           As I, perchance, hereafter shall think meet
           To put an antic disposition* on –
           That you, at such times seeing me, never shall,
           With arms encumbered* thus, or this head-shake,
           Or by pronouncing of some doubtful phrase,   175
           As* 'Well, well, we know,' or 'We could, an if* we would,'
           Or 'If we list* to speak,' or 'There be,* an if they might,'
           Or such ambiguous giving out, to note*
           That you know aught of me; this not to do,
           So grace* and mercy at your most need help you,   180
           Swear.

184   *commend me to you:* give you my warm regards.
186   *friending:* friendliness.
187   *lack:* be wanting. – The subject is *what* ('whatever') in line 185.
188   *still:* always. – A finger raised to the lips means 'Silence!'
189   *spite:* worrying situation. – Hamlet's misgivings as to how he will deal with the circum-
        stance he finds himself in come out clearly in these serious and forceful lines.

GHOST   [*Beneath*] Swear. [*They swear on Hamlet's sword.*]
HAMLET   Rest, rest, perturbéd spirit!
      – So, gentlemen,
      With all my love I do commend me* to you.
      And what so poor a man as Hamlet is   185
      May do t' express his love and friending* to you,
      God willing, shall not lack.* Let us go in together;
      And still* your fingers on your lips, I pray.
      The time is out of joint. – O ccurséd spite,*
      That ever I was born to set it right! –   190
      Nay, come, let's go together.
                                       [*Exeunt*

II. i.   About two months appear to have passed since the events at the end of Act I. Polonius tells a servant to go to Paris, to find out how Laertes is conducting himself there. As he leaves, Ophelia rushes in looking terrified and distracted. Hamlet has been to her in a dishevelled state, and has frightened her by gazing into her eyes and deeply sighing. Polonius is now convinced that Hamlet is deranged through unrequited love.

This scene begins quietly and moves to a climax with Ophelia's fear and distraction. Polonius seems to have changed: his schemes for Reynaldo to spy on his son are unpleasant, and he seems to revel in their unpleasantness. He appears older, more talkative, more rambling. Yet what he plans is legitimate: the play has reached a stage where in the search for reality appearances must be watched. Polonius's indirect surveillance of his son parallels Claudius's far graver and more direct watching of Hamlet.

4   *inquire,* for *enquiry.* – The usual form would have too many syllables for the line.
7   *me:* for me.
7   *Danskers:* Danes. – The word is like the Danish word for 'Dane'.
8   *keep:* stay, live – *what means* must mean 'how they get their money'.
10   *encompassment . . . question:* roundabout way of questioning. – Polonius is obviously pleased with his idea here, and expands it later (lines 61–4).
11   *come you . . . touch it:* you will come nearer than direct questions (*particular demand*) will get you. – If he asks people outright about Laertes' behaviour, they will be put on their guard, and may tell him nothing; but by a more roundabout way Reynaldo may easily get to know the truth.
15   *mark:* 'get', understand.
20   *forgeries:* defamation.
20   *rank:* foul. – Polonius does not consider it to be particularly dishonourable for a young man to indulge in drinking and brawling, but he does not want Laertes accused of graver vices.
23   *companions noted:* particular accompaniments.
26   *drabbing:* associating with 'drabs', women of bad reputation.
28   *as you may . . . charge:* so long as you moderate (*season*) what you have to say against him.
30   *open to incontinency:* open to [charges of] unrestrained lust – which would cause general scandal. Polonius is not sure of his own ground here; his mention of *drabbing* was what caused Reynaldo to question him.
31   *quaintly:* cleverly.

ACT II scene i

Elsinore. A room in POLONIUS'S *house.*

Enter POLONIUS *and* REYNALDO.

POLONIUS   Give him this money and these notes, Reynaldo.
REYNALDO   I will, my lord.
POLONIUS   You shall do marvellous wisely, good Reynaldo,
    Before you visit him, to make inquire*
    Of his behaviour.
REYNALDO   My lord, I did intend it.   5
POLONIUS   Mary, well said, very well said. Look you, sir,
    Inquire me* first what Danskers* are in Paris;
    And how, and who, what means, and where they keep,*
    What company, at what expense; and finding,
    By this encompassment* and drift of question,   10
    That they do know my son, come you* more nearer
    Than your particular demands will touch it.
    Take you, as 'twere, some distant knowledge of him;
    As thus, 'I know his father and his friends,
    And in part him.' – Do you mark* this, Reynaldo?   15
REYNALDO   Ay, very well, my lord.
POLONIUS   'And in part him – but', you may say, 'not well;
    But, if 't be he I mean, he's very wild;
    Addicted so and so' – and there put on him
    What forgeries* you please; marry, none so rank*   20
    As may dishonour him; take heed of that;
    But, sir, such wanton, wild, and usual slips
    As are companions noted* and most known
    To youth and liberty.
REYNALDO   As gaming, my lord.
POLONIUS   Ay, or drinking, fencing, swearing,   25
    Quarrelling, drabbing* – you may go so far.
REYNALDO   My lord, that would dishonour him.
POLONIUS   Faith, no, as you may season* it in the charge.
    You must not put another scandal on him,
    That he is open to incontinency.*   30
    That's not my meaning. But breathe his faults so
    quaintly*

35   *of general assault:* which assaults [young people] generally. – Polonius makes, by careful suggestions, the point that these vices are likely in young people when they are for the first time free of their parents' control: *liberty, outbreak, unreclaiméd* (i.e. 'not tamed by age and experience').

36   *Wherefore:* Why – Polonius anticipates the question.

38   *fetch of warrant:* a permitted trick – *to warrant* could mean 'to allow, permit' in Shakespeare's English.

39   *sullies:* blemishes.

42   *Your party . . . consequence* (line 45)*:* the man you are talking to, he you want to (*would*) sound out, if he has ever seen the youth you are talking about (*breathe of*) guilty of the vices already mentioned (*the prenominate crimes*), you can be sure he will fall in (*closes*) with you with words to the following effect (*this consequence*). – Polonius then gets carried away by trying out certain forms of address, and loses the thread of the conversation.

47   *addition:* title.

54   *t'other,* for *the other.*

55   *such, or such –* i.e. such and such a person.

56   *a':* he.

56   *o'ertook . . . rouse:* overcome by drink in his carousing (*rouse*).

61   *Your bait . . . –* He will have used falsehood as a means to get at the truth, like bait to catch a big fish (*this carp*).

62   *And thus . . . directions out* (line 64)*:* And in this way we who are wise and able (*of reach:* of ability) by roundabout ways (*windlasses*) and indirect attempts (*assays of bias*) make for the right direction. – The phrase *assays of bias* refers to the game of bowls; in this players roll the large ball by a circuitous curve instead of sending it straight to the target ball – the *bias* of a ball gives it this curved motion; *assays:* attempts.

65   *lecture:* instructions.

That they may seem the taints of liberty,
The flash and outbreak of a fiery mind,
A savageness in unreclaiméd blood,
Of general assault.*

REYNALDO   But, my good lord –   35
POLONIUS Wherefore* should you do this?
REYNALDO   Ay, my lord,
I would know that.
POLONIUS   Marry, sir, here's my drift;
And, I believe, it is a fetch of warrant.*
You laying these slight sullies* on my son,
As 'twere a thing a little soiled i' th' working,   40
Mark you,
Your party* in converse, him you would sound,
Having ever seen in the prenominate crimes
The youth you breathe of guilty, be assured
He closes with you in this consequence: 45
'Good sir', or so; or 'friend', or 'gentleman' –
According to the phrase, or the addition,*
Of man and country.
REYNALDO   Very good, my lord.
POLONIUS And then, sir, does he this – he does – What was
I about to say? – By the mass, I was about to say   50
something – where did I leave?
REYNALDO At 'closes in the consequence,' at 'friend or so,' and
'gentlemen.'
POLONIUS At 'closes in the consequence' – ay, marry,
He closes with you thus: 'I know the gentleman;
I saw him yesterday, or t'other* day,
Or then, or then; with such, or such;* and, as you say,   55
There was a'* gaming; there o'ertook* in's rouse;
There falling out at tennis'. Or perchance,
'I saw him enter such a house of sale' –
Videlicet, a brothel – or so forth. –
See you now;   60
Your bait of falsehood* takes this carp of truth.
And thus* do we of wisdom and of reach,
With windlasses and with assays of bias,
By indirections find directions out.
So, by my former lecture* and advice,   65
Shall you my son. You have me, have you not?
REYNALDO My lord, I have.

69   *his inclination in yourself:* his character for yourself. – Polonius seems suddenly to remember that he wants Reynaldo not to depend entirely on the evidence of others but to see Laertes' general behaviour for himself as well. In this part of the play Polonius becomes more and more pleased with his own plays on words.

71   *ply his music* – i.e. go his own way without interference.

77   *with his doublet all unbraced:* with his shirt all undone. – The doublet was an undergarment worn beneath an outer dress, such as a coat or cloak.

We have seen how Hamlet hit upon the idea of pretending to be mad, presumably so as to have time to watch the course of events and to consider how he should deal with them. The meaning of his behaviour towards Ophelia is, first, that he looks at her as a woman, and thinks of the weakness of her sex as exemplified in his mother – *Frailty, thy name is woman!* (I.ii.146) – and, second, that he is lonely in his predicament, not wanting to communicate it fully to anyone, yet for a moment he wonders whether Ophelia might have the moral strength to stand by him. But a look into her face is enough to persuade him that she has not the strength needed; he sighs and leaves her for ever.

78   *fouled:* dirty.

79   *down-gyvéd:* dropped down like gyves (fetters around the ankles).

81   *purport:* meaning.

82   *looséd:* released from his bonds – such as the gyvés just mentioned.

89   *falls to . . . draw it:* begins (*falls to*) gazing into my face so intently that it was as if he wanted to make a drawing of it.

94   *bulk:* body.

98   *their help* – i.e. the help of his eyes; he turned them (*bended their light*) towards Ophelia all the while.

101   *the very ecstasy of love:* exactly like love-madness – i.e. just that sort of madness which comes of unrequited love.

102   *Whose violent . . . itself:* the characteristic violence of which destroys (*fordoes*) itself.

POLONIUS	God be wi' ye! Fare ye well.
REYNALDO	Good my lord!
POLONIUS	Observe his inclination* in yourself.
REYNALDO	I shall, my lord.
POLONIUS	And let him ply* his music.
REYNALDO	Well, my lord.
POLONIUS	Farewell!

                                          70

                                        [*Exit* REYNALDO

Enter OPHELIA.

How now, Ophelia! What's the matter?

OPHELIA O, my lord, my lord, I have been so affrighted!

POLONIUS With what, i' th' name of God?   75

OPHELIA My lord, as I was sewing in my closet,
Lord Hamlet, with his doublet* all unbraced,
No hat upon his head, his stockings fouled,*
Ungartered, and down-gyvéd* to his ankle;
Pale as his shirt, his knees knocking each other,   80
And with a look so piteous in purport*
As if he had been looséd* out of hell
To speak of horrors — he comes before me.

POLONIUS Mad for thy love?

OPHELIA   My lord, I do not know;
But, truly, I do fear it.

POLONIUS   What said he?   85

OPHELIA He took me by the wrist, and held me hard.
Then goes he to the length of all his arm,
And, with his other hand thus o'er his brow,
He falls to* such perusal of my face
As he would draw it. Long stayed he so.   90
At last, a little shaking of mine arm,
And thrice his head thus waving up and down,
He raised a sigh so piteous and profound
That it did seem to shatter all his bulk,*
And end his being. That done, he lets me go;   95
And, with his head over his shoulder turned,
He seemed to find his way without his eyes;
For out o' doors he went without their help,*
And, to the last, bended their light on me.

POLONIUS Come, go with me. I will go seek the king.   100
This is the very ecstasy* of love,
Whose violent property* fordoes itself,
And leads the will to desperate undertakings,

111   *quoted:* observed.
112   *wrack:* destroy.
112   *beshrew my jealousy!:* a curse on my suspicion!
113   *proper to our age . . . opinions:* characteristic of (*proper to*) our old age to overreach our-
          selves in scheming – *cast:* scheme; *opinions:* capabilities, estimate of our
          capabilities.
117   *This must be known . . . love.* – Shakespeare often ends a scene or a long speech with a
          couplet, like this one, in which a great deal is packed into a small space. Here,
          assuming that the text is as Shakespeare wrote it, the general meaning must be:
          'I risk some disfavour by making this known, but, on the whole, more trouble
          will come if I keep it secret.' Literally it may perhaps be interpreted as follows:
          'We must make this known because, should their love be kept secret (*close*),
          there may be greater cause for sorrow if we conceal it than if we dare to
          mention (*hate to utter*) it.' Whatever he means exactly, it is clear that he is
          already acting according to the pattern he deplored a few lines back, of being
          over-cautious and scheming in a delicate situation.

II. ii.   The King asks Hamlet's old friends Rosencrantz and Guildenstern to find out why
          Hamlet's manner has changed. Polonius speaks of the diplomatic mission to Norway and
          Hamlet's madness: the ambassadors say there will be no more trouble between Denmark
          and Norway. Then Polonius reads a love-letter which Hamlet has written to Ophelia; he
          and the King agree to spy on Hamlet and Ophelia together. As the King and Queen leave,
          Hamlet comes in reading; Polonius is confused by Hamlet's answers to his questions: they
          are nonsensical yet they have some reasoning in them. As Polonius leaves, Rosencrantz
          and Guildenstern come in on their own mission: after a good deal of general bantering
          talk they admit they have been sent by the King; Hamlet tells them simply that he has lost
          all pleasure in the world.
             They tell him that a group of players is on its way into the castle. Hamlet knows the
          players and greets them good-humouredly. He remembers a good deal of a speech which
          one of the actors once delivered very effectively, and the actor picks it up from him: it is
          about the death of Priam, King of Troy, at the hands of Pyrrhus, and the lament of his
          queen, Hecuba. Hamlet persuades the group to present a play called 'The Murder of
          Gonzago' on the following night, and the actor he has been speaking with agrees to insert
          into the play a speech written by Hamlet himself.
             Left alone, Hamlet deplores his own inactivity; the actor was more moved by Hecuba's
          stage tragedy that he himself seems to be with real life. But his plan is now clear: the play
          and the speech he will write for it will present a crime similar to that which he believes
          caused his father's death. If the play is near to the truth, the King's behaviour will give
          him away as he watches it.
             Here Hamlet is seen gaining knowledge, and especially self-knowledge. Many doubts
          persist, not primarily over the course of any action he should be taking, but over the
          nature and implications of the events going on around him. Polonius, Rosencrantz and
          Guildenstern he places without much difficulty: they are each involved in plans to watch
          him, but he puzzles even himself with his changes of attitude, alternating between
          melancholy and elation. His puzzlement and his failure to respond to the majestic beauties
          of nature reflect lack of confidence in his appraisal of the situation, even though they are
          also in part a reflection of his attitude to the person he is addressing at the time. If ven-
          geance is to be taken at this point it will not come as a result of reasoning. Its source will be
          taken at this point it will not come as a result of reasoning. Its source will be passion and it
          is in this context of passion that the *passionate speech* of the First Player takes its proper
          place. Its style and subject-matter mark it off as artificial; an ordered representation of the
          uncontrolled frenzy in Pyrrhus' actions and their results is not true to life because passion
          alone will not bring the ends desired. (The Player King's speech (III.ii.174ff.), on the other
          hand, is realistic; for Hamlet it *holds the mirror up to nature*, the desired result is achieved
          by the commingling of passion and judgement.) Even though Hamlet is moved by the
          player being moved by the Hecuba speech, he sees by the player's change of face that
          passion is not proof of reality; the actor was acting.
             Now his passion begins to be tempered by thought; this is his first move forward, and he
          is aware of the need to confirm his suspicions of Claudius and his trust in the Ghost. He
          evolves the scheme of the play test. (It is in accordance with a dramatic convention that
          Hamlet speaks of his plan as if he had just thought of it, whereas he has already taken
          action to put it into effect.)

As oft as any passion under heaven
That does afflict our natures. I am sorry.   105
What, have you given him any hard words of late?
OPHELIA No, my good lord; but, as you did command,
I did repel his letters, and denied
His access to me.
POLONIUS   That hath made him mad. –
I am sorry that with better heed and judgement   110
I had not quoted* him. I feared he did but trifle,
And meant to wrack* thee; but, beshrew* my jealousy!
It seems it is as proper to our age*
To cast beyond ourselves in our opinions,
As it is common for the younger sort   115
To lack discretion. Come, go we to the king;
This must be known,* which, being kept close, might move
More grief to hide than hate to utter love.
Come.

[*Exeunt*

scene ii

A room in the castle.

Enter KING, QUEEN, ROSENCRANTZ, GUILDENSTERN,
and ATTENDANTS.

KING Welcome, dear Rosencrantz and Guildenstern!
Moreover that* we much did long to see you,
The need we have to use you did provoke
Our hasty sending. Something have you heard
Of Hamlet's transformation; so call it,   5
Since nor* th' exterior nor the inward man
Resembles that* it was. What it should* be,

2   *Moreover that:* Besides the fact that.
6   *nor:* neither.
7   *that:* what. – Hamlet has changed both in outward appearance and in spirit.
7   *should:* can.

11   *of:* from.
12   *since so . . . haviour:* since then so close to him (*neighboured*) in his youthful vigour and
             bearing (*haviour,* for *behaviour*).
13   *vouchsafe your rest:* kindly agree to stay. – The King is moving very carefully, and adopting
             a polite tone; the two guests notice this, and point out later (lines 26–31) that
             he, as King, could just as well command them to do what he wants.
16   *occasion:* favourable opportunities.
18   *opened . . . remedy:* if disclosed, will come within my power to remedy.
22   *gentry:* courtesy.
24   *supply and profit:* aid and benefit.
26   *fits:* befits – *remembrance* must include some suggestion of reward.
28   *dread:* revered.
30   *in the full bent:* to the greatest extent – like a bow fully *bent* and ready to shoot.
34   *gentle Rosencrantz* – The Queen half playfully changes the order of their names so that the
             adjective *gentle* can be attached to the one which the King did not attach it to.
             There is here an echo of an 'epic formula', a convention used in epic poetry:
             where a number of characters are mentioned by name in a list, an honouring
             epithet is attached to the last name.
38   *practices:* what we do.
40   *Th' ambassadors from Norway* – We have seen (I.i.80ff.) how trouble had arisen between
             Denmark and Norway over the incursions of the Norwegian prince Fortinbras
             into Danish territory. The matter is now brought up again, to set off dramatic-
             ally the other main theme at this point (the relationship between Hamlet and
             Ophelia), to show that some considerable time has passed – the envoys have
             been to Norway on a mission and have just returned – and re-emphasize the
             need for a powerful ruler over the troubled state of Denmark.

More than his father's death, that thus hath put him
So much from th' understanding of himself,
I cannot dream of. I entreat you both,   10
That, being of* so young days brought up with him,
And since* so neighboured to his youth and haviour,
That you vouchsafe your rest* here in our court
Some little time; so by your companies
To draw him on to pleasures, and to gather   15
So much as from occasion* you may glean,
Whether aught, to us unknown, afflicts him thus,
That, opened,* lies within our remedy.

QUEEN   Good gentlemen, he hath much talked of you;
And sure I am two men there are not living   20
To whom he more adheres. If it will please you
To show us so much gentry* and good will
As to expend your time with us awhile,
For the supply* and profit of our hope,
Your visitation shall receive such thanks   25
As fits* a king's remembrance.

ROSENCRANTZ   Both your majesties
Might, by the sovereign power you have of us,
Put your dread* pleasures more into command
Than to entreaty.

GUILDENSTERN   But we both obey,
And here give up ourselves, in the full bent,*   30
To lay our service freely at your feet,
To be commanded.

KING   Thanks, Rosencrantz and gentle Guildenstern.
QUEEN   Thanks, Guildenstern and gentle Rosencrantz.*
And I beseech you instantly to visit   35
My too-much-changéd son. – [To the Attendants] Go, some
of you,
And bring these gentlemen where Hamlet is.

GUILDENSTERN   Heavens make our presence and our practices*
Pleasant and helpful to him!

QUEEN   Ay, amen!

[Exeunt ROSENCRANTZ, GUILDENSTERN, and some ATTENDANTS

Enter POLONIUS.

POLONIUS   Th' ambassadors from Norway,* my good lord,   40
Are joyfully returned.

KING   Thou still hast been the father of good news.

43   *liege:* sovereign – one to whom *allegiance* is owed.
47   *Hunts not . . . policy – policy* here must mean 'general prudence in state business', the
        quality most looked for in a lord chamberlain. He seeks this like a hunting
        dog on the trail of its prey. But *policy,* as used in Shakespeare's English, can
        have undertones of craftiness, dishonest pursuit of one's aims. This is not a
        meaning which Polonius himself has in mind, but it is one which Shakespeare's
        audience might very well have been expected to catch. This 'dramatic irony'
        puts the audience in a position where they can see wider implications in the
        words of a speaker than the speaker can himself. Polonius offers them as bait
        a solution to the problem of Hamlet's madness, but when they strive to get at
        it he insists that audience is first given to the envoys from Norway.
52   *fruit:* dessert – what follows the main courses of the meal.
53   *do grace to them:* pay respects to them – with a joke on *grace* as what *precedes* a meal, the
        opposite in this sense of *fruit,* 'dessert'. (To 'say grace' is to thank God for the
        food one is about to eat.) Polonius's word-play affects even the most serious
        of his listeners.
55   *distemper:* derangement (of mind).
56   *I doubt . . . main:* I suspect it is none other than the chief (cause—the one we know about).
58   *sift him:* study his character closely.
59   *our brother Norway:* the King of Norway, our brother – in the sense that they are both
        kings; the phrase 'brother officer' is still used.
60   *desires:* good wishes. – The king sent these good wishes and they are reciprocated.
61   *Upon our first:* As soon as he had heard us.
62   *to him appeared To be* – i.e. he was under the impression that they were . . .
66   *That so . . . borne in hand:* that he was so wickedly deluded (*borne in hand*) in his sickness,
        age, and weakness.
67   *arrests On:* orders against – orders, that is, to stop his warlike activities.
71   *th' assay of arms:* armed attack.
77   *give quiet pass:* allow him to pass through peacefully (with his soldiers).
79   *regards:* conditions.

POLONIUS Have I, my lord? Assure you, my good liege,*
I hold my duty, as I hold my soul,
Both to my God and to my gracious king.   45
And I do think – or else this brain of mine
Hunts not the trail of policy* so sure
As it hath used to do – that I have found
The very cause of Hamlet's lunacy.
KING O, speak of that; that do I long to hear.   50
POLONIUS Give first admittance to th' ambassadors;
My news shall be the fruit* to that great feast.
KING Thyself do grace to them,* and bring them in.

[*Exit* POLONIUS.

He tells me, my dear Gertrude, he hath found
The head and source of all your son's distemper.*   55
QUEEN I doubt* it is no other but the main:
His father's death, and our o'erhasty marriage.
KING Well, we shall sift him.*

Enter POLONIUS, *with* VOLTIMAND *and* CORNELIUS.

                              Welcome, my good friends!
Say, Voltimand, what from our brother Norway?*
VOLTIMAND Most fair return of greetings and desires.*   60
Upon our first,* he sent out to suppress
His nephew's levies; which to him appeared*
To be a preparation 'gainst the Polack;
But, better looked into, he truly found
It was against your highness; whereat grieved –   65
That so* his sickness, age, and impotence,
Was falsely borne in hand – sends out arrests*
On Fortinbras; which he, in brief, obeys;
Receives rebuke from Norway; and, in fine,
Makes vow before his uncle never more   70
To give th' assay of arms* against your majesty.
Whereon old Norway, overcome with joy,
Gives him three thousand crowns in annual fee,
And his commission to employ those soldiers,
So levied as before, against the Polack;   75
With an entreaty, herein further shown, [*Gives him a paper*]
That it might please you to give quiet pass*
Through your dominions for this enterprise,
On such regards* of safety and allowance
As therein are set down.

80   *likes us:* pleases me – The King is here undoubtedly using the 'royal *we*', i.e. he calls
      himself *we*, not *I*, and refers to himself as *us*, not *me*. In many other places it is
      not clear whether he is talking about himself alone, or including Gertrude,
      (which he is likely to wish to do), e.g. at I.ii.112ff.

81   *our more considered time:* when I have a more suitable occasion for reflection.

86   *expostulate:* discuss. – Polonius evidently senses that the King and Queen are pleased with
      what has so far transpired, and he now wishes to take the centre of the stage.
      He wants to talk, and a simple, courteous address to the King and Queen (*My
      liege, and madam*) suggests to him a way to begin: 'majesty' is as good a topic
      as any other. He then embarks on a speech full of the accepted types of rhetoric
      current in Shakespeare's day, where meaning is sacrificed to the elaborate play
      of words and phrases. The Queen quickly tires of this and asks for *More matter,
      with less art,* i.e. more substance and less rhetoric.

90   *brevity . . . wit* – This has become a proverbial saying; Polonius's actions are once again in
      striking contrast to the advice he gives, even to himself; *wit:* intelligence, good
      understanding.

91   *limbs . . . flourishes* – i.e. in contrast to the *soul*, which is the inner being, these are limbs
      and external expressions.

95   *that* – i.e. the rhetorical figure, the play on the idea of madness. The phrase here suggests
      that Polonius would have liked to pursue it further, and embellish it more.

96   *art* – The Queen uses *art* to mean 'rhetoric' or 'playing on the use of words'. Polonius
      catches up her word, but uses it in a somewhat different sense, to mean
      'pretence', something which is artificial, not natural. But he continues to use a
      good deal of *art* in the Queen's sense of the word.

98   *figure:* figure of speech – The figure is referred to as *it* in the next line.

101   *effect,* the result of a *cause,* is a word which starts Polonius off on another long play of
      words. And he has been brought to it by sentences which add nothing to what
      the King and Queen already know, and could therefore very well be left
      unsaid.

103   *this effect . . . cause:* this effect, which is a defect, is the result of (*comes by*).

105   *Perpend:* consider – a very learned word, like *gather* and *surmise* in their contexts in line
      108.

108   *gather, and surmise:* inform yourselves of the facts (from this evidence) and imagine (what
      they mean). – He reads them a love-letter addressed by Hamlet to Ophelia. It
      is written in a very affected and exalted style, but is meant seriously; we must
      assume that Hamlet wrote it before Ophelia was forbidden by her father to
      receive any communication from him (II.i.107–8).

111   *an ill phrase:* a poor expression. – He dislikes it, evidently, because *beautified* is an
      'ungrammatical' variant of *beautiful.*

115   *faithful:* truthful (or perhaps 'conscientious'). – The verse extolling the lover's constancy
      is again according to the custom of the time, and is meant seriously.

KING	It likes us* well;	80

And at our more considered time* we'll read,
Answer, and think upon this business.
Meantime we thank you for your well-took labour.
Go to your rest; at night we'll feast together.
Most welcome home!

[*Exeunt* VOLTIMAND *and* CORNELIUS

POLONIUS   This business is well ended.   85
My liege, and madam – to expostulate*
What majesty should be, what duty is,
Why day is day, night night, and time is time,
Were nothing but to waste night, day, and time.
Therefore, since brevity* is the soul of wit,   90
And tediousness the limbs and outward flourishes,*
I will be brief: your noble son is mad.
Mad call I it; for, to define true madness,
What is 't but to be nothing else but mad?
But let that* go.

QUEEN   More matter, with less art.   95
POLONIUS   Madam, I swear I use no art* at all.
That he is mad, 'tis true; 'tis true, 'tis pity,
And pity 'tis 'tis true; a foolish figure,*
But farewell it, for I will use no art.
Mad let us grant him, then. And now remains   100
That we find out the cause of this effect* –
Or rather say, the cause of this defect,
For this effect defective* comes by cause.
Thus it remains, and the remainder thus.
Perpend.*   105
I have a daughter – have whilst she is mine –
Who, in her duty and obedience, mark,
Hath given me this. [*He takes out a letter*] Now gather,*
and surmise.
[*Reads*] *To the celestial and my soul's idol, the most*
beautified Ophelia –   110
That's an ill phrase,* a vile phrase – *beautified* is a vile
phrase. But you shall hear. Thus:
[*Reads*] *In her excellent white bosom, these,* &c. –
QUEEN   Came this from Hamlet to her?
POLONIUS   Good madam, stay awhile; I will be faithful.*   115
[*Reads*]   *Doubt thou the stars are fire,*
               Doubt that the sun doth move,

118   *Doubt:* Suspect – This is the meaning in the third line of the stanza; cf. I.ii.254: *I doubt some foul play.*
120   *ill at these numbers:* not good at writing verses (*numbers*) like these. – But it was the custom for a man to write some verses addressed to his lady, however poor they might be.
121   *reckon my groans:* count my sighs of love – and also 'put my sufferings into *numbers*', i.e. verses. This is a play on the word *numbers*, yet it is meant quite seriously, as part of the *art* or rhetoric of this kind of writing.
124   *whilst this machine . . . him:* for as long as he has this earthly body (*machine*).
126   *more above, hath:* moreover, she has.
127   *As they fell out . . . and place:* as they took place, at various times, in various ways and places. – The second half of the line adds nothing to what Polonius wishes to say; it is another example of his wordiness in expressing what is obvious and not worth mentioning.
131   *fain prove so:* willingly prove to be so.
136   *played the desk . . . book:* played the part of a desk or notebook – not speaking himself, any more than a desk or notebook can say what is being written on them, but acting as a silent holder of letters (like a desk) or as a means by which the lovers could write to one another (like passing notes in a notebook).
137   *given . . . winking:* closed the eyes of my heart – i.e. winked at, pretended not to see the romance going on between them.
139   *round:* directly.
140   *bespeak:* speak to.
141   *out of thy star* – i.e. out of your sphere (see note to line I.v.17), and therefore not of your social status.
142   *prescripts:* commands.
143   *lock . . . resort:* lock herself in and prevent him from going to see her – *resort:* visiting.
144   *tokens* – i.e. signs of his love, e.g. presents.
145   *the fruits . . . advice:* my advice and (profited by) the fruits of it – i.e. took it and benefited from it.
148   *watch:* state of wakefulness – not being able to sleep at nights.
149   *lightness:* feeling of lightness in the head.
149   *declension:* decline. – Polonius's *short tale* of Hamlet's supposed madness is in carefully worked, artificial language, and sounds ironically in the ears of the audience, who are well aware that Hamlet is only mad by artifice, not in fact.
153   *I'd,* short for *I would.*

> *Doubt* truth to be a liar,*
> *But never doubt I love.*
>
> *O dear Ophelia, I am ill at these numbers;* I have not art to*   120
> *reckon* my groans. But that I love thee best, O most best,*
> *believe it. Adieu*
>
> > > *Thine evermore, most dear lady, whilst this*
> > > *machine* is to him,* **HAMLET.**

This, in obedience, hath my daughter shown me,   125
And more above,* hath his solicitings,
As they fell out* by time, by means, and place,
All given to mine ear.

KING   But how hath she
Received his love?

POLONIUS   What do you think of me?

KING As of a man faithful and honourable.   130

POLONIUS I would fain* prove so. But what might you think,
When I had seen this hot love on the wing –
As I perceived it, I must tell you that,
Before my daughter told me – what might you,
Or my dear majesty your queen here, think,   135
If I had played the desk* or table-book,
Or given my heart a winking,* mute and dumb,
Or looked upon this love with idle sight?
What might you think? No. I went round* to work,
And my young mistress thus I did bespeak:*   140
'Lord Hamlet is a prince, out of thy star;*
This must not be.' And then I prescripts* gave her,
That she should lock* herself from his resort,
Admit no messengers, receive no tokens.*
Which done, she took the fruits* of my advice;   145
And he, repulséd – a short tale to make –
Fell into a sadness; then into a fast;
Thence to a watch;* thence into a weakness;
Thence to a lightness;* and, by this declension,*
Into the madness wherein now he raves,   150
And all we mourn for.

KING *[To the* QUEEN*]*   Do you think 'tis this?

QUEEN It may be, very likely.

POLONIUS Hath there been such a time – I'd* fain know that –
That I have positively said ' 'Tis so,'
When it proved otherwise?

KING   Not that I know.   155

158   *circumstances:* detailed evidence – which helps to prove or disprove a statement.

160   *the centre –* i.e. the centre of the earth.

160   *try:* judge.

161   *four hours –* i.e. for a long while. *Four* could be used in Shakespeare's day for an indefinite number.

163   *loose:* release. – This word is used for animals at stud.

164   *Be you . . . arras then:* Let you and me then be standing behind an arras. – An *arras* was a piece of tapestry hanging like a curtain some way away from a wall. There would be room for them to stand between the arras and the wall.

166   *from his reason . . . thereon:* out of his mind because of it (his love for her).

167   *no assistant . . . carters:* not a state office-holder but the manager of a farm with its carters. – It has been suggested that the mention of a farm here links this line with *loose my daughter* in the first line of the speech.

169   *poor wretch –* Only the Queen shows any feeling of pity for Hamlet. She expressed sympathetic concern for him when his love-letter was read. Now, in pity and affection, fitting a mother's feelings for her son, she calls him *poor wretch.*

171   *board him presently:* address him directly. – Since Polonius adds *O, give me leave,* it seems that at least one of the others, reluctant to abet the spying on Hamlet, tries to restrain him. The Queen is most likely to feel in this way.

173   *God-a-mercy –* This phrase must originally have meant: 'May God reward you'. It is used by characters in Shakespeare with a meaning like 'thank you', particularly in acknowledging polite greetings from others who are below them socially.

175   *a fishmonger –* Polonius does not understand what Hamlet means, and Hamlet, pretending to be mad, may very well simply be using the first word that comes into his head. But there are two other possibilities, either or both of which may be intended here. First, since Hamlet in what follows is so much concerned with sex relations, and from certain evidence elsewhere in the literature of this time, *fishmonger* may mean a go-between in illicit love, a seller of women for immoral purposes. In lines 185ff., Hamlet seems to suggest that Polonius is trying to 'sell' his daughter to him. Second, as suggested by Coleridge, Hamlet may be accusing Polonius of having been sent to 'fish out' his secret; but this would be more the work of a fisherman than a fishmonger. What is clear is that Hamlet bitterly dislikes Polonius; he mistrusts his motives and will go to any extreme to confuse him and make him look foolish. It is evident, too, that Hamlet suspects a trick is being played on him, and therefore deliberately confuses the issue.

177   *so honest a man –* He is evidently referring to an 'honest' tradesman, such as a fishmonger might be.

182   *a good kissing carrion:* flesh good for kissing. – The link between this and the talk about honesty may be explained thus: honesty, purity of motive, must be a hard thing to find, for even the purity of the sun causes corruption when it shines down on the carcass of a dead dog. In fact the sun 'breeds' life, maggots, in the dead body . . . 'now your daughter – have you one? – being flesh good for kissing, [will breed]. See, therefore, that she does not walk in the sunshine (of my princely favour, cf. I.ii.67).' The mixture of references to love and death is, of course, deliberately made to shock Polonius, but all he can make of it is the constant reference to his daughter. The idea of the sun 'breeding' in the dead dog, and the 'sun' of the prince's favour shining on Ophelia and perhaps causing 'conception' is something that he is too slow-witted to grasp.

188   *How . . . that?:* What do you say to that?

POLONIUS   [*Pointing to his head and shoulder*] Take this from this, if
this be otherwise;
If circumstances* lead me, I will find
Where truth is hid, though it were hid indeed
Within the centre.*

KING   How may we try* it further?   160
POLONIUS   You know, sometimes he walks four hours* together
Here in the lobby.
QUEEN   So he does, indeed.
POLONIUS   At such a time I'll loose* my daughter to him.
Be you and I behind an arras* then;
Mark the encounter. If he love her not,   165
And be not from his reason* fall'n thereon,
Let me be no assistant* for a state,
But keep a farm and carters.
KING   We will try it.
QUEEN   But, look, where sadly the poor wretch* comes reading.
POLONIUS   Away, I do beseech you, both away.   170
I'll board* him presently. – O, give me leave.

                   [*Exeunt* KING, QUEEN, *and* ATTENDANTS

Enter HAMLET, *reading a book.*

How does my good Lord Hamlet?
HAMLET   Well, God-a-mercy.*
POLONIUS   Do you know me, my lord?
HAMLET   Excellent well; you are a fishmonger.*   175
POLONIUS   Not I, my lord.
HAMLET   Then I would you were so honest* a man.
POLONIUS   Honest, my lord?
HAMLET   Ay, sir; to be honest, as this world goes, is to be one man
picked out of ten thousand.   180
POLONIUS   That's very true, my lord.
HAMLET   For if the sun breed maggots in a dead dog, being a good
kissing carrion* . . . Have you a daughter?
POLONIUS   I have, my lord.
HAMLET   Let her not walk i' th' sun. Conception is a blessing, but not 185
as your daughter may conceive. – Friend, look to 't.
POLONIUS   [*Aside*] How* say you by that? Still harping on my daughter.
– Yet he knew me not at first; he said I was a fishmonger. He
is far gone, far gone. And truly in my youth I suffered much   190
extremity for love, very near this. I'll speak to him again. –
[*To* HAMLET] What do you read, my lord?

194   *matter:* subject-matter. – Polonius blunders into the mistake of using a word with two meanings and Hamlet takes *matter* to mean 'dispute, trouble', and asks *Between who?*

197   *the satirical rogue* – i.e. the author he is reading. But Hamlet is not taking what he says from the book; he is making it up as a further means of humiliating Polonius. He says the author is a *satirical rogue*, i.e. that he writes bitter attacks on people to make them feel ridiculous. Hamlet goes on to give what amounts to a description of Polonius, pretending that it comes from the book.

199   *purging:* discharging. – The pus which the eyes of old men discharge is likened to amber and the sap which comes from the bark of the plum-tree when it is cut.

200   *hams:* thighs.

202   *hold . . . honesty:* do not consider it proper.

203   *old:* as old.

206   *out of the air* – Polonius is apparently thinking, in accordance with a current belief, that it would be better for Hamlet to confine himself to a small room, where he might recover more quickly from what appears to be his madness. Again Polonius has blundered in his use of words, and Hamlet turns his unhappy remark against him.

208   *pregnant:* apt. – But even then, Polonius goes on, the aptness is a matter of chance which is often not evident when a man is in his senses.

209   *happiness* – i.e. fitness of expression – a 'happy phrase'.

210   *prosperously . . . of:* express so advantageously.

211   *suddenly:* very soon. – Even when Polonius talks to himself he cannot avoid elaborate sentences and turns of phrase.

216   *withal:* with – *withal* is the usual form at the end of a clause in Shakespeare's English.

Polonius leaves, apparently still believing that Hamlet is truly mad, and blind to the devices Hamlet has used to make him appear ridiculous. He walks off, and is out of earshot by the time Hamlet makes his unkind remark (line 219). The change of tone in Hamlet's speech is emphasized by the entry of his old friends Rosencrantz and Guildenstern, who have been asked by the King and Queen to do what they can to restore Hamlet to a better humour. He greets them heartily, but quickly guesses that they have been sent on a mission; their expressions are somewhat forced and unnatural, and they take a good deal of time in general conversation before they get to the point of the meeting.

226   *indifferent:* ordinary – i.e. not distinguished in any way.

228   *button* – i.e. the top; they are not at the high point of good fortune. Fortune is personified as a woman.

HAMLET   Words, words, words.

POLONIUS   What is the matter,* my lord?

HAMLET   Between who?   195

POLONIUS   I mean, the matter that you read, my lord.

HAMLET   Slanders, sir. For the satirical rogue* says here that old men
have grey beards; that their faces are wrinkled; their eyes
purging* thick amber and plum-tree gum; and that they
have a plentiful lack of wit, together with most weak hams* –   200
all which, sir, though I most powerfully and potently
believe, yet I hold it not honesty* to have it thus set down.
For yourself, sir, shall grow old* as I am, if, like a crab, you
could go backward.

POLONIUS   [Aside] Though this be madness, yet there is method in 't.   205
– [To HAMLET] Will you walk out of the air,* my lord?

HAMLET   Into my grave?

POLONIUS   Indeed, that is out o' th' air. – [Aside] How pregnant* sometimes his replies are! A happiness* that often madness hits on,
which reason and sanity could not so prosperously* be   210
delivered of. I will leave him, and suddenly* contrive the
means of meeting between him and my daughter. – [To
HAMLET] My honourable lord, I will most humbly take my
leave of you.

HAMLET   You cannot, sir, take from me any thing that I will more   215
willingly part withal* – except my life, except my life, except
my life.

POLONIUS   Fare you well, my lord.

HAMLET   These tedious old fools!

Enter ROSENCRANTZ *and* GUILDENSTERN.

POLONIUS   You go to seek the Lord Hamlet; there he is.   220

ROSENCRANTZ   [To POLONIUS] God save you, sir!   [*Exit* POLONIUS

GUILDENSTERN   My honoured lord!

ROSENCRANTZ   My most dear lord!

HAMLET   My excellent good friends! How dost thou, Guildenstern?
Ah, Rosencrantz! Good lads, how do ye both?   225

ROSENCRANTZ   As the indifferent* children of the earth.

GUILDENSTERN   Happy, in that we are not overhappy;
On Fortune's cap we are not the very button.*

HAMLET   Nor the soles of her shoe?

ROSENCRANTZ   Neither, my lord.   230

HAMLET   Then you live about her waist, or in the middle of her
favours?

233   *her privates we:* we are her intimates – with the play on words suggested by the rest of the
           conversation.
240   *hither* – They have evidently come from abroad, perhaps from the university at Witten-
           berg. The King had certainly summoned them from a distance (lines 3–4
           above).
244   *confines, wards:* places of confinement, prison cells.
247   *none to you:* not one (a prison) as far as you are concerned.
247   *there is nothing . . . so* – i.e. things in themselves are neither good nor bad; it is what we
           think about them which makes them one or the other.
249   *ambition:* deeply felt desires. – He is perhaps referring to a longing he thinks Hamlet may
           feel to become King of Denmark.
252   *bad dreams* – i.e. dreams of his murdered father which will force him out of the little world
           he says he would be content with and into the world of action, the action which
           will avenge his father's death.
254   *the shadow of a dream* – Desires and longings are even less real than dreams – they are just
           shadows of dreams. In these lines the word *shadow* is used to mean 'that which
           has no substance, an image of reality'. Plato thought that the world we see
           around us was only a 'shadow' of true reality.
258   *our beggars bodies . . . shadows* – Hamlet says after this that he *cannot reason*; we should
           not, therefore, expect to get plain good sense from these lines, particularly
           because they depend on playing with the many meanings of words. The general
           argument must be: Guildenstern has said that *the very substance of the ambitious*
           is nothing but shadow. Kings, therefore, and boastful stage players (*out-
           stretched heroes*) are nothing but shadows, being full of ambition. Beggars on
           the other hand, are not ambitious, and must therefore be the opposite of
           shadows, i.e. substance, bodies. – This is what Guildenstern meant, but the
           passage is an example of the playing with ideas by means of words which was
           a fashionable courtly pursuit in Shakespeare's day.
260   *fay:* faith.
261   *wait upon:* accompany.
262   *sort you:* associate you.
264   *dreadfully attended:* very badly served (by my other servants) – and also, perhaps,
           'accompanied with the horror (of my own dreadful dreams)'.
264   *in the beaten way of friendship:* along the well-used path of friendship – i.e. talking as friend
           to friend.
265   *what make you:* what are you doing.
268   *too dear a halfpenny:* too dear at a halfpenny – i.e. not worth a halfpenny, of no value.

GUILDENSTERN Faith, her privates* we.

HAMLET In the secret parts of Fortune? O, most true; she is a strumpet.
What's the news?   235

ROSENCRANTZ None, my lord, but that the world's grown honest.

HAMLET Then is doomsday near. But your news is not true. Let me
question more in particular: what have you, my good friends,
deserved at the hands of Fortune, that she sends you to
prison hither?*   240

GUILDENSTERN Prison, my lord!

HAMLET Denmark's a prison.

ROSENCRANTZ Then is the world one.

HAMLET A goodly one, in which there are many confines,* wards,
and dungeons, Denmark being one o' th' worst.   245

ROSENCRANTZ We think not so, my lord.

HAMLET Why, then, 'tis none to you;* for there is nothing* either
good or bad, but thinking makes it so. To me it is a prison.

ROSENCRANTZ Why, then, your ambition* makes it one; 'tis too narrow for
your mind.   250

HAMLET O God, I could be bounded in a nut-shell, and count myself
a king of infinite space, were it not that I have bad dreams.*

GUILDENSTERN Which dreams, indeed, are ambition; for the very substance
of the ambitious is merely the shadow* of a dream.

HAMLET A dream itself is but a shadow.   255

ROSENCRANTZ Truly, and I hold ambition of so airy and light a quality that
it is but a shadow's shadow.

HAMLET Then are our beggars bodies,* and our monarchs and out-
stretched heroes the beggars' shadows. Shall we to th'
court? For, by my fay,* I cannot reason.   260

ROSENCRANTZ & We'll wait upon* you.
GUILDENSTERN

HAMLET No such matter. I will not sort you* with the rest of my
servants; for, to speak to you like an honest man, I am most
dreadfully attended.* But, in the beaten way* of friendship,
what make you* at Elsinore?   265

ROSENCRANTZ To visit you, my lord; no other occasion.

HAMLET Beggar that I am, I am even poor in thanks; but I thank you.
And sure, dear friends, my thanks are too dear a halfpenny.*
Were you not sent for? Is it your own inclining? Is it a free
visitation? Come, deal justly with me. Come, come; nay,   270
speak.

GUILDENSTERN What should we say, my lord?

273   *to the purpose:* (let it be) to the point. – This is in answer to Guildenstern's question in the previous line, where *should* has the force of the modern English *can:* 'What can we say, my lord?' Now Hamlet's suspicions are aroused, and the other two come very guarded in what they say.

275   *colour:* disguise.

278   *conjure:* ask you to tell me in all seriousness.

279   *consonancy* – literally 'agreement'; he must be referring to the good fellowship they enjoyed when they were younger, *being of so young days brought up* together, as the Queen has said (line 11).

281   *by what more . . . withal:* by whatever there is of more significance (between us) (*what more dear*) which a better initiator of discussion (*proposer*) than I could charge you with. – For *proposer*, see also Glossary.

282   *even:* just.

284   *I have . . . you:* I am watching you.

285   *hold not off:* do not keep silent.

287   *so shall . . . feather* (line 289): by doing so (telling you why you were sent for) my foresight will anticipate (*prevent*) your disclosing (*discovery*) the truth, and nothing will be revealed (*moult no feather*) of the secrecy you promised to the King and Queen. – In other words, 'I will tell you why you came, and there is no need for you to break your promise to the King and Queen by telling me the secret reason for your visit.' If a bird moults no single feather, no part of its body is uncovered; there is no *discovery*.

290   *forgone . . . exercises:* given up all my usual practices. – No particular practice seems to be referred to, but Shakespeare's audience would think of certain pursuits expected of a young prince, such as fencing, dancing and riding. He no longer does those things which used to interest him.

291   *it goes so heavily . . . disposition:* I am so depressed in spirit. – This begins Hamlet's own detailed account of his melancholy.

292   *a sterile promontory* – This is another strange image. The meaning in the context must be 'an unproductive waste', but it is hard to see the full force of the word *promontory* here. It may refer to a sandy headland sticking out into the sea, away from the fertile plains. The *promontory* may be an image of life thrusting out into the great seas of eternity; cf. 'this bank and shoal of time' in *Macbeth* (I.vii.6). It is as likely to be a reference to the physical surroundings of the theatre of Shakespeare's day, the stage jutting out into the audience area being a counterpart of the *promontory, this goodly frame, the earth.* (See Introduction, p. xxvi, and the note on *canopy* below.)

293   *canopy* – A canopy is a covering held up by poles over a throne or bed. Canopies were sometimes painted to look like the sky, and it is fitting for Hamlet the prince to think of the sky as a canopy over a throne. He could also indicate the painted roof over the stage of the theatre as he spoke, which thus gave the words a kind of double imagery; the sky – the princely canopy – the painted roof over the stage.

293   *brave:* splendid.

294   *fretted . . . fire:* adorned with the golden fire of the sun – *fretted* means 'decorated with carved ornament', and is applied especially to roofs. Hamlet's figurative use of these words builds up a beautiful image. The contrast between this and the *foul and pestilent congregation* (gathering together) *of vapours* is very telling.

297   *faculty:* ability to do things.

298   *moving:* movement.

298   *express:* well-made. – This goes with *form*.

299   *apprehension:* intelligence.

301   *quintessence of dust:* purest and most perfect form of dust. – Hamlet's words rise to a great climax as he speaks of the beauty and capacity of man, but the enchantment is broken with this word *dust*. Whatever a man's excellence may be, he finishes as dust. The Bible (*Genesis* 3: 19) says, '. . . dust thou art, and unto dust shalt thou return'.

302   *by your smiling . . .* – Hamlet has spoken of *Man*, meaning 'human beings', but his companions take it (or pretend to take it) that he is now thinking of man as opposed to woman, and they smile. He takes pains to assure them that he no longer has delight even in the company of women. Rosencrantz deftly turns the talk in a different direction by bringing up, for the first time, the matter of the players

HAMLET   Why, anything – but to the purpose.* You were sent for; and there is a kind of confession in your looks, which your modesties have not craft enough to colour.* I know the good king and queen have sent for you.   275

ROSENCRANTZ   To what end, my lord?

HAMLET   That you must teach *me*. But let me conjure* you, by the rights of our fellowship, by the consonancy* of our youth, by the obligation of our ever-preserved love, and by what   280
more* dear a better proposer could charge you withal, be even* and direct with me, whether you were sent for, or no.

ROSENCRANTZ   [*Aside to* GUILDENSTERN] What say you?

HAMLET   [*Aside*] Nay, then, I have an eye* of you. – (*To the other two*) If you love me, hold not off.*   285

GUILDENSTERN   My lord, we were sent for.

HAMLET   I will tell you why; so shall my anticipation* prevent your discovery, and your secrecy to the king and queen moult no feather. I have of late – but wherefore I know not – lost all my mirth, forgone* all custom of exercises; and, indeed, it   290
goes so heavily* with my disposition that this goodly frame, the earth, seems to me a sterile promontory;* this most excellent canopy,* the air, look you, this brave* o'erhanging firmament, this majestical roof fretted* with golden fire – why, it appears no other thing to me than a foul and pestilent   295
congregation of vapours. What a piece of work is man! How noble in reason! How infinite in faculty!* In form and mov- ing* how express* and admirable! In action how like an angel! In apprehension* how like a god! The beauty of the world! The paragon of animals! And yet, to me, what is this quint-   300
essence of dust?* Man delights not me; no, nor woman neither, though by your smiling* you seem to say so.

ROSENCRANTZ   My lord, there was no such stuff in my thoughts.

HAMLET   Why did you laugh, then, when I said 'man delights not me'?

ROSENCRANTZ   To think, my lord, if you delight not in man, what lenten   305
entertainment* the players shall receive from you. We coted*

---

302 (*cont'd*)   who are coming to 'delight' the royal household with their plays.
306   *lenten entertainment:* treatment of guests during Lent. – Lent is the fasting period of the Christian Church, and even guests cannot expect lavish entertainment during that time.
306   *coted:* overtook.

309   *He that plays the king* . . . – The mention of the players sets Hamlet at once on a train of thought. Perhaps the fact that he first mentions the Player King means that the idea of setting a trap for Claudius has at once occurred to him. He goes on to enumerate a number of characters who would take stock parts in any play that the company are likely to present; he is clearly enthusiastic about their visit.

310   *of:* from – *tribute* here means something, perhaps money, given as a mark of respect – Prince Hamlet will give tribute to the 'king'.

311   *his foil and target:* light fencing sword and light shield. – A real knight would have heavier weapons, but these light ones are enough for a player-knight.

311   *gratis:* for nothing – i.e. he, too, will be rewarded.

312   *the humorous man:* the man who plays the part of the odd, fantastic character in the play. – He was not the comic character but the one who had certain characteristically strange ways of behaviour (humours) which singled him out as unusual; if he was lucky, the difficulties and quarrels he became involved in in the plays were eventually resolved in peace. Jaques in *As You Like It* is a famous example of 'the humorous man'.

313   *tickle o' the sere:* easily moved to laughter – literally, 'easily made to go off', like a gun which is provided with a catch (*sere*) to make it go off at the lightest touch on the trigger.

313   *the lady* . . . *halt for it* – It is impossible to say precisely what this means. One suggestion is, 'the actor who takes the lady's part will say freely what is in "her" mind, or, if it is not written in the part to do so, "she" will spoil the blank verse to get it all in'. Female parts in Shakespeare's day were always acted by boys or young men. Perhaps Shakespeare is referring here to the old joke about women always talking at length and with great directness; since the male characters are going to do well in the play he has in mind, the female character ought also to have freedom with the words of the part, such as one would associate with women talking.

318   *How chances* . . . *travel:* How does it happen that they are on the move? – They have evidently come from another country, and the *city* mentioned by Rosencrantz (line 317) may be Wittenberg. Cf. lines 401–2: Hamlet asks one of the players, *Comest thou to beard me in Denmark?*

318   *Their residence* . . . *both ways:* Remaining in one place (*residence*) was better for them in respect of both reputation and profit.

320   *I think* . . . *innovation:* I think that the withdrawal of permission to act (in the court and the city) (*inhibition*) has come about because of the current conspiracy (*innovation*). – This is certainly a reference to what Shakespeare's own company of actors were experiencing in London at about the time *Hamlet* was first produced.

    Two series of events, probably connected with one another, seem to have led up to the situation touched upon here. First, a company of boy actors became popular and drew audiences away from the Globe theatre, where Shakespeare's company acted, to the Blackfriars, where the boys presented plays which were often bitter and satirical. This new vein for stage plays became fashionable, and it appears that Shakespeare's company decided to move into the provinces for a season of touring. This new fashion may be the *innovation* referred to. Second, the satirical tone of the boy actors' plays may have been matched by genuine or imagined references to the current political situation in the plays of Shakespeare's company (e.g. *Richard II*, from which one objectionable scene had to be dropped during Queen Elizabeth's lifetime). There is evidence to suggest that the company fell out of favour because of the support its members gave to the Earls of Essex and Southampton in their conspiracy against the queen, and were prohibited from appearing in London or at least at Court; this may be the *inhibition*. Shakespeare implies that a similar incident has driven the players out of their home-town and country, and into Denmark.

    In this passage the word *innovation* is an example of a disagreeable thing being referred to by a word which makes it sound more agreeable; an *innovation* is a change, here clearly a 'change for the worse', but the word has less harsh an effect than, say, *conspiracy* or *revolution*. The whole sentence in the text is strained and forced, as if the topical reference had been introduced with difficulty. Such references continue in lines 322ff.

them on the way, and hither are they coming to offer you
service.

HAMLET He that plays the king* shall be welcome. His majesty shall
have tribute of me;* the adventurous knight shall use his   310
foil* and target; the lover shall not sigh gratis;* the humorous
man* shall end his part in peace; the clown shall make those
laugh whose lungs are tickle o' the sere;* and the lady* shall
say her mind freely, or the blank verse shall halt for 't. –
What players are they?   315

ROSENCRANTZ Even those you were wont to take such delight in, the
tragedians of the city.

HAMLET How chances it they travel? Their residence,* both in
reputation and profit, was better both ways.

ROSENCRANTZ I think their inhibition* comes by the means of the late   320
innovation.

HAMLET Do they hold the same estimation* they did when I was in
the city? Are they so followed?

ROSENCRANTZ No, indeed, they are not.

HAMLET How comes it? Do they grow rusty?   325

---

322   *hold . . . estimation:* have the same reputation – evidently in Wittenberg (*the city*).

327   *an aery . . . question:* a bird's brood of children (*aery*), little hawks not yet fully trained (*eyases*), who shout out at the tops of their voices. – Shakespeare's company being in disgrace, a rival group of actors, most of whom were boys who sang the services in the Chapel Royal and St. Paul's Cathedral, rose to fame. They seem to have been especially famous for presenting the plays of Ben Johnson, some of which openly attack other playwrights of the day. We may take all these lines to line 345 as an attack in the 'war of the theatres'. The idea of the children looking like sweet nestlings and talking shrilly on the stage, but being little birds of prey, is an important part of the attack.

The meaning of the phrase *on the top of question* is doubtful. A possible alternative to the one given above is 'above (the noise of) conversation'; the explanation would then be that their fame makes their voices loud and irritating to other speakers.

329   *berattle . . . stages:* fill (with noise) the public theatres. – The point about the *common stages* is brought home by the phrase *so they call them*; the emphasis is fitting because the boy actors had for a long time enjoyed a reputation for giving plays at court, which was not, of course, a *common stage.*

331   *goose-quills:* pens – such as were once cut from the feathers of the goose. Well-to-do men, *wearing rapiers,* were afraid of what the pens of playwrights would write in satire about them.

333   *escoted:* paid for.

333   *pursue the quality:* follow the profession (of actors). – He implies that if they act only until their voices break, they will never become really accomplished actors.

334   *Will they not say . . . succession* (line 337) – This sentence presents a number of difficulties. The train of thought seems to be: 'If they do in fact follow the profession of actor (and not give it up when their voices break), grow to be '*common players*' – which is really most likely, if they have nothing more profitable to do (*their means are no better*) – will they not say in time to come that the writers who are now writing plays for them did them wrong by making them abuse (*exclaim against*) what they were to become (*their own succession:* their future as grown-up actors)?'

Such an explanation fits well into the historical background of this part of the play; the boy actors had parts which satirized adult players (e.g. those in Shakespeare's company) as part of the 'war of the theatres'.

339   *tarre:* provoke.

340   *no money bid . . . question* – This sentence presents further difficulties; the general meaning seems to be: 'only discussions (*argument*) in which the poet and the actor fell to blows (*went to cuffs*) over the matter (*question*) were considered to be of any interest'. Other discussions were unimportant, 'had *no money bid* for them'.

344   *carry it away:* win the fight.

345   *Hercules . . . too* – In a classical story, Hercules changed places with Atlas, who carried the sky on his shoulders, so that Atlas could get the golden apples of the Hesperides for him. It became usual to show Hercules holding the world on his shoulders (the world including the sky, the universe), and this aptly became the sign of the Globe theatre, where Shakespeare's Company put on their plays at this time. The mention of Hercules here is prompted by *carry it away* in the previous line; it is the closest possible reference to the recent history of Shakespeare's own players.

Hamlet's thoughts now turn again to his own sorrows; the death of his father and the rise of his uncle as king in his father's place have caused a change of fashion, too.

347   *mows:* strange faces, grimaces.

349   *his picture in little:* a miniature picture of him. – People who used to make faces at Claudius before he became king now pay a lot of money for a picture of him which they can gaze at.

349   *'Sblood* – literally, 'By God's blood', an oath.

350   *more than natural* – i.e. beyond the natural feelings of kindness and humanity.

351   *the players* – Their arrival has been announced by the trumpets. It was quite usual for groups of players to be given a formal welcome like this when they arrived at a great house. Amusements were not plentiful, and it was a great day when the actors arrived and began making preparations for presenting plays.

ROSENCRANTZ Nay, their endeavour keeps in the wonted pace. But there is,
sir, an aery* of children, little eyases, that cry out on the top
of question, and are most tyrannically clapped for 't. These
are now the fashion, and so berattle* the common stages – so
they call them – that many wearing rapiers are afraid of   330
goose-quills,* and dare scarce come thither.

HAMLET What, are they children? Who maintains 'em? How are
they escoted?* Will they pursue the quality* no longer than
they can sing? Will they not say* afterwards, if they should
grow themselves to common players – as it is most like, if   335
their means are no better – their writers do them wrong, to
make them exclaim against their own succession?

ROSENCRANTZ Faith, there has been much to-do on both sides; and the
nation holds it no sin to tarre* them to controversy. There
was, for a while, no money bid* for argument unless the poet   340
and the player went to cuffs in the question.

HAMLET Is 't possible?

GUILDENSTERN O, there has been much throwing about of brains.

HAMLET Do the boys carry it away?*

ROSENCRANTZ Ay, that they do, my lord; Hercules* and his load too.   345

HAMLET It is not very strange; for my uncle is king of Denmark, and
those that would make mows* at him while my father lived
give twenty, forty, fifty, an hundred ducats a-piece for his
picture in little.* 'Sblood,* there is something in this more
than natural,* if philosophy could find it out.   350

[*Flourish of trumpets within*

GUILDENSTERN There are the players.*

HAMLET Gentlemen, you are welcome to Elsinore. Your hands, come.*
The appurtenance* of welcome is fashion* and ceremony.

---

352   *Your hands, come* – He insists on shaking hands with Rosencrantz and Guildenstern,
although they hesitate to do so with a prince.
353   *appurtenance of welcome:* what fittingly goes with the act of welcoming.
353   *fashion:* customary display.

354   *comply . . . garb:* observe the formalities of courtesy with you in this way (*garb*).
354   *extent . . . than yours* (line 356) – Hamlet, like some other characters in Shakespeare's plays,
becomes heavily ceremonious when he is talking about ceremony. The
grammar of his sentence here is very involved; if we are right in thinking
(note to line 353 above) that *fashion* means 'customary display', Hamlet is saying, I will greet you in this showy way so that you do not appear less welcome
than the players.' A more literal explanation is as follows: '. . . so that my
display of friendliness (*extent*) towards the players (which, I tell you, must
at least look polite (*show fairly*) on the surface (*outward*)) shall not seem to be
better treatment (*more . . . like entertainment*) than that which you yourselves
received (*yours*)'.
        Nowadays a formal display of welcome does not always imply a true feeling
of friendliness; but in Shakespeare's day good breeding included the ability
to make a formal show of true feelings. Here there is no contrast between the
sort of display he speaks of and true feelings of friendly welcome; he is not
expected to be informally welcoming – a formal welcome is the one most
expected and prized of a prince.
357   *deceived:* mistaken. – He is thinking of their belief that he is mad.
359   *north-north-west* – i.e. when the wind is blowing from one point of the compass, from time
to time.
360   *a hawk . . . handsaw* – Hamlet clearly means that on other occasions (when the wind is
blowing from another quarter) his powers of discernment are as good as anyone else's. Two explanations of the *hawk* and the *handsaw* are suggested.
        (i) *handsaw* should be *hernshaw*, another name for a heron. (It is likely that
a copyist taking down the play in shorthand for printing might have been
unfamiliar with the word, or heard it incorrectly.) Then the hawk, a bird of
prey, is imagined as chasing the heron; the heron, as birds of heavy flight
generally do, flies with the wind to escape pursuit; and if the wind is blowing
from the south, the bird will be flying away from the sun. The hunter will be
able to distinguish them, therefore, since he will have his back to the sun and
not be dazzled by it.
        (ii) *hawk*, as a variant of *hack*, is used (but not elsewhere in Shakespeare) to
refer to the square board with a handle used by plasterers to hold their plaster
as they are working with it. The phrase could then simply refer to Hamlet's
ability to distinguish one tool (one thing) from another.
        Neither explanation has any particular link with the patterns of imagery
in the play, and the phrase may, perhaps, demand another explanation which
we know nothing of. It has a proverbial sound, with the alliteration of the *h*'s;
and, in favour of the explanation to do with birds, it should be added that a
proverb to do with distinguishing birds is known from a book of about the
same date as *Hamlet:* '[She] doth not knowe a Buzzard from a Hawke'.
364   *swaddling-clouts:* bandages used to wrap round newborn children – in the belief that they
helped to keep the baby's limbs straight; *clouts* is a form of *clothes.*
365   *Happily:* Perhaps.
366   *twice* – i.e. for the second time.
368   *You say right . . .* – Hamlet says this out loud so that Polonius can hear him, as if it were part
of a different conversation from the one they are having. He does not want
Polonius to know that they were, in fact, talking about him and noticing him as
he came up to them.
370   *Roscius* was a famous Roman actor, and a friend of Cicero; it became the custom to refer
to a good actor as a 'Roscius'. Hamlet spoils Polonius's efforts at bringing
sensational news by being the first to mention something about acting.
373   *Buz, buz!* – This was an interjection implying, 'Stop telling us news we know already.'
375   *on his ass* – This is probably further ridicule of Polonius; Hamlet pretends that Polonius
meant: 'The actors are come hither . . . upon mine honour'. Hamlet says 'his
honour' is an ass, and that is how the actors must have arrived if what he says
is true. But this line, which has a ballad rhythm, may be from an old song.
376   *tragedy* (etc.) This list is a satire on the scholar's classification of different types of drama.
A *pastoral* is a literary piece (here a play) dealing with themes of country life.
378   *scene . . . unlimited* – These phrases refer to the 'unities' of drama. Aristotle noted that it
was the practice of Greek tragedians to restrict the action of their plays to
events happening within a period of twenty-four hours, and to those which

Let me comply* with you in this garb, lest my extent* to the
players (which, I tell you, must show fairly outward) should   355
more appear like entertainment than yours. You are welcome;
but my uncle-father and aunt-mother are deceived.*

GUILDENSTERN In what, my dear lord?

HAMLET I am but mad north-north-west;* when the wind is southerly
I know a hawk* from a handsaw.   360

Enter POLONIUS.

POLONIUS Well be with you, gentlemen!

HAMLET Hark you, Guildenstern – [*To* ROSENCRANTZ] and you too –
at each ear a hearer: that great baby you see there is not yet
out of his swaddling-clouts.*

ROSENCRANTZ Happily* he's the second time come to them; for they say an   365
old man is twice* a child.

HAMLET I will prophesy he comes to tell me of the players. Mark it. –
You say* right, sir; o' Monday morning; 'twas then, indeed.

POLONIUS My lord, I have news to tell you.

HAMLET My lord, I have news to tell *you*. When Roscius* was an   370
actor in Rome –

POLONIUS The actors are come hither, my lord.

HAMLET Buz, buz!*

POLONIUS Upon mine honour –

HAMLET Then came each actor on his ass* –   375

POLONIUS The best actors in the world, either for tragedy,* comedy, history, pastoral, pastoral-comical, historical-pastoral, tragical-his-
torical, tragical-comical-historical-pastoral, scene individable,*

---

378 (*cont'd*)   had a direct bearing on one single plot. These became known as the 'unities' of
time and action; later a third 'unity' was postulated, that of place; events were
to be shown as happening in only one place, i.e. there was no change of scene.
    Here *scene individable* probably means a play in which the 'unity of place' is
adhered to; *poem unlimited* means one in which the 'unities' of time and place
are not observed.

379   *Seneca . . . Plautus* – These were Latin dramatists well known to university students and the courts of Shakespeare's day. Seneca (died A.D. 65) wrote tragedies on the ancient stories of Greece, and his work has recourse to a good deal of stage sensation, such as murder (the 'tragedy of blood'), bombastic speeches, and the use of supernatural effects. (Shakespeare's own plays, particularly his early tragedy *Titus Andronicus*, show considerable influence from Seneca). Plautus (died 184 B.C.) was the first and greatest of the writers of comedy in Latin. His plays are characterized by such stage devices as disguise, the gods playing the parts of men, and the confusion of identity between twins. (Shakespeare's *Comedy of Errors* is based on a translation into English of Plautus's comedy *Menæchmi*.)

380   *the law of writ . . . liberty* – (perhaps) 'saying (on the stage) exactly what is written, or taking freedom with the words (i.e. making some of them up going along)'. These are the best actors (*the only men*) either for following the lines of the dramatist or for making lines up as the play goes along. Some have thought, however, that *the law of writ* refers to the 'unities' (see note 378 above), and *the liberty* to the neglect of this law.

382   *Jephthah* was a military leader and judge of Israel whose story is given in the Bible (*Judges* 11). He sacrificed his daughter to God in fulfilment of a rash vow; before she died she went into the wasteland to lament that she had never had a husband. Ophelia, too, is doomed to die unmarried, and Hamlet, although talking what appears to be nonsense to Polonius, may have this similarity unconsciously in his mind. The *treasure* was the daughter.

        Jephthah was the subject of a ballad, or popular song with a story, well-known in Shakespeare's day. This is the song Hamlet quotes from in the following lines.

386   *passing:* extremely.

391   *that follows not:* that is not the expected result. – But when Polonius uses *follows* in the next line, Hamlet pretends to misunderstand him, taking him to mean 'come next in order'. He continues with the ballad.

394   *God wot:* indeed – literally, 'God knows'.

396   *like:* likely.

397   *the first row . . . chanson:* the first verse (*row*) of this religious song – *pious:* religious (since the subject comes from the Bible). Hamlet has by now succeeded in confusing Polonius completely, and this makes a good point for the visiting actors to enter.

398   *my abridgement:* that which cuts me short in what I am saying – i.e. the visiting actors. *Abridgement* also meant 'entertainment', in the sense of a pastime which 'shortened' the time; Hamlet may be playing on this meaning. When Hamlet begins to talk to the actors, his manner changes; he is simple, friendly and sincere; he has a light-hearted joke with the 'woman' in the company, who is in reality a boy dressed up. The men he calls *masters* (line 399), i.e. 'gentlemen', and greets individually, e.g. in line 399:

        I am glad to see thee well.

        His playing with words in what follows is in the tradition of stage conversation; he is clearly eager to get on well with the actors, and remembers many of them intimately.

401   *valanced:* fringed (with a beard).

402   *beard:* confront – with a play on the idea of 'beard' in *valanced* above.

403   *By'r lady* – i.e. 'By our Lady, the Virgin Mary', a mild oath deliberately used to bring in yet again the word *lady* in talking to the boy dressed as one.

405   *the altitude . . . chopine:* the height of a shoe with a high heel. – *Chopines* were fashionable at the time, and since they were shoes on high cork bases they made the wearer look taller than she really was. Hamlet, still teasing the boy gently on his appearance as a woman, is saying that he has grown but does so obliquely by making reference to a woman's shoe.

406   *cracked within the ring:* (i) broken and without its clear ring; (ii) with a crack in it reaching the circle round the sovereign's head (on a coin). – Any coin in this condition was considered to be no longer current, *like a piece of uncurrent gold*; if the boy's voice had broken he would no longer be any use for taking women's parts.

or poem unlimited. Seneca* cannot be too heavy, nor
Plautus too light. For the law of writ* and the liberty, these   380
are the only men.

HAMLET O Jephthah,* judge of Israel, what a treasure hadst thou!
POLONIUS What a treasure had he, my lord?
HAMLET Why,

One fair daughter, and no more,   385
The which he lovéd passing* well.

POLONIUS [Aside] Still on my daughter.
HAMLET Am I not i' th' right, old Jephthah?
POLONIUS If you call me Jephthah, my lord, I have a daughter that I
love passing well.   390
HAMLET Nay, that follows not.*
POLONIUS What follows, then, my lord?
HAMLET Why,

As by lot, God wot,*

and then, you know,   395

It came to pass, as most like* it was –

the first row* of the pious chanson will show you more; for
look, where my abridgement* comes.

Enter four or five PLAYERS.

You are welcome, masters; welcome, all; I am glad to see
thee well; welcome, good friends. – O, my old friend! Why,   400
thy face is valanced* since I saw thee last. Comest thou to
beard* me in Denmark? – [To a player dressed as a woman]
What, my young lady and mistress! By'r lady,* your lady-
ship is nearer to heaven than when I saw you last by the
altitude* of a chopine. Pray God, your voice, like a piece of   405
uncurrent gold, be not cracked within the ring.* – Masters,
you are all welcome. We'll e'en to 't* like French falconers,
fly at anything we see. We'll have a speech straight. Come,
give us a taste of your quality.* Come, a passionate speech.
FIRST PLAYER What speech, my good lord?   410

---

407   *e'en to 't . . . falconers:* get down to business (*to 't*) just (*e'en*) like French falconers. – The
French were expert falconers, but the English thought they did not choose
their prey with sufficient care. Hamlet wants to hear the players in some
parts, and is not much concerned with what these parts are.
409   *quality:* profession.

412   *above:* more than.

413   *caviare to the general:* like caviare to common people. – Caviare, a delicacy made from
the roe of a fish called the sturgeon, was first brought to England in the reign
Elizabeth I, but people found they did not enjoy it when they first tasted it.
If they had it more often, they acquired a taste for it: but since it was expensive
the ordinary man could never afford to do this. The phrase here means that
the play did not please the ordinary people.

414   *received:* considered.

415   *cried . . . top of:* sounded out above mine – because the opinion of these other people was
considered more valuable than mine.

416   *digested:* arranged. – The plot of the play was well set out in the various scenes.

417   *modesty . . . cunning:* moderation . . . skill. – The play was skilfully set down, without
gross displays of passion. (See note to line 425 below on the actual nature of the
play.)

417   *one* – i.e. someone, one of the people Hamlet speaks of as having a good opinion of the play.

417   *sallets:* tasty morsels. – *Sallet* is a form of the modern English word *salad*, and the word
therefore links with the idea *savoury* in the next line. The matter was not
spiced with anything improper which might make it tempting. Hamlet later
says that Polonius needs such 'savoury' things in a play to hold his attention:
he's for . . . a tale of bawdry, or he sleeps
(475–6)

419   *affection:* affectation.

420   *an honest method* – (perhaps) 'a fair presentation of the plot'. The *method* of a book was a
summary of its contents.

421   *more handsome than fine:* more fittingly beautiful than superficially attractive. – Everything Hamlet says about the play suggests that it was highbrow and deeply
moving, not showy.

422   *Aeneas' tale to Dido* – In the epic poem *Aeneid*, composed by the Latin poet Vergil, the
hero Aeneas, a prince of Troy, is on a long voyage of adventure. After seven
years he lands with his men at Carthage, on the north coast of Africa. There he
meets Dido, the queen of Carthage, who listens greedily to the account he gives
of his adventures. In the course of his story he tells her about the struggle at
Troy between the aged king Priam and his adversary Pyrrhus. Before the
Greek adventures sailed to what is now Asia Minor to sack the city of Troy, it
had been prophesied that the Greek soldier Pyrrhus, son of Achilles, was
necessary for its capture. He was one of the heroes who entered the city concealed in a great wooden horse (line 429), and it was he who later killed the
aged king Priam. Priam's son, Paris, had in a sense been the cause of the war
because he had eloped with Helen, the beautiful Greek princess, whom the
Greeks were determined to get back. This war is the subject of the *Iliad* of
Homer; and, in the *Aeneid*, Aeneas says of the sack of Troy: 'I witnessed that
tragedy myself, and I took a great part in those events.' Book II of the *Aeneid*
tells the story; lines 526–558 give the account of Priam's death. Pyrrhus kills
Priam, and the speech goes on to describe the mourning of Priam's wife,
Hecuba, over her husband's dead body.

425   *The rugged Pyrrhus . . . – rugged:* long-haired (and therefore fierce-looking).
The speech which Hamlet begins to quote here, and which is picked up and
completed by the player, presents a number of problems.
First, as to its origin:
Marlowe, Shakespeare's contemporary, began a play called *Dido, Queen of
Carthage,* on the same theme, which was completed by Nashe. But the lines in
Hamlet are not from that play as we now have it, though Shakespeare may have
had it in mind at this point. There is no evidence to suggest that Shakespeare
did not compose these lines himself.
This leads to the second consideration, the style of the lines.
They are written in a pompous rhetorical style, showing the bare story
drawn out with mechanically formal phrases and exaggerated similes and
metaphors. This is the style of Shakespeare's earlier contemporaries, the sort
of passionate speechifying which, for instance, Bottom makes use of in *A
Midsummer Night's Dream:*
. . . a part to tear a cat in, to make all split.

HAMLET I heard thee speak me a speech once – but it was never acted;
or, if it was, not above* once; for the play, I remember,
pleased not the million; 'twas caviare to the general.* But it
was as I received* it, and others, whose judgements in such
matters cried in the top* of mine   an excellent play, well   413
digested* in the scenes, set down with as much modesty as
cunning.* I remember, one* said there were no sallets* in the
lines to make the matter savoury, nor no matter in the phrase
that might indict the author of affection,* but called it an
honest method,* as wholesome as sweet, and by very much   420
more handsome than fine.* One speech in it I chiefly loved;
'twas Aeneas' tale* to Dido; and thereabout of it especially
where he speaks of Priam's slaughter. If it live in your
memory, begin at this line – let me see, let me see—
        The rugged Pyrrhus, like th' Hyrcanian* beast*   425

---

425 *(cont'd)*

        The raging rocks
        And shivering shocks
        Shall break the locks
            Of prison gates;
        And Phibbus' car
        Shall shine from far
        And make and mar
            The foolish Fates. (*M.N.D.*I.ii.23–32)

This instance (from a play written before *Hamlet*, c. 1595) suggests that at
that date Shakespeare was sufficiently aware of the faults of the style to be
willing to parody it. It is puzzling, therefore, that in *Hamlet* he should put
into the mouths of his characters many appreciative comments on this speech.
It was one which impressed Hamlet, a university student who had been
abroad to study, and stayed fixed in his mind. Some commentators have
suggested that all Hamlet says about the speech, and the play it is supposed
to come from, is ironical, but such an explanation is extremely unlikely: there
would be no dramatic point in talking in this way about it, and the 'truth'
about the lines never transpires.

Third, then, what was the view of the lines which the audience was expected
to take? It is most likely that Shakespeare found them somewhat outmoded
but not as flat and conventional as we now feel them to be. Such uninspired
passages as *sable arms, Black as his purpose* and *Out, out, thou strumpet,
Fortune* were fresher to an Elizabethan audience than they are to us, and are
not worse than Shakespeare himself sometimes wrote in his earlier plays. He
may not have appreciated fully how far his own style in *Hamlet* had out-
stripped the earlier conventions, and would yet have recalled the success of his
earlier plays. It was not improbable then that in history the court of Elsinore
might have been enchanted by lines which appear tarnished when placed
beside his own. And, whatever their origin or value, the main function of the
style they are written in is to be in obvious contrast to the style of the play
itself; and this they are. But there is no intention to parody the style or the
play from which the lines may have come.

425 *th' Hyrcanian beast* – a classical reference to the tiger; the ancients thought of Hyrcania,
    a province lying south and south-east of the Caspian Sea, as a land full of
    dangerous wild animals, especially tigers. It was a stock classical reference
    which Hamlet justifiably guessed might have followed *rugged*.

427   *sable:* black. – This, like *gules* (red), is a technical term used in *heraldry* to denote the colours on coats of arms, as is referred to in lines 431–2. The black of his weapons (*arms*) and face is changed to a new 'badge', the red of his victim's blood. Black is ill-omened; his aims (*purpose*) were also 'black'. 'Trick' (line 432) is also a term from heraldry; it means 'draw diagrams of coats of arms'.

4.29   *couchéd . . . horse:* hidden inside the ill-omened horse. – This was the Wooden Horse of Troy, a huge statue on wheels of a horse, made of wood and hollow inside. The Greek soldiers sent forward to enter Troy were concealed in this horse; the Trojans hauled it into their city, not knowing what was inside, and from it the soldiers escaped to begin their work of destruction.

430   *complexion:* natural appearance.

431   *dismal:* ill-omened.

432   *gules:* red – in heraldry.

433   *horridly tricked:* horribly marked – *trick* is also a heraldic term (see note to line 427).

434   *impasted . . . streets:* made into a paste by (the action of) the hot, dry streets.

435   *lend:* give.

435   *tyrannous:* cruel. – This meaning is more frequent in Shakespeare than the more precise 'like a tyrant, tyrannical'.

437   *o'er-sizéd . . . gore:* covered over with solidifying blood – *o'er-sizéd* means, literally, covered over with a substance like size, which gives a glassy, polished effect to rough surfaces.

438   *carbuncles:* fiery-red precious stones. – The horrors of blood have now been built up to a melodramatic climax; this falls away with *Old grandsire Priam* in the next line, and so ends the first part of the speech which Hamlet remembers so well.

441   *'Fore God:* (I swear) before God – an oath.

444   *Striking too short* – i.e. striking out with his sword but not hitting any Greeks; the sword is *Rebellious to his arm* (next line), i.e. (literally) it refuses to do what his arm orders it to do. It is *Repugnant to command* (line 446), i.e. it offers resistance to commands.

447   *drives:* rushes (at).

448   *the whiff and wind . . .* – Although Pyrrhus struck wide of the mark, the wind from his sword was enough to knock the old king down. This is a circumstance which appears in Marlowe and Nashe's *Dido*, but not in the *Aeneid*, where Priam's death is quick and deliberate. The alliteration *whiff* and *wind* is characteristic of the style of this speech.

448   *fell:* fierce.

449   *unnervéd:* weak. – The nerves were taken to be the seat of bodily strength.

449   *senseless Ilium* – literally, 'inanimate Troy'; i.e. the city of Troy, though *senseless* (unfeeling, inanimate), seemed to feel this blow which brought down Priam, and crashed in flames (lines 449–50). Ilium is another name for Troy.

450   *flaming top . . . base:* with its towers in flames stoops to its (*his*) base. – Although in fact *senseless*, Troy is still spoken of as a person stooping; even *top* here may have a meaning secondary to 'high point', that of 'forelock', which is common in Shakespeare in figurative phrases, and would here signify further personification.

452   *Takes . . . ear:* captures Pyrrhus's ear – i.e. dazes him so that for a time he cannot act. Once again Troy is personified as 'taking something prisoner', even though *senseless*.

453   *declining:* falling.

453   *milky* – i.e. 'milk-white'. Priam was an old man.

455   *as a painted tyrant:* like a tyrant in a picture. There were pictures of fierce rulers with swords in their hands which they held up and never brought down.

456   *a neutral . . . matter:* one unattached (*neutral*) to either side—what he really wanted to do (*his will*) and the business he had to do (*matter*). – For a moment he was detached from both these considerations.

458   *against:* in expectation of. – Pyrrhus's moment of inaction is likened to the calm before a thunder-storm.

459   *rack:* mass of cloud, driven along in normal weather by the wind in the upper air.

460   *the orb below* – i.e. the earth.

461   *hush:* quiet.

461   *anon:* in a moment.

462   *region:* heavens.

— 'tis not so — it begins with Pyrrhus:
The rugged Pyrrhus — he whose sable* arms,
Black as his purpose, did the night resemble
When he lay couchèd* in the ominous horse —
Hath now this dread and black complexion* smeared   430
With heraldry more dismal;* head to foot
Now is he total gules;* horridly tricked*
With blood of fathers, mothers, daughters, sons,
Baked and impasted* with the parching streets,
That lend* a tyrannous* and damnèd light   435
To their vile murders. Roasted in wrath and fire,
And thus o'er-sizèd* with coagulate gore,
With eyes like carbuncles,* the hellish Pyrrhus
Old grandsire Priam seeks. —
So proceed you.   440

POLONIUS   'Fore God,* my lord, well spoken, with good accent and good
discretion.

FIRST PLAYER   *Anon he finds him*
Striking too short* at Greeks; his antique sword,
Rebellious to his arm, lies where it falls,   445
Repugnant to command. Unequal matched,
Pyrrhus at Priam drives;* in rage strikes wide;
But with the whiff* and wind of his fell* sword
Th' unnervèd* father falls. Then senseless Ilium,*
Seeming to feel this blow, with flaming top*   450
Stoops to his base; and with a hideous crash
Takes prisoner* Pyrrus' ear. For, lo! his sword,
Which was declining* on the milky* head
Of reverend Priam, seemed i' th' air to stick.
So, as a painted tyrant,* Pyrrhus stood   455
And, like a neutral* to his will and matter,
Did nothing.
But, as we often see, against* some storm,
A silence in the heavens, the rack* stand still,
The bold winds speechless, and the orb below*   460
As hush* as death, anon* the dreadful thunder
Doth rend the region;* so, after Pyrrhus' pause,

463 *new a-work:* newly to work. – He is forced into action again by the passion of his desire for revenge.

464 *the Cyclops' hammers . . . armour* – In classical mythology the Cyclops were a race of one-eyed giants; they were assistants to the god (Hephaestus) who was charged with the making of armour and metal ornaments for gods and horses. They were thought of as working inside volcanoes. Mars was the God of War, second only to Jupiter in the Roman pantheon. *Mars his:* Mars's.

465 *for proof eterne:* to remain of proved strength for ever.

466 *remorse:* pity. – The blows used to beat out Mars's armour were never less feeling than that which Pyrrhus dealt old Priam; i.e. Pyrrhus's blow was without any trace of pity.

468 *strumpet:* immoral woman. – Fortune, like an immoral woman, seems to 'love' some people at one time, but her favours cannot be trusted or counted on. Fortune is often associated with the wheel (as in line 470 below). As the wheel revolves, what was once at the top is now at the bottom; one can in the same way be high in Fortune's favour and quickly fall away to the depths of despair. She sits blindfold and turns her wheel; she cannot see who is in favour and who out, so that her influence is not open to any logical explanation. Anyone may rise and fall in her favour.

470 *fellies:* arcs of the wooden circle of the wheel; *nave* (next line): hub.

472 *the fiends* – i.e. the devils in hell.

474 *shall:* must go.

475 *jig* – a lively, comic performance in rhyme given in an interval or at the end of a full-length play. Jigs were often broadly humorous, and became associated with lively dance music; *jig* thus came later to mean a lively dance tune.

476 *Hecuba* – Priam's wife. In the *Aeneid* a moving picture is given of Hecuba drawing her aged husband to the altar where she and her daughters had gone for sanctuary. Hamlet awaits the pathos of this scene after the horrors of Pyrrhus's attack.

477 *mobled:* veiled. – The word *mobled* is certainly unusual, and Shakespeare meant it to appear so. Hamlet questions its use here, and Polonius approves it. It may have been pronounced to rhyme with *hobbled*.

481 *bisson rheum:* blinding tears. – With the city in flames she wept so profusely that she 'threatened' the fire with her tears, i.e. she might have put it out.

481 *clout:* piece of cloth.

482 *late:* of late. – This change is an example of the work of Fortune's wheel; the queen now has a piece of cloth over her head where she recently wore a crown (*diadem*).

483 *o'er-teeméd:* worn out from bearing many children. – Hecuba was said to have had fifty sons and fifty daughters.

484 *caught up:* snatched up.

485 *Who this had seen . . . pronounced:* whoever had seen this would have spoken words of treason, with a tongue full of poison, against the ruling power of Fortune. – Fortune rules like a monarch and should be obeyed like one; but this sight was so horrible that anyone who saw it would have been justified in uttering bitter words of treason against this ruler, Fortune, because the suffering seemed to have been awarded so unjustly.

487 *if . . . gods* (line 493, at the end of the speech): if the gods themselves had seen her (Hecuba) then . . . the immediate burst of wailing (*instant . . . clamour*, line 490) that she made . . . would have made the heavenly bodies (*the burning eyes of heaven*, line 492) full of tears (*milch*, line 492).

493 *passion in the gods:* (the clamour would have aroused – *made*) sympathy in the gods themselves.

494 *whe'r:* whether – used sometimes to introduce a general question; here the question is rhetorical and spoken 'aside', no answer being expected: 'Has he (Hamlet) not changed colour? Has he not tears in his eyes?' (*turned his colour:* turned pale).

497 *Good my lord:* My good Lord – a courteous mode of address which leads us to expect that Hamlet is treating Polonius seriously on this occasion.

497 *bestowed:* lodged. – It was the custom to accommodate within the great houses any groups of wandering players who came to perform.

498 *used:* treated.

498 *abstract:* summary, account.

> *Aroused vengeance sets him new a-work;**
> *And never did the Cyclops' hammers* fall*
> *On Mars his armour, forged for proof eterne,**   465
> *With less remorse* than Pyrrhus' bleeding sword*
> *Now falls on Priam. –*
> *Out, out, thou strumpet,* Fortune! All you gods,*
> *In general synod, take away her power;*
> *Break all the spokes and fellies* from her wheel,*   470
> *And bowl the round nave down the hill of heaven,*
> *As low as to the fiends!**

POLONIUS This is too long.

HAMLET It shall* to th' barber's, with your beard. – [*To the* FIRST
PLAYER] Prithee, say on – he's for a jig* or a tale of bawdry, or   475
he sleeps – say on; come to Hecuba.*

FIRST PLAYER *But who, O, who had seen the mobled* queen – .*

HAMLET 'The mobled queen'?

POLONIUS That's good; 'mobled queen' is good.

FIRST PLAYER *Run barefoot up and down, threat'ning the flames*   480
> *With bisson rheum,* a clout* upon that head*
> *Where late* the diadem stood, and for a robe,*
> *About her lank and all o'er-teeméd* loins*
> *A blanket, in th' alarm of fear caught up* –*
> *Who this had seen,* with tongue in venom steeped,*   485
> *'Gainst Fortune's state would treason have pronounced.*
> *But if* the gods themselves did see her then,*
> *When she saw Pyrrhus make malicious sport*
> *In mincing with his sword her husband's limbs,*
> *The instant burst of clamour that she made –*   490
> *Unless things mortal move them not at all –*
> *Would have made milch the burning eyes of heaven,*
> *And passion* in the gods.*

POLONIUS [*Aside*] Look, whe'r* he has not turned his colour, and has
tears in's eyes! – [*To the* FIRST PLAYER] Pray you, no more.   495

HAMLET 'Tis well; I'll have thee speak out the rest soon. – [*To* POLONIUS]
Good my lord,* will you see the players well bestowed?*
Do you hear, let them be well used,* for they are the abstract*
and brief chronicles of the time. After your death you were

500   *you were better:* it will be better for you to – *you* in this phrase was originally in the dative case, meaning 'to, for you', and the verb was impersonal, with the subject *it* understood. The grammar of the phrase is reflected in the translation into modern English.

502   *their desert:* what they deserve.

503   *God's bodykins* – an oath, literally 'By God's body', with the suffix – *kin*, 'the little one', to lighten the gravity of the blasphemy.

503   *after:* according to.

510   *you* – The mode of address in this sentence perhaps indicates a move from friendly exchange to more serious, purposeful instruction. Hamlet's detailed directions are all with the form *you*, not *thou*. The *you* in line 510 probably means 'you, the company', i.e. it is the plural pronoun.

513   *for a need:* if necessary.

513   *study:* learn – as lines of his part in the play.

515   *set down:* write out.
      This long scene began with Rosencrantz and Guildenstern, and Hamlet speaks to them again briefly here before the scene closes. As they leave, the fast-moving action of the scene comes to a quiet close as Hamlet, full of doubts and remorse, thinks over the First Player's performance. He is amazed that fiction has moved the player powerfully, whereas the fact of his own father's murder has so far failed to spur him to action.

521   *wi'ye:* with you.

526   *conceit:* imagination.

527   *her* – i.e. his soul's; the soul was sometimes referred to as feminine.

527   *his visage wanned:* his face turned pale.

528   *in's aspect:* in the way he looked. – The rhythm of the lines requires *aspéct* to be stressed on the second syllable, not as in modern English.

529   *function:* action.

530   *nothing* – i.e. nothing in real life; just fiction, a story told in the form of a play.

534   *the cue for passion* – For an actor, a *cue* is the last words of a speech before his own, which he remembers as indicating where he should come in. Hamlet is, of course, deliberately using an image from the theatre to compare the player's action with his own inactivity.

536   *cleave . . . speech:* split everyone's ear with terrifying speeches; *general:* public.

537   *free:* innocent – i.e. those who are free from guilt.

538   *Confound:* confuse.

better* have a bad epitaph than their ill report while you   500
live.

POLONIUS   My lord, I will use them according to their desert.*

HAMLET   God's bodykins,* man, better. Use every man after* his
desert, and who should 'scape whipping? Use them after
your own honour and dignity. The less they deserve, the   505
more merit is in your bounty. Take them in.

POLONIUS   Come, sirs.

HAMLET   Follow him, friends; we'll hear a play tomorrow. [*Exit*
POLONIUS *with all the* PLAYERS *but the First.*] [*To the* FIRST
PLAYER] Dost thou hear me, old friend; can you* play the   510
Murder of Gonzago?

FIRST PLAYER   Ay, my lord.

HAMLET   We'll ha 't tomorrow night. You could, for a need,* study* a
speech of some dozen or sixteen lines, which I would set
down* and insert in 't; could you not?   515

FIRST PLAYER   Ay, my lord.

HAMLET   Very well. – Follow that lord; and look you mock him not.
[*Exit* FIRST PLAYER.] [*To* ROSENCRANTZ *and* GUILDENSTERN]
My good friends, I'll leave you till night. You are welcome to
Elsinore.

ROSENCRANTZ   Good my lord!   520

HAMLET   Ay, so, God be wi' ye!*

[*Exeunt* ROSENCRANTZ *and* GUILDENSTERN

Now I am alone.
O, what a rogue and peasant slave am I!
Is it not monstrous, that this player here,
But in a fiction, in a dream of passion,   525
Could force his soul so to his own conceit,*
That, from her* working, all his visage wanned,*
Tears in his eyes, distraction in 's aspect,*
A broken voice, and his whole function* suiting
With forms to his conceit? And all for nothing!*   530
For Hecuba!
What's Hecuba to him, or he to Hecuba,
That he should weep for her? What would he do,
Had he the motive and the cue* for passion
That I have? He would drown the stage with tears,   535
And cleave* the general ear with horrid speech,
Make mad the guilty, and appal the free,*
Confound* the ignorant, and amaze, indeed,
The very faculties of eyes and ears.

541   *muddy-mettled:* dull-spirited; *mettle:* spirit, courage.
541   *peak . . . unpregnant of:* mope about like John the dreamer, not stirred into activity by. –
        John-a-dreams seems to have been a nickname for a dreamy, faraway type of
        man.
545   *defeat:* destruction.
548   *the lie i' th' throat:* the total lie – a lie not just in the mouth but as from the whole body.
        To 'give' such a lie means to accuse a person of complete falsehood: '(Who)
        accuses me of total falsehood through and through?'
549   *me:* to me.
550   *'Swounds:* By God's wounds – a strong oath.
551   *it cannot be But:* it can only be that.
551   *pigeon-livered:* gentle. – The gentleness of doves and pigeons was thought to be because
        they had no gall in their livers; gall was taken to be the cause of that kind of
        temperament which resented insult or injury.
552   *make oppression bitter:* make distress (from other sources) bitter (to himself).
553   *region kites:* kites of the air; *region* (air) was used in line 462.
555   *kindless:* unnatural. – See I.ii.65 and the note to it on *kind.*
557   *most brave . . .* – Hamlet thinks ironically of his ranting, calling it 'most brave', and now
        reproves himself for using words instead of actions, unpacking words, not
        deeds, from his heart.
561   *fall a-:* begin to.
563   *Fie upon 't* – an oath, 'Curse it!'
563   *About:* Get to work.
565   *cunning:* brilliant skill.
566   *presently:* at once.
569   *organ:* organ of the voice. – The guilty person's speech organs will speak miraculously
        whether he wants them to or not.

        Hamlet goes on to speak of his plan as if he had just thought of it, whereas
        he has already taken action to put it into effect. By putting his thoughts into
        words he is 'telling' the audience what he proposes to do: the play will tell a
        story similar to Claudius's own; as Claudius watches the play he will realize
        that someone knows the truth about him. Hamlet will watch him closely,
        because the King will certainly do something to reveal his guilt.

572   *tent . . . quick:* probe him down to the tender part of the wound. – A *tent* was a tight
        roll of linen for searching a wound and removing impurities from it.
572   *blench:* flinch.
574   *May be the devil* – i.e. not the wandering soul of a dead man, but the devil in disguise.
577   *very potent . . . spirits:* very powerful over people who are suffering from such afflictions
        (as my weakness and melancholy).
578   *Abuses:* deceives.
579   *relative:* conclusive – i.e. more relevant, more closely related to the facts. The evidence of
        the ghost may not be as conclusive as he first thought.

Yet I,   540
A dull and muddy-mettled* rascal, peak,*
Like John-a-dreams, unpregnant of my cause,
And can say nothing – no, not for a king
Upon whose property and most dear life
A damned defeat* was made. Am I a coward?   545
Who calls me villain? breaks my pate across?
Plucks off my beard, and blows it in my face?
Tweaks me by th' nose? gives me the lie i' th' throat*
As deep as to the lungs? who does me* this, ha?
'Swounds,* I should take it. For it cannot be   550
But* I am pigeon-livered,* and lack gall
To make oppression* bitter; or, ere this,
I should have fatted all the region kites*
With this slave's offal – bloody, bawdy villain!
Remorseless, treacherous, lecherous, kindless* villian!   555
O, vengeance!
Why, what an ass am I! This is most brave,*
That I, the son of a dear father murdered,
Prompted to my revenge by heaven and hell,
Must, like a whore, unpack my heart with words,   560
And fall* a-cursing, like a very drab,
A scullion!
Fie upon 't!* Foh! – About,* my brain! I have heard
That guilty creatures sitting at a play
Have by the very cunning* of the scene   565
Been struck so to the soul that presently*
They have proclaimed their malefactions;
For murder, though it have no tongue, will speak
With most miraculous organ.* I'll have these players
Play something like the murder of my father   570
Before mine uncle. I'll observe his looks;
I'll tent* him to the quick. If he but blench,*
I know my course. The spirit that I have seen
May be the devil.* And the devil hath power
T' assume a pleasing shape; yea, and perhaps   575
Out of my weakness and my melancholy,
As he is very potent* with such spirits,
Abuses* me to damn me. I'll have grounds .
More relative* than this. – The play's the thing
Wherein I'll catch the conscience of the king.   [*Exit*   580

III. i.   The King and Polonius spy on Hamlet and Ophelia together. Hamlet ponders on suicide
and the terrors of life after death. He guesses he is being watched, and the advice he gives
to Ophelia (*Get thee to a nunnery* . . .) convinces the King that he is not mad and not in
love with her. In the King's opinion, the best way to relieve his trouble is to send him away
to England; a pretext for this is quickly found.

This scene represents a further stage in the probing of Hamlet's state of mind. Polonius
and the two courtiers have failed; Ophelia, acting for her father, almost succeeds. In an
aside, Claudius admits his guilt; the audience hears Hamlet, who is unaware of this
admission, extending his doubts about the Ghost to the whole supernatural world, and
expressing his fears of the life after death. By the end of his most famous speech he has
come to terms with his dilemma: action has disappeared in speculation; his predicament
involves a woman (the weakness of Ophelia reminds him of his own mother's weakness of
character). He is near to revealing himself by directly threatening the King in his hearing
. . . *all but one* . . . ; *not to be* has crystallized into both an acknowledgement of the supernatural (the Ghost did not deceive) and a determination to *take up arms*, i.e. act to avenge
the wrongs he has suffered.

1   *drift of circumstance*: roundabout method (of conversation).
3   *Grating*: vexing.
7   *forward to be sounded*: prepared to be questioned (on the subject).
12   *disposition*: inclination. – He was evidently unwilling to speak, and forced himself to do
            so against his real inclination. The account that Rosencrantz and Guildenstern
            give of their conversation with Hamlet before the players arrived (II.ii) is quite
            incorrect and misleading. They evidently want to cover up the fact that they
            did not manage to deceive Hamlet and were forced to admit to him that they
            had been sent to inform on him. Hamlet was very ready to ask questions of
            them; it was they who were reluctant to reply.
13   *Niggard of question*: Disinclined to ask questions – i.e. begin a conversation.
14   *assay . . . pastime*: try to persuade him to take part in any amusement – *assay* means,
            literally, 'challenge (him) to take part in a trial of strength or skill'.
17   *o'er-raught*: overtook – *raught* is an old past tense form of *reach*.
19   *about the court*: somewhere in the castle.
23   *the matter* – i.e. the play; the word sounds rather condescending, and Polonius no doubt
            intends it to do so.
24   *content*: please.
26   *give . . . edge*: incite him further.
29   *closely*: secretly.

ACT III scene i

Elsinore. A room in the castle.

Enter KING, QUEEN, POLONIUS, OPHELIA,
ROSENCRANTZ, *and* GUILDENSTERN.

KING And can you, by no drift of circumstance,*
Get from him why he puts on this confusion,
Grating* so harshly all his days of quiet
With turbulent and dangerous lunacy?
ROSENCRANTZ He does confess he feels himself distracted;   5
But from what cause he will by no means speak.
GUILDENSTERN Nor do we find him forward to be sounded;*
But, with a crafty madness, keeps aloof
When we would bring him on to some confession
Of his true state.
QUEEN   Did he receive you well?   10
ROSENCRANTZ Most like a gentleman.
GUILDENSTERN But with much forcing of his disposition.*
ROSENCRANTZ Niggard of question,* but, of our demands,
Most free in his reply.
QUEEN   Did you assay* him
To any pastime?   15
ROSENCRANTZ Madam, it so fell out that certain players
We o'er-raught* on the way: of these we told him;
And there did seem in him a kind of joy
To hear of it. They are about* the court,
And, as I think, they have already order   20
This night to play before him.
POLONIUS   'Tis most true.
And he beseeched me to entreat your majesties
To hear and see the matter.*
KING With all my heart; and it doth much content* me
To hear him so inclined. –   25
Good gentlemen, give him a further edge,*
And drive his purpose on to these delights.
ROSENCRANTZ We shall, my lord.
                    [*Exeunt* ROSENCRANTZ *and* GUILDENSTERN
KING   Sweet Gertrude, leave us too;
For we have closely* sent for Hamlet hither,

95

31   *Affront:* meet face to face.
32   *lawful espials:* lawful spies – *lawful* because as real or step-parents they may consider
         themselves morally justified in what the King suggests they should both do:
         spy on their children together.
35   *by him . . . behaved:* from him, by the way he acts.
41   *wonted way:* usual way of life.
42   *To . . . honours:* to the credit of both of you.
42   *I wish it may:* I hope it (the exercise of my virtues) will.
43   *Gracious:* My gracious lord. – Polonius's way of addressing the King here is very unusual,
         and may be a mark of his eccentricity.
44   *bestow:* place in position.
44   *this book* is evidently a prayer-book, as is suggested by the lines which follow, and line 90,
         thy orisons.
45   *That show . . . loneliness:* so that the appearance of religious devotion may be some excuse
         (*colour*) for your being alone.
46   *with devotion's visage . . . himself* (line 49): with the appearance of devotion and acts of
         piety we give a pleasant appearance to (*sugar o'er*) the devil himself. – Polonius
         confuses the matter completely by adding this general observation to the
         detailed instruction; it can only mean, in effect, that people often try to cover
         up wickedness with the appearance of goodness – which is exactly what he has
         suggested Ophelia should do, since her appearance alone is planned as an
         enticement to Hamlet. Polonius stoops to a mean action and at the same time
         warns his daughter against doing it. Dramatically it fits the King's deeds
         perfectly, and it is he who feels the sting of it; for the first time his conscience
         is pricked.
51   *plastering art* – i.e. painting the face. The King's speech aside carries on the image of an
         agreeable exterior covering up villainous deeds. The word *painted* in line 53
         means, therefore, 'feigned'; 'The face of the harlot . . . is no uglier to the face-
         paint she uses than my actions are to the feigned words I use to cover them'.
55   *withdraw* – i.e. to the places agreed upon, where they can watch secretly what happens
         between Ophelia and Hamlet.
56   *To be . . .* – (perhaps) 'Should the necessary action take place, or not take place?' This is
         close to saying, 'Shall I lose my life or not?' since death will be the result of any
         action he may take. The rhetorical questions which follow (*whether . . . or*
         (line 59) . . .) explain or imply what the first words mean: is it better to leave
         things as they are or to take action which will probably cause his death, either
         by suicide or as retribution for killing the King.
59   *take arms . . . end them:* make a stand against the mass of troubles, and by doing so put an
         end to them. – The *end* of the troubles could be brought about either by killing
         the King or by taking his own life. But as the speech moves on, Hamlet's
         thoughts seem to turn more specifically to suicide; he begins to doubt the
         value of this solution, because man cannot be sure of what will happen after
         death, and has no proof that human suffering stops at that point.
         Some commentators have objected to the expression *take arms against a sea*,
         since a literal interpretation makes strange sense. But Shakespeare is writing
         poetry, and the free play of metaphors is an essential part of it.
60   *to sleep* – The idea of death as a sleep plays an increasingly important part. It is a concept
         with which Shakespeare's audience was perfectly familiar; the Bible uses such
         images as 'sleep in the dust' for death, and their Burial Service referred to death
         as sleep. Hamlet's thoughts move on in this vein: but supposing death, unlike
         sleep, is an end in itself, and with it all earthly troubles are finished, then it is
         very desirable. Yet in sleep there is the possibility of dreaming (*perchance to
         dream*, line 65); will there be dreams after death? Is it for this that human
         beings are so reluctant to take their own lives, and would rather bear earthly
         sorrows and troubles?
61   *No:* nothing.
61   *to say:* supposing; if it is true that.

	That he, as 'twere by accident, may here	30
	Affront* Ophelia.	
	Her father and myself – lawful espials* –	
	Will so bestow ourselves that, seeing, unseen,	
	We may of their encounter frankly judge,	
	And gather by him,* as he is behaved,	35
	If 't be th' affliction of his love or no	
	That thus he suffers for.	

QUEEN   I shall obey you. –
And for your part, Ophelia, I do wish
That your good beauties be the happy cause
Of Hamlet's wildness. So shall I hope your virtues   40
Will bring him to his wonted way* again,
To both your honours.*

OPHELIA   Madam, I wish* it may.

                                 [*Exit* QUEEN

POLONIUS Ophelia, walk you here. – [*To the* KING] Gracious,* so please you,
We will bestow* ourselves. – [*To* OPHELIA] Read on this book,*
That show* of such an exercise may colour   45
Your loneliness. – We are oft to blame in this –
'Tis too much proved – that with devotion's visage*
And pious action we do sugar o'er
The devil himself.

KING   [*Aside*] O, 'tis too true!
How smart a lash that speech doth give my conscience!   50
The harlot's cheek, beautied with plastering art,*
Is not more ugly to the thing that helps it
Than is my deed to my most painted word.
O heavy burden!

POLONIUS I hear him coming. Let's withdraw,* my lord.   55

                             [*Exeunt* KING *and* POLONIUS

Enter HAMLET.

HAMLET To be, or not to be* – that is the question.
Whether 'tis nobler in the mind to suffer
The slings and arrows of outrageous fortune,
Or to take arms* against a sea of troubles,
And by opposing end them? – To die – to sleep* –   60
No* more; and by a sleep to say* we end
The heart-ache, and the thousand natural shocks

63   *flesh is heir to* – i.e. that human beings are born to suffer. The *flesh* is heir to these in the sense that the human race has 'handed down' from father to son and grandson and so an inheritance of sorrow and tragedy.

65   *rub:* difficulty. – In the game of bowls, the *rub* was the obstacle in the ground which prevented the ball from going in its proper course.

67   *shuffled . . . coil:* shaken off the turmoil (*coil*) of this present life (*mortal*). – Many have taken *coil* in this passage to mean 'the human body', i.e. what 'coils' round or surrounds the spirit; but there is no evidence to suggest that *coil* had this meaning in Shakespeare's day.

68   *give us pause:* make us hesitate. – The subject is '(the question of) *what dreams may come*'

68   *respect:* consideration.

69   *of so long life:* last so long. – It is this consideration, dreams in the sleep of death, which makes calamity (in life) last so long, since man is reluctant to put an end to it by taking his own life.

70   *scorns of time:* insults of this world. – Hamlet is thinking of the punishments and insults which the world (*time*) brings.

71   *contumely:* humiliating speech or behaviour.

72   *the law's delay* – i.e. the delays caused by the processes of law. If one goes to law one learns not to expect the processes to move quickly.

73   *The insolence of office:* the proud rudeness of people who hold official positions.

73   *spurns . . . takes:* insults (*spurns*) which people who are good and quiet (*patient merit*) take from those who are *unworthy* (those, that is, who are not as good as the people they insult).

75   *he* links with *who* in line 70.

75   *quietus . . . bodkin:* bring about his release (from life – *quietus*) with nothing but (*bare*) a dagger (*bodkin*). – A *quietus* (used as a technical term) was a statement which released an accountant from his responsibility for the accounts he was working on; the full Latin phrase was *quietus est*, 'it is at peace', i.e. there is no further dispute over the exact amount in the account. This reference may be an extension of the thoughts on the *law's delay* and the *insolence of office* (lines 72–3). Some have thought that *bare* here means 'naked, unsheathed', but the explanation above gives better sense: all the troubles and burdens of life can be quickly finished by using a small instrument, a dagger.

76   *fardels:* packs, burdens.

79   *bourn:* boundary, confines.

83   *conscience:* conscious thought, reflection. – In saying that *conscience* (in this sense) makes cowards of us all, Hamlet shows that he has his own case principally in mind.

84   *the native hue . . . thought:* the natural colour (*native hue*) of resolution is made to look sick by the paleness (*pale cast*) of reflection – *cast:* a tinge of colour. The image is of the face which loses its healthy red colour and becomes pale when the body is sick.

86   *pitch:* height – a technical term used to indicate the high point in the flight of a falcon. The early Folios have *pith* here, which also makes sense.

87   *With this regard:* when considered in this way.

87   *their currents turn awry* – This is a very noticeable change of metaphor from the *pitch* and *moment* in the line before. Action is now seen as a current of water, a river; its direction is changed, turned *awry*, by the conscious thought which Hamlet refers to. The Folios have *away* here, which perhaps gives more perfect sense, a total diversion from the previous course of the *currents*.

88   *Soft you now:* Gently. – Hamlet is telling himself to soften the passion of his words. Ophelia was set to reading a prayer-book (line 44), and now she comes in, evidently reading prayers. Hamlet had been sent for secretly by the King (line 29) and now comes upon Ophelia, as if by accident. Yet since Ophelia spoke to her father about Hamlet's appearance as a madman (II.i.76ff.), she has followed Polonius's orders and refused to see Hamlet (II.i.107–109). Hamlet certainly suspects another trick; he wants to know where Polonius is, doubtless believing that they are being watched (line 132).

He does not adopt, or forgets, the pose of madness when he first speaks to her; for the solemnity of his previous thoughts has carried him away. She begins by most gently and courteously asking after his health, how he has been since many days ago (*this many a day* – line 92) when they last talked together. But Hamlet's pose of madness quickly returns and he begins to talk to her with increasing rudeness and fouler implications.

That flesh is heir to;* 'tis a consummation
Devoutly to be wished. To die – to sleep –
To sleep! perchance to dream. Ay, there's the rub;*   65
For in that sleep of death what dreams may come,
When we have shuffled* off this mortal coil,
Must give us pause.* There's the respect*
That makes calamity of so long life.*
For who would bear the whips and scorns* of time,   70
The oppressor's wrong, the proud man's contumely,*
The pangs of déspised love, the law's delay,*
The insolence of office,* and the spurns*
That patient merit of the unworthy takes,
When he* himself might his quietus* make   75
With a bare bodkin? Who would fardels* bear,
To grunt and sweat under a weary life,
But that the dread of something after death –
The undiscovered country from whose bourn*
No traveller returns – puzzles the will,   80
And makes us rather bear those ills we have
Than fly to others that we know not of?
Thus conscience* does make cowards of us all,
And thus the native hue* of resolution
Is sicklied o'er with the pale cast of thought;   85
And enterprises of great pitch* and moment,
With this regard,* their currents turn awry,*
And lose the name of action. [*He sees* OPHELIA *praying.*] –
Soft you now!*
The fair Ophelia! –
[*To* OPHELIA] Nymph, in thy orisons*   90
Be all my sins remembered.

OPHELIA   Good my lord,*
How does your honour for this many a day?

HAMLET I humbly thank you. Well, well, well.

OPHELIA My lord, I have remembrances* of yours

---

90   *orisons:* prayers.
91   *Good my lord:* My good lord.
94   *remembrances:* gifts – from a lover to the loved one, as tokens of true love. For a long time
      (*long*) Ophelia has wished (*longed*) to give them back (*re-deliver*) them to
      Hamlet, as a mark that the association between them is at an end.

97   *aught:* anything. – Hamlet may mean that he never gave her anything of real value—his heart, his life—or that the Hamlet who gave the tokens to her is not the same as the Hamlet she now sees. In either case, Ophelia appears too modest, her words too contrived (*longéd long*, line 95; *Rich gifts wax poor*, line 102), to understand fully what is happening in Hamlet's mind, and has no strength of character to help him.

99   *words . . . rich:* words (when he gave her the tokens) arranged so sweetly (*of so sweet breath composed*) that they (*As*) made the presents appear even more rich.

101   *Take these again:* take them back. – They have lost the *perfume* of kindness.

102   *wax:* become.

106   *fair* – There is a stage tradition that at line 104, when Hamlet says:
             Ha, Ha! Are you honest?
             a noise is made by the King and Polonius, who are hidden behind the arras to spy on the Prince and Ophelia together. Hamlet hears this, realizes at once that he has been tricked into the meeting, and begins asking these disconcerting questions like a madman. There is a contrast in the words *honest* and *fair* which is meant to put women in a very unfavourable light: if a women is *honest*, i.e. virtuous, she will not be *fair*, since all beautiful women are deceivers and seducers. His mother's recent behaviour has driven him to think in this way.

109   *discourse:* familiar contact. – He means that her virtue should prevent everyone from addressing her beauty, since the beauty will deceive. Ophelia purposely misunderstands him, taking him to mean, 'your honesty and your beauty should never be allowed to have familiar intercourse with one another'.

110   *commerce:* friendly intercourse.

113   *bawd:* woman who exploits other women for immoral purposes. – Beauty, he says in effect, will more readily spoil virtue (*honesty*) than virtue will turn beauty to good ends.

115   *the time . . . proof:* the present age (*time*) proves it to be true. – He is thinking again about his mother's recent actions.

119   *so inoculate . . . of it:* be engrafted on to our first state to such an extent that no flavour of it remains. – The imagery is from gardening: new stems are grafted on to old ones (*old stock*) but there is in the new fruit some flavour of the old. The *old stock* is vice stirred by beauty; the grafting of *virtue* cannot change its entire nature.
             Hamlet's notions of feminine charms and designs are perhaps genuinely confused here; hence his first admitting and then denying his love.

122   *a nunnery* – where she will never be able to marry. The advice is fair, since by now Hamlet must have a premonition that, in taking revenge, he and many of those with him will be overtaken by tragedy. When the world she knows is falling away, the life of a nun might be her only safe shelter.

123   *indifferent honest:* moderately virtuous.

124   *me:* myself. – The vices that Hamlet goes on to accuse himself of are not true in fact, but he knows what exists in his own mind, where they are all possibilities. He aims to make himself appear in Ophelia's eyes too vile for any scrap of her love for him to remain.

126   *beck:* call, bidding.

129   *arrant:* thorough.

130   *Go thy ways:* Go away. – But before Ophelia can leave him he asks her directly where her father is, in order to test her. Her reply is a lie; this adds further intensity to Hamlet's words against women, and he unfairly ascribes all the faults of women to her.

That I have longed long to re-deliver.   95
I pray you, now receive them.

HAMLET   No, not I;
I never gave you aught.*

OPHELIA My honoured lord, you know right well you did;
And, with them, words* of so sweet breath composed
As made the things more rich. Their perfume lost,   100
Take these again;* for to the noble mind
Rich gifts wax* poor when givers prove unkind.
There, my lord.   [*She hands the presents back to him*]

HAMLET Ha, ha! Are you honest?

OPHELIA My lord?

HAMLET Are you fair?*   105

OPHELIA What means your lordship?

HAMLET That if you be honest and fair, your honesty should admit no
discourse* to your beauty.

OPHELIA Could beauty, my lord, have better commerce* than with   110
honesty?

HAMLET Ay, truly; for the power of beauty will sooner transform
honesty from what it is to a bawd* than the force of honesty
can translate beauty into his likeness. This was sometime a
paradox, but now the time* gives it proof. I did love you   115
once.

OPHELIA Indeed, my lord, you made me believe so.

HAMLET You should not have believed me, for virtue cannot so
inoculate* our old stock but we shall relish of it. I loved you
not.   120

OPHELIA I was the more deceived.

HAMLET Get thee to a nunnery.* Why wouldst thou be a breeder of
sinners? I am myself indifferent* honest. But yet I could
accuse me* of such things, that it were better my mother had
not borne me. I am very proud, revengeful, ambitious; with   125
more offences at my beck* than I have thoughts to put them
in, imagination to give them shape, or time to act them in.
What should such fellows as I do crawling between earth
and heaven? We are arrant* knaves, all; believe none of us.
Go thy ways* to a nunnery. – Where's your father?   130

OPHELIA At home, my lord.

HAMLET Let the doors be shut upon him, that he may play the fool
nowhere but in 's own house. Farewell.

OPHELIA [*Aside*] O, help him, you sweet heavens!

HAMLET If thou dost marry, I'll give thee this plague for thy dowry –   135

137   *calumny:* false charges (against your behaviour).
138   *thou wilt needs:* you must – strongly emphasized – 'if indeed you have to'.
139   *monsters* – This is a very powerful word; it means here an inhumanly wicked person, one
           who is 'unnatural' in his behaviour. Women, Hamlet contends, can drive men
           to such a condition.
142   *paintings* – i.e. painting the face, make-up.
144   *You jig . . . your ignorance* (line 145): You walk about with dance-like steps (*jig*), you drag
           your feet (*amble*), you talk in a lisping voice, and you give fancy names
           (*nickname*) to the things which God has created, and pretend that this affected
           behaviour, which is designed to entice men (*wantonness*) comes from innocence
           of what is the normal way (*ignorance*). – This long accusation relates to Hamlet's
           main theme, that women are treacherous deceivers.
145   *Go to . . . on 't:* Away with you! I will have no more of it.
147   *all but one* – This refers to Claudius, of course, who is listening behind the arras. Hamlet
           storms out, with only the vaguest ideas of how his purposes may be effected.
           But the words *all but one* may have been an inducement to some sort of action.
           Ophelia's speech is all love and sorrow for his condition. Coleridge wrote of it,
           'Ophelia's soliloquy is the perfection of love – so exquisitely unselfish.'
151   *expectancy . . . state:* hope and embellishment (*rose*) of this country (*state*) which he
           adorned (*fair*).
152   *glass . . . form:* mirror of fashion and the model (*mould*) on which men formed their
           behaviour (*form*). – He had been looked up to see as a pattern of good taste.
154   *deject:* dejected, downcast.
155   *music vows* – i.e. vows (of love), which were as music to her ears.
157   *jangled out of tune:* rung noisily in the wrong order. – This simile extends the metaphor
           of *music* (line 155), and also touches upon the general Elizabethan notion of
           harmony: what was in the 'proper' order was good, reasonable, harmonious.
           Adverse happenings came because the proper, harmonious order was dis-
           turbed. This could apply even to a shooting star – a bad portent, for harmony
           could only be maintained if stars kept to their proper courses. (Cf. I.v.17 and
           IV.vii.15 and the notes to these lines.)
158   *blown youth:* youth in full blossom. – The idea of the flower (*rose*, line 151, and *sucked the
           honey*, line 155) is returned to here.
159   *ecstasy:* madness. – The Greek word from which *ecstasy* comes means 'being outside
           oneself', i.e. not according to one's true nature.
161   What the King has to say to Polonius, and the first part of Polonius's reply, are evidently
           not for Ophelia to hear. On the Shakespearean stage she would be standing at
           the outer edge, well away from the point back-stage at which they enter. We
           can assume that her father addresses her when he and the King reach her at
           the front (line 177).
161   *affections:* feelings.
162   *Nor what . . . madness:* and what he said (*spake*) . . . did not sound like madness either. –
           The negative aspect is emphasized here: *Nor . . . not.*
164   *melancholy . . . brood:* disposition to sadness (*melancholy*) sits brooding (*on brood*). –
           Melancholy was thought of as being one kind of 'humour', i.e. a general
           physical and mental disposition which governed one's view of life. The fact
           that it was thought to 'reign' over one's behaviour accounts for *sits* here.
165   *I do doubt . . . danger:* I fear (*do doubt*) that the hatching and what comes out (*disclose*) will
           be dangerous. – The image of new-born birds coming out of their shells began
           with *brood* in the line before.
168   *set it down:* decreed – i.e. issued written orders.
169   *For the demand . . . tribute:* in order to demand the tribute they are neglecting to pay us. –
           This tribute, known as *Danegeld*, was first paid to the Danes by King Ethelred
           II of England (991); in return, the Danes agreed not to invade and plunder the
           country.
170   *Haply:* Perhaps.
171   *variable objects:* various things to look at.
172   *something-settled:* somewhat settled.
173   *puts him . . . himself:* causes him to be very different in this way from his usual manner
           (*fashion of himself*). – His brain, constantly working over this matter (*still
           beating*), makes his behaviour quite strange.

be thou as chaste as ice, as pure as snow, thou shalt not
escape calumny.* Get thee to a nunnery, go. Farewell. Or, if
thou wilt needs* marry, marry a fool; for wise men know
well enough what monsters* you make of them. To a nunnery, go, and quickly too. Farewell.   140

OPHELIA [Aside] O heavenly powers, restore him!

HAMLET I have heard of your paintings* too, well enough. God has
given you one face, and you make yourselves another. You
jig,* you amble, and you lisp, and nickname God's creatures,
and make your wantonness your ignorance. Go to,* I'll no   145
more on 't; it hath made me mad. I say, we will have no more
marriages. Those that are married already, all but one,*
shall live; the rest shall keep as they are. To a nunnery, go.
                                                        [Exit

OPHELIA O, what a noble mind is here o'erthrown!
The courtier's, soldier's, scholar's eye, tongue, sword,   150
Th' expectancy* and rose of the fair state,
The glass* of fashion and the mould of form,
Th' observed of all observers – quite, quite down!
And I, of ladies most deject* and wretched,
That sucked the honey of his music* vows,   155
Now see that noble and most sovereign reason,
Like sweet bells jangled* out of tune and harsh;
That unmatched form and feature of blown* youth
Blasted with ecstasy.* O, woe is me
To have seen what I have seen, see what I see!   160

Enter KING *and* POLONIUS.

KING* Love! His affections* do not that way tend;
Nor* what he spake, though it lacked form a little,
Was not like madness. There's something in his soul
O'er which his melancholy* sits on brood;
And I do doubt* the hatch and the disclose   165
Will be some danger; which for to prevent,
I have in quick determination
Thus set it down:* he shall with speed to England,
For the demand of* our neglected tribute.
Haply,* the seas, and countries different,   170
With variable objects,* shall expel
This something-settled* matter in his heart,
Whereon his brains still beating puts* him thus
From fashion of himself. What think you on 't?

180   *hold:* consider.
182   *griefs:* grievances, causes of sorrow.
182   *round:* frank.
183   *placed . . . in the ear Of* – i.e. listening secretly to.

III. ii.   Hamlet gives the players some last-minute advice before Polonius haste..s in, eager to get the play started. Hamlet talks to Horatio, first praising him and then explaining the purpose of the play. Hamlet talks distractedly to the royal party as they enter.

There is a dumb-show; a king is poisoned in his sleep, and after gestures of mourning his queen receives the amorous advances of the poisoner.

There is a short prologue, and the play begins.

The player-queen, Baptista, and the player-king, Gonzago, talk of love and death. She is devoted to him, and if she lost him, nothing would persuade her to marry again. He lies down and falls asleep.

The real King and Queen are now aroused.

The player-king's nephew, Lucianus, pours poison into Gonzago's ear; he wants the kingship and Baptista.

The King jumps up, stopping the play; his guilt is revealed. When he leaves, Hamlet is elated; Horatio confirms his impressions of the King. Rosencrantz and Guildenstern, when they break in, show they are now on the King's side; Hamlet admits to nothing, but confuses them with ambiguous remarks. He bewilders Polonius, making him agree to contradictory statements. Alone, he speaks of the oppression of supernatural forces driving him to vengeance, and vows he will do nothing to harm his mother.

This scene includes the play-within-the-play, which is the turning-point of the whole drama; suspicions are confirmed and from now on the action centres on the struggle between Hamlet and his uncle. It takes place in the great hall of the castle at Elsinore. This would be furnished (in the imagination of Shakespeare's audience) with a simple stage at one end, surrounded by hangings and lit by lamps. Hamlet, sitting at Ophelia's feet, is with the rest of the audience in comparative darkness below the stage.

The nature of the struggle between Hamlet and the King is clarified by Hamlet's intellectual endeavour to balance passion and thought (*blood and judgement*). This endeavour is for him the way to attain an objectively correct view of nature. One stage in the progress towards this awareness is the player-king's speech (III.ii.174ff.). This speech looks at first sight undramatic, and long enough to hold up the gathering speed of the plot. Indeed it is the part of the player-king's role in the play which least resembles old Hamlet (who evidently had no reservations about his wife's virtue and devotion). But it is significant in at least two ways. First, its ordered movement of rhyming couplets, presenting wise generalizations on the nature of man and his actions, contrasts vividly with the language of the rest of the play and clearly marks off for the audience the play-within-the-play. Second, like Hamlet's advice to the player at the beginning of the scene, it stands for a temperate view of action and life, unlike (for instance) the player-queen's extravagant protestations of devotion.

The second consideration suggests that this is the speech Hamlet himself wrote for the play. By the end of the speech, the proposition has become universalized: we must expect purposes not to lead to results: *our devices still* [i.e. always] *are overthrown*, however passionate the desires may have been. As the dumb-show foreshadowed the play-within-the play – or rather showed what course it would have taken if the King had not stopped it – this reflection looks chiefly to the second half of the play.

Now begins the long train of pressures on Claudius. Hamlet can in some measure control them, because his purposes are clear; he has been shown learning about the nature of man and how he may master it. But reason has not excluded passion; it has come to reckon with it.

1   *speech* – This may be the speech Hamlet said he would write for insertion in the play (II.ii.514), though it is never made clear which actual lines are referred to. The entire theme of the Gonzago murder is relevant and meets Hamlet's needs exactly. But his advice here may, after all, refer to a speech which the actors have just been running through. Hamlet's suggestions as to how it should be delivered are, of course, given for this particular occasion. He was not averse loud declamation of speeches in other settings, e.g. the 'Pyrrhus speech' at II.ii.425ff. Here he wants the words spoken *trippingly*, i.e. lightly.

POLONIUS It shall do well; but yet do I believe   175
          The origin and commencement of his grief
          Sprung from neglected love. – How now, Ophelia!
          You need not tell us what Lord Hamlet said;
          We heard it all. – [*To the* KING] My lord, do as you please;
          But, if you hold* it fit, after the play   180
          Let his queen mother all alone entreat him
          To show his griefs.* Let her be round* with him.
          And I'll be placed,* so please you, in the ear
          Of all their conference. If she find him not,
          To England send him, or confine him where   185
          Your wisdom best shall think.
KING   It shall be so;
          Madness in great ones must not unwatched go.
                                              [*Exeunt*

scene ii

A hall in the castle.

Enter HAMLET *and two or three of the* PLAYERS.

HAMLET Speak the speech,* I pray you, as I pronounced it to you,
        trippingly on the tongue; but if you mouth* it, as many of
        your players* do, I had as lief* the town crier* spoke my lines.
        Nor do not saw* the air too much with your hand, thus [*He*

---

2   *mouth:* shout – with exaggerated movements of the mouth.
3   *your players* – i.e. players in general, 'the ones you all know about'. Hamlet is not thinking
            especially of their own company.
3   *I had as lief:* I would like it just as much as if . . . – i.e. not at all.
3   *the town crier* was a local government officer employed to go around the town with a bell
            and announce orders and news in a loud voice for all to hear.
4   *saw* – i.e. cut as with saw.

5   *use all gently:* do everything quietly, without violence – with a *temperance* of manner (line 7). Hamlet fears that if the play is acted with too much noise and heightened stage effects it will lose some of its power to reach the heart.

9   *robustious:* violent.

9   *periwig-pated* – i.e. with his head (*pate*) covered by a wig. It seems that in Shakespeare's day wigs were seldom worn except by actors; they did not become common in ordinary use until the reign of Charles II, in the middle of the seventeenth century.

10   *the groundlings:* the poorer theatre-goers who stood on the ground in the open courtyard of the theatre, where there was no flooring or seating (see Introduction, p. xxiii). – They are referred to as that part of the audience with the least cultivated taste.

11   *capable of:* able to appreciate.

11   *inexplicable:* senseless.

13   *Termagant . . . Herod* – These were characters which played extremely violent parts in the traditional 'Mystery Plays' of medieval England. Mystery plays were performed by members of leagues of tradesmen (known as the 'mysteries' of the various trades), and generally told some version of the story of Christianity. *Termagant* was seen as a turbulent god of the Saracens. *Herod* is the furious tyrant who in history ruled the Jews at the time Christ was born; *it out-herods Herod* means '(such a performance) is more extreme than even Herod was'.

17   *your tutor* – i.e. your guide (in how you play the part).

19   *modesty:* moderation.

19   *from* – i.e. remote from.

21   *to hold . . . to nature* – This is a well-known comment on the aims of a play. It does not mean that every play should be like real life, but that the acting should not be outlandish or exaggerated.

22   *scorn her own image:* (show) contempt (*scorn*) how she looks. – If plays are acted with moderation, qualities in them such as *virtue* and contempt will be seen clearly, and, as in a mirror, we shall see something of ourselves too, in relation to these qualities.

23   *pressure:* impression.

24   *come tardy off:* not well finished off.

25   *unskilful:* uneducated – contrasting with *judicious* later in the line.

26   *censure . . . must:* the judgement of one of which – i.e. one judicious person.

26   *in your allowance:* you will admit.

27   *others* – i.e. the *unskilful,* the uneducated.

29   *profanely* – He does not want to utter profanity though he goes on to suggest that these players he is talking about cannot be Christians.

32   *journeymen:* day-labourers – paid by the day, and therefore not of the quality of a skilled craftsman.

34   *indifferently:* somewhat.

35   *clowns* – These comic figures took the parts in plays which brought in humour, usually as a relief from tragic action. They were the spiritual descendants of the 'vices' in the older religious plays, who used to bring in light humorous relief into the Bible stories. Hamlet objects to the way clowns like to draw attention to themselves on the stage by saying and doing things outside the script of the play.

37   *there be of them:* there are some of them.

37   *some quantity . . . spectators:* some stupid (*barren*) members of the audience.

39   *question* – i.e. matter, part of the plot.

makes gestures in the air with his hands]; but use all gently.*   5
For in the very torrent, tempest, and, as I may say, whirlwind
of your passion, you must acquire and beget a temperance
that may give it smoothness. O, it offends me to the soul to
hear a robustious,* periwig-pated* fellow tear a passion to
tatters, to very rags, to split the ears of the groundlings,* who,   10
for the most part, are capable of* nothing but inexplicable*
dumb-shows and noise. I would have such a fellow whipped
for o'erdoing Termagant;* it out-herods Herod. Pray you,
avoid it.

FIRST PLAYER   I warrant your honour.   15

HAMLET   Be not too tame neither, but let your own discretion be your
tutor.* Suit the action to the word, the word to the action;
with this special observance, that you o'erstep not the
modesty* of nature. For anything so overdone is from* the
purpose of playing, whose end, both at the first and now,   20
was and is, to hold,* as 'twere, the mirror up to nature; to
show virtue her own feature, scorn* her own image, and the
very age and body of the time his form and pressure.* Now,
this overdone, or come tardy off,* though it make the unskilful* laugh, cannot but make the judicious grieve; the   25
censure* of the which one must, in your allowance,* o'er-
weigh a whole theatre of others.* O, there be players that I
have seen play – and heard others praise, and that highly –
not to speak it profanely,* that, neither having the accent of
Christians, nor the gait of Christian, pagan, nor man, have   30
so strutted and bellowed that I have thought some of nature's
journeymen* had made them, and not made them well, they
imitated humanity so abominably.

FIRST PLAYER   I hope we have reformed that indifferently* with us, sir.

HAMLET   O, reform it altogether. And let those that play your clowns*   35
speak no more than is set down for them. For there be of
them* that will themselves laugh to set on some quantity* of
barren spectators to laugh too; though, in the mean time,
some necessary question* of the play be then to be considered; that's villainous, and shows a most pitiful ambition   40
in the fool that uses it. Go, make you ready.

[*Exeunt* PLAYERS

Enter POLONIUS, ROSENCRANTZ, *and* GUILDENSTERN.

[*To* POLONIUS] How now, my lord! Will the king hear this
piece of work?

44   *presently:* immediately.
48   *Horatio* – Hamlet continues to have a special regard for Horatio. Since Hamlet has just given Rosencrantz and Guildenstern a plain hint that they should leave him, we are to believe that he has some indication of Horatio's arrival, and wants to be alone with him.
50   *thou art e'en . . . withal:* you are indeed (*e'en*) as honourable (*just*) a man as I ever met with (*coped withal*) in my dealings with people (*conversation*).
53   *advancement:* advantage – especially in respect to one's position in the world. Hamlet is saying that there can be no reason for him to flatter Horatio, because he has no status or wealth (*revenue*) and can give Hamlet nothing in return. Hamlet's view of life is here very cynical; he takes it that no one compliments anyone else except with an eye to his own advantage.
56   *let the candied tongue . . . fawning* (line 58): let the sugared tongue (of the flatterer) lick the absurd pomp (of a person of higher status), and let the joints of the knee bend in profit (*pregnant*) when material advantage (*thrift*) is likely to result from this flattering behaviour (*fawning*). – The image is very bold and tightly packed in these lines; the tongue with sugared words of flattery on it, and the knee which bows humbly to others of higher status are, Hamlet thinks, fully justified if material advantage comes to the flatterer. It is again a cynical, disillusioned comment on life.
59   *dear:* precious, highly valued.
60   *could of men distinguish:* discriminate among men – i.e. distinguishing the good from the bad.
60   *election:* choice. – Hamlet makes the choice sound reasoned and calculated by using *election* here and *sealed* (marked deliberately) in the following line.
63   *A man . . . thanks:* a man who has taken both the reverses (*buffets*) and the blessings (*rewards*) of fortune with the same thanks. – This and what immediately follows show that Hamlet recognizes Horatio's character as something very different from his own. It is characteristic of human relationships that Hamlet and Horatio should therefore be close to one another.
65   *blood and judgement* – i.e. passion and reason. It was thought that the source of passion, rash action, was the blood.
66   *a pipe* – This image foreshadows the incident of the recorders later in the scene (line 322ff.). The stops of the pipe (mentioned in the following line) are the holes which are covered or uncovered to vary the notes.
68   *passion's slave:* the slave of passion – one who is entirely obedient to his passions and takes no account of what his reason tells him.
69   *my heart's core:* the centre of my heart – i.e. the deepest, inner point of my being. It has been suggested that the use of the word *core* here is partly due to a pun on the Latin word *cor* (heart).
70   *Something too much of this:* I have given you rather (*something*) too much on this subject.
75   *the very comment . . . soul:* your most intent observation.
76   *occulted:* hidden.
77   *itself unkennel in one speech:* reveal itself during one particular speech. – The speech is the one he mentioned at II.ii.513:

> *You could, for a need, study a speech of some dozen or sixteen lines, which*
> *I would set down and insert in* [the play].

78   *damnéd* – i.e. not a ghost which can be believed but one which has deceived us, a visitation from hell, sent by the devil.
79   *as foul . . . stithy:* as black (evil) as Vulcan's workshop. – Vulcan was the Roman god of fire, associated with volcanic islands, and having the Cyclops working for him (see II.ii.464: *the Cyclops' hammers*). The reference here is linked with the idea of hell (*a damnéd ghost*).

POLONIUS   And the queen, too, and that presently.*

HAMLET   Bid the players make haste.   [*Exit* POLONIUS   45
Will you two help to hasten them?

ROSENCRANTZ &   We will, my lord.
GUILDENSTERN

[*Exeunt* ROSENCRANTZ *and* GUILDENSTERN

HAMLET   What, ho, Horatio!*

Enter HORATIO.

HORATIO   Here, sweet lord, at your service.

HAMLET   Horatio, thou art e'en* as just a man   50
As e'er my conversation coped withal.

HORATIO   O, my dear lord –

HAMLET   Nay, do not think I flatter;
For what advancement* may I hope from thee,
That no revenue hast but thy good spirits
To feed and clothe thee? Why should the poor be
flattered?
                                                          55
No, let the candied tongue* lick absurd pomp,
And crook the pregnant hinges of the knee
Where thrift may follow fawning. Dost thou hear?
Since my dear* soul was mistress of her choice,
And could of men* distinguish, her election*   60
Hath sealed thee for herself. For thou hast been
As one, in suffering all, that suffers nothing;
A man* that fortune's buffets and rewards
Has ta'en with equal thanks. And blest are those
Whose blood* and judgement are so well commingled   65
That they are not a pipe* for Fortune's finger
To sound what stop she please. Give me that man
That is not passion's slave,* and I will wear him
In my heart's core,* ay, in my heart of heart,
As I do thee. – Something* too much of this. –   70
There is a play tonight before the king;
One scene of it comes near the circumstance,
Which I have told thee, of my father's death.
I prithee, when thou seest that act a-foot,
Even with the very comment* of thy soul   75
Observe my uncle. If his occulted* guilt
Do not itself unkennel* in one speech,
It is a damnéd* ghost that we have seen,
And my imaginations are as foul*

83   *censure . . . seeming:* giving our opinions on what sort of face he shows.
84   *If he steal . . . theft:* if he gets away with anything at all (i.e. the slightest change in his
            manner) while this play is on, and escape (*scape*) my notice (*detecting*), I will
            pay for it – literally, pay for the thing 'stolen' (*theft*).
86   *idle:* mad. – He must take on the stupid manner which he has already been affecting in
            front of the courtiers.
*   *flourish:* loud trumpet call.
88   *cousin* – an address used for any close relative.
89   *the chameleon's dish* – It was popularly believed that the chameleon (a kind of lizard) lived
            on air alone. Hamlet has deliberately taken *fares* to suggest 'food' ('good fare'),
            and talks about eating.
90   *promise-crammed* – They have both made promises; Claudius has promised him he will be
            next in succession (I.ii.109); Hamlet has promised he will avenge his father's
            murder (I.v.102–3). But so far these have not been put into action.
92   *are not mine:* have no bearing on what I have just said.
94   *i' th' university* – In Shakespeare's time, students at Oxford and Cambridge frequently
            performed plays in the college halls. Polonius goes on to say how he took the
            part of Julius Caesar in a university play. (Shakespeare's own *Julius Caesar* was
            perhaps written only a few months before *Hamlet.*)
97   *Capitol* – Caesar was in fact killed in the Theatre of Pompey, not the Capitol. But the
            mistake is often made, as in Shakespeare's own *Julius Caesar* and *Antony and
            Cleopatra.*
99   *brute:* brutal – with a pun on Brutus. Hamlet continues to treat Polonius very unkindly;
            perhaps this is a feature of his assumed 'madness'.
101 *they stay . . . patience:* they are waiting for (*stay upon*) your permission (*patience*) to begin.
103 *metal:* material.

As Vulcan's stithy. Give him heedful note;   80
For I mine eyes will rivet to his face,
And, after, we will both our judgements join
In censure* of his seeming.

HORATIO   Well, my lord;
If he steal* aught the whilst this play is playing,
And scape detecting, I will pay the theft.   85

HAMLET They're coming to the play; I must be idle;*
Get you a place.

*Danish March. A flourish.**

Enter KING, QUEEN, POLONIUS, OPHELIA, ROSENCRANTZ,
GUILDENSTERN, *and other* LORDS *attending, with the* GUARD
carrying torches.

KING How fares our cousin* Hamlet?

HAMLET Excellent, i' faith; of the chameleon's dish:* I eat the air,
promise-crammed.* You cannot feed capons so.   90

KING I have nothing with this answer, Hamlet; these words are
not mine.*

HAMLET No, nor mine now. – [*To* POLONIUS] My lord, you played
once i' th' university,* you say?

POLONIUS That did I, my lord; and was accounted a good actor.   95

HAMLET And what did you enact?

POLONIUS I did enact Julius Caesar. I was killed i' th' Capitol;* Brutus
killed me.

HAMLET It was a brute* part of him to kill so capital a calf there. – Be
the players ready?   100

ROSENCRANTZ Ay, my lord; they stay* upon your patience.

QUEEN Come hither, my dear Hamlet, sit by me.

HAMLET No, good mother; here's metal* more attractive.
                                    [*He indicates* OPHELIA

POLONIUS [*To the* KING] O, ho! Do you mark that?

HAMLET Lady, shall I lie in your lap?   105
                              [*Lying down at* OPHELIA'S *feet*

OPHELIA No, my lord.

HAMLET I mean, my head upon your lap?

OPHELIA Ay, my lord.

HAMLET Do you think I meant country matters?

OPHELIA I think nothing, my lord.   110

HAMLET That's a fair thought to lie between maids' legs.

OPHELIA What is, my lord?

HAMLET Nothing.

117   *your only jig-maker:* (I am) the only jig-maker among you here – i.e. the only person who is gay. A jig was a short, lively comedy. Hamlet has accused Polonius of sleeping at plays except when there is a *jig* (II.ii.475).

119   *within's:* within these.

122   *a suit of sables:* clothing trimmed with rich black fur – black, indeed, like the devil's suit, but rich and grand, not clothes for mourning.

124   *by'r Lady* – He swears by Our Lady, the Virgin Mary.

125   *shall he suffer . . . on:* he will have to bear being forgotten.

126   *the hobby-horse* – The *epitaph* must be from a ballad, now lost; it is quoted in other plays of the period. The hobby-horse was a man present at country games who had the figure of a horse strapped round his waist. The line of the ballad may refer to this part of the May games being discontinued under pressure from the Puritans.

*   Hautboys: Oboes – musical instruments (pipes with reeds).

*   The dumb-show – This is the story of the play performed in actions, but without words. The story is, of course, that of the death of Hamlet's father. It is puzzling, therefore, that the King, Claudius, shows no reaction to it until it is repeated in words (line 143 and onwards). It is difficult to see why Shakespeare presented the story of the play twice, since the dumb-show should have made the matter perfectly clear. Dumb-shows were not unknown on the English stage at the time (there is one in *Macbeth*, IV.i), but they were never, so far as we know, linked with a repetition of the same story with words added. It seems, however, that the theatre in Denmark had such a tradition. An English diarist, Abraham de la Pryme, records how, in the year 1688, a body of Danish soldiers were stationed in the north of England, and how they 'acted a play in their language'. He noticed that 'all the postures were shown first . . . and when they had run through all so, they then began to act . . .' (Joseph Hunter: *New Illustrations of the Life, Studies, and Writings of Shakespeare*, London, 1845, ii.249.) Ophelia's remark: *Belike this show imports the argument of the play* (line 130), shows that she, at least, was unfamiliar with a tradition of mime in this form.
        But since the directions for the dumb-show give the action very clearly, the King's silence needs some further explanation. The best and most likely, perhaps, is that Claudius and his Queen were not watching. We know that great lords treated their players with little respect (in the last act of *A Midsummer Night's Dream*, for instance), and it is possible that the Danish custom of the dumb-show was a device to draw the attention of the audience to the play, to stop them from talking to one another and prepare to listen.

*   *show of protestation* – i.e. she shows by her action that she is affirming ('protesting') something very strongly, here her love for her husband.

*   *takes her up* – i.e. brings her to her feet from the kneeling position.

*   *declines:* leans.

*   *lays him:* lies.

*   *Anon:* At once.

*   *loth:* reluctant.

129   *miching malicho* – (perhaps) 'secret mischief'. (The word *miching* may be associated with the word *micher*, 'truant', which occurs in Shakespeare and elsewhere; *malicho* has been associated with the Spanish word *malhecho*, meaning 'misdeed'. (The First Folio prints it as a foreign word.) If this explanation is correct, Hamlet must mean that both the poisoner and he himself are causing 'secret mischief'.

130   *Belike . . . play:* Perhaps this dumb-show indicates (*imports*) the plot (*argument*) of the play.

*   PROLOGUE – i.e. the person who speaks the prologue of the play.

132   *keep counsel:* keep secrets, keep things to themselves.

134   *Be not you:* If you are not.

136   *naught:* wicked.

OPHELIA   You are merry, my lord.

HAMLET   Who, I?   115

OPHELIA   Ay, my lord.

HAMLET   O God, your only jig-maker.* What should a man do but be
merry? For, look you, how cheerfully my mother looks, and
my father died within's* two hours.

OPHELIA   Nay, 'tis twice two months, my lord.   120

HAMLET   So long? Nay, then, let the devil wear black, for I'll have a
suit of sables.* O heavens! Die two months ago, and not
forgotten yet? Then there's hope a great man's memory may
outlive his life half a year; but, by'r Lady,* he must build
churches, then, or else shall he suffer* not thinking on, with   125
the hobby-horse,* whose epitaph is, 'For, O, for, O, the
hobby-horse is forgot.'

Hautboys play. The dumb-show* enters.*

Enter a KING *and a* QUEEN *very lovingly; the* QUEEN *embracing
him, and he her. She kneels, and makes show of protestation*
unto him. He takes her up,* and declines* his head upon her
neck; lays him* down upon a bank of flowers; she, seeing him
asleep, leaves him. Anon* comes in a fellow, takes off his
crown, kisses it, and pours poison in the* KING'S *ears, and exit.
The* QUEEN *returns; finds the* KING *dead, and makes passionate
action. The* POISONER, *with some two or three* MUTES, *comes in
again, seeming to lament with her. The dead body is carried
away. The* POISONER *woos the* QUEEN *with gifts; she seems
loth* and unwilling awhile, but in the end accepts his love.*

[*Exeunt*

OPHELIA   What means this, my lord?

HAMLET   Marry, this is miching *malicho;** it means mischief.

OPHELIA   Belike* this show imports the argument of the play.   130

Enter PROLOGUE.*

HAMLET   We shall know by this fellow. The players cannot keep
counsel;* they'll tell all.

OPHELIA   Will he tell us what this show meant?

HAMLET   Ay, or any show that you'll show him. Be* not you ashamed
to show, he'll not shame to tell you what it means.   135

OPHELIA   You are naught,* you are naught. I'll mark the play.

PROLOGUE   For us, and for our tragedy,
                           Here stooping to your clemency,
                           We beg your hearing patiently.   [*Exit*

140 *posy:* a motto written on the inside of an engagement or wedding ring – usually in the form of a single rhyme, e.g. 'God above / increase our love', 'Let love abide / till death divide.' Hamlet is ridiculing the simple rhyming of the prologue. (The word *posy* is associated with *poetry*.)

The play-within-the-play which follows is in the old style of English tragedy, characterized by a heavy, rhetorical style of speaking, by rhyme, and by the lengthy repetition of a single idea in different forms. In the first four lines spoken by the Player King, for instance, all the elaborate arithmetic means in the end only: 'It is thirty years since . . .'. The rhyming of the lines and other old-fashioned devices do much to distinguish this interlude from the main dialogue of the play. There are some quaint words in it: *cart* (chariot), *sheen* (light), *woe is me* (alas), and some references to classical mythology.

It is not possible to point to any passage in this play as the *dozen or sixteen lines* Hamlet said he would write for himself (II.ii.514–5). Perhaps the best explanation is that there was a play which the players knew well called *The Murder of Gonzago*. The plot of this play was in some respects remarkably like the account of his father's death, as told by the ghost. By altering it somewhat (but in a way which is not apparent from the text) he brought the plot even closer to the event as he believed it to have taken place, and the finished play was so close to reality as he understood it that the King could not fail to see it was aimed at him. But he restrains himself until the scene of the poisoning, and this is the point that Hamlet and Horatio recall afterwards (line 273). No play called *The Murder of Gonzago* is known to have existed; and even if it had, no one could imagine it would have followed Claudius's own history so closely that it needed no adaptation at all.

143 *Phoebus' cart:* the chariot of Phoebus (the sun god of the Greeks). – A Greek story told how the sun was Phoebus' chariot draw across the sky each day by horses.

144 *Neptune's salt wash . . . ground* – i.e. the sea and the land. Neptune was the Roman god of the sea; Tellus was the ancient Italian goddess of the earth; *orbéd:* round, like an orb.

145 *with borrowed sheen* – i.e. with light (*sheen:* shine) borrowed from the sun. There are twelve *moons* (months) in each of the thirty years.

147 *Hymen* – the God of Marriage, who was thought to join the hands of husband and wife in the marriage ceremony.

148 *commutual:* given to and received from each other.

150 *count o'er . . . done:* count before (*ere*) our love for one another is finished.

151 *woe is me:* alas.

152 *cheer:* cheerfulness.

153 *I distrust you:* I am worried about you.

154 *Discomfort . . . must:* it must not in the least (*nothing*) grieve (*Discomfort*) you, my lord. – The whole phrase has been inverted here to fit into the rhyme scheme.

155 *hold quantity . . . extremity:* vary together; they either have nothing in them at all (*aught*), or exist together in extremes (*extremity*). – In women, fear and love always exist together.

157 *proof:* experience.

158 *sized:* of a particular size. – She goes on to say that her fear for him is of the same size, a point which she has already made in general.

162 *My operant powers . . . do:* my active (*operant*) powers are ceasing (*leave*) to perform (*to do*) their functions. – He feels he may soon die.

163 *behind* – i.e. after me.

165 *confound the rest:* may the rest (of what you were going to say) be cursed.

168 *None wed . . . first* – This is a crude example of dramatic irony; the Player Queen perhaps means, 'No woman shall marry a second husband except she who kills the first.' Something very like this has already been seen in the dumb-show, but the Player Queen refers to it as if it could never happen.

169 *Wormwood* – something bitterly wounding to a person's feelings. Literally, *wormwood* is the name of a bitter herb.

170 *instances:* causes.

170 *move:* bring about.

171 *respects of thrift:* considerations of gain, not (*none*) of love.

172 *A second time . . . bed:* If a second husband ever makes love to me, I shall be killing my husband a second time.

HAMLET Is this a prologue, or the posy* of a ring?   140
OPHELIA 'Tis brief, my lord.
HAMLET As woman's love.

Enter two PLAYERS *us King and Queen.*

PLAYER KING Full thirty times hath Phoebus' cart* gone round
Neptune's salt wash* and Tellus' orbéd ground,
And thirty dozen moons with borrowed sheen*   145
About the world have times twelve thirties been,
Since love our hearts, and Hymen* did our hands,
Unite commutual* in most sacred bands.

PLAYER QUEEN So many journeys may the sun and moon
Make us again count o'er* ere love be done!   150
But, woe is me,* you are so sick of late,
So far from cheer* and from your former state,
That I distrust* you. Yet, though I distrust,
Discomfort* you, my lord, it nothing must;
For women's fear and love hold quantity,*   155
In neither aught, or in extremity.
Now, what my love is, proof* hath made you know;
And as my love is sized,* my fear is so.
Where love is great, the littlest doubts are fear;
Where little fears grow great, great love grows there.   160

PLAYER KING Faith, I must leave thee, love, and shortly too;
My operant powers* their functions leave to do.
And thou shalt live in this fair world behind,*
Honoured, beloved; and haply one as kind
For husband shalt thou –

PLAYER QUEEN   O, confound the rest!*   165
Such love must needs be treason in my breast.
In second husband let me be accurst!
None wed the second* but who killed the first.

HAMLET [*Aside*] Wormwood,* wormwood.

PLAYER QUEEN The instances* that second marriage move*   170
Are base respects of thrift,* but none of love.
A second time* I kill my husband dead
When second husband kisses me in bed.

PLAYER KING I do believe you think what now you speak;
But what we do determine oft we break.   175

176   *Purpose:* Resolution. – Our resolutions depend entirely on (*the slave to*) memory; they are born in a moment of passion (*violent birth*), but their strength (*validity*) is poor.

178   *Which* – i.e. the *Purpose.*

179   *fall . . . they* – These words still refer to *Purpose*, but are in the plural forms since they are influenced by the simile-word *fruit*, which is taken as a plural.

180   *Most necessary 'tis:* It is inevitable. – In making resolutions we are, as it were, indebted only to ourselves, and it is not surprising that we do not always pay ourselves back.

185   *enactures:* fulfilment. – Lines 184–5 contain a clause which is perhaps the most elaborate of all in this complicated, rhetorical speech. 'The violence of grief or the violence of joy destroy not only themselves but the fulfilment (of resolutions) they brought with them'.

186   *Where joy . . .* – This and the following line mean that great joy and great sorrow exist together, and it is a matter of chance events, based on trivial causes (*slender accident*), which one happens to be uppermost at one time. The careful balance of the words, bringing together opposites in a carefully worked pattern (*Grief joys, joy grieves*) is characteristic of the rhetorical style in which this passage is cast.

188   *is not for aye:* does not last for ever.

188   *nor:* and so.

192   *flies* for *fly* – i.e. fly away, desert him.

193   *The poor advanced:* the poor man who has improved his position in life.

194   *hitherto:* up to this point.

194   *on fortune tend:* follow fortune.

195   *who not needs:* he who is not in need of anything.

196   *who in want . . . enemy:* he who in need puts a false friend to the test (*try*) at once confirms (*seasons*) him as an enemy.

198   *orderly:* in an orderly fashion – as good discourses should be concluded.

199   *Our wills . . . run:* What we wish to happen (*Our wills*), and what is planned for us by fate (our *fates*) are so much at variance (*contrary run*).

200   *devices:* schemes.

200   *still:* constantly.

201   *their ends . . . own:* the outcome (*ends*) (of our thoughts) is not in our own hands at all.

203   *die thy thoughts:* your thoughts must die, come to nothing.

204   *Nor earth . . . food:* Let the earth not give me food. – The Player Queen goes on to deliver a sort of curse against herself, which calls for many terrible consequences if she should marry again after losing her husband. The finite verbs in this passage are with one exception (note 205) in the subjunctive mood (e.g. *An anchor's cheer . . . be my scope! Each opposite . . . meet*—not *is, meets*, etc.), giving the meaning: 'Let this happen, and this, and this, if I ever marry a second time.' Note especially *pursue me lasting strife* (let unending strife pursue me – line 210).

205   *Sport:* Entertainment, amusement.

205   *lock* – This, by exception in this passage, is an imperative: 'Lock, shut away, from me all amusement (*Sport*) and rest.

207   *anchor's cheer . . . scope:* Let my end (in view) (*scope*) be the fare (*cheer*) of a hermit (*anchor*, i.e. *anchorite*) in confinement. – Anchorites were men or women who voluntarily cut themselves off from everyday life, and lived simply, in a cell attached to a church. Some editors have taken *cheer* to be a slip for *chair*, on the suggestion of a line in Joseph Hall's *Satires* (II.iv.p.18 in the edition of 1602):
       Sit seven yeres pining in an anchore's cheyre;
but it is likely that this line is a deliberate distortion of an established phrase, *anchor's cheer*, as in the line under discussion.

208   *Each opposite . . . have well:* Let everything which is in opposition to (*opposite*) looks of pleasurable fulfilment (i.e. turns pale (*blanks*) *the face of joy*) meet what I wish to turn out well. – May all her fondest wishes, she says in effect, remain unfulfilled.

210   *hence* – in the next world.

214   *fain I would beguile:* I would gladly while away (*beguile*, literally, 'cheat' the time by diverting my attention from it). – These words are charged with irony for those who know or guess that he will never wake from this sleep.

216   *twain:* two.

Purpose* is but the slave to memory,
Of violent birth, but poor validity;
Which* now, like fruit unripe, sticks on the tree,
But fall,* unshaken, when they mellow be.
Most necessary 'tis* that we forget   180
To pay ourselves what to ourselves is debt;
What to ourselves in passion we propose,
The passion ending, doth the purpose lose.
The violence of either grief or joy
Their own enactures* with themselves destroy;   185
Where joy* most revels, grief doth most lament,
Grief joys, joy grieves, on slender accident.
This world is not for aye;* nor* 'tis not strange
That even our loves should with our fortunes change;
For 'tis a question left us yet to prove,   190
Whether love lead fortune, or else fortune love.
The great man down, you mark his favourites flies;*
The poor advanced* makes friends of enemies.
And hitherto* doth love on fortune tend.*
For who not needs* shall never lack a friend;   195
And who in want* a hollow friend doth try,
Directly seasons him his enemy.
But, orderly* to end where I begun —
Our wills and fates* do so contrary run
That our devices* still* are overthrown;   200
Our thoughts are ours, their ends* none of our own.
So think thou wilt no second husband wed;
But die* thy thoughts when thy first lord is dead.
PLAYER QUEEN   Nor earth to me give* food, nor heaven light!
Sport* and repose lock* from me day and night!   205
To desperation turn my trust and hope!
An anchor's cheer* in prison be my scope!
Each opposite* that blanks the face of joy
Meet what I would have well, and it destroy!
Both here and hence* pursue me lasting strife   210
If, once a widow, ever I be wife!
HAMLET   If she should break it now!
PLAYER KING   'Tis deeply sworn. Sweet, leave me here awhile;
My spirits grow dull, and fain I would beguile*
The tedious day with sleep.   [Sleeps
PLAYER QUEEN   Sleep rock thy brain;   215
And never come mischance between us twain!*   [Exit

218   *protest:* promise (in public).

220   *argument:* plot. – This question of the King's seems to support the suggestion that he was not paying any attention to the dumb-show.

224   The Mouse-trap – Hamlet's name for the play, thought out at a moment's notice, recalls *catch* in II.ii.511.

224   *Tropically:* (Speaking) figuratively (a *trope* is a figure of speech). – It is not a play about a real mouse-trap, but about a situation which catches someone in the way a mouse is caught in a trap. The play is an *image* (line 225)—a representation.

225   *duke's:* king's—since Gonzago is referred to elsewhere as a king. It is evident that at the time Shakespeare was writing the titles *king*, *duke* and *count* were not carefully differentiated. They all stood for a ruler with sovereign power. Here, of course, the title *king* best suits Hamlet's purpose. The source of this story of Gonzago has never been discovered, even though Hamlet says, *The story is extant, and writ in choice Italian* (line 247 below).

226   *knavish:* wicked.

227   *we that . . . souls* – Here *free* means 'innocent', i.e. 'free from guilt', as at II.ii.537. The contrast between *Your majesty* and *we* is deliberate: cf. *Those that are married already, all but one* (III.i.147).

228   *let the galled . . . unwrung:* although the brokendown horse (*jade*), rubbed painfully by the collar (*galled*), may wince with pain, it is not our *withers* (neck-joints) which are wrenched (*-wrung*). – A form of these lines was a proverbial saying; it means, that we need worry only about what affects ourselves.

      This is one of the places in *Hamlet* where the rush of unusual words is too intense to be a source of pleasure in the good use of English. Hamlet may be given these words to say as a means of showing that his growing exasperation has to be concealed behind a curtain of obscure words. Other versions of the saying are much simpler, e.g.:

      the gall'd horse will soonest wince   (*Damon and Pythias*, 1582)

230   *the king* – i.e. Gonzago, called 'the duke' in line 225.

231   *a chorus* – i.e. a speaker at a play who explains or comments on the course of events, as in *Romeo and Juliet* and *Henry V*. In ancient Greek tragedy the chorus consisted of a number of interested spectators who performed the same function; today a chorus is a group of singers.

232   *interpret . . . dallying:* I could give the dialogue (*interpret*) between you and your lover if I could see you as puppets flirting (*dallying*) together. – Puppet-shows are shows in which dolls are made to act like human beings. There was, in Shakespeare's day, a person behind the scenes who made them move and another who spoke the dialogue fitted to the actions of the puppets; he was called 'the interpreter of the puppets'. Here Hamlet openly insults Ophelia by taking up her friendly remark about him being *as good as a chorus*, and turning it against her, saying that if he could see her and her lover dallying like puppets in a puppet-show, he would provide the dialogue. These bitter words further his purpose in debasing love in her eyes, as he does in the speeches beginning at III.i.122. *Get thee to a nunnery . . .*

234   *keen:* bitter.

235   *edge:* desire (for you). – Hamlet's remark is certainly indecent. It probably means, 'If you accept my desire for you, it will bring you to child-bed (*groaning*)'. The use of *edge* plays on Ophelia's word *keen*.

236   *better . . . worse* – i.e. even more witty (since now he is indulging in word-play) but less decent.

237   *mistake* – Many editors have changed this word (which appears here in all the early editions of the play) to *must take*. But *mistake* is most likely to be correct, or rather the joke brought out by the spelling *mis-take*, i.e. 'take misguidedly'. The reference is to the order of the marriage service in the Prayer Book of the Church of England, where the betrothed man and woman say they take each other in marriage 'for better or worse, richer or poorer'.

238   *pox:* a pox on it – a swear word. Hamlet is telling the player to stop making expressions of horrible villainy and to begin speaking his part.

239   *the croaking raven . . . revenge* – This is a condensed quotation from an old play, *The True Tragedy of Richard Third*, known to have been popular in Shakespeare's day:
      The screeking raven sits croking for revenge
      Whole herds of beasts comes bellowing for revenge.

HAMLET   *[To the* QUEEN] Madam, how like you this play?

QUEEN   The lady doth protest* too much, methinks.

HAMLET   O, but she'll keep her word.

KING   Have you heard the argument?* Is there no offence in 't?   220

HAMLET   No, no, they do but jest, poison in jest, no offence i' th' world.

KING   What do you call the play?

HAMLET   *The Mouse-trap.** Marry, how? Tropically.* This play is the image of a murder done in Vienna: Gonzago is the duke's*   225
name; his wife, Baptista. You shall see anon; 'tis a knavish* piece of work: but what o' that? Your majesty, and we* that have free souls, it touches us not; let the galled jade* wince, our withers are unwrung.

Enter PLAYER *as* LUCIANUS.

This is one Lucianus, nephew to the king.*   230

OPHELIA   You are as good as a chorus,* my lord.

HAMLET   I could interpret* between you and your love, if I could see the puppets dallying.

OPHELIA   You are keen,* my lord, you are keen.

HAMLET   It would cost you a groaning to take off my edge.*   235

OPHELIA   Still better,* and worse.

HAMLET   *[To the* PLAYER] So you mistake* your husbands. – Begin, murderer; pox,* leave thy damnable faces, and begin. Come – the croaking raven* doth bellow for revenge.

---

239 *(cont'd)*   These lines explain why Hamlet says the raven *doth bellow* here.
It was thought that the croaking of a raven was a forewarning of death. In the old play the king is talking about the terrors of his conscience: after all the murders he has been responsible for, the raven croaks for revenge against him, i.e. for his death. Hamlet must mean, 'The raven is waiting for the murder and the revenge which will follow.' He quotes from a play to hurry the players along; as in previous remarks of his, the language here is involved and close-packed.

240   *Thoughts black . . . :* The thoughts are black, etc. – The style of discourse here is especially
    strained and rhetorical.

241   *Confederate season:* an opportunity conspiring (to help the murderer). – The use of this
    word *confederate* here is very strained.

241   *else . . . seeing* – (perhaps) 'no other living thing looking on'; or maybe, 'no living thing
    seeing anything besides'.

242   *mixture rank* – i.e. the poison; *rank:* evil smelling, as at III.iii.36:
    my offence is rank
    The poison is made of herbs collected at midnight (*midnight weeds*), a time when
    they were thought to be most potent.

243   *Hecate's ban . . . infected:* three times (*thrice*) corrupted (*blasted*) by the curse (*ban*) of
    Hecate, three times infected (with poisonous potency). – Hecate (pronounced
    'hekit' here and elsewhere in Shakespeare) was a goddess of the underworld,
    associated with witchcraft and magic; she figures as the leader of the witches in
    Macbeth. The balance of this line is in the rhetorical style which characterizes
    the speeches of the play-within-the-play.

244   *dire:* dreadful.

245   *On wholesome . . . immediately:* (you poison) exercise your evil influence (*usurp*) on this
    healthy (*wholesome*) life without delay.

246   *for's estate:* in order to usurp his high rank – i.e. become king himself. It is as if Hamlet
    has seized on Lucianus' word *usurp* in the previous line, where it is used
    figuratively, and adapted the idea behind it to suit his own ends; the murderer
    'usurps' the estate.

250   *false fire* – literally, guns fired without being loaded with ammunition. Hamlet pretends
    in this metaphor that the play about Gonzago is not aimed at Claudius; and, as
    this is so, he wonders why Claudius should be frightened.

251   *fares:* is. – The Queen sees the King jump up, and asks him how he is.

252   *Give o'er*, for *give over:* stop.

253   *light* – The audience had evidently been sitting in darkness in the castle hall. But the king's
    request for light is also metaphorical: the darkness of the guilt arising from his
    crime is closing in upon him. When lights are brought he rushes away with
    the rest of the company.

255   *the stricken deer* – This is evidently from an old ballad, though no source for it has been
    discovered. But it is not impossible that Shakespeare wrote the stanza himself
    to sound like a ballad. The lines refer to a tradition that a wounded deer leaves
    the herd and goes away to weep. The uninjured deer (*hart ungallèd*) disports
    itself without showing any sympathy. That is what life (*the world*) is like; some
    are born to suffer, others not. Hamlet is now exultant, and in this scene grows
    steadily more excited as the success of his 'mouse-trap' delights him. But he
    too is really a *stricken deer*, not a *hart ungallèd*, although in his excitement he
    seems to forget this.

259   *a forest of feathers* – This apparently alludes to the feathers worn profusely by actors on
    the stage as part of their costume; *this . . . and a forest of feathers* must then
    mean, 'this (example of play-writing) and a crowd of actors to go with it'. But
    it must be admitted that here, as elsewhere in this scene, Hamlet indulges in
    the use of obscure words and references which, although dramatically
    significant as manifesting his highly-wrought excitement, do not make for
    conciseness and clarity.

260   *turn Turk:* take a turn for the worse – literally, change from a Christian to an infidel, i.e.
    if Hamlet had to earn his living.

260   *two Provincial roses . . . shoes:* two bows tied like damask roses on my open-work (*raced*)
    shoes. – A type of shoe with an open-work pattern and bows tied up in the
    shape of five double roses (perhaps 'roses from Provence' in France) was
    fashionable.

261   *fellowship:* partnership.

261   *cry:* company. – The word is used satirically; it would normally refer to a pack of hounds,
    but players were known to shout out their lines as Hamlet said (at the beginning
    of III.ii), and *cry* would thus be an appropriate name for a company of them.

263   *Half a share* – The players who acted in the theatres of Shakespeare's day did not draw
    salaries for their work but had a share in the profits. The amount they were
    entitled to depended on their number and on the share of the profits that went
    to the 'housekeepers', i.e. the proprietors of the theatres. Fully fledged actors

LUCIANUS Thoughts black,* hands apt, drugs fit, and time agreeing;   240
          Confederate* season, else no creature seeing;*
          Thou mixture rank,* of midnight weeds collected,
          With Hecate's ban* thrice blasted, thrice infected,
          Thy natural magic and dire* property,
          On wholesome life* usurp immediately.   245
                              [*He pours the poison into the King's ear*
HAMLET   He poisons him i' th' garden for's estate.* His name's Gon-
          zago. The story is extant, and writ in choice Italian; you shall
          see anon how the murderer gets the love of Gonzago's wife.
OPHELIA   The king rises.
HAMLET   What, frighted with false fire!*   250
QUEEN   [*To the* KING] How fares* my lord?
POLONIUS Give o'er* the play.
KING   Give me some light!* – Away!
ALL   Lights, lights, lights.
                              [*Exeunt all but* HAMLET *and* HORATIO
HAMLET   Why, let the stricken deer* go weep,   255
                  The hart ungalléd play;
              For some must watch, while some must sleep;
                  So runs the world away. –
          Would not this, sir, and a forest of feathers* – if the rest of
          my fortunes turn Turk* with me – with two Provincial roses*   260
          on my raced shoes, get me a fellowship* in a cry* of players,
          sir?
HORATIO   Half a share.*
HAMLET   A whole one, I.

---

263 (*cont'd*)   would get one share (say in all a tenth or less of the takings); others might get
                  half a share; others might not be shareholders at all but simply draw wages
                  (paid them by the actors) as hired men. Horatio thinks Hamlet is a good
                  enough actor to deserve half a share; Hamlet thinks himself good enough for
                  a whole one.

265   *For thou dost know* . . . – This stanza, except for the last word of it, also looks like a quotation, although no source for it has been found.

265   *Damon* – In a classical story, Damon and Pythias were two young men between whom the deepest friendship existed. *Damon dear* means 'my dear, close, friend'.

266   *dismantled . . . himself:* was deprived of (a ruler who was like) Jove himself – i.e. the king of the gods.

268   *pajock* – Hamlet has put this strange word in place of *ass*, which would give good sense, and would go with *was* in the scheme of rhymes. The meaning of the word *pajock* is unknown; many editors have taken it to be a form of *peacock*; in Shakespeare's day, and for many centuries before, the peacock had a bad reputation for being a bad mate, and having the 'voice of a fiend, the head of a serpent, and the pace of a thief'. But it may be a form of *patchocks*, a name used by the poet Edmund Spenser for the poorer type of Englishmen in the Ireland of his day. However, the meaning of the stanza is clear: Denmark has been deprived of a god-like king and a villain rules in his place.

271   *Didst perceive:* Did you notice (how the King reacted)?

275   *recorders:* high-pitched pipes.

277   *belike:* perhaps. – These two lines also sound like a quotation which Hamlet deliberately changes.

277   *perdy,* from the French oath *par Dieu:* by God.

279   *vouchsafe:* be kind enough to allow.

282   *sir* – Hamlet is not compelled by good manners to call Guildenstern 'sir'; but in his present mood he is bitterly ironical, twisting verses to suit his own ends, interrupting his friends when they speak, and, as here, mocking them when they call him 'sir'.

283   *in his retirement . . . distempered:* has gone to his private rooms and is extremely angry – *distempered* could mean upset in either mind or body. Guilderstern means the former; Hamlet pretends to understand the latter.

285   *choler:* rage. – This is Guildenstern's meaning, but this use of *choler* reflects the belief that anger is caused by acid in the stomach. Hamlet pretends to understand *choler* in this physical sense – bile. His remarks which follow: *Your wisdom should show itself* . . . are in an ironically pompous style of condescending advice.

287   *purgation:* cleansing – both from solid waste in the body and figuratively, from an accusation or suspicion of guilt. Hamlet is therefore playing on the word by saying both (i) 'to purge him would make him worse than he was before, not cure him', and (ii) 'to purge him of his crime would make him even more angry than he is already.

289   *frame:* order.

290   *start not . . . affair:* do not jump (*start*) so wildly away from the matter I have raised (*my affair*). – Hamlet says he will be *tame*, i.e. not *start . . . wildly*.

291   *Pronounce:* Proclaim – again an ironic word.

295   *breed:* kind. – Hamlet has interrupted Guildenstern's speech (lines 292–3) with a satirical and irrelevant welcome, and so prevented him from coming directly to the Queen's message.

296   *wholesome:* reasonable. – Another meaning of *wholesome* is 'healthy', contrasting with *diseased* in line 301.

302   *you shall command:* you will have at your disposal.

                    For thou dost know,* O Damon* dear,   265
                        This realm dismantled* was
                    Of Jove himself; and now reigns here
                        A very, very – pajock.*

HORATIO   You might have rhymed.

HAMLET   O good Horatio, I'll take the ghost's word for a thousand   270
pound. Didst perceive?*

HORATIO   Very well, my lord.

HAMLET   Upon the talk of the poisoning –

HORATIO   I did very well note him.

HAMLET   Ah, ha! – Come, some music! Come, the recorders!* –   275
                    For if the king like not the comedy,
                        Why, then, belike* – he likes it not, perdy.* –
                    Come, some music!

Enter ROSENCRANTZ *and* GUILDENSTERN.

GUILDENSTERN   Good my lord, vouchsafe* me a word with you.

HAMLET   Sir, a whole history.   280

GUILDENSTERN   The king, sir –

HAMLET   Ay, sir,* what of him?

GUILDENSTERN   Is, in his retirement,* marvellous distempered.

HAMLET   With drink, sir?

GUILDENSTERN   No, my lord, with choler.*   285

HAMLET   Your wisdom should show itself more richer to signify this
to his doctor. For, for me to put him to his purgation* would
perhaps plunge him into far more choler.

GUILDENSTERN   Good my lord, put your discourse into some frame,* and
start* not so wildly from my affair.   290

HAMLET   I am tame, sir. – Pronounce.*

GUILDENSTERN   The queen, your mother, in most great affliction of spirit,
hath sent me to you –

HAMLET   You are welcome.

GUILDENSTERN   Nay, good my lord, this courtesy is not of the right breed.*   295
If it shall please you to make a wholesome* answer, I will do
your mother's commandment; if not, your pardon and my
return shall be the end of my business.

HAMLET   Sir, I cannot.

GUILDENSTERN   What, my lord?   300

HAMLET   Make you a wholesome answer. My wit's diseased. But, sir,
such answer as I can make, you shall command;* or, rather,
as you say, my mother; therefore no more, but to the matter.
My mother, you say –

306   *amazement and admiration:* worry and bewilderment. – Yet again, Hamlet pretends to
        misunderstand these words, and, in the case of *admiration*, gives it a more
        modern sense, 'approving wonder', in his next lines.
308   *Impart:* Tell.
310   *We*, not 'I', since Hamlet has now put on a regal attitude.
311   *trade:* business – again an ironic use.
313   *these pickers and stealers:* these hands. – He is looking at them as he swears. The phrase
        'to pick and steal' was fixed, perhaps because of a sentence in the catechism
        of the English Church: 'Keep my hands from picking and stealing.'
314   *distemper:* bad mood.
315   *your own liberty . . . griefs:* your own deliverance (*liberty*) (from your bad humour) if you
        refuse to speak about (*deny*) your griefs.
317   *I lack advancement* – This is a characteristically inconsequential answer, perhaps sparked
        off by the odd phrase spoken by Rosencrantz, *your cause of distemper*, instead
        of 'the cause of your distemper'. Rosencrantz is using a strained, courtly style;
        the word *cause* may have reminded Hamlet of 'pleading for a cause or favour';
        hence his reply.
18   *voice:* support.
320   *the proverb* – an old saying, in some such form as 'While the grass grows, the simple
        horse starves.' The application to the present situation is not altogether clear;
        perhaps he means, 'While I am waiting to succeed to the throne, I may die',
        like a simple horse who is too slow to take advantage of the fresh grass (new
        opportunities) around him.
323   *To withdraw with you* – (perhaps) 'Let me speak to you in private (so that the players shall
        not hear what we are talking about).' This remark of Hamlet's has never been
        satisfactorily explained, but it must be dependent upon what follows; leaving
        the matter of the recorders for a moment, he wants to ask Guildenstern a
        straight question.
323   *go about . . . a toil:* get me to run with the wind, as if you wanted to drive me into a net
        (*toil*). – These are metaphors from hunting; huntsmen tried to get their quarry
        (e.g. deer, hares) to run with the wind into the nets; otherwise the animal
        hunted would scent the net and the men who had prepared it.
325   *if my duty . . . unmannerly* – Yet again a remark is made which is difficult to explain; even
        Hamlet does not know what this elaborate and strained expression really
        means. One interpretation is: 'You have evidently found me too bold in
        carrying out my duty (allegiance to the King, lines 318–9), so any gesture of
        affection for you (such as inviting you to confide in us, lines 314–6) would be
        very unfitting. But the courtly, elaborate style has greatly obscured any
        meaning that Guildenstern might have wished to express.
332   *I know . . . it:* I know nothing about the fingering (*touch*) needed to play it.
333   *as easy as lying* – Hamlet's words in this passage make a vague pattern of imagery: he
        talks of the music of the recorder as if it were human speech. He begins by
        telling Guildenstern that playing the recorder is *as easy as lying*, since Rosen-
        crantz and Guildenstern have not dealt honestly or frankly with him (II.ii.
        224ff.). He goes on to say that if certain holes in the recorder (*ventages*) are
        covered (*Govern:* control) it will *discourse* very *eloquent* music; the covering-
        up may relate equally to the concealment of information, which is one aspect
        of lying. Even if such an interpretation is not in fact so precise as suggested
        here, there is certainly a close relationship between the music of the recorder
        and human speech, particularly the words of Guildenstern and his associate,
        which Hamlet mistrusts and goes on to decry.
333   *ventages:* the finger-holes of the recorder.
336   *stops:* finger holes. – Hamlet shows how they are covered with the fingers.
337   *command . . . utterance* – Guildenstern falls in with Hamlet's imagery: *command* is
        suggested by *Govern* (line 333), *utterance* by *discourse* and *eloquent*. And in
        doing so he falls into the trap which Hamlet has laid for him: Hamlet can then
        accuse Guildenstern of trying to play on *him*, make him speak, *sound me from
        my lowest note*, etc. Hamlet has turned the image against Guildenstern; there is
        much 'music' in him, but Guildenstern cannot make him speak.
340   *would:* want to.
343   *compass:* range of notes.

ROSENCRANTZ	Then thus she says: your behaviour hath struck her into amazement* and admiration.
HAMLET	O wonderful son, that can so astonish a mother – But is there no sequel at the heels of this mother's admiration? Impart.*
ROSENCRANTZ	She desires to speak with you in her closet, ere you go to bed.
HAMLET	We* shall obey, were she ten times our mother. Have you any further trade* with us?
ROSENCRANTZ	My lord, you once did love me.
HAMLET	And do still, by these pickers* and stealers.
ROSENCRANTZ	Good my lord, what is your cause of distemper?* You do surely bar the door upon your own liberty* if you deny your griefs to your friend.
HAMLET	Sir, I lack advancement.*
ROSENCRANTZ	How can that be, when you have the voice* of the king himself for your succession in Denmark?
HAMLET	Ay, sir, but 'While the grass grows' – the proverb* is something musty.

Enter PLAYERS *with recorders.*

	O, the recorders – Let me see one. [*They give him a recorder.*] – To withdraw* with you – Why do you go about to recover* the wind of me, as if you would drive me into a toil?
GUILDENSTERN	O, my lord, if my duty* be too bold, my love is too unmannerly.
HAMLET	I do not well understand that. Will you play upon this pipe?
GUILDENSTERN	My lord, I cannot.
HAMLET	I pray you.
GUILDENSTERN	Believe me, I cannot.
HAMLET	I do beseech you.
GUILDENSTERN	I know no touch* of it, my lord.
HAMLET	'Tis as easy as lying.* Govern these ventages* with your finger and thumb, give it breath with your mouth, and it will discourse most eloquent music. Look you, these are the stops.*
GUILDENSTERN	But these cannot I command* to any utterance of harmony; I have not the skill.
HAMLET	Why, look you now, how unworthy a thing you make of me! You would* play upon me; you would seem to know my stops; you would pluck out the heart of my mystery; you would sound me from my lowest note to the top of my compass.* And there is much music, excellent voice, in this

305

310

315

320

325

330

335

340

344   *organ* – i.e. (i) himself, his body, but also (ii) the musical instrument.

344   *'Sblood* – an oath, 'By God's blood!'

346   *fret:* (i) vex; (ii) fit with a fret – i.e. a piece of wire on the fingering board of a stringed instrument to guide the playing. (On modern instruments this function is performed by a bar of wood.)

350   *yonder:* that . . . (over there). – Hamlet now shows how easily he can play' on Polonius, making him say anything Hamlet wants him to. Polonius is an easy instrument to play on, because he is intent on humouring what he believes to be a dangerous madman.

353   *backed* – It is, of course, the camel, not the weasel, which has a prominent back; Polonius, by making this random choice of something distinctive in a weasel, shows himself to be particularly foolish.

356   *Then:* In that case – i.e. 'You agree to everything I say, so I will consent to go to my mother, in accordance with your request.'

356   *by and by:* at once.

357   *to the top of my bent:* to extreme lengths – like a bow being bent as far as it will go.

362   *the very witching time* – The darkness of the night was thought to be the special time for supernatural powers to show themselves. At midnight especially, witches were thought to ride, spirits to come out of hiding, and graveyards to give up their dead.

364   *Contagion:* evil, poisonous influence.

368   *The soul of Nero* – Nero was an emperor of Rome who had his own mother murdered. His evil character did something to bring the Roman Empire to destruction.

369   *unnatural:* without 'natural' feelings – i.e. the feelings of ordinary humanity. Cf. note on *kin* and *kind* (I.ii.65).

372   *How in my words . . . shent:* however much (*How . . . soever*) my words may wound and humiliate her (*she be shent*).

373   *give them seals* – i.e. 'confirm them (my words) by putting them into action'.

little organ,* yet cannot you make it speak. 'Sblood,* do you
think I am easier to be played on than a pipe? Call me what   345
instrument you will, though you can fret* me, you cannot
play upon me—

Enter POLONIUS.

God bless you, sir!
POLONIUS My lord, the queen would speak with you, and presently.
HAMLET Do you see yonder* cloud that's almost in shape of a camel? 350
POLONIUS By th' mass, and 'tis like a camel, indeed.
HAMLET Methinks it is like a weasel.
POLONIUS It is backed* like a weasel.
HAMLET Or like a whale?
POLONIUS Very like a whale.   355
HAMLET Then* will I come to my mother by and by.* – [*Aside*] They
fool me to the top of my bent.* – [*To the others*] I will come by
and by.
POLONIUS I will say so.
HAMLET 'By and by' is easily said.   [*Exit* POLONIUS   360
Leave me, friends.
[*Exeunt* ROSENCRANTZ, GUILDENSTERN, HORATIO, *and* PLAYERS
'Tis now the very witching time* of night,
When churchyards yawn, and hell itself breathes out
Contagion* to this world. Now could I drink hot blood,
And do such bitter business as the day   365
Would quake to look on. Soft! Now to my mother. –
O heart, lose not thy nature; let not ever
The soul of Nero* enter this firm bosom.
Let me be cruel, not unnatural;*
I will speak daggers to her, but use none;   370
My tongue and soul in this be hypocrites –
How in my words* soever she be shent,
To give them seals,* never, my soul, consent!   [*Exit*

III. iii.   The King makes final preparations to get Hamlet away to England. He has been summoned to his mother's room, and Polonius resolves to spy on him there. The King, now alone, tries to pray. Hamlet finds him kneeling, and so has him at his mercy; but he does not kill him.

So far the play has dealt with a single plot, centring on Hamlet and the King. At this point the counter-plot, which treats of Rosencrantz and Guildenstern's passage to England, is touched upon. But it is not yet ripe, and the rest of the scene reverts to the further positioning of Hamlet and the King, leading to a dramatic climax, Hamlet's discovery of Claudius at prayer. Hamlet does not take his life because his judgement prevails over his passion, and his moral sensibility revolts at the cowardly and unprincely deed of stabbing his victim from behind. Moreover, as the player-king said, purposes if pursued passionately result in their opposites. Hamlet's perception of the after-world is very real, not just a peg on which to hang excuses. He doubted the benevolence of his father's ghost, and believes equally that Claudius would die forgiven if he were killed at prayer. Claudius does not see Hamlet, but is aware of his own inadequacy: his repentance is hollow because he asks forgiveness without offering to give up the gains of his crimes.

1	*nor stands . . . us:* and it is not safe for me.
3	*your commission . . . dispatch:* I will see that your warrant is made ready at once. – This is the letter to the King of England (III.i.168) about the arrangement for collecting the tribute, and so on. Rosencrantz and Guildenstern must already know about this arrangement in detail.
4	*shall along:* shall go along.
5	*The terms . . . endure:* The conditions of my administration of government (*estate*) cannot stand.
6	*near us* – The Quartos read *neer's*; the Folios *dangerous*, which seems to be a poorer reading since it repeats a large part of the meaning of *Hazard:* risk.
7	*ourselves provide:* prepare ourselves – in accordance with the King's order (line 2 above).
8	*Most holy . . . fear it is:* It is a most holy and religious source of concern. – The King is here looked upon as a ruler appointed by God to order and provide for his people. As Rosencrantz goes on to point out, the whole nation is dragged to disaster if the King, who is their centre and on whom they all depend, is in peril of his life. These considerations, drawn from the world-view of the England of Shakespeare's day, are adduced by Guildenstern and Rosencrantz as an excuse for undertaking at the King's request a venture which will, if it goes well, lead to the death of Prince Hamlet.
11	*The single . . . life:* The private individual who lives for himself. – This private person is compared with the King, who lives for all his subjects.
13	*noyance:* harm.
14	*weal:* welfare.
15	*The cease . . . alone:* The passing-away (*cease*) of a king (*majesty*) is not just a death in itself.
16	*gulf:* whirlpool.
17	*massy:* massive.
20	*mortised:* joined by fitting into a *mortise* or hole in a piece of wood. – The tongue of wood which fits into the hole is the *tenon.*
22	*Attends:* accompanies.
23	*a general groan* – i.e. sorrow for everyone; when the King sighs, the whole nation must grieve; the King, under God and appointed by God, suffers for all his people.
24	*Arm you:* Prepare yourselves.
25	*fear:* thing to be feared. – The King talks of it as a prisoner; 'it' (i.e. Hamlet) is too much at liberty (*free-footed*), and must be chained (equipped with *fetters*).
27	*closet:* private apartment.
28	*arras* – See II.ii.164. This hanging screen of tapestry was far enough away from the wall to allow people to hide behind it. Such hangings were evidently put up to keep the large halls and rooms of the houses warm in cold weather.
29	*the process:* what goes on (between them).
29	*tax him home:* censure him to the utmost.

scene iii

A room in the castle.

Enter KING, ROSENCRANTZ, *and* GUILDENSTERN.

KING   I like him not; nor stands* it safe with us
To let his madness range. Therefore prepare you;
I your commission* will forthwith dispatch,
And he to England shall along* with you.
The terms* of our estate may not endure   5
Hazard so near us* as doth hourly grow
Out of his lunacies.

GUILDENSTERN   We will ourselves provide.*
Most holy* and religious fear it is
To keep those many many bodies safe
That live and feed upon your majesty.   10

ROSENCRANTZ   The single and peculiar life* is bound,
With all the strength and armour of the mind,
To keep itself from noyance;* but much more
That spirit upon whose weal* depends and rests
The lives of many. The cease* of majesty   15
Dies not alone, but, like a gulf,* doth draw
What's near it with it. 'Tis a massy* wheel,
Fixed on the summit of the highest mount,
To whose huge spokes ten thousand lesser things
Are mortised* and adjoined; which, when it falls,   20
Each small annexment, petty consequence,
Attends* the boisterous ruin. Ne'er alone
Did the king sigh, but with a general groan.*

KING   Arm you,* I pray you, to this speedy voyage;
For we will fetters put upon this fear,*   25
Which now goes too free-footed.

ROSENCRANTZ &   We will haste us.
GUILDENSTERN

[*Exeunt* ROSENCRANTZ *and* GUILDENSTERN

Enter POLONIUS.

POLONIUS   My lord, he's going to his mother's closet.*
Behind the arras* I'll convey myself,
To hear the process;* I'll warrant she'll tax him home.*

30   *as you said* – It was Polonius himself who made this suggestion (III.i.179); he thinks it
    will be more acceptable to the King if he attributes the suggestion to him, and
    flatters him with the wisdom of it.

31   *meet:* fitting.

32   *them* – i.e. mothers.

33   *of vantage:* in addition.

    The King is now left alone. He speaks out his secret thoughts; and the horror of his
    crime, as he reveals it to himself, leads him to earnest prayer for the salvation of his soul.

37   *the primal, eldest curse* – In the Bible (*Genesis* 4:8ff.) the story is told of how the two sons
    of Adam and Eve, the first man and woman, fell to quarrelling, and how one,
    Cain, murdered his brother Abel. For this, God brought a curse on Cain, who
    became the first of all outcasts. This is the first (*primal*) and oldest (*eldest*)
    curse brought on man.

39   *Though . . . will:* – even though my inclination (to do so) is as strong (*sharp*) as my deter-
    mination (*will*) (to do so). – He is 'inclined' to pray, and wants to do so, but
    his guilt is stronger than both, and prevents him.

41   *to double business bound:* committed to do two things at the same time.

42   *in pause:* hesitating.

43   *both neglect* – i.e. neglect to do both.

45   *rain enough* – Rain from heaven is an image of mercy, forgiveness:
        The quality of mercy is not strained;
        It droppeth as the gentle rain from heaven
        Upon the place beneath. (*Merchant of Venice,* IV.i.180–2.)
    The image is continued with *wash* (washing away the sin of the wicked) and
    white as snow (pure, free from guilt).

46   *Whereto serves mercy:* What is the purpose of mercy.

47   *confront . . . offence:* to oppose and overcome (*confront*) the face (*visage*) of guilt.

49   *forestallèd . . . fall:* prevented from falling (into temptation).

50   *pardoned being down:* forgiven if we *have* fallen (into temptation).

52   *serve my turn:* be of use to me.

56   *offence* – i.e. the profits of the offence; what he called the *effects* in line 54 above.

57   *corrupted currents:* wicked courses. – Some editors have thought that *currents* here is a
    short form of *occurrents:* events, as at v.ii.339.

58   *shove by justice:* push justice to one side (*by*). – *Offence's . . . hand* is said to be *gilded*, i.e.
    golden, in the sense that the results of the offence are richly rewarding—the
    wicked prize of the following line.

61   *There* – i.e. *above*, in heaven. The word *There* must be fully stressed in both places in this
    sentence.

61   *shuffling:* trickery, deception.

62   *his:* its – as normally for things as well as persons in Shakespeare.

62   *compelled, for àre compelled.* – In the next world we shall be compelled to act as witnesses
    (*give in evidence* – line 64) even if this means giving evidence against ourselves;
    this cannot be forced upon witnesses in this world.

63   *the teeth and forehead* – i.e. right in the face of our faults, without any concealment. Cf.
    the visage of offence, line 47.

64   *rests:* remains.

65   *can:* is able to do.

68   *limèd:* trapped. – A bird trapped in bird-lime gets more entrapped the more it struggles
    to get free.

69   *assay:* an attempt.

And, as you said,* and wisely was it said,   30
'Tis meet* that some more audience than a mother
(Since nature makes them* partial) should o'erhear
The speech of vantage.* Fare you well, my liege;
I'll call upon you ere you go to bed,
And tell you what I know.

KING   Thanks, dear my lord.   35

[*Exit* POLONIUS

O, my offence is rank, it smells to heaven;
It hath the primal, eldest curse* upon 't —
A brother's murder! — Pray can I not,
Though inclination* be as sharp as will.
My stronger guilt defeats my strong intent;   40
And, like a man to double business bound,*
I stand in pause* where I shall first begin,
And both* neglect. What if this curséd hand
Were thicker than itself with brother's blood,
Is there not rain* enough in the sweet heavens   45
To wash it white as snow? Whereto serves mercy*
But to confront* the visage of offence?
And what's in prayer but this twofold force —
To be forestalléd* ere we come to fall,
Or pardoned being down?* Then I'll look up;   50
My fault is past. But, O, what form of prayer
Can serve my turn?* 'Forgive me my foul murder'? —
That cannot be, since I am still possessed
Of those effects for which I did the murder —
My crown, mine own ambition, and my queen.   55
May one be pardoned, and retain th' offence?*
In the corrupted currents* of this world
Offence's gilded hand may shove* by justice,
And oft 'tis seen the wicked prize itself
Buys out the law. But 'tis not so above;   60
There* is no shuffling* — there the action lies
In his* true nature, and we ourselves compelled,*
Even to the teeth* and forehead of our faults,
To give in evidence. What then? What rests?*
Try what repentance can.* What can it not?   65
Yet what can it when one cannot repent?
O wretched state! O bosom black as death!
O liméd* soul, that, struggling to be free,
Art more engaged! Help, angels! Make assay.*

73   *pat:* without delay.

The speech which follows is a revelation of Hamlet's character. He can act impetuously, on the spur of an impulse, but he cannot act when there is time to take thought, when the situation *would be scanned* (line 75). And once his resolution fails at this point (and it does fail, although the King is in his hands in a way which will never happen again), he makes excuses for himself: his revenge will not be fulfilled if, murdering the King while he is praying, he sends his soul straight to heaven. Hamlet thinks he must wait to catch the King at some vice or other, and then kill him. But the opportunity does not occur.

75   *would be scanned:* must be carefully considered.

79   *hire and salary:* (an action for which Claudius might) hire me and pay me a reward – i.e. to murder in this way would be to earn the king's gratitude, not kill him for revenge, since he would go straight to heaven.

80   *full of bread* – i.e. having indulged his wordly lusts. The full understanding of this phrase depends on a knowledge of a passage in the Bible (*Ezekiel* 16 : 49):
this was the iniquity of thy sister. Sodom, pride, fulness of bread, and abundance of idleness was in her.
The Ghost has said something of the same sort himself (I.v.76):
Cut off even in the blossom of my sin.
The main point is that his death came swiftly, before he had time to confess his sins to God. Claudius, on the other hand, is confessing his sins in prayer even now.

81   *broad blown . . . May:* in full blossom, and as full of life (*flush*) as springtime (*May*).

82   *how . . . stands:* what his final reckoning is turning out to be – *audit* suggests a balance between the profits (good deeds) and the losses (sins) he made on earth, and connects with *hire and salary,* line 79. The Ghost has already told Hamlet of his father's condition, but Hamlet here wants to know what rewards or punishments are in store for his father.

83   *circumstance . . . thought* – (perhaps) 'the evidence such as it is (to people in this world) (*our circumstance*) and the conclusions which reason may lead us to (*course of thought*)'.

84   *'Tis heavy with him:* his existence is sorrowful.

85   *take him . . . soul:* kill him while he is in the act of confessing his sins.

86   *seasoned:* mature, quite ready.

88   *know thou . . . hent:* (i) experience a grip (*hent*) which has a more terrible purpose (*horrid*); *or* (ii) experience a more terrible intention; *or* (iii) wait till you can take advantage of a more horrible opportunity. – Suggestion (iii) assumes that *hent* is a form of *hint* in its Shakespearean sense, 'opportunity'. The difficulty here arises from the fact that Shakespeare does not use *hent* as a noun elsewhere in his plays, and it is used as a noun only rarely elsewhere.

92   *relish:* trace.

95   *stays:* is waiting.

96   *This physic . . . days:* this practice of the art of healing (*physic*) only prolongs your days of sickness. – It is not clear whether Hamlet is addressing the King or himself. If he is addressing the King, his remark must be rhetorical, i.e. not to be heard by the King, and must mean that the King has not been given his life but simply allowed to go on in his illness of mind. But if Hamlet is addressing himself, it must mean that he is already feeling remorse for not taking the King's life as the opportunity offered.

Bow, stubborn knees; and, heart with strings of steel,   70
Be soft as sinews of the new-born babe!
All may be well.   [*He moves to one side and kneels down*

Enter HAMLET.

HAMLET   Now might I do it pat,* now he is praying;
And now I'll do 't – and so he goes to heaven;
And so am I revenged – that would be scanned.*   75
A villian kills my father, and, for that,
I, his sole son, do this same villain send
To heaven.
O, this is hire and salary,* not revenge.
He took my father grossly, full of bread,*   80
With all his crimes broad blown,* as flush as May;
And how his audit stands* who knows save heaven?
But, in our circumstance* and course of thought,
'Tis heavy* with him. And am I, then, revenged,
To take him* in the purging of his soul,   85
When he is fit and seasoned* for his passage?
No.
Up, sword, and know thou a more horrid hent.*
When he is drunk asleep, or in his rage,
Or in th' incestuous pleasure of his bed;   90
At gaming, swearing; or about some act
That has no relish* of salvation in 't –
Then trip him, that his heels may kick at heaven,
And that his soul may be as damned and black
As hell, whereto it goes. My mother stays;*   95
This physic* but prolongs thy sickly days.   [*Exit*

KING   [*Rising*] My words fly up, my thoughts remain below;
Words without thoughts never to heaven go.   [*Exit*

III. iv. As Hamlet enters his mother's room, Polonius hides behind the wall-covering. Hamlet's manner makes the Queen think he is mad. As she calls for help, Polonius answers, and Hamlet, taking him to be the King, runs his sword through the arras and kills him. Hamlet is trying to persuade his mother of the evil that she has done when his father's ghost enters, telling him not to delay in carrying out his resolves. He explains that his madness is a pretence, and urges his mother to give up Claudius.

When Gertrude shouts for help and an answering noise comes from behind the arras, Hamlet's passion, already aroused, makes him seize on this as the propitious moment to kill the King. However, he has not killed the King but only the King's willing accomplice, who has now paid the price of his own trickery. The Queen sees the flagrancy of her own involvement in recent events, and Hamlet passionately denounces Claudius in front of her. The Ghost, which she cannot see, brings Hamlet back to his senses; he tries to dissuade his mother from living any longer with her second husband.

1	*lay home to:* deal firmly with – i.e. bring each point home.
4	*heat* – i.e. heated opposition.
4	*sconce me* – All the early editions read *silence* for *sconce* here. If *silence* is in fact the correct reading, it can only mean 'I will keep silent from now on'; this may suggest that he is going to hide, but no more. However, the emendation to *sconce*, 'hide', gives good sense: 'I'll hide myself just (*even*) here', and is generally accepted by editors.
5	*be round with him:* speak to him plainly – *round:* plain-spoken.
7	*I'll warrant you:* I promise you (I will).
11	*you* – Hamlet addresses his mother in this way, but she addresses him *thou*. (See Introduction, p. xlii).
13	*Go, go . . . tongue* – Hamlet has already (line 11) made a retort which mocks the Queen's words by repeating them with some changes. Here the mockery of *come—go, answer—question, idle* (foolish)—*wicked* is very pointed.
15	*the rood:* the cross (on which Christ was crucified).
18	*I'll set those . . . speak:* I will confront you with people who will be able to talk to you. – Hamlet has so far taken up every short utterance that his mother has made, and prevented her from going on.
25	*A rat?* There is a suggestion here (as elsewhere) that a rat is a spy, hiding in dark corners and watching people. Cf. the modern English expression *to smell a rat,* i.e. to have suspicions about a person's motives.
25	*ducat:* a gold coin. – Hamlet makes up this alliterative phrase, *dead . . . ducat,* to signify that the life he has taken is worth very little, only a common gold coin.

scene iv

The Queen's closet.

Enter QUEEN *and* POLONIUS.

POLONIUS He will come straight. Look you lay home* to him.
          Tell him his pranks have been too broad to bear with,
          And that your Grace hath screened and stood between
          Much heat* and him. I'll sconce* me even here.
          Pray you, be round* with him.   5
HAMLET   [*Within*] Mother, mother, mother!
QUEEN   I'll warrant you;* fear me not. – Withdraw;
          I hear him coming.

                                        [POLONIUS *goes behind the arras*

Enter HAMLET.

HAMLET   Now, mother, what's the matter?
QUEEN   Hamlet, thou hast thy father much offended.   10
HAMLET   Mother, you* have my father much offended.
QUEEN   Come, come, you answer with an idle tongue.
HAMLET   Go, go,* you question with a wicked tongue.
QUEEN   Why, how now, Hamlet!
HAMLET   What's the matter now?
QUEEN   Have you forgot me?
HAMLET   No, by the rood,* not so.   15
          You are the queen, your husband's brother's wife;
          And – would it were not so! – you are my mother.
QUEEN   Nay, then, I'll set* those to you that can speak.
HAMLET   Come, come, and sit you down; you shall not budge;
          You go not till I set you up a glass   20
          Where you may see the inmost part of you.
QUEEN   What wilt thou do? Thou wilt not murder me? –
          Help, help, ho!
POLONIUS [*Behind*] What, ho! help, help, help!
HAMLET   [*Drawing his rapier*] How now! A rat?* Dead for a ducat,*   25
          dead!   [*Makes a pass with his rapier through the arras*
POLONIUS [*Behind*] O, I am slain!   [*Falls and dies*
QUEEN   O me, what hast thou done?
HAMLET   Nay, I know not. Is it the king?

31   *kill a king!* – This remark of the Queen's, said with shocked surprise, has been taken by many readers to suggest that the Queen is genuinely unaware that Hamlet's father, her first husband, was murdered. But it probably does no more than repeat the first part of Hamlet's implied accusation and show the Queen's terror at what may now be revealed.

33   *thy better* – i.e. the King, who Hamlet thought was hiding behind the arras.

34   *find'st* – i.e. findest *that*. Polonius has met his death because he was too occupied with other people's affairs (*busy*).

35   *Leave:* Stop.

38   *If damnéd . . . sense:* if familiarity (*custom*) with evil (*damnéd*) has not hardened it like brass (*brazed*) to such an extent that it is of tested strength (*proof*) and fortified (*bulwark*, a noun used as an adjective) against feeling (*sense*).

43   *the rose* – an image of the charm, grace and beauty of love.

45   *blister* – Prostitutes were marked with a sign or 'blister' on their foreheads.

47   *contraction:* engagement (to be married).

48   *sweet religion . . . words:* (such a deed as) makes the gracious forms of religion just a string of words. – This is reminiscent of the King's observation at the end of the previous scene:
        Words without thoughts never to heaven go.

49   *glow* – i.e. with hot blushes at the enormity of the crime.

50   *solidity . . . mass:* earth – which, with its sad face (*tristful visage*), is as appalled as the heavens.

51   *as against the doom:* as if it were in expectation of (*against*) the day of judgment – i.e. the time after death when men will receive their rewards and punishments.

53   *index* – The meaning of this word as used here has not been satisfactorily explained. (i) In Shakespeare's day, books often had a detailed table of contents, called 'the index', at the beginning; this suggests the use of the word to mean 'preface, prologue'. If that is the meaning here, the Queen is saying that Hamlet's last speech sounds like the prologue to a play; they have both used the word *act*, and now the Queen, who has been told of this *act* in a sort of prologue (*index*), wants to know what the *act* in fact was. (ii) Another possibility is that *index* means a list of sins, such as those punishable by excommunication from the church.

55   *counterfeit presentment:* presentation in a portrait. – There is no element of trickery or deceit in the word *counterfeit* as used by Shakespeare.

57   *Hyperion's* – in Greek mythology Hyperion was a person of giant size and superhuman powers; he was looked upon as the son of earth and heaven, and father of the sun, the moon and the dawn. (The giant race were called Titans.)

57   *front of Jove:* the forehead of Jupiter. – Jupiter (*Jove*) was looked upon by the ancient Romans as the lord of heaven and the deity who determined the course of all human affairs.

58   *Mars* – the Roman god of war.

59   *station:* a way of standing.

59   *Mercury* – the winged messenger of the gods, their *herald*.

60   *lighted* – i.e. alighted, descended.

62   *set his seal:* leave his mark – in order to confirm that the thing is genuine (*give the world assurance*).

QUEEN O, what a rash and bloody deed is this!

HAMLET A bloody deed! – Almost as bad, good mother,
    As kill a king, and marry with his brother.   30

QUEEN As kill a king!*

HAMLET   Ay, lady, 'twas my word. –
              [Lifts up the arras, and sees POLONIUS
    Thou wretched, rash, intruding fool, farewell!
    I took thee for thy better.* Take thy fortune;
    Thou find'st* to be too busy is some danger. –
    [To the QUEEN] Leave* wringing of your hands. Peace; sit
    you down,   35
    And let me wring your heart; for so I shall,
    If it be made of penetrable stuff,
    If damnéd custom* have not brazed it so
    That it is proof and bulwark against sense.

QUEEN What have I done, that thou dar'st wag thy tongue   40
    In noise so rude against me?

HAMLET   Such an act
    That blurs the grace and blush of modesty;
    Calls virtue hypocrite; takes off the rose*
    From the fair forehead of an innocent love,
    And sets a blister* there; makes marriage-vows   45
    As false as dicers' oaths. O, such a deed
    As from the body of contraction* plucks
    The very soul, and sweet religion* makes
    A rhapsody of words. Heaven's face doth glow;*
    Yea, this solidity* and compound mass   50
    With tristful visage, as against* the doom,
    Is thought-sick at the act.

QUEEN   Ay me, what act
    That roars so loud, and thunders in the index?*

HAMLET Look here, upon this picture, and on this [He shows her
    pictures of her father and his uncle],
    The counterfeit presentment* of two brothers.   55
    See, what a grace was seated on this brow –
    Hyperion's* curls, the front of Jove* himself;
    An eye like Mars,* to threaten and command;
    A station* like the herald Mercury*
    New lighted* on a heaven-kissing hill;   60
    A combination and a form indeed
    Where every god did seem to set his seal,*
    To give the world assurance of a man.

65   *mildewed ear* – i.e. an ear of corn which has gone bad, and is turning other ears rotten also (*Blasting his wholesome brother*).

67   *on this fair . . . moor:* stop feeding (*leave to feed*) on this fine mountain and grow fat (*batten*) on this wasteland (*moor*). – The image is of an animal feeding on the fresh green mountain slopes or on the coarse grass of infertile land.

70   *The hey-day . . . tame:* the state of excitement (*hey-day*, meaning literally 'high-day') in the passions of the body is easily controlled (*tame*). – At his mother's age there was no chance of her passions overcoming her good sense (*judgement*). The lines which follow are bitterly insulting to her.

72   *Sense:* sexual desire.

73   *motion:* impulses.

74   *apoplexed:* paralysed.

75   *Nor sense . . . difference* (line 77)*:* and sexual desire (*sense*) was never so enslaved (*thralled*) by excitement (*ecstasy*) that it did not retain (*But it reserved*) some measure of discrimination (*quantity of choice*) to give guidance (*serve*) where the difference is as striking as here.

78   *cozened . . . blind:* cheated you at blindman's buff. This is a game in which one player is blindfold and tries to catch the others.

80   *sans all:* without anything else. – This is a particularly cruel observation; Hamlet, playing on the word *sense* (which here refers to the bodily senses) means that, even if his mother had lost all her bodily senses except that of smell, she should have 'smelt out' the wickedness of Claudius, her second husband.

82   *so mope:* act so stupidly.

84   *mutine:* rebel – *thou* refers to *shame* in the previous line.

84   *matron's:* mother's.

85   *To flaming youth . . . wax:* let virtue be as wax to flaming youth – i.e. let virtue melt before the fiery passions of youth (and be virtue no longer).

86   *her own fire* – i.e. the fire which belongs to *flaming youth*.

89   *reason panders will:* reason helps desire to gratify itself. – Hamlet has reached the peak of invective. Images of hot and cold, passion and reason, have come thickly into his speech, and the Queen can stand no more.

91   *grainéd . . . tinct:* ingrained spots as will not lose (*leave*) their colour (*tinct*).

93   *enseaméd:* greased (with sweat).

98   *tithe:* the tenth part.

99   *precedent:* former.

99   *a vice of kings:* clown of a king. – The *Vice* was the stock character in a certain type of play, the 'Morality', which seems to have reached the height of its popularity shortly before Shakespeare began to write his plays. Moralities were composed to teach moral lessons, and the characters in them represented human qualities, good and bad. The Vice at one time evidently represented evil, but by Shakespeare's day his status had been lowered to the level of a clown or buffoon, frequently shown in conflict with the Devil. In Shakespeare's *Twelfth Night* (iv.ii.107ff.) there is a song which mentions him:

> I'll be with you again,
>   In a trice,
>   Like to the old Vice,
> Your need to sustain;
> Who with dagger of lath,
> In his rage and his wrath,
>   Cries, Ah, ha! to the devil.

When the Vice appeared like a clown, he wore the traditional dress made of different coloured scraps of cloth. Hamlet later (line 103) calls him
   A king of shreds and patches.

This was your husband. – Look you know, what follows:
Here is your husband, like a mildewed ear,*   65
Blasting his wholesome brother. Have you eyes?
Could you on this fair* mountain leave to feed,
And batten on this moor? Ha! have you eyes?
You cannot call it love, for at your age
The hey-day* in the blood is tame, it's humble,   70
And waits upon the judgement; and what judgement
Would step from this to this? [*Pointing to the pictures in
turn*] Sense,* sure, you have,
Else could you not have motion.* But, sure, that sense
Is apoplexed;* for madness would not err,
Nor sense* to ecstasy was ne'er so thralled   75
But it reserved some quantity of choice
To serve in such a difference. What devil was 't
That thus hath cozened* you at hoodman-blind?
Eyes without feeling, feeling without sight,
Ears without hands or eyes, smelling sans all,*   80
Or but a sickly part of one true sense
Could not so mope.*
O shame! Where is thy blush? Rebellious hell,
If thou canst mutine* in a matron's* bones,
To flaming youth* let virtue be as wax,   85
And melt in her own fire.* Proclaim no shame
When the compulsive ardour gives the charge,
Since frost itself as actively doth burn,
And reason panders* will.

QUEEN   O Hamlet, speak no more.
Thou turn'st mine eyes into my very soul;   90
And there I see such black and grainéd* spots
As will not leave their tinct.

HAMLET   Nay, but to live
In the rank sweat of an enseaméd* bed,
Stewed in corruption, honeying and making love
Over the nasty sty –

QUEEN   O, speak to me no more;   95
These words, like daggers, enter in mine ears;
No more, sweet Hamlet!

HAMLET   A murderer and a villain,
A slave that is not twentieth part the tithe*
Of your precedent* lord; a vice of kings;*

100   *cutpurse:* thief. – Purses were normally worn outside the clothing, fixed to a belt. Cf.
         modern English *pickpocket.*

101   *diadem:* crown.

         Ghost – It is clear from what follows that only Hamlet can see the Ghost on this occasion;
         and to him it seems to be wearing everyday clothes, not the armour of the first
         appearance. The ghost of the dead King comes most appropriately after Hamlet
         has reached a high pitch of frenzy in his abuse of the present king.

107   *your tardy . . . chide:* to reprove your slow-moving (*tardy*) son.

108   *lapsed . . . passion* – (probably) 'allowing the opportunity (*time*) and his passion for revenge
         to slip away (*lapse*)'.

109   *important acting:* urgent carrying out.

109   *dread:* revered.

113   *amazement:* bewilderment. – The Ghost says, in an involved and formal style, that
         Hamlet's mother looks bewildered by what is going on – her son evidently
         talking to nobody.

115   *Conceit:* imagination. – The Ghost is naturally sympathetic to Gertrude in her misery. It
         sees that her imagination, appalled now with the horror of what she has done,
         is working feverishly, and may cause her bodily harm; the Ghost therefore
         tells Hamlet to intervene.

118   *bend . . . vacancy:* turn your eyes to (look at) empty space (*vacancy*).

119   *incorporal:* incorporeal, without body – without anything that can be touched.

122   *Your bedded . . . Start up:* your hair, laid in a smooth layer (*bedded*), jumps up, as if there
         were life in these outgrowths (of the body). – His hair stands on (*an*) end with
         emotion. The image *bedded* is suggested by *sleeping* in the previous line.

124   *distemper:* mental illness.

127   *His form . . . capable:* The shape he assumes (*form*), taken together with (*conjoined*) the
         cause he pleads, would make even stones capable of feeling if he addressed
         (*preaching to*) them.

120   *convert My stern effects:* change my most serious intentions. – The *piteous action* of the
         Ghost was his look when his attitude changed from demanding revenge to
         pleading for sympathy to be shown to Gertrude (lines 113–16). Hamlet, only
         too ready to pity, fears the effect of this upon himself. And the Queen is
         completely confused because she cannot tell who he is talking to.

131   *Will want . . . blood:* will not take on its true character; there will perhaps be tears instead
         of blood. – The image of colour here is deeply felt: both tears and blood can
         come in drops, but the former are transparent, 'white', while the latter are red.

A cutpurse* of the empire and the rule   100
That from a shelf the precious diadem* stole,
And put it in his pocket!

QUEEN   No more!

HAMLET   A king of shreds and patches –

Enter GHOST.*

Save me, and hover o'er me with your wings,
You heavenly guards! – [*To the* GHOST] What would your
gracious figure?   105

QUEEN   Alas, he's mad!

HAMLET   Do you not come your tardy* son to chide,
That, lapsed* in time and passion, lets go by
Th' important* acting of your dread* command?
O say!   110

GHOST   Do not forget: this visitation
Is but to whet thy almost blunted purpose.
But, look, amazement* on thy mother sits.
O, step between her and her fighting soul –
Conceit* in weakest bodies strongest works –   115
Speak to her, Hamlet.

HAMLET   How is it with you, lady?

QUEEN   Alas, how is 't with *you*,
That you do bend* your eye on vacancy,
And with th' incorporal* air do hold discourse?
Forth at your eyes your spirits wildly peep,   120
And, as the sleeping soldiers in th' alarm,
Your bedded hair,* like life in excrements,
Start up, and stand an end. O gentle son,
Upon the heat and flame of thy distemper*
Sprinkle cool patience. Whereon do you look?   125

HAMLET   On him, on him! Look you, how pale he glares!
His form* and cause conjoined, preaching to stones
Would make them capable. – [*To the* GHOST] Do not look
upon me,
Lest with this piteous action you convert*
My stern effects, then what I have to do   130
Will want* true colour; tears perchance for blood.

QUEEN   To whom do you speak this?

HAMLET   Do you see nothing there?

QUEEN   Nothing at all; yet all that is I see.

136   *habit:* clothes – his ordinary clothes, not the armour he was wearing when he first appeared.
138   *coinage:* fabrication.
139   *This bodiless . . . in:* madness (*ecstasy*) is very skilful in creating these apparitions. – As in line 119, the Queen is evidently at pains to emphasize that there is no *body* there – *incorporal* (line 119) (Latin *corpus:* a body) and *bodiless.*
144   *I the matter . . . gambol from:* I will repeat in words the substance of what has taken place (*matter*) – (a *test*) which true madness would jump away from.
146   *flattering unction* – i.e. unction, ointment, which promises to give relief, but does not do so. He begs the Queen not to use his madness as a healing balm to cover up her own crime.
147   *trespass:* crime.
151   *avoid . . . come* – *what* here must refer to temptations to further indulgence; in the first half of the line, *what* refers to the *trespass* of line 147.
152   *the compost* – decayed vegetable matter used as manure. The image here means, 'Do not make your former evil deeds worse by adding new ones to them.'
153   *Forgive me . . . him good* (line 156) – These lines are difficult to explain, since it is strange that anyone should ask pardon for his virtues. The general drift of the passage suggests that Hamlet is concerned that his rightness in this cause must be apologized for because there is so much wickedness around him. There is also some element of humility in Hamlet's words: in reproving his mother so harshly he may be setting himself up as more virtuous than he really is.
　　　　I could accuse me of such things that it were better my mother had not borne me (III.i.123–5).
　　　　Here is a possible explanation of the present passage: 'You will have to forgive this virtuous attitude I am taking up, for in the pampered softness of these short-winded (*pursy*) times, even virtue must excuse itself to vice; yes, it must bow and plead for permission to do vice some good.' The image from *fatness* and *pursy* is of a man grown fat and yet delicate and short of breath through over-indulgence. Cf. line 173
　　　　I'll blessing beg of you
　　　　which seems to follow the same line of thought.
157   *cleft . . . in twain:* split . . . into two. – The Queen addresses Hamlet with the affectionate *thou.*
158   *it* – i.e. the Queen's heart. Hamlet has taken her words more literally than she could have expected.
161   *if:* even if.
162   *That monster . . . in this:* Custom, that monster which eats up all finer feeling (*sense*), the evil spirit of habits, is nevertheless a good angel in this respect.
165   *a frock . . . put on:* clothing or uniform which is readily (*aptly*) put on. – In other words, good actions can become as customary as bad ones; the image of clothing is perhaps suggested by *habits* which can mean both 'habitual action' and 'dress'.
169   *use:* custom.
170   *master* – Only the later Quartos give this word here; earlier editions omit the verb entirely. It is most likely that, on considerations of the metre of the line, a different verb with a single syllable is correct here: *curb, quell, shame* and others have been suggested.

HAMLET Nor did you nothing hear?

QUEEN   No, nothing but ourselves.

HAMLET Why, look you there! Look, how it steals away!   135
My father, in his habit* as he lived!
Look, where he goes, even now, out at the portal!

                                                    [*Exit* GHOST

QUEEN This is the very coinage* of your brain;
This bodiless creation ecstasy*
Is very cunning in.

HAMLET   Ecstasy!   140
My pulse, as yours. doth temperately keep time,
And makes as healthful music. It is not madness
That I have uttered; bring me to the test,
And I the matter* will re-word which madness
Would gambol from. Mother, for love of grace,   145
Lay not that flattering unction* to your soul,
That not your trespass* but my madness speaks.
It will but skin and film the ulcerous place,
Whilst rank corruption, mining all within,
Infects unseen. Confess yourself to heaven;   150
Repent what's past; avoid* what is to come;
And do not spread the compost* on the weeds,
To make them ranker. Forgive* me this my virtue;
For in the fatness of these pursy times
Virtue itself of vice must pardon beg,   155
Yea, curb and woo for leave to do him good.

QUEEN O Hamlet, thou hast cleft* my heart in twain.

HAMLET O, throw away the worser part of it,*
And live the purer with the other half.
Good night. But go not to my uncle's bed;   160
Assume a virtue, if* you have it not
That monster,* custom, who all sense doth eat,
Of habits devil, is angel yet in this,
That to the use of actions fair and good
He likewise gives a frock* or livery,   165
That aptly is put on. Refrain tonight;
And that shall lend a kind of easiness
To the next abstinence; the next more easy;
For use* almost can change the stamp of nature,
And either master* the devil, or throw him out   170
With wondrous potency. Once more, good night.

172   *desirous to be blest:* determined to pray for God's blessing (through repentance).

173   *For . . . lord:* As for this lord here – *same* is used sarcastically.

176   *their* – i.e. heaven's, God's. He is destined to be the instrument (*scourge,* literally 'whip') and agent (*minister*) by which God's punishment is effected. A *scourge* came to mean a wicked man used by God to punish wickedness in others, damning himself in the process; a *minister* punished sin without involving himself in wickedness.

177   *bestow:* dispose of.

177   *answer:* explain.

182   *Not this . . .* – The speech which follows represents a further stage in Hamlet's emotion. Here the mass of images he employs suggests that he is somewhat distracted, and so does his satirical beginning, where he says things which are the opposite of what he really desires.

183   *bloat:* soft-bodied, puffed out. – Cf. *pursy,* line 154 above.

184   *wanton,* for *wantonly.*

184   *mouse* – a pet name for the loved one in earlier English.

185   *reechy:* dirty.

187   *ravel . . . out:* disentangle, make plain and clear.

189   *in craft:* by design – contrasting with *essentially;* he is just pretending to be mad.

190   *For who . . . queen* – literally, 'For who, who is just (*but*) a queen . . .'; but this seems to make very little sense. Hamlet continues to be ironical in all he says; this suggests that the phrase *but a queen* means, in fact, just the opposite, 'nothing less than a queen'. In the lines to . . . *hide?* (line 192), Hamlet must therefore mean something as follows: 'For who, that is nothing less than a queen, . . . would conceal (*hide*) such deeply-felt (*dear*) matters (*concernings*) from (even) a toad (*paddock*), a bat, a cat (*gib*)?' None of these creatures was looked upon with much respect; the implication is, still less would she conceal these things from a king.

194   *Unpeg the basket* – What follows is a brief account of a fable which cannot now be traced. The exact content and meaning of the fable, as it is referred to here, is unclear, since here as elsewhere Hamlet is talking ironically, and is quite likely using an illustration with a moral quite opposite to what really suits the situation. The story must be something like this: 'Undo the basket with live birds in it which hangs from the roof-top; let the birds fly out, and then, like the monkey (*ape*) in the story, make your way into the basket yourself and experiment (*try conclusions*) (by jumping out of the basket as if you were a bird) and fall and break your neck.'
It is very hard to see how this is to be applied to the situation in the play. Here is a possible explanation: Hamlet in reality does not want his mother to tell the King that his madness is not real. But he has no faith in her discretion (he has said ironically that she is *fair, sober, wise* (line 190)); she is quite likely to 'let the birds out of the basket', i.e. give away his secret. But if she does, she is likely to come to a sad end, like the monkey which let the birds fly away and then took their place. The 'meaning' of the fable may possibly be carried one stage further: it is no use for the Queen now to start feigning in the way Hamlet is feigning his madness, because she will suffer for it if she does.

199   *breathe:* speak. – The usage persists in modern English: 'I shan't breathe a word.'

201   *to England* – This is as planned at the end of III.i. The king pretended that the trip was primarily for Hamlet's health, but in fact both he and Polonius would like to get Hamlet away from Denmark.

201   *Alack:* Alas.

202   *concluded on:* decided.

203   *There's letters sealed:* Letters have been written and sealed (to this effect).

204   *adders fanged:* poisonous snakes with fangs – i.e. he has no faith at all in Rosencrantz and Guildenstern.

205   *sweep my way:* prepare my way for me – literally, 'sweep a path'. Hamlet begins again with the exaggerated style of speaking he has used earlier. Cf. *mandate:* commission to act on behalf of another.

207   *'tis the sport . . . petar:* it is good fun (*sport*) to see the military engineer (*enginer*) blown into the air (*hoist,* past participle of *hoise*) by his own bomb (*petar*). – He means that what they are plotting against him may be turned against them in a most satisfying way.

And when you are desirous* to be blest,
I'll blessing beg of you. — For this same lord,*

[*Pointing to* POLONIUS

I do repent; but heaven hath pleased it so,
To punish me with this, and this with me,   175
That I must be their* scourge and minister.
I will bestow* him, and will answer* well
The death I gave him. So, again, good night. —
I must be cruel, only to be kind;
Thus bad begins, and worse remains behind. —   180
One word more, good lady.

QUEEN   What shall I do?

HAMLET Not this,* by no means, that I bid you do:
Let the bloat* king tempt you again to bed;
Pinch wanton* on your cheek; call you his mouse;*
And let him, for a pair of reechy* kisses,   185
Or paddling in your neck with his damned fingers,
Make you to ravel* all this matter out,
That I essentially am not in madness,
But mad in craft.* 'Twere good you let him know;
For who,* that's but a queen, fair, sober, wise,   190
Would from a paddock, from a bat, a gib,
Such dear concernings hide? Who would do so?
No, in despite of sense and secrecy,
Unpeg the basket* on the house's top,
Let the birds fly, and, like the famous ape,   195
To try conclusions, in the basket creep,
And break your own neck down.

QUEEN Be thou assured, if words be made of breath
And breath of life, I have no life to breathe*
What thou hast said to me.   200

HAMLET I must to England;* you know that?

QUEEN   Alack,*
I had forgot. 'Tis so concluded on.*

HAMLET There's letters sealed.* And my two school-fellows —
Whom I will trust as I will adders fanged* —
They bear the mandate; they must sweep* my way,   205
And marshal me to knavery. Let it work;
For 'tis the sport* to have the engineer

208   *'t shall go hard . . . moon:* things will turn out badly indeed (*'t shall go hard*) if I do not dig (*delve*) a yard deep under their works with explosives in them (*mines*), and blow them sky-high (*at*, 'up to', *the moon*). – He means that he will plant his own mines to blow up theirs.

211   *in one line two crafts* – The literal meaning is evidently 'two ships in a line' and so collid-ing. But the words are full of irony: *line* may have the secondary meaning 'fortification', thus continuing the idea of *mines* and *petar* above; *crafts* may also have the meaning 'cunning natures'.

212   *set me packing:* (i) make me begin plotting; and (perhaps) (ii) send me off in a hurry – though the verb in this usage should be *send*, not *set*, a fact which makes this second explanation doubtful.

213   *the guts*, i.e. the dead body (literally, the entrails).

217   *draw* suggests *lug* (line 213) as well as the phrase 'life draws to an end'; Hamlet's use of language is ironical even here, in the presence of death.

*   *severally:* separately, one by one.

Hoist with his own petar. And 't shall go hard*
But I will delve one yard below their mines,
And blow them at the moon. O, 'tis most sweet   210
When in one line* two crafts directly meet —
This man shall set me packing.*
I'll lug the guts* into the neighbour room. —
Mother, good night. — Indeed, this counsellor
Is now most still, most secret, and most grave,   215
Who was in life a foolish prating knave.
[*To the body*] Come, sir, to draw* toward an end with you. —
Good night, mother.
               [*Exeunt severally,* HAMLET *dragging* POLONIUS *away*

IV. i.   When the Queen tells Claudius about Polonius's death, he thinks first of his own safety – the thrust was obviously aimed at him – and then of the effect on the people. Rosencrantz and Guildenstern are to watch Hamlet and get him out of the country as soon as possible.

    This short scene, and the two which follow, further the action in the most direct way. Hamlet is now himself a murderer, and consequently at Claudius's mercy. Although Hamlet is powerless in this situation, his command of himself increases; he can treat the world with contempt.

1   *sighs* – i.e. the Queen's disturbed manner. Rosencrantz and Guildenstern are, as usual, in attendance, and have to be dismissed.

4   *Bestow . . . us:* Give us this place – i.e. 'Leave us'.

7   *contend Which:* strive against one another to decide which. – The Queen keeps up the pretence of Hamlet's madness; the King, in what follows, shows himself satisfied with this as an explanation.

10   *Whips:* he whips.

11   *brainish apprehension:* headstrong fit of imagination.

13   *It had . . . us:* Just the same would have happened to me.

16   *answered:* accounted for.

17   *laid . . . providence:* blamed on me my foresight (*providence*).

18   *short . . . haunt:* from roaming freely (*short*) under control (*restrained*) and away from the company of other people (*haunt*).

22   *divulging:* becoming known.

22   *feed . . . life* – i.e. eat away the most vital part (*pith*) of the body. The imagery is of physical disease in place of mental disease.

25   *ore:* gold. – The Queen in motherly love says something which puts Hamlet in a better light; his tears were like a streak of gold in a rock containing baser metals. (This rock is called *ore* in everyday English; Shakespeare has evidently confused the word with the Latin *aurum*: gold.) But perhaps what the Queen says is pure invention on her part.

32   *countenance* – (perhaps) 'take into account'.

ACT IV scene i

A room in the castle.

Enter KING, QUEEN, ROSENCRANTZ, *and* GUILDENSTERN.

KING There's matter in these sighs,* these profound heaves.
You must translate; 'tis fit we understand them.
Where is your son?
QUEEN Bestow this place on us* a little while.
　　　　　　　　　[*Exeunt* ROSENCRANTZ *and* GUILDENSTERN
Ah, my good lord, what have I seen tonight!　　　　　　5
KING What, Gertrude? How does Hamlet?
QUEEN Mad as the sea and wind, when both contend*
Which is the mightier. In his lawless fit,
Behind the arras hearing something stir,
Whips* out his rapier, cries 'A rat, a rat!'　　　　　　10
And, in this brainish apprehension,* kills
The unseen good old man.
KING 　　　　　　　　　O heavy deed!
It had been so with us,* had we been there.
His liberty is full of threats to all,
To you yourself, to us, to every one.　　　　　　15
Alas, how shall this bloody deed be answered?*
It will be laid* to us, whose providence
Should have kept short,* restrained, and out of haunt
This mad young man. But so much was our love,
We would not understand what was most fit;　　　　　　20
But, like the owner of a foul disease,
To keep it from divulging,* let it feed*
Even on the pith of life. Where is he gone?
QUEEN To draw apart the body he hath killed,
O'er whom his very madness, like some ore*　　　　　　25
Among a mineral of metals base,
Shows itself pure; he weeps for what is done.
KING O Gertrude, come away!
The sun no sooner shall the mountains touch,
But we will ship him hence; and this vile deed　　　　　　30
We must, with all our majesty and skill,
Both countenance* and excuse. – Ho, Guildenstern!

149

33   *go join . . . aid:* go and get some more assistance – since Hamlet is now (as it seems) a
      dangerous lunatic.
40   *untimely:* out of its proper time – i.e. inappropriately.
40   *So, haply, slander* – There is a blank in place of these words in the Folios and Quartos, but
      it is evident that the line and the sense are incomplete without an addition of
      some kind. The words given here are those generally adopted by editors; they
      were first suggested, in a slightly different form, by the Shakespearean scholar
      Lewis Theobald in his *Shakespeare Restored,* 1715.
          The lines *So, haply . . . woundless air* (line 44) may be explained as follows:
      'In this way, with luck (*haply*), slander, whose whisper carries its poisoned
      shot from one side of the world to the other (*diameter,* i.e. it travels so quickly,
      that it does not have to go round the world but simply through it), as straight
      (*level*) as a cannon fires at the white centre of a target (*blank*), may miss my
      name and instead hit the air, which cannot be wounded (*woundless*).' – This
      long explanation shows by contrast the neat suggestiveness of Shakespeare's
      lines, in which the image of slanderous talk as a gun firing at the person
      slandered is implied in a number of single words, *cannon, blank, shot, miss, hit.*

IV. ii.   Hamlet, assuming his ironic manner which the others take as madness, refuses to say
          where Polonius's body lies. He agrees to go to the King.

1   *stowed* – i.e. put away, hidden. He is referring to Polonius's body.
5   *whereto 'tis kin:* to which it is related. – In the burial service in the Prayer Book, the priest
          says, 'Dust to dust, earth to earth, ashes to ashes'.
10   *counsel:* secrets, confidence. – Is he perhaps thinking of his own discovery that they
          were the King's accomplices: *so shall . . . your secrecy to the king and queen
          moult no feather* (II.ii.287–9).
11   *to be demanded of a sponge:* to be questioned by a sponge – ready to soak up all the infor-
          mation given.
11   *replication:* reply.

Enter ROSENCRANTZ *and* GUILDENSTERN.

Friends both, go join* you with some further aid.
Hamlet in madness hath Polonius slain,
And from his mother's closet hath he dragged him.   35
Go seek him out; speak fair, and bring the body
Into the chapel. I pray you, haste in this.
                    [*Exeunt* ROSENCRANTZ *and* GUILDENSTERN
Come, Gertrude, we'll call up our wisest friends,
And let them know both what we mean to do,
And what's untimely* done. So, haply, slander* —   40
Whose whisper o'er the world's diameter,
As level as the cannon to his blank,
Transports his poisoned shot — may miss our name,
And hit the woundless air. — O, come away!
My soul is full of discord and dismay.   45
                                    [*Exeunt*

scene ii

Another room in the castle.

Enter HAMLET.

HAMLET   Safely stowed.*

ROSENCRANTZ &   [*Within*] Hamlet! Lord Hamlet!
GUILDENSTERN

HAMLET   What noise? Who calls on Hamlet? O, here they come.

Enter ROSENCRANTZ *and* GUILDENSTERN.

ROSENCRANTZ   What have you done, my lord, with the dead body?

HAMLET   Compounded it with dust, whereto* 'tis kin.   5

ROSENCRANTZ   Tell us where 'tis, that we may take it thence,
          And bear it to the chapel.

HAMLET   Do not believe it.

ROSENCRANTZ   Believe what?

HAMLET   That I can keep your counsel,* and not mine own. Besides,   10
          to be demanded of a sponge!* — What replication* should be
          made by the son of a king?

ROSENCRANTZ   Take you me for a sponge, my lord?

14   *countenance:* favour.
15   *authorities:* positions of authority – i.e. high appointments.
16   *like an ape . . . jaw* – The words *doth nuts* appear in the First Quarto but not in the Folios.
         In any case the text is probably faulty here, since *like* at the beginning of a
         clause is un-Shakespearean; he wrote *as* in this position. The meaning is
         sufficiently clear: the monkey keeps the nuts in the corner of its mouth,
         delaying the pleasure of swallowing them at last.
21   *knavish:* wicked.
24   *The body . . . body* – These words have not been satisfactorily explained. Hamlet seems to
         the others to be talking nonsense, and that is surely the impression his lines
         are meant to convey. Perhaps the first *king* means the King of Heaven, God—
         i.e. the body, no longer alive, is with its heavenly king.
27   *Hide fox . . . after* – Once again, this is best taken as deliberate nonsense. Perhaps it refers
         to a children's game: 'You hide, be the fox, and we will all go after you.'

IV. iii.   The King now makes a desperate effort to be rid of Hamlet, who treats his enquiries about
            Polonius with ironic contempt. Hamlet is told that he is to go to England, and the King,
            left alone, reveals that Hamlet will be killed as soon as he arrives there.

3   *we:* I – as elsewhere.
4   *of:* by.
6   *th' offender's scourge is weighed* – i.e. the instrument used to punish the offender is taken
            into consideration (*weighed*).
9   *Deliberate pause:* the ultimate result of careful deliberation – *pause* suggests 'hesitation,
            holding back', the opposite of *sudden sending.* Cf.:
                I stand in pause where I shall first begin (III.iii.42)
10   *appliance:* remedy.
14   *Without:* outside (the room).

HAMLET   Ay, sir, that soaks up the king's countenance,* his rewards,
his authorities.* But such officers do the king best service in   15
the end. He keeps them, like an ape doth nuts,* in the corner
of his jaw; first mouthed, to be last swallowed. When he
needs what you have gleaned, it is but squeezing you, and,
sponge, you shall be dry again.

ROSENCRANTZ   I understand you not, my lord.   20

HAMLET   I am glad of it. A knavish* speech sleeps in a foolish ear.

ROSENCRANTZ   My lord, you must tell us where the body is, and go with us
to the king.

HAMLET   The body* is with the king, but the king is not with the body.
The king is a thing –   25

GUILDENSTERN   A thing, my lord?

HAMLET   Of nothing. Bring me to him. Hide fox,* and all after.

[*Exeunt*

scene iii

Another room in the castle.

Enter KING, *attended.*

KING   I have sent to seek him, and to find the, body.
How dangerous is it that this man goes loose!
Yet must not we* put the strong law on him.
He's loved of* the distracted multitude,
Who like not in their judgement, but their eyes;   5
And where 'tis so, th' offender's scourge* is weighed,
But never the offence. To bear all smooth and even,
This sudden sending him away must seem
Deliberate pause.* Diseases desperate grown
By desperate appliance* are relieved,   10
Or not at all.

Enter ROSENCRANTZ.

　　　　　　How now! What hath befall'n?

ROSENCRANTZ   Where the dead body is bestowed, my lord,
We cannot get from him.

KING   　　　　　　　　But where is he?

ROSENCRANTZ   Without,* my lord; guarded, to know your pleasure.

21   *convocation . . . worms:* assembly of politically-minded (*politic*) worms. – The meaning of
          politic is uncertain here: perhaps they are 'politically minded' because they
          are feeding on a politician; perhaps the word means simply 'discreet', i.e.
          working unobstrusively.
              The talk which follows is on the subject of man eventually being conquered
          by worms; it is a common theme in earlier literature.

21   *e'en:* just now.

21   *Your worm* – This use of the possessive *your* with nouns is colloquial and sounds con-
          descending; the speaker wants to sound extremely familiar with the subject
          and to imply that the listener is absurdly ignorant.

22   *for:* as regards.

22   *fat,* for *fatten.*

22   *all creatures else:* all other creatures.

24   *is but variable service:* are only (*but*) a different order of dishes at the meal (*service*).

30   *a progress* – a state journey made by a king in order to get to know his country and people.

34   *th' other place* – i.e. hell. The King will be able to look for him there, but not in heaven.

40   *do tender:* care for – *which* refers to *safety.*

40   *dearly:* deeply.

42   *fiery* – i.e. with the speed of spreading fire.

43   *at help:* favourable.

44   *Th' associates tend:* the companions of your journey are waiting.

44   *is bent For:* is turned in the direction of. – Hamlet is not really surprised when he hears he
          is to leave for England, since the plan has already been made known to him
          (III.iv.200).

47   *a cherub* – Cherubs were thought of as angels who stood around the throne of God and
          who acted as tokens of the presence of God among his people. They were
          thought of as full of the knowledge of human and divine affairs; Hamlet
          speaks, therefore, of an all-knowing heavenly being.

49   *Thy loving father* – Hamlet has acknowledged his mother; the King wants Hamlet to
          acknowledge him as his father, i.e. step-father.

KING   Bring him before us.   15
ROSENCRANTZ Ho, Guildenstern! Bring in my lord.

          Enter HAMLET *and* GUILDENSTERN.

KING   Now, Hamlet, where's Polonius?
HAMLET   At supper.
KING   At supper! Where?
HAMLET   Not where he eats, but where he is eaten. A certain convoca-   20
           tion* of politic worms are e'en* at him. Your* worm is your
           only emperor for* diet. We fat* all creatures else* to fat us,
           and we fat ourselves for maggots. Your fat king and your
           lean beggar is but variable* service – two dishes, but to one
           table; that's the end.   25
KING   Alas, alas!
HAMLET   A man may fish with the worm that hath eat of a king, and
           eat of the fish that hath fed of that worm.
KING   What dost thou mean by this?
HAMLET   Nothing but to show you how a king may go a progress*   30
           through the guts of a beggar.
KING   Where is Polonius?
HAMLET   In heaven; send thither to see. If your messenger find him
           not there, seek him i' th' other place* yourself. But, indeed, if
           you find him not within this month, you shall nose him as   35
           you go up the stairs into the lobby.
KING   [*To some* ATTENDANTS] Go seek him there.
HAMLET   He will stay till ye come.
                                        [*Exeunt* ATTENDANTS

KING   Hamlet, this deed, for thine especial safety –
           Which we do tender,* as we dearly* grieve   40
           For that which thou hast done – must send thee hence
           With fiery* quickness. Therefore prepare thyself;
           The bark is ready, and the wind at help,*
           Th' associates* tend, and everything is bent*
           For England.
HAMLET   For England!
KING   Ay, Hamlet.
HAMLET   Good.   45
KING   So is it, if thou knew'st our purposes.
HAMLET   I see a cherub* that sees them. – But, come; for England! –
           Farewell, dear mother.
KING   Thy loving father,* Hamlet.

51   *one flesh* – an echo of the Prayer Book (marriage service): 'they two [the husband and wife] shall be one flesh', after they are married.

53   *at foot:* close behind.

55   *everything . . . else leans:* everything else . . . which the undertaking depends on (*leans*).

57   *England* – i.e. the King of England.

57   *hold'st at aught:* consider as of any value – *aught:* anything.

58   *As my . . . sense:* for so my great power should make you aware (*give thee sense*) of (the need for) it (*thereof*).

59   *cicatrice:* scar of a wound. – The Danes began intensive raids on England early in the ninth century, and kept them up for two centuries, until, in 1016, the Saxon king was overthrown and the Danish king took his place.

60   *free* – i.e. no longer enforced by Danish armies.

61   *coldly set . . . process:* estimate lightly (*coldly set:* treat with indifference) my royal mandate (*process*).

62   *imports at full:* sets out in detail.

63   *conjuring* – (perhaps) 'earnestly requesting, adjuring'. The Quartos read *congruing*, 'agreeing', but this reading makes unsatisfactory sense; as the letters are about the mandate, they must agree with it.

64   *present:* immediate.

65   *hectic:* wasting fever.

67   *Howe'er my haps:* whatever (else) may happen to me.

IV. iv.   A military expedition from Norway moves across the stage. The soldiers are on their way to fight the Poles over a piece of disputed territory worth virtually nothing to either side. When they have gone, Hamlet compares the urgent and large-scale action of this army, over a trivial point of honour, with his own inaction in the face of the gravest offence.

Only the first 8 lines of this scene appear in the Folios; the remainder is taken from the First Quarto. The scene contributes little to the immediate dramatic effect, but provides some pageantry (which Shakespeare's audience welcomed) and adds further evidence to confirm the soundness of Hamlet's mind: his speech at the end, with its sharp delineation of the inglorious contrast between him and the Norwegian prince, is in the finest, most characteristic style.

3 ·   *conveyance:* safe conduct.

3   *a promised march* – i.e. a march already agreed upon. At II.ii.81 the King said he would think over the request and decide whether to allow it or not. Shakespeare skilfully contrives that Fortinbras should give his Captain instructions of a kind which incidentally explain this particular incident in the play; he thus avoids a direct exposition of what is taking place.

5   *would aught with us:* wants to see us – literally, 'wishes to have anything (*aught*) (in the way of dealings) with us'.

6   *in his eye:* in the royal presence.

8   *softly:* slowly.

HAMLET   My mother. Father and mother is man and wife; man and   50
          wife is one flesh;* and so, mý mother. – [*To* ROSENCRANTZ *and*
          GUILDENSTERN] Come, for England!   [*Exit*
  KING   Follow him at foot;* tempt him with speed aboard;
          Delay it not; I'll have him hence tonight.
          Away! For everything* is sealed and done   55
          That else leans on th' affair. Pray you, make haste.
                    [*Exeunt* ROSENCRANTZ *and* GUILDENSTERN
          And, England,* if my love thou hold'st* at aught –
          As* my great power thereof may give thee sense,
          Since yet thy cicatrice* looks raw and red
          After the Danish sword, and thy free* awe   60
          Pays homage to us – thou mayst not coldly set*
          Our sovereign process, which imports* at full,
          By letters conjuring* to that effect,
          The present* death of Hamlet. Do it, England;
          For like the hectic* in my blood he rages,   65
          And thou must cure me. Till I know 'tis done,
          Howe'er my haps,* my joys were ne'er begun.   [*Exit*

scene iv

A plain in Denmark.

Enter FORTINBRAS *and a* CAPTAIN, *with an army, marching
across the stage.*

FORTINBRAS   Go, captain, from me greet the Danish king.
          Tell him that, by his licence, Fortinbras
          Claims the conveyance* of a promised march*
          Over his kingdom. You know the rendezvous.
          If that his majesty would aught* with us,   5
          We shall express our duty in his eye,*
          And let him know so.
  CAPTAIN   I will do 't, my lord.
FORTINBRAS   [*To his troops*] Go softly* on.
                    [*Exeunt all but* CAPTAIN

Enter HAMLET, ROSENCRANTZ, GUILDENSTERN, *and others.*

  HAMLET   Good sir, whose powers are these?

11   *How purposed:* Where do they propose to go.
14   *old Norway* – i.e. the aged King of Norway.
15   *main:* main part – i.e. the country as a whole.
20   *To pay . . . it:* I would not rent (*farm*) it on payment (*To pay*) of even (so little as) five
          ducats.
22   *ranker:* higher.
22   *in fee:* freehold – i.e. held in absolute possession.
23   *Polack:* Pole.
26   *debate:* settle by fighting. – All the early Quarto editions of the play give these lines to
          Hamlet, but, since the first two at least state facts which cannot possibly be
          known to him, these should almost certainly be given to the Captain. If this is
          the correct arrangement, Hamlet begins with *This is th' imposthume . . .*, which
          then makes good sense.
27   *imposthume* – inward swelling in the body, full of poisonous matter, abscess.
28   *without:* outside. – The abscess breaks inside the body.
32   *inform against me:* bring charges against me – as in law. This fact, that incidents happen
          and turn Hamlet's thoughts back into himself, is reflected in the arrangement of
          this scene, which, as elsewhere (e.g. I.ii; II.ii), begins with action and finishes
          with Hamlet, alone on the stage, talking to himself about his inaction.
34   *market of his time:* the most profitable use he makes of his time – i.e. selling it, as at a
          market.
36   *large discourse:* widely ranging powers of reasoning.
39   *fust:* grow mouldy.
40   *Bestial oblivion:* animal forgetfulness.
40   *craven scruple Of thinking:* cowardly misgivings arising from (*of*) thinking.
44   *to do:* (still) to be done.
45   *Sith:* When. – *Sith* is an old form of *since*.
47   *of such . . . charge:* so . . . costly.

CAPTAIN	They are of Norway, sir.	10
HAMLET	How purposed,* sir, I pray you?	
CAPTAIN	Against some part of Poland.	
HAMLET	Who commands them, sir?	
CAPTAIN	The nephew to old Norway,* Fortinbras.	
HAMLET	Goes it against the main* of Poland, sir,	15
	Or for some frontier?	
CAPTAIN	Truly to speak, sir, and with no addition,	
	We go to gain a little patch of ground	
	That hath in it no profit but the name.	
	To pay* five ducats, five, I would not farm it;	20
	Nor will it yield to Norway or the Pole	
	A ranker* rate, should it be sold in fee.*	
HAMLET	Why, then, the Polack* never will defend it.	
CAPTAIN	Yes, it is already garrisoned.	
HAMLET	Two thousand souls and twenty thousand ducats	25
	Will not debate* the question of this straw.	
	This is th' imposthume* of much wealth and peace,	
	That inward breaks, and shows no cause without*	
	Why the man dies. – I humbly thank you, sir.	
CAPTAIN	God be wi' you, sir. [*Exit*	
ROSENCRANTZ	Will 't please you go, my lord?	30
HAMLET	I'll be with you straight. Go a little before.	

[*Exeunt all but* HAMLET

How all occasions do inform* against me,
And spur my dull revenge! What is a man
If his chief good and market* of his time
Be but to sleep and feed? A beast, no more.   35
Sure, he that made us with such large discourse,*
Looking before and after, gave us not
That capability and godlike reason
To fust* in us unused. Now, whether it be
Bestial oblivion,* or some craven scruple*   40
Of thinking too precisely on th' event –
A thought which, quartered, hath but one part wisdom
And ever three parts coward – I do not know
Why yet I live to say, 'This thing's to do',*
Sith* I have cause, and will, and strength, and means   45
To do 't. Examples, gross as earth, exhort me:
Witness this army, of such mass and charge,*
Led by a delicate and tender prince,
Whose spirit, with divine ambition puffed,

50   *Makes mouths . . . event:* makes grimaces, mocks at the outcome (*event*), which cannot yet
           be foreseen (*invisible*).
53   *Rightly to be great . . . stake* (line 56): It is not a mark of true greatness to take offence
           (*stir*) without good reason (*argument*), but (it is a mark of greatness) to dispute
           over a trivial matter (*find quarrel in a straw*) if it is a question of honour. –
           Hamlet thinks that the reason for Fortinbras's expedition is utterly insignifi-
           cant, and again realizes to his shame that his own honour is by contrast
           genuinely at stake. There can be no excuse whatever for his own inactivity.
61   *a fantasy . . . fame:* a whim of fancy, an imaginary point of honour.
63   *Whereon the numbers . . . cause* – i.e. on which the numbers of men involved are too great
           to fight out the dispute; there is not enough room on the disputed plot of
           ground for the army to make a battlefield.
64   *continent:* container.

IV. v.   Ophelia comes on to the stage, driven to insanity by the loss of her father and the realiza-
         tion that Hamlet does not love her. She sings pathetic scraps of love-songs, and the King,
         as he hears her speak, laments the calamities that have led to her sad state.
           It is announced that Laertes has come with a band of men threatening the life of the
         King, whom he takes to be his father's killer. Ophelia re-enters, singing distractedly, and
         giving out flowers from her garland, each a symbol of her sorrow. The King denies that he
         is implicated, but Laertes is unconvinced – why was the noble Polonius given such a
         simple, hasty funeral?
           Although Hamlet does not appear in this scene, Ophelia's genuine distraction is to be
         seen against his own developed presence of mind and judgement. Laertes' passionate
         accusations and threats show him to be at this stage, like Hamlet, a menace to Claudius;
         some clever persuasion by Claudius is needed before Laertes pauses to think about
         who is guilty.

2   *distract,* for *distracted:* mad.
3   *will needs:* must.
3   *What would she have?:* What does she want?
5   *hems:* clears her throat, splutters.
6   *Spurns . . . straws:* kicks out (*Spurns*) angrily (*enviously*) at trifles.
7   *nothing:* nonsense.
8   *the unshaped . . . collection:* the artless (*unshaped:* unformed) use of it (*speech*) makes those
           who hear her try to put it together by inference (*collection*) (and so make some
           sense of it) – *move:* urge.
9   *aim:* guess.
10   *botch . . . up:* patch up, fit together as best they can.
11   *Which . . . –* The meaning of the passage in this and the following two lines (to *unhappily*)
           is not clear *Which* is probably best taken as referring to *the words* in the
           previous line; *yield* here means 'give out'. The general sense of the passage is,
           'her words, as given out with winks and nods and certain gestures, certainly
           give the impression that there is some thought behind them, though there is
           nothing clear-cut (*sure*), and what there is is spoken tragically (*unhappily*)'.
           Horatio is touching on the whole matter of Ophelia's distraction with great
           care, deliberately avoiding outright statements of fact. Ophelia's winks and
           nods would give the impression that she has some secret understanding with
           hearers who are in her confidence.
14   *'Twere good:* It would be a good thing if.
15   *ill-breeding minds:* minds which conceive evil.

Makes mouths* at the invisible event,   50
Exposing what is mortal and unsure
To all that fortune, death, and danger dare,
Even for an egg-shell. Rightly to be great*
Is not to stir without great argument,
But greatly to find quarrel in a straw   55
When honour's at the stake. How stand I, then,
That have a father killed, a mother stained,
Excitements of my reason and my blood,
And let all sleep? While, to my shame, I see
The imminent death of twenty thousand men,   60
That for a fantasy* and trick of fame
Go to their graves like beds, fight for a plot
Whereon the numbers* cannot try the cause,
Which is not tomb enough and continent*
To hide the slain? – O, from this time forth   65
My thoughts be bloody, or be nothing worth!   [Exit

scene v

Elsinore. A room in the castle.

Enter QUEEN *and* HORATIO.

QUEEN   I will not speak with her.
HORATIO She is importunate, indeed distract;*
         Her mood will needs* be pitied.
QUEEN   What would she have?*
HORATIO She speaks much of her father; says she hears
         There's tricks i' th' world; and hems,* and beats her heart;   5
         Spurns* enviously at straws; speaks things in doubt,
         That carry but half sense. Her speech is nothing,*
         Yet the unshaped* use of it doth move
         The hearers to collection; they aim* at it,
         And botch* the words up fit to their own thoughts,   10
         Which,* as her winks and nods and gestures yield them,
         Indeed would make one think there might be thought,
         Though nothing sure, yet much unhappily.
         'Twere good* she were spoken with, for she may strew
         Dangerous conjectures in ill-breeding* minds.   15

18   *toy:* trifling circumstance. – The general sense of the Queen's words is, 'To the guilty conscience, every little event seems to be leading to disaster; the guilty person is so intent on covering up his guilt that he betrays himself'.

18   *amiss:* disaster.

19   *artless jealousy:* suspicion unskilfully concealed.

20   *spills itself:* destroys itself. Guilt brings a person to destruction in its very attempts to conceal itself.

*   Ophelia's song brings together, in obscure hints, her thoughts of her father and of Hamlet's love for her. The song laments the death of both, and these are the causes of her distraction. The song is evidently an old ballad; there are melodies traditionally associated with the songs in this scene.

25   *cockle hat* – i.e. a hat with a cockle-shell on it as a mark that the wearer was a pilgrim who had been across the sea. In old stories it is a favourite trick of lovers to disguise themselves as pilgrims.

26   *shoon:* shoes – an archaic form especially associated with ballads.

27   *What imports this song:* What does this song signify?

28   *mark:* take notice. – She then sings the second stanza of the song; the third begins at line 35.

37   *Larded:* decked out – used literally of a dish served with garnishing.

39   *showers* – of tears, with which the loved one was *bewept.*

41   *God 'ild you:* may God reward you (for your kindness) – *'ild* is short for *yield.*

41   *the owl was a baker's daughter* – Ophelia here seems to be recalling a folk tale, although no version of it has been traced. An early editor of Shakespeare, Francis Douce (1757–1834), claimed that he knew of the story referred to. In it, Jesus went into a baker's shop and asked for some bread. The baker-woman put a large piece of dough in the oven, but her daughter said it was too big and persuaded her to make it much smaller. Then by a miracle the small piece of dough rose to an enormous size in the oven. The daughter called out 'Heugh, heugh, heugh' in surprise, and Jesus turned her into an owl. – Ophelia may mean that she is completely changed, as different from what she once was as the owl is from what *it* once was. But the owl was associated with mourning, and this may also be referred to: 'the lamenting owl was, like me, once a daughter – the daughter of a baker'.

44   *Conceit upon:* (These are) thoughts about. – The King has apparently caught only the word *daughter* in what Ophelia has just said.

QUEEN   Let her come in.   [*Exit* HORATIO

        To my sick soul, as sin's true nature is,
        Each toy* seems prologue to some great amiss.*
        So full of artless jealousy* is guilt,
        It spills itself* in fearing to be spilt.   20

        Enter HORATIO, *with* OPHELIA, *distracted.*

OPHELIA Where is the beauteous majesty of Denmark?

QUEEN   How now, Ophelia!

OPHELIA [*Sings*]*

                    How should I your true-love know
                    From another one?
                    By his cockle hat* and staff,   25
                    And his sandal shoon.*

QUEEN   Alas, sweet lady, what imports* this song?

OPHELIA Say you? Nay, pray you, mark.*

        [*Sings*]   He is dead and gone, lady,
                        He is dead and gone;   30
                        At his head a grass-green turf,
                        At his heels a stone.

QUEEN   Nay, but, Ophelia –

OPHELIA Pray you, mark.

        [*Sings*]   White his shroud as the mountain snow –   35

        Enter KING.

QUEEN   [*To the* KING] Alas, look here, my lord.

OPHELIA [*Sings*]   Larded* with sweet flowers;
                        Which bewept to the grave did go
                        With true-love showers.*

KING   How do you, pretty lady?   40

OPHELIA Well, God 'ild you!* They say the owl* was a baker's
        daughter. Lord, we know what we are, but know not what
        we may be. God be at your table!

KING   Conceit upon* her father.

47   *Saint Valentine's day* – On this day (14th February) the birds were supposed to pair, and from this the custom arose of a man promising devotion for a year to the first girl he sees on that day; it is this custom which is referred to in the song:

> *I a maid at your window,*
> *To be your Valentine.*

  – The song is an old ballad.

48   *betime:* early.

51   *donned:* put on.

52   *dupped:* opened – literally, 'do up', as *don* in the previous line is 'do on'.

56   *la* – an exclamation to call attention to a statement, like 'indeed'. Ophelia evidently says this instead of an *oath* to swear to the truth of her story.

57   *By Gis:* By Jesus. – This is, of course, an oath.

60   *Cock:* God. – This and *Gis* in line 57 are perversions of the sacred names, made to avoid blasphemy.

67   *choose but weep:* avoid weeping.

72   *this'* for *this is*.

74   *single spies* – (perhaps) 'as single scouts'; *spies* evidently contrasting with *battalions*.

77   *remove:* removal. – Hamlet had to be removed through his own fault; *author:* agent.

77   *muddied:* disturbed – like standing water stirred up so that the mud rises.

79   *greenly:* unskilfully – as if lacking in ripeness and experience.

80   *in hugger-mugger:* in secret.

OPHELIA Pray you, let's have no words of this; but when they ask you   45
         what it means, say you this:

[*Sings*]   '*Tomorrow is Saint Valentine's day,**
              *All in the morning betime,**
              And I a maid at your window,
                 To be your Valentine.   50
              Then up he rose, and donned his clothes,*
                 And dupped the chamber-door;*
              Let in the maid, that out a maid
                 Never departed more.

KING Pretty Ophelia!   55
OPHELIA Indeed, la,* without an oath, I'll make an end on 't:

[*Sings*]   *By Gis* and by Saint Charity,*
                 Alack, and fie for shame!
              Young men will do 't, if they come to 't;
                 By Cock, they are to blame!*   60
              Quoth she, 'Before you tumbled me,
                 You promised me to wed.'

He answers.

              '*So would I ha' done, by yonder sun,*
                 An thou hadst not come to my bed.'

KING How long hath she been thus?   65
OPHELIA I hope all will be well. We must be patient. But I cannot
         choose but weep* to think they should lay him i' th' cold
         ground. My brother shall know of it. And so I thank you for
         your good counsel. — Come, my coach! — Good night, ladies;
         good night, sweet ladies; good night, good night.   [*Exit*   70
KING Follow her close; give her good watch, I pray you.
                                                          [*Exit* HORATIO
         O, this,* the poison of deep grief; it springs
         All from her father's death. O Gertrude, Gertrude,
         When sorrows come, they come not single spies,*
         But in battalions! First, her father slain;   75
         Next, your son gone; and he most violent author
         Of his own just remove.* The people muddied,*
         Thick and unwholesome in their thoughts and whispers,
         For good Polonius' death, and we have done but greenly,*
         In hugger mugger* to inter him. Poor Ophelia,   80
         Divided from herself and her fair judgement,

82   *pictures* – i.e. images of ourselves, not true persons.
83   *as much containing:* as important.
85   *Feeds on . . . clouds:* broods over his shocked surprise (*wonder* at his father's mysterious
             death), and keeps himself aloof.
86   *wants not buzzers:* does not lack those who whisper rumours.
87   *of:* about.
88   *Wherein necessity . . . ear* (line 90): in which the need (to sustain charges) (*necessity*), when
             facts are lacking (*of matter beggared*), will (cause the speaker to) stop at nothing
             to make accusations against me (*our person to arraign*) in people's ears – i.e. by
             whispered rumours.
91   *a murdering-piece* – a small cannon which shot out many scraps of metal at one time.
93   *Switzers:* (Swiss) bodyguard. – Switzerland seems frequently to have provided mercenary
             troops and hired bodyguards for kings of other countries.
95   *overpeering . . . list:* rising above its boundary – i.e. the shore. The image is of the rising
             tide quickly covering the flat lands of the seashore.
97   *head:* hostile body of men.
99   *as:* as if.
101 *The ratifiers . . . word:* custom, tradition, (which are) the confirmers and supports of every
             word pledged. – The point here is that every pledge made in the society has
             the support of age-old custom – the kingship, for instance, passing from father
             to son. But the rabble is prepared to break this traditional allegiance and declare
             Laertes king.
102 *Choose we:* Let us choose.
103 *Caps* – i.e. they applaud Laertes by throwing their caps into the air.
105 *cry:* bark. – The image is of a pack of dogs 'in full cry', barking as they follow the trail of
             the quarry—but here the scent is false.
106 *counter:* running backwards – said of dogs running backwards on the trail in the direction
             from which the hunt has come.
109 *without:* outside.
114 *That drop . . . bastard:* Any drop of blood that is calm in me shows that I am a bastard.
             – He disowns his father if any part of him remains calm in this situation.
115 *cuckold* – a husband whose wife is unfaithful to him.

Without the which we are pictures,* or mere beasts.
Last, and as much containing* as all these,
Her brother is in secret come from France;
Feeds on his wonder,* keeps himself in clouds,   85
And wants not buzzers* to infect his ear
With pestilent speeches of* his father's death,
Wherein necessity,* of matter beggared,
Will nothing stick our person to arraign
In ear and ear. O my dear Gertrude, this,   90
Like to a murdering-piece,* in many places
Gives me superfluous death.   [A noise within

QUEEN   Alack, what noise is this?
KING   Where are my Switzers?* Let them guard the door.

Enter a GENTLEMAN.

What is the matter?
GENTLEMAN   Save yourself, my lord!
The ocean, overpeering* of his list,   95
Eats not the flats with more impetuous haste
Than young Laertes, in a riotous head,*
O'erbears your officers. The rabble call him lord;
And, as* the world were now but to begin,
Antiquity forgot, custom not known,   100
The ratifiers* and props of every word,
They cry, 'Choose we;* Laertes shall be king!'
Caps,* hands, and tongues applaud it to the clouds:
'Laertes shall be king, Laertes king!'
QUEEN   How cheerfully on the false trail they cry!*   105
O, this is counter,* you false Danish dogs!
KING   The doors are broke.   [Noise within

Enter LAERTES, armed; DANES following.

LAERTES Where is this king? – [To the Danish Soldiers] Sirs, stand you
all without.*
DANES   No, let's come in.
LAERTES   I pray you, give me leave.   110
DANES   We will, we will.   [They retire outside the door
LAERTES I thank you – keep the door. – O thou vile king,
Give me my father!
QUEEN   Calmly, good Laertes.
LAERTES That drop of blood that's calm* proclaims me bastard;
Cries cuckold* to my father; brands the harlot   115

116   *unsmirchéd brow:* clean-skinned forehead. – The harlot was branded with a mark on the forehead; the calm drop of blood would brand his mother as a harlot.

119   *fear* – i.e. fear for, be concerned about. The King continues to use the first person plural when he refers to himself.

120   *divinity . . . king* – A king is 'hedged' in by God's protection since it is God who 'appoints' kings. They were not chosen by the people but ruled by 'divine right'.

121   *can but peep . . . would:* can only get a glimpse of what it wishes to do. – The pronoun *his* in the following line refers back to *it*, i.e. treason.

126   *demand his fill:* ask everything he wants – i.e. until he is filled, satisfied.

129   *grace* – i.e. the grace of God. Laertes utters these curses in a way which would have appeared very evil to Shakespeare's audiences. The stability of the country was seen to depend on a strong government, and the source of strong government was a powerful monarch. Since the monarch was 'appointed by God', treason against him was therefore an act against God's law and against common sense. But Laertes says, *To hell, allegiance!*

131   *both the worlds . . . negligence:* I treat both this world and the world to come with contempt. – So long as he avenges his father's death he does not care what happens to him in this life or after death.

133   *throughly:* thoroughly, completely.

133   *stay:* restrain.

135   *I'll husband them:* I'll use them (the *means*) economically. – He has little power, but what he has he vows to use effectively.

139   *swoopstake:* indiscriminately – like a gambler 'swooping' on the whole stake in a game of cards regardless of whether or not the points are in his favour. To be revenged, Laertes must know who are his friends and who are not.

143   *the kind . . . pelican Repast them* – It was once thought that the pelican pecked open its own breast and fed its young with its own blood if it could find no other food for them. It is by nature (*kind*) ready to give its life-blood for its young. The tradition arose probably because the pelican has a large pouch in its lower bill which it uses to store food in for its young; when the bill is open, it looks dark pink inside, like blood. – References to romantic traditions of this kind were thought to be part of the equipment of an educated person; hence the King's retort:

           now you speak. Like . . . a true gentleman.

       Repast: feed.

147   *sensibly:* feelingly.

148   *It* – i.e. the fact *That I am guiltless . . . And am most sensibly in grief . . .*

148   *level:* plain – *'pear,* for *appear* (the Quartos have *peare*).

Even here, between the chaste unsmirchéd* brow
Of my true mother.

KING   What is the cause, Laertes,
That thy rebellion looks so giant-like?
Let him go, Gertrude; do not fear* our person.
There's such divinity* doth hedge a king   120
That treason can but peep* to what it would,
Acts little of his will. – Tell me, Laertes,
Why thou art thus incensed? – Let him go, Gertrude –
Speak, man.

LAERTES Where is my father?

KING   Dead.

QUEEN   But not by him.   125

KING Let him demand* his fill.

LAERTES How came he dead? I'll not be juggled with.
To hell, allegiance! Vows, to the blackest devil!
Conscience and grace,* to the profoundest pit!
I dare damnation. To this point I stand,   ·   130
That both the worlds* I give to negligence,
Let come what comes; only I'll be revenged
Most throughly* for my father.

KING   Who shall stay* you?

LAERTES My will, not all the world.
And for my means, I'll husband* them so well,   135
They shall go far with little.

KING   Good Laertes,
If you desire to know the certainty
Of your dear father's death, is 't writ in your revenge,
That, swoopstake,* you will draw both friend and foe,
Winner and loser?   140

LAERTES None but his enemies.

KING   Will you know them, then?

LAERTES To his good friends thus wide I'll ope my arms,
And, like the kind life-rendering pelican,*
Repast them with my blood.

KING   Why, now you speak
Like a good child and a true gentleman.   145
That I am guiltless of your father's death,
And am most sensibly* in grief for it,
It* shall as level* to your judgement 'pear
As day does to your eye.

DANES [Within]   Let her come in.

152   *sense and virtue:* physical perception and essential power. – Burning, salt tears are the signs of the bitterest grief.

153   *paid by weight . . .* – The image here is of a pair of scales; a balance is used as a symbol of justice, where one side is adjusted automatically to changes in the other— no movement on one side (e.g. a misdeed) can take place without another movement (e.g. just retribution) on the other side. Ophelia's madness is the outcome of grave misdeeds; the gravity of these misdeeds will be paid for according to weight, i.e. the retribution will be as grave as the misdeeds, so much so that the retribution (*our scale,* the weight on our side) will outbalance the other side (*turn the beam*) and the wrong-doers will suffer more than they made others suffer. The beam is the horizontal bar from which the two scales hang.

154   *May* is associated with the freshness of spring and new birth.

157   *mortal:* subject to death, killable.

158   *Nature . . . it loves* (line 160): Human nature is refined (*fine*) in matters of love; and when it is refined in this way, it sends some highly valued part (*instance:* sample) of itself away to the object it loves. – Ophelia's sanity has left her and followed her father to his grave. There is some irony in the fact that the words *in love* are more likely to refer to sexual love, and in the song which Ophelia now sings the ideas of death and the passing away of love are interwoven; Polonius and Hamlet are together the sources of her insanity.

161   *barefaced* – i.e. the coffin was open.

162   *Hey non nonny* – These words form a meaningless refrain in the song, as not uncommonly in ballad poetry; they are usually associated with tragic events. No music is known for the ballad Ophelia sings here.

165   *persuade revenge:* urge us to take revenge.

166   *It could . . . thus:* it (your persuasion) could not move us as powerfully as this does. – Her madness is so touching that it has a power above rational persuasion.

167   *Down a-down* – another ballad refrain, which Ophelia in her distraction asks the others to join in singing.

168   *wheel* – Perhaps the spinning wheel, whirring round as the girls sang, is thought of as forming a fitting accompaniment to the song (*becomes it*).

168   *the false steward* – This evidently refers to a ballad, now lost.

170   *This nothing's . . . matter:* This nonsense has more meaning in it than any sense could have.

171   *rosemary* – Ophelia begins to use the language of flowers, apparently taking specimens of various kinds from the bunch she is carrying, and handing them to the people who are watching her. Each flower is associated with some message. The rosemary, standing for remembrance, she gives to Laertes, evidently taking him for her lover (she calls him *love*).

172   *pansies* are symbols of sorrow (*thoughts*); the name pansy comes from the French word *pensée:* thought.

174   *A document:* A piece of instruction.

174   *fitted:* agreeing, harmonising with one another.

175   *fennel . . . columbines* – Fennel stands for flattery, such as a king might expect to receive; *columbine* perhaps for unfaithfulness in love – in any case this flower was not looked upon with much favour in Shakespeare's day.

176   *rue* is associated with sorrow and repentance. (There is a verb *rue* in English, meaning 'have pity for'; this does not come from the same origin as *rue,* the flower, but doubtless became associated with it.) It seems that this flower was used in certain religious ceremonies for cleansing the afflicted; hence it is called here *herb of grace,* and is especially associated with Sundays.

178   *With a difference* – i.e. the Queen should wear it for repentance, since she has committed evil, whereas Ophelia wears it only for sorrow. (The phrase *with a difference* is associated with descriptions of coats-of-arms; a *difference* was a distinction made on one coat of arms to distinguish it from another belonging to a different member of the same family; but this imagery has no special significance here.)

178   *daisy* – This stands for deception in love-affairs.

179   *violets* – symbols of faithfulness, and so not among the flowers she is distributing. Before he left Denmark, Laertes had warned her of Hamlet's amorous trifling as *A violet in the youth of primy nature* (I.iii.7), like the spring flowers which quickly die. And now, although these flowers stood for faithfulness, she can have no

LAERTES   How now! What noise is that?   150

Enter OPHELIA.

O heat, dry up my brains! Tears seven-times salt,
Burn out the sense* and virtue of mine eye!
By heaven, thy madness shall be paid by weight,*
Till our scale turn the beam. O rose of May!*
Dear maid, kind sister, sweet Ophelia!   155
O heavens! Is 't possible a young maid's wits
Should be as mortal* as an old man's life?
Nature* is fine in love; and, where 'tis fine,
It sends some precious instance of itself
After the thing it loves.   160

OPHELIA   [*Sings*]   *They bore him barefaced* on the bier;*
                       Hey non nonny,* nonny, hey nonny;
                       And in his grave rained many a tear –
Fare you well, my dove!

LAERTES   Hadst thou thy wits, and didst persuade* revenge,   165
It could not move* thus.

OPHELIA   You must sing, *Down a-down,* and you call him a-down-a.* O,
how the wheel* becomes it! It is the false steward,* that stole
his master's daughter.

LAERTES   This nothing's* more than matter.   170

OPHELIA   [*To Laertes*] There's rosemary,* that's for remembrance;
pray you, love, remember. And there is pansies,* that's for
thoughts.

LAERTES   A document* in madness; thoughts and remembrance fitted.*

OPHELIA   [*To the* KING] There's fennel* for you, and columbines – [*To*   175
the QUEEN] There's rue* for you, and here's some for me – we
may call it herb of grace o'Sundays – O, you must wear your
rue with a difference.* – There's a daisy.* – I would give you
some violets,* but they withered all when my father died –
they say he made a good end –   180

[*Sings*]   *For bonny sweet Robin* is all my joy –*

---

179 (*cont'd*)   hope of marrying Hamlet, since he is the killer of her father and seems not to
                  be in his right mind.
181   *bonny sweet Robin* – a popular ballad of Shakespeare's day; the melody is preserved but
       the words are lost.

182   *Thought*: sorrow – as often elsewhere.
182   *passion*: suffering.
184   *a'*: he. – These verses are from another old song, perhaps adapted by Shakespeare to touch upon both her love for Hamlet (*He never will come again*) and the death of her father (*His beard was as white as snow*).
190   *poll*: head.
192   *cast away moan*: throw aside our grief.
194   *of*: on. – A formula such as '. . . on whose soul, and on all Christian souls, may God have mercy; Amen' was often used in inscriptions on memorials in medieval England. The last line of the song reminds Ophelia of this formula; and, fittingly, these are the last words she speaks before she goes to her death. All Christians would see a deeply tragic consequence in these sentiments of Christianity given utterance by a person who, because she takes her own life, will be denied the rites of a Christian burial.
194   *wi'*, for *with*. – The formula *God be wi' you* has been reduced to the modern English *Good-bye*.
196   *commune with*: share in.
198   *of whom . . . will*: of whoever you want among your wisest friends.
200   *collateral*: indirect – i.e. in league with some other *hand*.
201   *touched*: implicated – in the murder of Polonius; *touched* links with the image of *hand* as the instrument by which a deed is done.
207   *His means of death*: the way he died.
208   *hatchment* – the coat of arms of a dead man painted on a black background and shown at his funeral; Laertes says that the whole funeral ceremony was carried out hurriedly (*obscure burial*) without the honours due to a nobleman, and therefore the whole affair is suspect.
209   *ostentation*: funeral pomp.
212   *the great axe* – presumably the instrument of punishment or revenge.

LAERTES Thought* and affliction, passion,* hell itself,
          She turns to favour and to prettiness.

OPHELIA [*Sings*]   *And will a'* not come again?*
                            And will a' not come again?   185
                               No, no, he is dead.
                               Go to thy death-bed,
                            He never will come again.

                            His beard was as white as snow,
                            *All flaxen was his poll;**   190
                               He is gone, he is gone,
                               *And we cast away moan;**
                            God ha' mercy on his soul!

          And of* all Christian souls, I pray God. – God be wi'* you.
                                                              [*Exit*

LARTES   Do you see this, O God?   195
KING   Laertes, I must commune* with your grief,
          Or you deny me right. Go but apart,
          Make choice of whom* your wisest friends you will,
          And they shall hear and judge 'twixt you and me.
          If by direct or by collateral* hand   200
          They find us touched,* we will our kingdom give,
          Our crown, our life, and all that we call ours,
          To you in satisfaction; but if not,
          Be you content to lend your patience to us,
          And we shall jointly labour with your soul   205
          To give it due content.
LAERTES   Let this be so;
          His means of death,* his obscure burial –
          No trophy, sword, nor hatchment* o'er his bones,
          No noble rite nor formal ostentation* –
          Cry to be heard, as 'twere from heaven to earth,   210
          That I must call 't in question.
KING   So you shall;
          And where th' offence is let the great axe* fall.
          I pray you, go with me.
                                                        [*Exeunt*

IV. vi. There is news in a letter that Hamlet has escaped from the ship bound for England by getting aboard a pirate ship which attacked them. He is now back in Denmark; Rosencrantz and Guildenstern continue their passage to England.
    Claudius, already threatened by Laertes, has now to face Hamlet again.

5   *greeted:* addressed in letters.
10   *let to know:* informed.
12   *means:* way of getting.
13   *a pirate . . . appointmrnt:* a pirate ship fitted out formidably for war – *appointment:* equipment. Some readers have thought that Hamlet had arranged this pirate attack himself, but there is no evidence for this view, and, as Coleridge showed, this is one of the very few places in Shakespeare where the plot turns on an accident which is pure chance and in no way influenced by the will of the people involved. This, Coleridge points out, is quite in keeping with a play about a man who in the end determines issues 'by accident or by a fit of passion'.
15   *grapple* – the action of closing with an enemy ship by throwing an iron hook on the end of a rope on to the enemy ship and drawing the two ships together; in this way hand-to-hand fighting was made possible at sea.
18   *thieves of mercy:* merciful thieves.
21   *fly:* flee from.
21   *will:* which will.
22   *the bore of the matter* – The *bore* is the calibre, internal diameter, of the muzzle of a gun. The image suggests that Hamlet's words will be too light for the weight of the matter they tell of, as small shot is unsuitable for a large gun.
26   *He that . . . thine:* He who you know is your good friend – *thine* is used as we might end an intimate letter with *Yours* today.
28   *make you way:* show you the way (to the King).
29   *the speedier, that:* all the more quickly, so that.

scene vi

Another room in the castle.

Enter HORATIO *and a* SERVANT.

HORATIO What are they that would speak with me?
SERVANT Seafaring men, sir; they say they have letters for you.
HORATIO Let them come in. –   [*Exit* SERVANT
    I do not know from what part of the world
    I should be greeted,* if not from Lord Hamlet.   5

Enter SAILORS.

FIRST SAILOR God bless you, sir.
HORATIO Let him bless thee too.
FIRST SAILOR He shall, sir, an 't please him. There's a letter for you, sir. It
    comes from the ambassador that was bound for England – if
    your name be Horatio, as I am let to know* it is.   10
                            [*Hands him the letter*
HORATIO [*Reads*] *Horatio, when thou shalt have overlooked this, give*
    these fellows some means to the king; they have letters for*
    him. Ere we were two days old at sea, a pirate of very war-*
    like appointment gave us chase. Finding ourselves too slow
    of sail, we put on a compelled valour, and in the grapple I*   15
    boarded them. On the instant they got clear of our ship; so I
    alone became their prisoner. They have dealt with me like
    thieves of mercy. But they knew what they did; I am to do a*
    good turn for them. Let the king have the letters I have sent;
    and repair thou to me with as much speed as thou wouldest   20
    fly death. I have words to speak in thine ear will* make thee*
    dumb; yet are they much too light for the bore of the matter.*
    These good fellows will bring thee where I am. Rosencrantz
    and Guildenstern hold their course for England; of them I
    have much to tell thee. Farewell.   25

        He that thou knowest thine,*

            HAMLET

    Come, I will make you way* for these your letters;
    And do 't the speedier,* that you may direct me
    To him from whom you brought them.   30
                             [*Exeunt*

IV. vii The King finishes his work of convincing Laertes that Hamlet, not he himself, is guilty of Polonius's death and Ophelia's madness. At first Laertes mistrusts him: why is Hamlet still free? The King makes a good case: he will not kill him for fear of alienating his Queen's affection, and, the people love their prince. Instead he whips Laertes into a passionate desire for vengeance on Hamlet. He will have it by fencing with him in a test of skill; his foil will have its point unguarded and a cup of poisoned wine will be at hand.

The Queen enters with news that she has seen Ophelia drown; Ophelia has fallen into a river and her sodden clothes have dragged her body down. This pushes to the limit Laertes' thirst for revenge on Hamlet.

The structural contrasts of passion and reason are emphasized yet again: Laertes is now firm in his passion for revenge while Hamlet's widely respected reputation as a wise prince is asserted.

1	*my acquittance seal:* confirm my legal discharge from responsibility (for the crime). – This is a ponderous legalistic way of saying that Laertes must now realize that Claudius was not responsible for the crimes against Laertes' family.
2	*put me . . . for friend:* take me as a friend.
3	*Sith:* since.
3	*knowing:* acknowledging.
6	*feats, So crimeful . . . capital:* deeds so criminal . . . punishable by death.
9	*mainly:* greatly.
10	*much unsinewed:* very weak. – The King is careful to conceal at each point that he is on the defensive; he tries to anticipate objections before they are put forward.
13	*be it either which:* whichever of the two it may be. – The grammatical construction is strange here.
14	*She's so conjunctive . . . by her* (line 16): She is so closely united (*conjunctive*) to me in life and soul that, just as a star can move only within its own particular sphere, I cannot move except with her. – The imagery here depends upon an ancient notion that the stars kept to their courses because they each moved inside an invisible crystal globe in the heavens. The word *conjunctive* is used as a technical term in astrology, and therefore subscribes to this image. Cf. I.v.17: *Make thy two eyes, like stars, start from their spheres.*
17	*count, for account:* reckoning, trial.
18	*the general gender:* the common people. – For *general* in this sense, compare II.ii.413: *'twas caviare to the general.*
20	*Would . . . Convert* (in the following line): want . . . to convert. – The image here is of wood being petrified (turned to stone) if dipped in springs where the water is full of minerals; it can be explained in this context only if stone is considered to be more 'noble' than wood. The word *dipping* (line 19) links with this image.
21	*gyves:* shackles, instruments of imprisonment. – The point is evidently that the common people would want to take his imprisonment as something which was not shameful but an adornment (*graces*) to him.
22	*slightly timbered:* made of wood which is too light. – The arrows of his accusations would be too light to reach their target while there was so much popular feeling on Hamlet's side.
26	*A sister driven* – The words *have I* from the preceding line are understood, in the sense 'I find': 'I find a sister driven . . .
26	*terms:* condition.
27	*may . . . again:* can refer to what has now passed (and no longer applies).
28	*challenger . . . age:* challenger of the whole world, as if on a hill-top.
30	*sleeps, for sleep* – The King tells Laertes to have no misgivings, lose no sleep, on the score of revenge.
32	*with:* by. – It was looked upon as a grave insult if a man shook another by the beard.

scene vii

Another room in the castle.

Enter KING *and* LAERTES.

KING   Now must your conscience my acquittance seal,*
And you must put me* in your heart for friend,
Sith* you have heard, and with a knowing* ear,
That he which hath your noble father slain
Pursued my life.

LAERTES   It well appears – but tell me   5
Why you proceeded not against these feats,*
So crimeful and so capital in nature,
As by your safety, wisdom, all things else,
You mainly* were stirred up.

KING   O, for two special reasons,
Which may to you, perhaps, seem much unsinewed,*   10
But yet to me th' are strong. The queen his mother
Lives almost by his looks; and for myself –
My virtue or my plague, be it either which* –
She's so conjunctive* to my life and soul
That, as the star moves not but in his sphere,   15
I could not but by her. The other motive,
Why to a public count* I might not go,
Is the great love the general gender* bear him;
Who, dipping all his faults in their affection,
Would,* like the spring that turneth wood to stone,   20
Convert his gyves* to graces; so that my arrows,
Too slightly timbered* for so loud a wind,
Would have reverted to my bow again,
And not where I had aimed them.

LAERTES   And so have I a noble father lost;   25
A sister driven* into desperate terms* –
Whose worth, if praises may go back again,*
Stood challenger* on mount of all the age
For her perfections. – But my revenge will come.

KING   Break not your sleeps* for that. You must not think   30
That we are made of stuff so flat and dull
That we can let our beard be shook with* danger,
And think it pastime. You shortly shall hear more.

34   *I, not We,* since the King wants to show that he loved Polonius as a personal friend, not a subject. – The King clearly has something planned, but he is prevented from going on to give details by the dramatic entry of the messenger.

43   *naked:* destitute.

45   *eyes:* presence – a courtly turn of speech. Cf. IV.iv.6:
      We shall express our duty in his eye.

48   *should:* can.

49   *abuse:* piece of deception.

50   *character:* handwriting.

59   *So:* so long as.

59   *to a peace* – i.e. to come to terms (with him).

61   *As checking . . . voyage:* in that (*as*) he has abandoned his voyage. – The sport of falconry has the term *check* to mean 'give up the game being hunted and go after less important prey'.

63   *ripe . . . device:* mature in my contrivance.

66   *uncharge the practice:* not suspect anyone of the plot – *uncharge* means literally, 'not charge (anyone)'. Shakespeare probably invented the word for use here. In the English of his day, *practice* frequently had a bad sense, 'trick, plot, conspiracy'.

I* loved your father, and we love ourself;
And that, I hope, will teach you to imagine –   35

Enter a MESSENGER.

How now! What news?

MESSENGER   Letters, my lord, from Hamlet.
          [*Hands him the letters*] This to your majesty; this to the queen.
    KING   From Hamlet! Who brought them?
MESSENGER Sailors, my lord, they say; I saw them not.
           They were given me by Claudio; he received them   40
           Of him that brought them.

    KING   Laertes, you shall hear them. –
           [*To the* MESSENGER] Leave us.   [*Exit* MESSENGER

           [*Reads*] *High and mighty – You shall know I am set naked* on*
           your kingdom. Tomorrow shall I beg leave to see your kingly
           eyes when I shall, first asking your pardon thereunto,*   45
           recount the occasion of my sudden and more strange return.
                                                        HAMLET

           What should* this mean? Are all the rest come back?
           Or is it some abuse,* and no such thing?·

LAERTES   Know you the hand?

    KING   'Tis Hamlet's character.*   'Naked' –   50
           And in a postscript here, he says, '*alone*'.
           Can you advise me?

LAERTES   I'm lost in it, my lord. But let him come;
           It warms the very sickness in my heart,
           That I shall live and tell him to his teeth,   55
           'Thus diddest thou.'

    KING   If it be so, Laertes –
           As how should it be so? how otherwise? –
           Will you be ruled by me?

LAERTES   Ay, my lord;
           So* you will not o'errule me to a peace.*

    KING   To thine own peace. If he be now returned –   60
           As checking* at his voyage, and that he means
           No more to undertake it – I will work him
           To an exploit, now ripe* in my device,
           Under the which he shall not choose but fall.
           And for his death no wind of blame shall breathe;   65
           But even his mother shall uncharge* the practice,
           And call it accident.

68	*ruled:* commanded (by you).
69	*The rather:* but preferably.
70	*organ:* means (by which the result is brought about).
70	*falls:* turns out.
73	*Your sum of parts:* all your accomplishments put together – There is in modern English the phrase, 'a man of parts'. The King is slowly and carefully bringing up the matter of Laertes' skill in fencing. Laertes' interest is aroused, but he remains uncertain of what the King is referring to. It is evidently something that Hamlet envies him for.
76	*Of the unworthiest siege:* of the lowest rank – i.e. of the least importance.
76	*part:* accomplishment.
77	*A very riband* – i.e. a mere scrap of decoration, not a proper garment. The image is continued with *livery, sables, weeds* in the following lines.
78	*becomes:* befits, suits.
80	*settled age . . . graveness:* the rich dark fur (*sable*) and garments (*weeds*) of calm (*settled*) age, indicating prosperity (*health*) and gravity – *graveness* in contrast to the *light* and *careless* dress (*livery*) of young people.
84	*can well:* are well skilled.
85	*grew unto:* stuck tightly to.
87	*As he . . . incorpsed:* as if he had been made into one body.
87	*demi-natured:* become one half in nature.
88	*topped my thought:* rose above what my mind could grasp.
89	*in forgery . . . tricks:* in simply inventing (*forgery of*) positions and tricks. – His imagination comes short of what the horseman actually did. Again the King is indulging in exaggerated phrases so as to build up Laertes' expectation of what is to come.
93	*the brooch:* the precious jewel – especially one worn in a hat.
95	*He made . . . you:* He reluctantly admitted your superiority. – Even now the King does not mention fencing – it is superiority *in your defence* (line 97).
96	*such a masterly report:* a report which represented you as such a master.
97	*your defence* – i.e. your skill in the science of defence, fencing.
98	*rapier* – a light, slender sword used for thrusting in fencing bouts, and distinguished from the *foil*, which was blunted with a button on the end.
100	*scrimers:* fencers.
101	*had neither motion, guard:* would have no trained movement of the body (*motion*), no skilful position of defence (*guard*) – *motion* was a technical term used in fencing; it is used again at line 157.
102	*this report . . . envy* – i.e. the Frenchman's account of Laertes' skill in fencing poisoned (*Did . . . envenom*) Hamlet's mind by playing on his envy to such an extent.
105	*sudden:* immediate.
105	*play:* fence.

LAERTES My lord, I will be ruled;*
The rather,* if you could devise it so,
That *I* might be the organ.*

KING   It falls* right.   70
You have been talked of since your travel much,
And that in Hamlet's hearing, for a quality
Wherein, they say, you shine. Your sum of parts*
Did not together pluck such envy from him
As did that one; and that, in my regard,   75
Of the unworthiest siege.*

LAERTES   What part* is that, my lord?

KING A very riband* in the cap of youth,
Yet needful too; for youth no less becomes*
The light and careless livery that it wears
Than settled* age his sables and his weeds,   80
Importing health and graveness. – Two months since,
Here was a gentleman of Normandy –
I've seen myself, and served against, the French,
And they can well* on horseback. But this gallant
Had witchcraft in 't, he grew unto* his seat;   85
And to such wondrous doing brought his horse,
As he had been incorpsed* and demi-natured*
With the brave beast. So far he topped* my thought
That I, in forgery* of shapes and tricks,
Come short of what he did.

LAERTES   A Norman was 't?   90

KING A Norman.

LAERTES Upon my life, Lamond.

KING   The very same.

LAERTES I know him well; he is the brooch,* indeed,
And gem of all the nation.

KING He made confession* of you,   95
And gave you such a masterly* report,
For art and exercise in your defence,*
And for your rapier* most especially,
That he cried out, 'twould be a sight indeed,
If one could match you. Th' scrimers* of their nation,   100
He swore, had* neither motion, guard, nor eye,
If you opposed them. Sir, this report* of his
Did Hamlet so envenom with his envy
That he could nothing do but wish and beg
Your sudden* coming o'er, to play* with him.   105

111   *begun by time* – (perhaps) 'born in the course of time'', i.e. not innate in human beings but subject to the passing of time. But perhaps the text is wrong here, and *time* is an accidental copying of the same word in line 113. The general meaning is, however, clear.

112   *passages of proof:* occurrences which prove this to be true. – The King has flattered Laertes by praising the Frenchman whose report he quotes, then conveys the pretended invitation to a fencing-match, and now uses rhetoric to stir Laertes into violent action: *that I think . . . that I know . . . that I see*

115   *abate:* decrease its intensity. – If the flame has a long wick in it, it burns less brightly, particularly if a lot of the wick is blackened into *snuff.*

116   *at a like . . . still.* always (*still*) at the same level of excellence.

117   *plurisy.* excess. – Writers in Shakespeare's day seem to have confused this word *plurisy* with *pleurisy*, a disease of the tissues covering the lungs; they thought of the disease as a *plurisy*, i.e. excess, of blood.

118   *That we   . . easing* (line 123) – The general drift of this passage is: we should do at once what we want to do; otherwise all kinds of influences will persuade us not to do it. More literally. 'What we want to (*would*) do, we should do at the time we want to do it; for this 'want to' changes, and suffers as many reductions (*abatements*) and delays as there are tongues (to talk against it), hands (to work against it) and incidents (to prevent it from happening); and then the acknowledgement that we *should* have done it is like a wasteful (*spendthrift*) sign which eases us and also gives us pain.' The image here apparently depends on the old idea that sighs draw blood away from the heart and are thus bad for the body, even though they relieve sorrow in the breast. As our sighs relieve and harm at the same time, so our acknowledgement that we should have acted in time, but did not do so, relieves our conscience (since we are frank about it) but is harmful to our integrity.

123   *quick:* tenderest part – i.e. the essential core of the matter.

127   *murder sanctuarize:* give the protection of the church to a murderer. – In certain circumstances a murderer or other criminal could protect himself from the law by going to a church; here the law of the land had no power over him. The King has by his cunning persuasion worked Laertes' passions to the pitch that he says he would kill Hamlet even in a church; the King says in reply that no place, not even a church, should give protection ('sanctuary') to a murderer.

129   *close:* confined in secret.

131   *those:* those who.

132   *a double varnish* – which would make his fame shine twice as brightly in the eyes of the listeners.

134   *wager on your heads:* lay bets on your heads (as to who should win in a fight).

134   *remiss:* off his guard – not suspecting any villainy. (There is no sense of blame in *remiss* as it is used here.)

136   *peruse:* examine.

138   *unbated:* not blunted.

138   *a pass of practice:* an evilly-contrived thrust.

139   *Requite   . father:* take revenge on him for the death of your father.

140   *anoint my sword . . . unction* – i.e. Laertes will smear a 'salve' (*unction*) over his foil which will be deadly poison. The words *anoint* and *unction* recall the blessing of a priest in church, anointed with the holy oil, the unction of grace; Laertes' plans are just the opposite of this, and he is even prepared to violate the sanctuary of the church to carry them through. Whatever finer feelings he may have had before the King began to work on persuading him to kill Hamlet, he is now totally committed, and goes even further than the King by making this evil suggestion of the poisoned sword.

141   *mountebank:* quack doctor – one who pretends to have a knowledge of medicine but in fact has none.

142   *mortal:* deadly.

142   *that but . . . it:* that (you have only to) dip a knife in it, and.

143   *cataplasm:* plaster – for putting on to wounds.

                   Now, out of this —
LAERTES   What out of this, my lord?
  KING Laertes, was your father dear to you?
        Or are you like the painting of a sorrow,
        A face without a heart?
LAERTES   Why ask you this?
  KING Not that I think you did not love your father,   110
        But that I know love is begun by time;*
        And that I see, in passages of proof,*
        Time qualifies the spark and fire of it.
        There lives within the very flame of love
        A kind of wick or snuff that will abate* it,   115
        And nothing is at a like goodness* still;
        For goodness, growing to a plurisy,*
        Dies in his own too-much. That we would* do,
        We should do when we would; for this 'would' changes,
        And hath abatements and delays as many   120
        As there are tongues, are hands, are accidents;
        And then this 'should' is like a spendthrift sigh,
        That hurts by easing. But, to th' quick o'* th' ulcer:
        Hamlet comes back. What would you undertake,
        To show yourself your father's son in deed   125
        More than in words?
LAERTES   To cut his throat i' th' church.
  KING No place, indeed, should murder sanctuarize;*
        Revenge should have no bounds. But, good Laertes,
        Will you do this, keep close* within your chamber.
        Hamlet returned shall know you are come home.   130
        We'll put on those* shall praise your excellence,
        And set a double varnish* on the fame
        The Frenchman gave you; bring you, in fine, together,
        And wager* on your heads. He, being remiss,*
        Most generous, and free from all contriving,   135
        Will not peruse* the foils; so that, with ease,
        Or with a little shuffling, you may choose
        A sword unbated,* and, in a pass of practice,*
        Requite* him for your father.
LAERTES   I will do 't;
        And for that purpose I'll anoint* my sword.   140
        I bought an unction of a mountebank,*
        So mortal,* that but* dip a knife in it,
        Where it draws blood no cataplasm* so rare,

144   *simples . . . moon:* herbs for preparing medicines that have good quality (*virtue*) through having been collected by moonlight. – This was according to the belief that herbs for medicines and magic spells were most powerful if gathered by moonlight. Cf. III.ii.242:
Thou mixture rank, of midnight weeds collected.

147   *this contagion:* this contagious thing – i.e. the poison.

147   *gall:* injure by a rub or scratch.

150   *to our shape:* for the part we intend to act. – They must consider carefully when and how it will be most convenient to carry out their plan.

151   *And that . . . performance:* and if our aims (*drift*) are revealed by carrying them out badly.

152   *assayed:* attempted.

153   *a back . . . proof:* backing or supporter (*second*) which may stay firm if this (project) should blow up when it is being tried. – The word *second* is evidently taken from the idea of a personal supporter to another, e.g. in a fight; *blast in proof* is an image from gunnery, said of a gun which is not properly made and blows up when it is being tested.

155   *cunnings:* (respective) skills (in fencing).

157   *motion:* bodily exertion.

158   *As make:* for so you should make.

159   *And that:* and.

160   *A chalice . . . sipping:* a special cup (*chalice*) for the occasion (*nonce*), and he has only to sip from it (*whereon*). – The King continues to use a great deal of rhetoric to carry his point; his sentences are long and involved grammatically, and such words as *chalice* and *nonce* are unusual; *chalice* usually refers to the cup used at the holy communion service of the Christian Church; *nonce*, a form of *once*, was evidently archaic even in Shakespeare's day.

161   *stuck* – a thrust in fencing (short for the Italian technical term *stoccado*).

167   *a willow* – This tree is frequently seen in England growing along the banks of streams. Its roots are long and penetrating and it is therefore used for preventing the banks from caving in. These trees often overhang the water (*aslant a brook*), and the underside of their leaves is not green but silvery-grey (*hoar*, line 168). And because the branches of the tree hang down, it is sometimes called 'the weeping willow'; in the language of plants and flowers it is associated with forsaken love.

169   *fantastic:* extravagant.

170   *crow-flowers . . . purples* – Since Ophelia once spoke in the language of flowers (IV.v.171ff.), it is perhaps to be expected that these flowers too, which she chose to weave together before her death, give a message. Crowfoot (*crowflowers*) has a country name, 'fair maid of France'; *nettles* have leaves which sting severely; *daisies* (the 'eyes of the day') represent the spring of life, the bloom of pure virginity; *long purples* were, as explained below (line 170), called 'dead men's fingers'; the long purple is a kind of orchid, and some similar kinds have roots looking like the palm of a hand – hence the name. The message may therefore be taken to read: 'A beautiful girl is badly stung; her virgin bloom is under the cold hand of death'.

171   *liberal:* free-spoken – i.e. not careful in what they say.

171   *grosser:* more vulgar. – One of these names, 'rampant widow', would certainly not have pleased the Queen.

172   *cold:* chaste – and therefore too modest to use a vulgar name.

173   *her coronet weeds:* her garland of wild flowers. – This is the object of *hang*.

174   *an envious sliver:* a spiteful small branch.

179   *incapable:* unaware.

180   *native . . . element:* belonging to (*native*) and with qualities which made it possible to live in (*indued Unto*) that element – i.e. water.

182   *Till that:* before.

Collected from all simples* that have virtue
Under the moon, can save the thing from death   145
That is but scratched withal. I'll touch my point
With this contagion,* that, if I gall* him slightly,
It may be death.

KING   Let's further think of this,
Weigh what convenience both of time and means
May fit us to our shape.* If this should fail,   150
And that our drift* look through our bad performance,
'Twere better not assayed.* Therefore this project
Should have a back* or second, that might hold,
If this should blast in proof. Soft! – Let me see –
We'll make a solemn wager on your cunnings.* –   155
I ha't:
When in your motion* you are hot and dry –
As* make your bouts more violent to that end –
And that* he calls for drink, I'll have prepared him
A chalice* for the nonce, whereon but sipping,   160
If he by chance escape your venomed stuck,*
Our purpose may hold there. But stay! What noise? –

Enter QUEEN.

How now, sweet queen!
QUEEN   One woe doth tread upon another's heel,
So fast they follow. – Your sister's drowned, Laertes.   165
LAERTES   Drowned! O, where?
QUEEN   There is a willow* grows aslant a brook,
That shows his hoar leaves in the glassy stream;
There with fantastic* garlands did she come
Of crow-flowers,* nettles, daisies, and long purples   170
That liberal* shepherds give a grosser* name,
But our cold* maids do dead men's fingers call them.
There, on the pendent boughs her coronet* weeds
Clambering to hang, an envious sliver* broke;
When down her weedy trophies and herself   175
Fell in the weeping brook. Her clothes spread wide,
And, mermaid-like, awhile they bore her up;
Which time she chanted snatches of old tunes,
As one incapable* of her own distress,
Or like a creature native* and indued   180
Unto that element. But long it could not be
Till that* her garments, heavy with their drink,

183   *lay:* song.

> The Queen's description of Ophelia's drowning is best taken as fanciful. The vision of her floating for a time in the water while her clothes held her up, singing before her death, is moving and intensely dramatic in this place in the play where the plot is approaching the catastrophe. But one naturally asks why, if the Queen saw all this, she and others did not do something to rescue Ophelia from death by drowning. Again, in the next act she is buried with only those rites accorded to a suicide. *The corse . . . did . . . For do its own life*, (v.i.200), although the priest says *Her death was doubtful* (v.i.208). We are to suspect that she took her own life by leaping, fully clothed, into the brook.

188   *trick:* way, habit.
189   *When these . . . out:* When these (tears) have gone, this womanishness (*woman*) in me will be finished.
191   *fain:* gladly. – His fiery words are ready and will 'blaze out', be spoken.
192   *douts it:* puts it out. – His folly, the womanish tears, puts out the fire of his words.

> The King, as part of his plotting, pretends to the Queen that he has been trying to calm Laertes' fury. In fact, of course, he has been inciting it, and the death of Ophelia plays into his hands.

c) Comment on lang. & imagery of passage.

	Pulled the poor wretch from her melodious lay*	
	To muddy death.	
LAERTES	Alas, then, she is drowned?	
QUEEN	Drowned, drowned.	185
LAERTES	Too much of water hast thou, poor Ophelia,	

And therefore I forbid my tears. But yet
It is our trick;* nature her custom holds,
Let shame say what it will. When these* are gone,
The woman will be out. – Adieu, my lord.   190
I have a speech of fire, that fain* would blaze,
But that this folly douts* it.   [*Exit*

KING   Let's follow, Gertrude.
How much I had to do to calm his rage!
Now fear I this will give it start again;
Therefore let's follow.   195

                                            [*Exeunt*

v. i.   Two gravediggers talk irreverently as they dig a grave for Ophelia; they realize she has taken her own life. As Hamlet and Horatio approach, one of the gravediggers throws up two skulls, on each of which Hamlet soliloquizes.

Ophelia's funeral procession, with the King, the Queen and Laertes, moves on to the stage. Laertes complains of the scant Christian rites allowed to his sister, and grief makes him jump down into the grave, proclaiming his love for her and his desire to be buried with her. Hamlet intervenes, asserting that his own love for her was infinitely greater, and fights with Laertes in the grave. When they are separated, and Hamlet leaves, the King reminds Laertes of his vow to fight and kill Hamlet.

As the play moves nearer to the impending death struggle, the gravediggers provide some humorous relief. But the scene which begins with them introduces a further element into the structure of the play: they give the sole glimpse of the great world outside the court. And their activities lead Hamlet to the theme of wills and fates (*Our thoughts are ours, their ends none of our own*, as the Player King said): death has no respect for persons; a skull gives no indication of the sort of person it belonged to. If fate has decreed that Laertes shall hate him, his own friendly reasoned approach will be ineffectual. The first skull thrown up makes him think of a politician, undoubtedly with Claudius in mind; Yorick's skull belonged to a humble man who yet enjoyed the company of the court. All this meditation shows Hamlet able to reason confidently even at this juncture on destiny as it will fall on him and the others. His self-assurance is tested by Laertes, who is hysterical and not to be fended off by Hamlet's reasoned politeness. Then, even Hamlet breaks out in a passionate speech, ranting like Laertes. The Queen seizes on this and refers to his supposed madness, since by doing so she hopes to protect him. It is in the King's interest to prevent Laertes from rash action and to encourage him in the open duel he has planned.

GRAVEDIGGERS, called CLOWNS in the early editions of the play. In this usage, *clown* meant 'simple country fellow', but, because such people were represented in plays as a comic relief to more tragic events, the word *clown* became associated with comic performances. It is in the tradition of the time that the clown should be superficially simple but cleverly adept in twisting words to his own advantage

1   *seeks her own salvation* – a pleasanter way of saying, 'kills herself'.

3   *straight*: at once.

4   *The crowner . . . burial*: The coroner has considered her case and his finding is that she is to have a Christian burial. – The coroner's duty is to investigate cases of sudden death; since Ophelia is to have a burial according to the rites of the Church, the coroner evidently found that she did not take her own life. But subsequent events show that this was untrue.

8   se offendendo – This is the gravedigger's mistake for the Latin legal phrase *se defendendo*, 'in self-defence', used to announce that a person killed another in self-defence ('justifiable homicide'). It is not applicable to suicide, but the gravedigger's blunder has some irony in it: Ophelia's action did in fact *offend* herself.

9   *argues*: proves (that there has been).

10   *three branches* – This and what follows makes fun of an old scholastic discipline which made fine distinctions between various philosophical terms. Here the three *branches* mentioned by the gravedigger are not distinct but much about the same thing. The satire here and in the passage which follows may, however, be more comprehensive. In 1561 a case arising out of the death of Sir James Hales came before a coroner's court: it seems that Hales drowned himself in a fit of insanity, but his widow contested this decision because if her late husband had indeed committed suicide she would lose the right to property he held on lease. A good deal of legal argument was expended on the question whether he went to the water or the water came to him (cf. line 14ff). An act was spoken of as consisting of three parts (cf. lines 9–10): imagining the act, resolving to carry it out, and carrying it out to the end.

11   *Argal*, the gravedigger's mistake for *ergo* – Latin for 'therefore', a word used in scholastic arguments.

12   *goodman delver*: good mister digger.

15   *will he, nill he*: whether he wants to or not. (A form of this phrase, *willy-nilly*, is current in English today.)

17   *he that is not guilty . . .* – It is characteristic of the clown here to come to a conclusion which is no conclusion at all; he is saying in effect that a man who does not kill himself does not kill himself.

ACT V scene i

Elsinore. A churchyard.

Enter two GRAVEDIGGERS,* *carrying spades and other tools.*

FIRST GRAVEDIGGER Is she to be buried in Christian burial that wilfully seeks* her own salvation?

SECOND GRAVEDIGGER I tell thee she is; and therefore make her grave straight.* The crowner* hath sat on her, and finds it Christian burial.

FIRST GRAVEDIGGER How can that be, unless she drowned herself in her own defence? 5

SECOND GRAVEDIGGER Why, 'tis found so.

FIRST GRAVEDIGGER It must be *se offendendo*;* it cannot be else. For here lies the point: if I drown myself wittingly, it argues* an act. And an act hath three branches;* it is, to act, to do, and to perform. 10 Argal,* she drowned herself wittingly.

SECOND GRAVEDIGGER Nay, but hear you, goodman delver* –

FIRST GRAVEDIGGER Give me leave. [*He draws with his finger in the dust.*] Here lies the water; good. Here stands the man; good. If the man go to this water and drown himself, it is, will he, nill* he, he goes 15 – mark you that; but if the water come to him and drown him, he drowns not himself. Argal, he that is not guilty* of his own death shortens not his own life.

SECOND GRAVEDIGGER But is this law?

FIRST GRAVEDIGGER Ay, marry, is 't; crowner's quest law.* 20

SECOND GRAVEDIGGER Will you ha' the truth on 't? If this had not been a gentle-woman,* she should have been buried out o' Christian burial.

---

20 *crowner's quest law:* the law relating to coroner's inquests.
22 *a gentlewoman* – i.e. a well-to-do woman, not one of the common people.

189

23   *there thou sayest:* you are right there.
24   *have countenance* – (perhaps) 'be allowed'; *countenance* here seems to mean something like 'favour' – these people should enjoy the favour of permission to drown themselves.
25   *even Christian:* fellow Christian. – The word *even* suggests the idea that all Christians are equal before God.
26   *gentlemen* – It is clear from what follows that this word is used strictly to mean men who were legally entitled to use a coat of arms, i.e. well-to-do people from upper middle-class families. In the lines which follow there is double word-play: (i) *arms* is played on in the meanings 'coats of arms' and 'upper limbs of the human body'; (ii) the most ancient form of a coat of arms was said to have been the spade used by Adam, who, according to the Bible, was the first man. Adam was therefore a 'gentleman'. Yet the Bible says that Adam had to work with his hands in order to survive; so Adam used his *arms* when digging with his spade. Once again, this word-play is squarely in the tradition of contemporary stage-clowning.
27   *hold up:* carry on.
32   *art:* are you.
33   *Adam digged* – i.e. he had to work for his living by digging the ground. When God cursed him, God said, 'In the sweat of thy face shalt thou eat bread'. (*Genesis* 3: 19).
35   *confess thyself* – : make your confession – He is going on to say *and be hanged*, but he is interrupted. The phrase was proverbial, and its use here may have put the idea of hanging into the second gravedigger's mind (*gallows-maker*, line 39).
36   *Go to* – an expression of doubt about what someone else has just said. A colloquial expression with the same meaning in modern English is 'Get away with you.'
41   *does well* – i.e. is a good, amusing answer to the question. But the gravedigger's mind runs on to the gallows itself 'doing well'.
47   *unyoke:* your work is finished – i.e. you have done your day's work and can unyoke your team of oxen.
49   *To 't* – i.e. 'to the point then; tell me, then'.
50   *Mass* – a swear-word, 'By the Holy Mass'.
51   *your dull ass . . . beating:* a stupid donkey will not go faster (*mend his pace*) if you beat it. – The *your* here is said condescendingly, meaning 'the one you and we all know about'. (Cf. III.ii.3, *your players*, and IV.iii.21 *your worm . . .* etc.).

FIRST Why, there thou sayst.* And the more pity that great folk
GRAVEDIGGER should have countenance* in this world to drown or hang
themselves, more than their even Christian.* – Come, my 25
spade. There is no ancient gentlemen* but gardeners,
ditchers, and grave-makers. They hold up* Adam's profession.

SECOND Was he a gentleman?
GRAVEDIGGER

FIRST A' was the first that ever bore arms. 30
GRAVEDIGGER

SECOND Why, he had none.
GRAVEDIGGER

FIRST What, art* a heathen? How dost thou understand the
GRAVEDIGGER Scripture? The Scripture says, Adam digged.* Could he dig
without arms? I'll put another question to thee: if thou
answerest me not to the purpose, confess thyself* – 35

SECOND Go to.*
GRAVEDIGGER

FIRST What is he that builds stronger than either the mason, the
GRAVEDIGGER shipwright, or the carpenter?

SECOND The gallows-maker; for that frame outlives a thousand
GRAVEDIGGER tenants. 40

FIRST I like thy wit well, in good faith. The gallows does well;* but
GRAVEDIGGER how does it well? It does well to those that do ill. Now, thou
dost ill to say the gallows is built stronger than the church.
Argal, the gallows may do well to thee. To 't again, come.

SECOND 'Who builds stronger than a mason, a shipwright, or a 45
GRAVEDIGGER carpenter?'

FIRST Ay, tell me that, and unyoke.*
GRAVEDIGGER

SECOND Marry, now I can tell.
GRAVEDIGGER

FIRST To 't.*
GRAVEDIGGER

SECOND Mass,* I cannot tell. 50
GRAVEDIGGER

Enter HAMLET *and* HORATIO, *some distance away.*

FIRST Cudgel thy brains no more about it, for your dull ass* will
GRAVEDIGGER not mend his pace with beating; and when you are asked
this question next, say 'a grave-maker'. The houses that he

54   *Yaughan* – This reference has not been explained; it is evidently the name of a man or a
          place which supplied drink.
55   *stoup:* cup.
56   *In youth . . .* – The three stanzas which the gravedigger now sings are garbled versions of
          parts of a song printed in a collection of 'songs and sonnets' now known as
          Tottel's *Miscellany*. A manuscript copy of the song gives it as 'representing
          the image of Death'; it is therefore appropriate to the gravedigger, and, in fact,
          the last stanza he sings has to do with a grave.
              He makes nonsense of the lines, e.g. by mixing up some words with later
          passages in the song (*contract . . . the time* is a memory of *tract of time* in stanza 2
          of Tottel's version). The *O* and *Ah* represent him plunging his spade into the
          earth as he sings. In Tottel's song, the theme is of an old man lamenting the
          passing away of his youthful virility.
62   *a property of easiness:* a matter of indifference.
64   *daintier sense:* more refined sensibility. – Hamlet is trying to make the point that doing
          things infrequently makes people more sensitive about them, while doing the
          same things frequently makes the doer disregard their true significance.
67   *shipped . . . land* – i.e. (apparently) towards the land of Death; this line is an echo of one
          later in the song as it appears in Tottel:
                  And shipped me into the land
                  From whence I first was brought
          intil is a dialect form of *into*.
70   *jowls:* throws. – The word is especially fitting because of what follows: *jowl* can also
          mean 'jaw-bone'.
70   *Cain's jaw-bone* – According to tradition, Cain, the son of Adam and Eve, killed his brother
          Abel by hitting him with the jaw-bone of a donkey.
71   *the pate of a politician:* the head of an intriguer. – *Politician* is always used in a bad sense
          in the English of Shakespeare's day.
72   *o'er-reaches:* (i) reaches over; (ii) gets the better of. – Meaning (ii) suggests a simple fellow
          getting the better of a subtle intriguer.
73   *circumvent:* outwit – a *politican* so subtle that he might outwit God himself.
75   *which:* who.
78   *beg:* beg for.
80   *my Lady Worm's* – The skull which was once Lord Such-a-one's is now Lady Worm's,
          being eaten by worms.
80   *chapless:* jawless – the lower jaw having dropped off.
81   *mazzard:* head – a word used jokingly, probably from *mazer*, a large bowl. (The French
          word for *head* 'tête', comes from Latin *testa*, 'a pot'.)
82   *revolution:* change.
82   *and:* if.
83   *Did these bones . . . with 'em:* Were these bones bred at so little trouble that all one can
          do is play skittles with them? – Loggats was played with small logs which had
          to be thrown as near as possible to a 'jack'.
86   *For and:* and also. – Tottel has *And eke*.
90   *quiddits . . . quillets:* subtleties . . . over-precise dwelling on the meaning of words.

makes last till doomsday. Go, get thee to Yaughan;* fetch me
a stoup* of liquor.   [*Exit* SECOND GRAVEDIGGER   55
[*He digs, and sings*]

> *In youth,* when I did love, did love,*
> *Methought it was very sweet.*
> *To contract (O) the time, for (Ah) my behove,*
> *O, methought there was nothing meet.*

HAMLET Has this fellow no feeling of his business, that he sings at   60
grave-making?
HORATIO Custom hath made it in him a property* of easiness.
HAMLET 'Tis e'en so. The hand of little employment hath the daintier
sense.*

FIRST [*Sings*]   *But age, with his stealing steps,*   65
GRAVEDIGGER   *Hath clawed me in his clutch,*
> *And hath shipped* me intil the land,*
> *As if I had never been such.*

[*Throws up a skull*

HAMLET That skull had a tongue in it, and could sing once. How the
knave jowls* it to the ground, as if it were Cain's* jaw-bone,   70
that did the first murder! It might be the pate* of a politician,
which this ass now o'er-reaches;* one that would circumvent* God, might it not?
HORATIO It might, my lord.
HAMLET Or of a courtier, which* could say 'Good morrow, sweet lord!   75
How dost thou, good lord?' This might be my Lord Such-a-
one, that praised my lord Such-a-one's horse, when he
meant to beg* it – might it not?
HORATIO Ay, my lord.
HAMLET Why, e'en so. And now my Lady Worm's;* chapless,* and   80
knocked about the mazzard* with a sexton's spade. Here's
fine revolution,* and* we had the trick to see 't. Did these
bones* cost no more the breeding but to play at loggats with
'em? Mine ache to think on 't.

FIRST [*Sings*]   *A pickaxe, and a spade, a spade,*   85
GRAVEDIGGER   *For and* a shrouding-sheet;*
> *O, a pit of clay for to be made*
> *For such a guest is meet.*

[*Throws up another skull*

HAMLET There's another. Why may not that be the skull of a lawyer?
Where be his quiddits* now, his quillets, his cases, his   90

91   *suffer . . . knave:* allow this rough fellow.
92   *sconce:* head – a term used jokingly, like *mazzard.*
93   *action of battery* – legal action against someone who has attacked someone else by beating
            or wounding him. If the skull belonged to a lawyer, why does he not take
            action for battery against the gravedigger?
                In these and the following lines, a number of legal terms are used. Such
            passages have suggested to some that Shakespeare had legal training at some
            time in his life. Anyone, however, who owned property would have been
            likely to know a number of such terms, especially those relating to the
            conveyance of property.
94   *statutes . . . recoveries* (line 96)*:* bonds relating to debts (*statutes*), bonds for the award of
            bail (*recognizances*), processes of fines on land, statements by two people as to
            the tenant's entitlement to the land (*double vouchers*) and deeds of recovery for
            the tenant to be free of restriction as to the land passing within the landlord's
            family (*recoveries*).
96   *fine* – Hamlet plays on four meanings of *fine* in this sentence: 'Is this the end (*fine*) of his
            fines . . . to have his splendid (*fine*) head filled with powdered earth (*fine
            dirt*)?'
98   *vouch him . . . purchases:* assert his rights . . . in what he purchases.
99   *a pair of indentures* – An indenture is an agreement set out on a sheet and then cut into two
            parts with a wavy ('indentured') line; in any case of disagreement the two
            pieces can be fitted together to prove their genuineness.
100   *conveyances* – deeds of conveyance, transferring property from one owner to another.
101   *this box* – i.e. the grave. The underlying thought here is that in the end all a man 'inherits'
            is his grave; this, far from being the size of his lands, is barely enough to hold
            the documents concerned with transferring them.
103   *parchment:* skin prepared and used for writing on. – It was used regularly for legal
            documents.
105   *assurance:* (i) conveyance of lands by deed, (ii) security. – There can in fact be no perma-
            nent assurance in what is written on the skins of animals.
107   *sirrah* – a form of address used to servants.
111   *liest* – There is a good deal of word-play on *lie* (as 'lie in bed' and 'tell what is untrue')
            in what follows. When the gravedigger says the grave is his, he means that it
            is his work; he is digging it. Hamlet calls him *thou*; he calls Hamlet *you.*
115   *quick:* living.
122   *rest her soul* for *May God rest her soul.*
123   *absolute:* positive.
123   *by the card.* very precisely – perhaps with reference to the 'mariner's card', on which the
            points of the compass were carefully marked out.
124   *equivocation will undo us ·* double meanings will ruin us. – The gravedigger plays with the
            meanings of words in scenes such as this, and, in the courts of Shakespeare's
            day, it appears that equivocation was frequently practised when people
            defended themselves.
125   *picked:* refined.
127   *he galls his kibe ·* he chafes the chillblain on [the courtier's] hee.' – i.e. the peasant is annoy-
            ingly close to the courtier in this new-found refinement.

tenures, and his tricks? Why does he suffer* this rude knave
now to knock him about the sconce* with a dirty shovel, and
will not tell him of his action* of battery? Hum! This fellow
might be in's time a great buyer of land, with his statutes,*
his recognizances, his fines, his double vouchers, his   95
recoveries. Is this the fine* of his fines, and the recovery of
his recoveries, to have his fine pate full of fine dirt? Will his
vouchers vouch* him no more of his purchases, and double
ones too, than the length and breadth of a pair of indentures?*
The very conveyances* of his lands will hardly lie in this   100
box;* and must the inheritor himself have no more, ha?

HORATIO Not a jot more, my lord.

HAMLET Is not parchment* made of sheep-skins?

HORATIO Ay, my lord, and of calf-skins too.

HAMLET They are sheep and calves which seek out assurance* in that.   105
I will speak to this fellow. – [To the GRAVEDIGGER] Whose
grave's this, sirrah?*

FIRST Mine, sir. –
GRAVEDIGGER [Sings   O, a pit of clay for to be made
                              For such a guest is meet.   110

HAMLET I think it be thine, indeed; for thou liest* in 't.

FIRST You lie out on 't, sir, and therefore it is not yours. For my
GRAVEDIGGER part, I do not lie in 't, and yet it is mine.

HAMLET Thou dost lie in 't, to be in 't, and say it is thine. 'Tis for the
dead, not for the quick;* therefore thou liest.   115

FIRST 'Tis a quick lie, sir; 'twill away again, from me to you.
GRAVEDIGGER

HAMLET What man dost thou dig it for?

FIRST For no man, sir.
GRAVEDIGGER

HAMLET What woman, then?

FIRST For none, neither.   120
GRAVEDIGGER

HAMLET Who is to be buried in 't?

FIRST One that was a woman, sir; but, rest* her soul, she's dead.
GRAVEDIGGER

HAMLET How absolute* the knave is! We must speak by the card,* or
equivocation* will undo us. By the lord, Horatio, these three
years I have taken note of it; the age is grown so picked,* that   125
the toe of the peasant comes so near the heel of the courtier, he
galls his kibe.* – [To the GRAVEDIGGER] How long hast thou
been a grave-maker?

145   *Upon what ground?:* For what reason? – The gravedigger pretends to misunderstand him,
           taking *ground* to mean 'earth, land'; he is 'equivocating' again.
150   *scarce hold the laying in:* hardly keep until the laying-in (in the grave) – because they are
           pocky: rotten.
156   *whoreson* – a swear-word.
157   *you* – Like *you* and *your* in the preceding lines, this has no separate meaning; see notes to
           III.ii.3 and IV.iii.21–5.
161   *A pestilence . . . rogue* – This is said as a light, joking curse: 'May a plague fall upon him
           for being such a wildly gay fellow.'
162   *Rhenish:* wine from the Rhinelands.

FIRST GRAVEDIGGER	Of all the days i' th' year, I came to 't that day that our last king Hamlet o'ercame Fortinbras.
HAMLET	How long is that since?
FIRST GRAVEDIGGER	Cannot you tell that? Every fool can tell that: it was that very day that young Hamlet was born – he that is mad, and sent into England.
HAMLET	Ay, marry, why was he sent into England?
FIRST GRAVEDIGGER	Why, because a' was mad. A' shall recover his wits there; or, if a' do not, 'tis no great matter there.
HAMLET	Why?
FIRST GRAVEDIGGER	'Twill not be seen in him there; there the men are as mad as he.
HAMLET	How came he mad?
FIRST GRAVEDIGGER	Very strangely, they say.
HAMLET	How strangely?
FIRST GRAVEDIGGER	Faith, e'en with losing his wits.
HAMLET	Upon what ground?*
FIRST GRAVEDIGGER	Why, here in Denmark. I have been sexton here, man and boy, thirty years.
HAMLET	How long will a man lie i' th' earth ere he rot?
FIRST GRAVEDIGGER	I' faith, if a' be not rotten before a' die – as we have many pocky corses now-a-days that will scarce hold* the laying-in – a' will last you some eight year or nine year. A tanner will last you nine year.
HAMLET	Why he more than another?
FIRST GRAVEDIGGER	Why, sir, his hide is so tanned with his trade that a' will keep out water a great while; and your water is a sore decayer of your whoreson* dead body. Here's a skull now hath lain you* i' th' earth three-and-twenty years.
HAMLET	Whose was it?
FIRST GRAVEDIGGER	A whoreson mad fellow's it was. Whose do you think it was?
HAMLET	Nay, I know not.
FIRST GRAVEDIGGER	A pestilence* on him for a mad rogue! A' poured a flagon of Rhenish* on my head once. This same skull, sir, was Yorick's skull, the king's jester.
HAMLET	This?
FIRST GRAVEDIGGER	E'en that.

130

135

140

14'

150

155

160

165

169   *My gorge rises at it:* My stomach rises at the thought of it – i.e. of having kissed a face which is now a skull and having been carried on the back of what is now a skeleton.

        The skull is the final symbol in the play of Hamlet's apprehensions. In it are summed up all his thoughts on corruption and death, both at the level of the gravedigger's conversation and at the higher level of his mother's and his stepfather's sinful life, and the death and corruption this must inevitably lead to. The fact that Yorick was the court jester adds a fleeting element of comedy to his sad reflections.

172   *were wont . . . roar:* used to send everyone sitting at the table into fits of laughter (*on a roar*).

173   *chop-fallen:* dispirited – literally, with the *chop*, jaw, hanging down.

175   *favour:* face, appearance. – His point is that the Queen will look like this in time however much make-up she uses.

178   *Alexander* – i.e. Alexander the Great, King of Macedon in the days of the ancient Greek empire. He conquered a large part of the known world, but even so renowned a hero has turned to dust.

185   *bung-hole* – a hole in a barrel (e.g. a beer-barrel or a wine-cask), used for filling.

186   *curiously:* minutely.

187   *modesty enough . . . it:* sufficient moderation, and likelihood leading [the flight of imagination]. *Modesty* is to think *modestly*, without exaggeration, not *curiously* (line 186).

193   *Imperious Caesar:* Imperial Caesar – the great Roman general, statesman and historian. The stanza of four lines rhyming in couplets may be a quotation, though no source for it has been traced. More likely it is Hamlet's fancy for rhyming at moments of high emotional tension, brought on by imagination, which is the source. The lightness and excitement of the lines contrasts with the stirring speculation of what has gone before; a comparison can be made with lines III.ii.276–7.

        For if the King like not the comedy,
        Why, then, belike – he likes it not, perdy.

        Something of Hamlet's supposed madness comes out in these passages.

196   *expel . . . flaw:* keep out the gusts of wind (*flaw*) in winter.

199   *maiméd:* defective.

201   *Fordo:* destroy – *its* appears as *it*, a common form, in all the early editions.

201   *of some estate:* somewhat high in social rank.

202   *Couch we:* Let us lie hidden.

HAMLET   Let me see. [*Takes the skull*] – Alas, poor Yorick! – I knew him,
Horatio. A fellow of infinite jest, of most excellent fancy. He
hath borne me on his back a thousand times; and now, how
abhorred in my imagination it is! My gorge* rises at it. Here
hung those lips that I have kissed I know not how oft. Where   170
be your gibes now? Your gambols? Your songs? Your flashes
of merriment, that were wont* to set the table on a roar? Not
one now to mock your own grinning? Quite chop-fallen?*
Now get you to my lady's chamber, and tell her, let her paint
an inch thick, to this favour* she must come; make her laugh   175
at that. – Prithee, Horatio, tell me one thing.
HORATIO   What's that, my lord?
HAMLET   Dost thou think Alexander* looked o' this fashion i' th'
earth?
HORATIO   E'en so.   180
HAMLET   And smelt so? Pah!   [*Puts down the skull*
HORATIO   E'en so, my lord.
HAMLET   To what base uses we may return, Horatio! Why may not
imagination trace the noble dust of Alexander till he find it
stopping a bung-hole?*   185
HORATIO   'Twere to consider too curiously,* to consider so.
HAMLET   No, faith, not a jot; but to follow him thither with modesty*
enough, and likelihood to lead it. As thus: Alexander died,
Alexander was buried, Alexander returneth into dust; the
dust is earth; of earth we make loam, and why of that loam   190
whereto he was converted might they not stop a beer-
barrel?

> Imperious Caesar,* dead and turned to clay,
> Might stop a hole to keep the wind away;
> O, that that earth which kept the world in awe   195
> Should patch a wall t' expel* the winter's flaw! –

But soft! but soft! aside. – Here comes the king

Enter KING, QUEEN, LAERTES *and the Corpse, with* PRIESTS
and LORDS *in procession.*

The queen, the courtiers. Who is that they follow? –
And with such maiméd* rites? This doth betoken
The corse they follow did with desperate hand   200
Fordo* its own life. 'Twas of some estate.*
Couch we* awhile, and mark
[*Retiring with* HORATIO

LAERTES   [*To a* PRIEST] What ceremony else?

208   *warranty . . . doubtful* – This is certainly a reference to the question whether or not
       Ophelia took her own life; whether the Queen's account of the accident is
       true, or whether Ophelia's distraction was the real cause of her death, the
       dramatic point here is that Laertes does not think a Christian burial with full
       rites is being given to the body, and the stress which comes of this adds to
       his hatred of Hamlet. The First Folio has *warrantis* for *warrantly* in other
       early editions; the meaning is 'authorization', evidently from the coroner's
       court; the priest says that the funeral rites (*obsequies*) have been extended as
       far as he had permission to do.   .

209   *great command o'ersways* – i.e. the order of the King over-rules the coroner's order, though
       the priest will not actually say so.

210   *ground unsanctified . . . trumpet:* have been settled (*lodged*) in ground unblessed by the
       church (*unsanctified*) until the last trumpet – which will blow at doomsday
       and call the dead to rise up.

211   *for:* instead of.

213   *her virgin . . . strewments:* the garland (*crants*) and flowers strewn (*strewments*) on the
       grave of a young unmarried woman. – The garland was made of paper picked
       out with real and artificial flowers.

214   *the bringing home . . . burial:* the funeral bell and the burial rites bringing her to 'her long
       home' – i.e. to her grave.

219   *peace-parted souls:* souls which have departed (from this life) in peace – i.e. without any
       deadly sin.

221   *violets* – These flowers have been mentioned twice before, in connection with youth
       (I.iii.7) and, in the flower language, faithfulness (IV.v.179); in the second
       instance they were withered. Here, then, is the patterning of faithfulness,
       death and the renewal of spring, brought together in one image. Laertes turns
       from this beautiful contemplation to an angry tirade against the priest.

223   *howling* – i.e. in the torments of hell.

226   *I thought . . . decked:* I thought I would have decked . . .

229   *ingenious sense:* lively intelligence.

232   *quick:* alive. – The phrase used here is an echo from the Prayer Book, 'he shall come to
       judge the quick and the dead' (Apostles' Creed).

234   *Pelion . . . Olympus* – According to a classical legend, the giants called Titans tried to pile
       the mountains in the Pelion range, and Ossa, another mountain (see line 265),
       on top of Mount Olympus, so that they could climb up to the sky and be level
       with Zeus, the god of gods, and scale heaven. (All these mountains are in
       Greece.) The names therefore indicate high mountains; *skyish:* reaching to the
       sky.

236   *phrase:* expression.

237   *Conjures . . . stars:* influences, as if by magic, (*Conjures*) the planets. – *Conjures* takes the
       stress on the second syllable, *Conjúres*, not as in modern English. The planets
       were called *wandering stars* because it seemed that they did not keep to a
       'sphere', but wandered about the sky (see note to IV.vii.14).

238   *wonder-wounded:* struck with amazement. – These hearers *stand*, i.e. cannot move, but
       are struck still.

HAMLET   [*To* HORATIO *aside*] That is Laertes,
             A very noble youth. Mark.   205
LAERTES   What ceremony else?
FIRST PRIEST   Her obsequies have been as far enlarged
             As we have warranty.* Her death was doubtful;
             And, but that great command* o'ersways the order,
             She should in ground unsanctified* have lodged   210
             Till the last trumpet; for* charitable prayers,
             Shards, flints, and pebbles should be thrown on her.
             Yet here she is allowed her virgin crants,*
             Her maiden strewments, and the bringing home*
             Of bell and burial.   215
LAERTES   Must there no more be done?
FIRST PRIEST   No more be done.
             We should profane the service of the dead
             To sing a requiem and such rest to her
             As to peace-parted* souls.
LAERTES   Lay her i' th' earth;
             And from her fair and unpolluted flesh   220
             May violets* spring! – I tell thee, churlish priest,
             A minist'ring angel shall my sister be,
             When thou liest howling.*
HAMLET   What, the fair Ophelia!
QUEEN   [*Scattering flowers*] Sweets to the sweet. Farewell!
             I hoped thou shouldst have been my Hamlet's wife;   225
             I thought* thy bride-bed to have decked, sweet maid,
             And not have strewed thy grave.
LAERTES   O, treble woe
             Fall ten times treble on that cursèd head
             Whose wicked deed thy most ingenious sense*
             Deprived thee of! – Hold off the earth awhile,   230
             Till I have caught her once more in mine arms. [*He leaps into
             the grave*]
             Now pile your dust upon the quick* and dead,
             Till of this flat a mountain you have made
             T' o'ertop old Pelion* or the skyish head
             Of blue Olympus.
HAMLET   [*Advancing*   What is he whose grief   235
             Bears such an emphasis; whose phrase* of sorrow
             Conjures* the wandering stars, and makes them stand
             Like wonder-wounded* hearers? This is I,
             Hamlet the Dane.   [*Leaps into the grave*

242   *splenitive:* hot-headed. – The spleen is an organ in the body (on the left-hand side of the stomach) which helps to keep the blood pure; it was thought of as the 'seat' of bad temper in a man.

247   *theme:* matter.

248   *wag:* move.

254   *forbear him:* leave him alone.

256   *Woo't, for Wouldst thou:* Would you.

257   *drink up eisel:* drink vinegar. – To drink a draft of this is an unpleasant experience; but the true lover is prepared to do this and more to show his love for his mistress. (In the Folios, this word, in the form *Esile*, is printed in italics; some editors have suggested that it might be the name of a river.)

263   *Singeing . . . zone:* scorching its top against the region of the sun (*the burning zone*).

264   *Ossa* – See note to line 234.

264   *mouth:* proclaim passionately.

265   *mere:* complete.

268   *When that . . . disclosed:* When her two yellow nestlings (*golden couplets*) are hatched out (*disclosed*). – The dove lays only two eggs at a time, and the young birds, when they emerged from the egg, are covered in yellow down. The dove is a symbol of peace and quietness.

270   *use:* treat.

272   *Hercules* – a hero of ancient Greece, who performed immense tasks with his great strength.

273   *The cat . . . day.* This line is proverbial. It means that things will take their natural course whatever people do in an attempt to influence them: even Hercules cannot prevent the cat from mewing or the dog from asserting itself.

LAERTES [*Grappling with him*] The devil take thy soul!
HAMLET Thou pray'st not well.   240
          I prithee, take thy fingers from my throat;
          For, though I am not splenitive* and rash,
          Yet have I something in me dangerous,
          Which let thy wisdom fear. Hold off thy hand!
   KING Pluck them asunder.
  QUEEN   Hamlet, Hamlet!
    ALL   Gentlemen –   245
HORATIO Good my lord, be quiet.
          [*The* ATTENDANTS *separate them, and they come out of the grave*
HAMLET Why, I will fight with him upon this theme*
          Until my eyelids will no longer wag.*
  QUEEN O my son, what theme?
HAMLET I loved Ophelia. Forty thousand brothers   250
          Could not, with all their quantity of love,
          Make up my sum. – [*To* LAERTES] What wilt thou do for
          her?
   KING O, he is mad, Laertes.
  QUEEN For love of God, forbear him.*
HAMLET 'Swounds, show me what thou'lt do.   255
          Woo't* weep? Woo't fight? Woo't fast? Woo't tear
          thyself?
          Woo't drink up eisel?* Eat a crocodile?
          I'll do't. – Dost thou come here to whine?
          To outface me with leaping in her grave?
          Be buried quick with her, and so will I.   260
          And if thou prate of mountains, let them throw
          Millions of acres on us, till our ground,
          Singeing* his pate against the burning zone,
          Make Ossa* like a wart! Nay, an thou'lt mouth,*
          I'll rant as well as thou.
  QUEEN   This is mere* madness;   265
          And thus awhile the fit will work on him;
          Anon, as patient as the female dove
          When that her golden couplets* are disclosed,
          His silence will sit drooping.
HAMLET   Hear you, sir;
          What is the reason that you use* me thus?   270
          I loved you ever. But it is no matter;
          Let Hercules* himself do what he may,
          The cat* will mew, and dog will have his day.   [*Exit*

275   *in . . . speech:* in the light of what I said last night.

276   *the present push:* immediate trial.

278   *living:* lasting. – There is something ominous in this remark of the King's; perhaps he means also that Hamlet, now alive, will when he dies provide a monument, a symbol of memory, to the grave.

v. ii.   Hamlet tells Horatio how he turned the tables on Rosencrantz and Guildenstern; he now wants to make peace with Laertes. Osric, a foppish courtier, explains Laertes' challenge to him.

        Laertes accepts Hamlet's gesture of friendship, but says he must go through with the duel as a point of honour. The bouts begin as arranged and Hamlet wins the first two. The Queen drinks to him in the poisoned cup, despite the King's protests. In the third bout the swords become interchanged, and each man mortally wounds the other. The Queen dies, Laertes accuses the King, and Hamlet promptly kills him. Laertes reconciles himself with Hamlet, and dies. Hamlet, as he dies, dissuades Horatio from taking his own life, and gives his support to Fortinbras (who now comes in with his victorious army) as the next King of Denmark. English ambassadors report that Rosencrantz and Guildenstern were killed as soon as they got to England. Horatio is permitted to arrange for Hamlet's body to lie in state, and it is carried away to the accompaniment of gunfire and martial music.

        The account of the death of Rosencrantz and Guildenstern is postponed until this scene, perhaps because it shows here most effectively how Hamlet has changed since he left for England; this is a quick, deliberate action of his own contriving. And of course the ambassadors have taken time to get to Denmark. The stratagem contrived by the courtiers has brought about their own death; intentions have led to their opposites.

        Osric's part is a second piece of lighter relief. But also he illustrates humanity which in the end is reduced to sameness – he is *spacious in the possession of dirt.* Hamlet is sad and full of foreboding, yet also confident, seeing Claudius's schemes closing in upon their creator. He cannot be dissuaded from the fight, for if it must be, it must be, and like Osric he will, win or lose, take nothing with him when he dies.

        Hamlet, as Claudius foresaw, is too magnanimous to examine the foils; his judgement is blurred by generosity, and so he meets his death; in the final action Claudius is defeated by his own devices, and Laertes admits he is justly killed.

1   *so much for this* – They have been talking earnestly about some matter before the scene opens. Hamlet is somewhat distant, calling Horatio 'sir' more than once.

2   *circumstance:* details.

6   *the mutines in the bilboes:* mutineers in their fetters. – Bilboes were iron bars with shackles fitted in ships and used to punish mutinous sailors. When a man was locked in one, he, like Hamlet, would be too troubled to sleep much.

6   *Rashly* – The next five lines are about rashness, and in them Hamlet diverts from the account of his own escape to some general remarks: a rash action sometimes turns out better than a carefully planned one; it seems that the results of our schemes are in the hands of Providence. For Hamlet this observation is an important departure, since up to this point he has been planning, although only vaguely; and that has brought him nowhere.

9   *pall:* fail.

9   *learn:* teach.

10   *shapes . . . will:* shapes our destiny, however much we roughly cut it about (*Rough-hew*).

13   *My sea-gown . . . me:* my rough sailor's gown thrown over my shoulders (*scarfed*).

14   *them* – i.e. the dispatches.

15   *Fingered:* stole.

15   *in fine:* finally.

16   *Making so bold . . . to unseal:* venturing so far . . . as to unseal.

20   *Larded:* enriched.

21   *Importing:* deeply concerning. – The *grand commission* contained fearful menaces against the King of England if he did not put Hamlet to death at once.

22   *such bugs . . . life:* such objects of terror and alarm associated with me. – The *bugs,* or bugbears' were imagined objects of fear. Hamlet means that there were in this communication many exaggerated accounts of what he had been doing.

23   *on the supervise . . . bated:* at the first reading, without any delay (*no leisure bated,* i.e. no time taken for leisure).

KING I pray you, good Horatio, wait upon him. –

[*Exit* HORATIO

[*To* LAERTES] Strengthen your patience in* our last night's
speech;   275
We'll put the matter to the present push.* –
Good Gertrude, set some watch over your son. –
This grave shall have a living* monument.
An hour of quiet shortly shall we see;
Till then, in patience our proceeding be.   280

[*Exeunt*

scene ii

A hall in the castle.

Enter HAMLET *and* HORATIO.

HAMLET So much for this,* sir. Now shall you see the other;
You do remember all the circumstance?*
HORATIO Remember it, my lord!
HAMLET Sir, in my heart there was a kind of fighting
That would not let me sleep. Methought I lay   5
Worse than the mutines* in the bilboes. Rashly,*
And praised be rashness for it, let us know,
Our indiscretion sometime serves us well,
When our deep plots do pall.* And that should learn* us
There's a divinity that shapes* our ends,   10
Rough-hew them how we will –
HORATIO   That is most certain.
HAMLET Up from my cabin,
My sea-gown* scarfed about me, in the dark
Groped I to find out them.* Had my desire;
Fingered* their packet; and, in fine,* withdrew   15
To mine own room again. Making so bold,*
My fears forgetting manners, to unseal
Their grand commission, where I found, Horatio –
O royal knavery! – an exact command –
Larded* with many several sorts of reasons,   20
Importing* Denmark's health, and England's too,
With, ho! such bugs* and goblins in my life
That, on the supervise,* no leisure bated,

24   *stay:* wait for.

30   *Ere I could . . . play:* before I could even get my will to begin the prologue, it had begun the play. – The image is of the theatre, where a play began with an introductory speech telling the audience something about the action. In this case, Hamlet says, there was no introduction or plan at all; his brain conceived the plan in a moment without careful thought.

32   *fair:* well – i.e. legibly.

33   *did hold it . . . A baseness:* considered it, as our statesmen (*statists*) do, a sign of vulgarity.

36   *yeoman's service* – i.e. good and faithful service. Yeomen were small freeholders, famous for their bravery and independent attitude.

37   *effect:* general drift.

38   *conjuration.* appeal.

39   *tributary:* subject (paying tribute). – The King of England at this time paid tribute to the King of Denmark as his overlord.

41   *As peace . . . amities* – This passage is hard to explain satisfactorily—it is perhaps not as Shakespeare wrote it, but no satisfactory amendment has been suggested. The general drift of the lines must be: 'since peace should always (*still*) wear her garland of wheat-ears and be a link between their friendships'. The goddess Peace, with a garland of wheat-ears, suggests freedom from war, when men are at liberty to till their fields and grow crops, *comma* may stand for *compact* or some such word.

43   *As-es . . . charge:* clauses beginning *As . . .*, all of great importance (*charge*). – Dr Johnson suggested a play of words here; read in another way the words could mean 'donkeys (*asses*) with heavy loads (*charge*) on them'.

44   *That* links with *conjuration* (line 38).

45   *debatement . . . less:* any further deliberation.

46   *the bearers put:* put the bearers (of the dispatches) – i.e. Rosencrantz and Guildenstern.

47   *Not shriving-time allowed:* with no time allowed to make confession (*shriving*). – This was a consideration which prevented Hamlet from taking the King's life when he was at prayer·   *am I then, revenged,*
         To take him in the purging of his soul,
         When he is fit and seasoned for his passage?   (III.iii.84ff.).
The soul of a dying man was thought to be cursed if he made no confession of his sins, but blessed if he confessed them. By doing this, Hamlet has no mercy on the courtiers who went to sea with him. Some commentators think that he was cruelly negligent of any course of justice by so doing, since Rosencrantz and Guildenstern did not know the messages they were carrying. Others feel that in everything they did these courtiers were blind followers of the King's wishes, ready to do anything he asked to help in carrying out his designs, and their punishment is therefore deserved. Horatio certainly has misgivings about what Hamlet has done, and Hamlet goes to some lengths to account for it (lines 57–62 below).

48   *ordinant:* controlling. – Providence was on Hamlet's side, since he happened to have a ring with him which bore the royal seal of Denmark on it. He was therefore able to seal the false letter he wrote with the royal seal of the King. This seal is *th' impression* of line 52.

50   *the model . . . seal:* the counterpart of the Danish seal – which Hamlet had broken.

51   *writ:* piece of writing.

52   *subscribed:* signed.

53   *changeling* – literally, a child left by the fairies in place of one they had stolen; here it is figuratively applied to the counterfeit letter substituted for the other one.

54   *what to this was sequent:* what followed upon this.

56   *go to 't* – i.e. go to their death; Horatio does not choose to speak too plainly about it.

58   *their defeat . . . grow:* their downfall springs naturally (*Does . . . grow*) from their deliberate intrusion into the affair. – Hamlet, at least, believes that they quite willingly became involved in the plot, and used their subtlety to further it; *insinuation* suggests the twisting and turning of a body to get into a certain position.

60   *the baser nature . . . opposites* (line 62): one who is not of noble birth comes (in fencing) between the thrust (*pass*) and the fierce (*fell*), angry sword-points of powerful opponents (*opposites*). – The word *mighty* also carries a contrast to *baser*, i.e. nobly born.

No, not to stay* the grinding of the axe,
My head should be struck off.

HORATIO   Is 't possible?   25
HAMLET Here's the commission. Read it at more leisure.
But wilt thou hear me how I did proceed?
HORATIO I beseech you.
Being thus be-netted round with villainies –
Ere I could* make a prologue to my brains,   30
They had begun the play – I sat me down;
Devised a new commission; wrote it fair.* –
I once did hold* it, as our statists* do,
A baseness to write fair, and laboured much
How to forget that learning; but, sir, now   35
It did me yeoman's* service. – Wilt thou know
The effect* of what I wrote?
HORATIO   Ay, good my lord.
HAMLET An earnest conjuration* from the king –
As England was his faithful tributary;*
As love between them like the palm might flourish;   40
As peace* should still her wheaten garland wear,
And stand a comma 'tween their amities;
And many such-like As-es* of great charge –
That,* on the view and knowing of these contents,
Without debatement* further, more or less,   45
He should the bearers put* to sudden death,
Not shriving-time* allowed.
HORATIO   How was this sealed?
HAMLET Why, even in that was heaven ordinant.*
I had my father's signet in my purse,
Which was the model* of that Danish seal;   50
Folded the writ* up in the form of th' other;
Subscribed* it; gave 't th' impression; placed it safely,
The changeling* never known. Now, the next day
Was our sea-fight; and what to this was sequent*
Thou know'st already.   55
HORATIO So Guildenstern and Rosencrantz go to 't.*
HAMLET Why, man, they did make love to this employment;
They are not near my conscience; their defeat*
Does by their own insinuation grow.
'Tis dangerous when the baser nature* comes   60
Between the pass and fell incensèd points
Of mighty opposites.

63   *Does it not . . . upon:* Does it not, do you think, now make it imperative for me (*stand me . . . upon*) – and the sentence is broken off, to be taken up again at line 67. The phrase *think'st thee* appears to be a combination of *thinkest thou* and *thinks it thee*, literally, 'seems it to you'.

65   *th' election . . . hopes:* the election (of a new king) and my hopes (of becoming a king myself)'.

66   *angle:* fish-hook.

66   *proper:* own.

67   *cozenage:* trickery.

67   *perfect conscience To quit him:* in accordance with a clear conscience to take vengeance on (*quit*) him.

69   *canker . . . come In:* diseased growth (*canker*) among humanity enter into.

71   *It must* – i.e. It will inevitably. Horatio cautiously suggests that no time must be lost, since if the King gets to know what has happened in England, Hamlet's fate will be swift and sure. Hamlet characteristically finds reasons once again for putting off action. But he goes so far as to say *The interim is mine* (line 73), i.e. the interval between now and the arrival of the news is in his hands. This observation is more likely to lead to action than his former ranting against the King, and the arrival of news from England must be the point at which he will either kill the King or be killed himself. A man can be quickly killed, at the word 'One'.

77   *by the image . . . his:* when I look at my own cause, I see a reflection of his. – Like himself, Laertes has good cause to lament recent events, which touch them both.

78   *court* – All the early editions have *count* here, but that word does not make good sense.

79   *bravery:* showy display.

83   *this water-fly* – Osric is the type of person who is always busy over nothing, like a fly bobbing aimlessly up and down over water. He has exaggeratedly courtly manners, exemplified in much play with his hat, which he takes off and swings while he is bowing, and in extravagant ways of talking and addressing people. Examples of his exaggerated courtly diction are: *Sweet lord, if your lordship were at leisure* (assuming he is not) . . . *impart* (i.e. 'tell')—line 90; *bade me signify to you* (i.e. 'told me to tell you')—line 100.

85   *Thy state* – i.e. the state of Horatio's soul.

87   *Let a beast . . . mess:* Imagine that an animal is lord over all other animals, and (you will find) Osric's food-trough (*crib*) standing among the King's own eating companions (*mess*). – Hamlet is talking of Osric in terms of an animal among animals, the *lord of beasts* he mentions becoming the king—Osric not being the king of beasts, but in the king's company, a courtier. 'Messes' were small groups of people who ate together at banquets; the word *mess*, meaning an eating-place, is still used in the fighting forces.

88   *chough:* jackdaw – a bird with a chattering cry. Hamlet is referring to Osric's way of talking, his use of the fashionable phrases of the court.

89   *dirt* – i.e. land.

92   *diligence of spirit* – Hamlet is mocking Osric's style of talking.

93   *your bonnet . . . use:* your hat to its right use. – The word *bonnet* is now not normally used for a man's hat.

95   *'tis very cold* – Here Hamlet uses for the second time a device to make courtiers look ridiculous; he makes them agree to one thing, then contradicts himself, and they contradict themselves similarly—evidently to be courteous and also to humour Hamlet in his supposed madness. We are reminded of the incident (III.ii.350ff.) when Polonius pretends to see in the clouds the shapes that Hamlet describes.

98   *complexion:* (bodily) constitution.

HORATIO   Why, what a king is this!

HAMLET Does it not,* think'st thee, stand me now upon –
He that hath killed my king, and whored my mother;
Popped in between th' election* and my hopes;   65
Thrown out his angle* for my proper* life,
And with such cozenage* – is 't not perfect* conscience
To quit him with this arm? And is 't not to be damned
To let this canker* of our nature come
In further evil?   70

HORATIO It must* be shortly known to him from England
What is the issue of the business there.

HAMLET It will be short. The interim is mine;
And a man's life's no more than to say 'One'.
But I am very sorry, good Horatio,   75
That to Laertes I forgot myself;
For, by the image* of my cause, I see
The portraiture of his. I'll court* his favours.
But, sure, the bravery* of his grief did put me
Into a towering passion.

HORATIO   Peace! Who comes here?   80

Enter OSRIC.

OSRIC Your lordship is right welcome back to Denmark.

HAMLET I humbly thank you, sir – [*Aside to* HORATIO] Dost know this
water-fly?*

HORATIO [*Aside to* HAMLET] No, my good lord.

HAMLET [*Aside to* HORATIO] Thy state* is the more gracious, for 'tis a   85
vice to know him. He hath much land, and fertile. Let a
beast* be lord of beasts, and his crib shall stand at the king's
mess. 'Tis a chough;* but, as I say, spacious in the possession
of dirt.*

OSRIC Sweet lord, if your lordship were at leisure, I should impart   90
a thing to you from his majesty.

HAMLET I will receive it, sir, with all diligence* of spirit. Put your
bonnet* to his right use; 'tis for the head.

OSRIC I thank your lordship; it is very hot.

HAMLET No, believe me, 'tis very cold;* the wind is northerly.   95

OSRIC It is indifferent cold, my lord, indeed.

HAMLET But yet methinks it is very sultry and hot for my complexion.*

OSRIC Exceedingly, my lord; it is very sultry – as 'twere – I cannot

*

HAMLET moves him . . . – Osric has been bowing and sweeping his hat in extravagant
    gestures; Hamlet asks him to remember his request, *Put your bonnet to his
    right use* (line 92). Osric answers *For mine ease,* a conventional reply, meaning,
    probably, 'Allow me to show the proper marks of respect.'

105   *absolute.* perfect.

106   *differences:* characteristic, distinguishing features. – It has been suggested that the
    metaphor here is from heraldry, a shield with a 'difference'; compare Ophelia's
    words
            you must wear your rue with a difference (IV.v.178).

106   *soft . . . showing:* gentle birth and distinguished appearance.

107   *feelingly:* understandingly.

108   *the card . . . gentry:* the guide (*card*) and directory (*calendar*) of good breeding (*gentry,* i.e.
    gentility). – The *card* is like that which is perhaps referred to at v.i.123, on
    which the points of the compass were set out as a guide; the *calendar* is a general
    directory of times at which things should be done. Laertes is said to be a model
    on which all who profess to be gentlemen could base their behaviour.

109   *the continent . . . see:* the sum (*continent*) of those qualities (*part*) which a gentleman would
    wish to see. – The image of the *card* (containing the points of the compass) is
    extended to *continent* and *part,* i.e. of a map.

110   *definement:* description – Hamlet's reply is in the style of Osric's own speech, using
    unnecessarily long and difficult words and involved sentences. This style
    makes particular use of involved words of Latin origin (sometimes invented
    for the occasion) where a simple short word would convey exactly the same
    meaning.

110   *perdition:* loss.

111   *inventorially:* in detail – as in an inventory, or detailed list of goods.

112   *and yet but yaw . . . sail:* and yet it (dividing him inventorially) would go along very un-
    steadily (*yaw*) compared with the speed with which it (the recollection of
    Laertes' good qualities) sails into the mind. – The imagery is of the sea and
    ships; but the passage is not to be taken seriously.

113   *the verity of extolment:* the truthfulness of praise.

114   *great article:* of large scope – with the word *article* evidently taken from *inventorially,* i.e.
    the particulars of the inventory.

114   *his infusion:* the essential qualities 'infused' in him.

114   *dearth:* high value, scarcity.

115   *to make true diction:* to speak truly.

115   *his semblance:* his like – i.e. anyone who is like him is nothing but a reflection of himself.

116   *who else . . . more:* whoever else would follow (*trace*) him is nothing more than his shadow
    (*umbrage*).

117   *infallibly:* unerringly

119   *The concernancy.* The import (of the message).

120   *more rawer:* more vulgar. – The eccentric style here reaches its limit: to describe Laertes
    is 'to wrap him in breath', but the breath they are using is coarse and vulgar
    compared with Laertes.

122   *Is't not possible . . . tongue* – (perhaps) 'Is it not possible for you to understand (the style
    of speech you use) when it is on someone else's tongue?' Hamlet has out-
    stripped Osric in the use of this form of English, and has left him completely
    bewildered.

124   *What imports . . . gentleman:* What is the reason for your naming (*nomination*) this gentle-
    man?

126   *purse* links with *golden* in this sentence, as an image of Osric's word-store.

131   *not much approve me:* not be much to my credit. – Osric was going to say 'you are not
    ignorant of Laertes', and something more about his good qualities, but Hamlet
    interrupts him, taking it to mean *ignorant* alone, i.e. uninformed about things
    in general, uneducated. Osric picks up the theme again in his reply.

134   *to know . . . himself:* for a man to know someone else well, he has to know himself.

135   *imputation . . . them·* reputation (*imputation*) given him by people in general (*them*).

136   *in his meed he's unfellowed:* in his merit (*meed*) he has no match.

140   *Barbary* – the lands along the north coast of Africa, famous for fine horses.

	tell how. – But, my lord, his majesty bade me signify to you 100
	that he has laid a great wager on your head. Sir, this is the
	matter –
HAMLET	I beseech you, remember –

[HAMLET *moves* him to put on his hat

OSRIC Nay, good my lord. For mine ease, in good faith. Sir, here is
newly come to court Laertes; believe me, an absolute*   105
gentleman, full of most excellent differences,* of very soft*
society and great showing. Indeed, to speak feelingly* of him,
he is the card* or calendar of gentry, for you shall find in him
the continent* of what part a gentleman would see.

HAMLET Sir, his definement* suffers no perdition* in you; though, I   110
know, to divide him inventorially* would dizzy the arithmetic of memory, and yet but yaw* neither, in respect of his
quick sail. But, in the verity* of extolment, I take him to be
a soul of great article,* and his infusion* of such dearth* and
rareness, as, to make true diction* of him, his semblable* is   115
his mirror; and who else* would trace him, his umbrage,
nothing more.

OSRIC Your lordship speaks most infallibly* of him.

HAMLET The concernancy,* sir? Why do we wrap the gentleman in
our more rawer* breath?   120

OSRIC Sir?

HORATIO Is 't not possible* to understand in another tongue? You will
do 't, sir, really.

HAMLET What imports* the nomination of this gentleman?

OSRIC Of Laertes?   125

HORATIO [*Aside to* HAMLET] His purse* is empty already. All's golden
words are spent.

HAMLET Of him, sir.

OSRIC I know you are not ignorant –

HAMLET I would you did, sir; yet, in faith, if you did, it would not   130
much approve* me. – Well, sir.

OSRIC You are not ignorant of what excellence Laertes is –

HAMLET I dare not confess that, lest I should compare with him in
excellence; but, to know* a man well, were to know himself.

OSRIC I mean, sir, for his weapon; but in the imputation* laid on   135
him by them, in his meed* he's unfellowed.

HAMLET What's his weapon?

OSRIC Rapier and dagger.

HAMLET That's two of his weapons. But, well.

OSRIC The king, sir, hath wagered with him six Barbary* horses.   140

141   *imponed* – Perhaps this is Osric's affected pronunciation of *impawned*: wagered. The early Quartos have *impaund* here. The King has wagered the horses against Laertes' winning the match; if he *does* win he will get the horses. Laertes has wagered the rapiers and poniards against Hamlet winning the match; if Hamlet wins, the King gets the prizes.

142   *poniards:* daggers.

142   *assigns:* fittings.

142   *hangers:* straps – four in number, which attached the sword to the girdle. Osric affectedly refers to them as *the carriages* in his next sentence.

144   *responsive to:* in keeping with.

145   *liberal conceit:* tasteful design – the meaning of *liberal* here being derived from 'what pleases a liberal person, a person of good taste'.

147   *edified by the margent:* instructed by what is written in the margin. – He means that Hamlet could not possibly understand what Osric is trying to say without the help of explanations, like the guiding notes and glosses printed in the margins of old books.

150   *german:* appropriate. – It is cannon, not swords, that are moved by carriages.

151   *I would it might be:* I would prefer it (the word) to be.

156   *passes:* fencing bouts.

157   *shall not exceed . . . nine* – This evidently means that to win the match Laertes must score three more hits than Hamlet scores; and there are to be twelve bouts (*a dozen passes*) instead of the usual nine. Each bout ends with a hit. In other words, the King has bet that Laertes will not score more than eight hits in the total of twelve bouts. Hamlet thinks that he can keep Laertes to a maximum of two hits more than his own, and so win the match. He says (line 194), *I shall win at the odds,* i.e. 'with the chances in my favour'.

158   *would:* could. – They could put the wager to the test immediately.

159   *answer* – Hamlet takes this to refer to an answer to the challenge, but Osric explains that he means the encounter itself, *the opposition of your person,* i.e. offering himself as an opponent in the contest.

163   *the breathing . . . day* – i.e. the usual time for relaxation and exercise during the day.

167   *re-deliver you:* return your answer.

168   *flourish:* verbal adornment.

171   *no tongues . . . turn:* no other tongues to serve his purpose.

172   *This lapwing . . . head* – The lapwing, a black-and-white bird, was said to run from the nest as soon as it was hatched, i.e. with the shell still on his head. Osric (he is referred to as *young Osric* in line 180) is called a lapwing because his manner shows that he is inexperienced in life, and in the ways of the court, overdoing the habits and styles of speech he has learnt there.

173   *comply:* use the formalities of courtesy – i.e. the manners and speech-styles of the court. Hamlet said Osric did this even at his mother's breast, showing that he was born a courtier.

174   *bevy:* flock of birds – such as the lapwing.

175   *drossy:* frivolous.

175   *the tune of the time:* the mood of the age.

176   *outward . . . encounter:* exterior polite manner in handling people. – They have polished social manners which are quite superficial.

176   *yesty collection:* superficial ('foamy') knowledge.

177   *fanned . . . opinions* – This phrase presents many difficulties. For *fanned* in the text here, the Folios read *fond* (meaning, presumably, 'foolish') and the Quartos have other readings. The word *fanned* has been attracted by *winnowed*, it seems; *to winnow* is to fan grain (e.g. corn) free of chaff. The general meaning seems to be: the superficial knowledge and facility with words carries these people through the most carefully considered opinions expressed by other people (people who have 'winnowed the grain' of their thoughts, and blown away everything that was unworthy). But just blow off these superficial scraps of knowledge (like froth) and you will find them on examination (*trial*) to be bubbles which burst (*the bubbles are out*).

180   *commended him:* sent his greetings – i.e. sent a message.

against the which he has imponed,* as I take it, six French
rapiers and poniards,* with their assigns,* as girdle, hangers,*
and so. Three of the carriages, in faith, are very dear to fancy,
very responsive* to the hilts, most delicate carriages, and of
very liberal conceit.*   145

HAMLET   What call you the carriages?

HORATIO [Aside to HAMLET] I knew you must be edified* by the
margent ere you had done.

OSRIC   The carriages, sir, are the hangers.

HAMLET   The phrase would be more german* to the matter if we could   150
carry cannon by our sides. I would* it might be 'hangers' till
then. But, on. Six Barbary horses against six French swords,
their assigns, and three liberal-conceited carriages; that's the
French bet against the Danish. Why is this 'imponed', as you
call it?   155

OSRIC   The king, sir, hath laid that in a dozen passes* between yourself and him, he shall not exceed* you three hits. He hath laid
on twelve for nine; and it would* come to immediate trial, if
your lordship would vouchsafe the answer.*

HAMLET   How if I answer no?   160

OSRIC   I mean, my lord, the opposition of your person in trial.

HAMLET   Sir, I will walk here in the hall. If it please his majesty, 'tis
the breathing* time of day with me; let the foils be brought,
the gentleman willing, and the king hold his purpose, I will
win for him an I can; if not, I will gain nothing but my shame   165
and the odd hits.

OSRIC   Shall I re-deliver* you e'en so?

HAMLET   To this effect, sir; after what flourish* your nature will.

OSRIC   I commend my duty to your lordship.

HAMLET   Yours, yours. [Exit OSRIC] – He does well to commend it him-   170
self; there are no tongues* else for's turn.

HORATIO This lapwing* runs away with the shell on his head.

HAMLET   He did comply* with his dug, before he sucked it. Thus has
he – and many more of the same bevy,* that I know the
drossy* age dotes on – only got the tune* of the time, and   175
outward habit* of encounter; a kind of yesty* collection,
which carries them through and through the most fanned*
and winnowed opinions; and do but blow them to their trial,
the bubbles are out.

Enter a LORD.

LORD   My lord, his majesty commended him* to you by young   180

181   *attend:* wait for.
182   *if your pleasure . . . play:* if you still wish to contest (in a fencing match, or *play*).
183   *that:* if.
185   *pleasure* – This is evidently used with a double meaning: to the Lord it means that what
            Hamlet has already said about his willingness to fight (*my purposes*) remains
            firm, and he now awaits a command from the King (*the king's pleasure*); to
            himself Hamlet means that his *purposes* to kill the King and avenge his father's
            death are unshaken, and will pursue the King while he is indulging himself, and
            not busy with something which will ensure that his soul will go to heaven.
            Cf.

> Now might I do it pat, now he is praying;
> . . . and so he goes to heaven (III.iii.73–4).

185   *his fitness speaks:* he expresses his readiness. – The *his* apparently refers to the King,
            though some editors have thought it referred to Laertes.
187   *down* – i.e. from the upper chambers of the castle into the hall. The anticipation of the
            final events leading to the catastrophe is now becoming more and more
            intense.
188   *In happy time* – i.e. the time is suitable.
189   *use . . . entertainment:* give a warm and friendly welcome.
198   *gain-giving:* misgiving (*gain*, here, means 'against', as in *gainsay*). – It is women rather
            than men who usually have these vague forebodings and fears of what will
            happen in the future.
201   *repair hither:* coming here.
203   *the fall of a sparrow* – This is an echo from the Bible. Jesus says, '. . . one of them [the
            sparrows] shall not fall on the ground without your Father (i.e. God's provi-
            dence)' (*Matthew* 10: 29).
203   *If it be now . . .* – Hamlet is resigned to fate, and unwilling to take any measures to counter-
            act it; *we defy angury*. He does not, therefore, suspect anything wrong in the
            arrangements for the fencing match, and has his own plan of action ready. The
            attendants are ready with the foils, and when they come in he takes all the
            arrangements on trust.
205   *aught:* anything – i.e. no-one keeps any part of what he leaves behind him at death. (This
            is the reading of the Folios; the Quartos have other versions which do not
            seem to make such good sense. A Quarto reading, *. . . no man knows aught . . .*,
            could be interpreted as meaning, 'Since no man knows anything of the real
            nature of the life he leaves behind him, why should he be concerned about
            leaving it in good time?')
206   *betimes:* in good time.
210   *This presence knows:* Those who are present here know.
212   *sore distraction:* grievous derangement of the mind.
213   *exception:* disapproval. – This word and *nature* and *honour* are the objects of *Roughly
            awake*.

      The lines from *This presence knows* (210) to *Hamlet's enemy* (221) are weak as
      poetry, and the matter in them seems quite unworthy of Hamlet at a point
      where he is at last prepared to act. This elaborate pleading for pardon is un-
      called for, and leads nowhere. Some critics have questioned whether these
      lines are in fact Shakespeare's.

Osric, who brings back to him, that you attend* him in the
hall. He sends to know if your pleasure* hold to play with
Laertes, or that* you will take longer time.

HAMLET I am constant to my purposes; they follow the king's
pleasure * If his fitness* speaks, mine is ready, now or when-   185
soever, provided I be so able as now.

LORD The king and queen and all are coming down.*

HAMLET In happy time.*

LORD The queen desires you to use some gentle entertainment* to
Laertes before you fall to play.   190

HAMLET She well instructs me.   [*Exit* LORD

HORATIO You will lose this wager, my lord.

HAMLET I do not think so. Since he went into France, I have been in
continual practice; I shall win at the odds. But thou wouldst
not think how ill all's here about my heart; but it is no   195
matter.

HORATIO Nay, good my lord —

HAMLET It is but foolery; but it is such a kind of gain-giving* as would
perhaps trouble a woman.

HORATIO If your mind dislike anything, obey it. I will forestall their   200
repair hither,* and say you are not fit.

HAMLET Not a whit, we defy augury. There's a special providence in
the fall of a sparrow.* If it be now,* 'tis not to come; if it be
not to come, it will be now; if it be not now, yet it will come.
The readiness is all. Since no man has aught* of what he   205
leaves, what is 't to leave betimes?* Let be.

Enter KING, QUEEN, LAERTES, LORDS, OSRIC, *and* ATTENDANTS
with foils and gauntlets: a table and flagons of wine on it.

KING Come, Hamlet, come, and take this hand from me.
                    [*The* KING *puts* LAERTES' *hand into* HAMLET'S

HAMLET Give me your pardon, sir. I've done you wrong;
But pardon 't, as you are a gentleman.
This presence* knows,   210
And you must needs have heard, how I am punished
With sore* distraction. What I have done,
That might your nature, honour, and exception*
Roughly awake, I here proclaim was madness.
Was 't Hamlet wronged Laertes? Never Hamlet.   215
If Hamlet from himself be ta'en away,
And when he's not himself does wrong Laertes,

225   *shot mine arrow* . . . – Hamlet is saying that he has acted blindly and irresponsibly, like a man who shoots an arrow over a house, and, on the other side, which he cannot see, hurts his own brother with it.

226   *nature* – This contrasts with *terms of honour* in the next line but one. His natural feelings are satisfied, but the code of honour he is supposed to live by at the court, and as explained by the *elder masters* (line 230), may not allow him to be content with Hamlet's apology.

227   *Whose motive:* the incitement of which (to anger).

229   *will no:* do not want any.

231   *a voice* . . . *ungored:* an opinion and a precedent for making peace, so that my reputation (*name*) remains uninjured (*ungored*).

234   *embrace:* welcome.

235   *frankly:* without restraint – like *freely* in the preceding line.

237   *foil:* setting of a jewel (to show it to advantage). – Hamlet is playing on the word *foil*, which has so far been used for fencing foils. The position now is that the fencing match is to be a friendly one, since any enmity which may have existed between them is at an end.

239   *Stick fiery off:* stand out in blazing relief.

243   *Your Grace* . . . *weaker side* – The King has backed (*laid the odds o'*) Hamlet to win although Hamlet is, in his own judgement, the *weaker side*. The King explains that he is not worried about this, but because he knows how Laertes' fencing has improved, he stipulated odds in Hamlet's favour—Hamlet need score only four hits in twelve to prevent Laertes from winning the match.

245   *bettered:* much improved (in skill) – i.e. since he had training in Paris.

247   *have all a length:* are all of the same length – *a:* one.

251   *quit* . . . *exchange:* repay Laertes in the third bout for any hit he scored in the first or second.

Then Hamlet does it not, Hamlet denies it.
Who does it, then? His madness. If 't be so,
Hamlet is of the faction that is wronged;   220
His madness is poor Hamlet's enemy.
Sir, in this audience,
Let my disclaiming from a purposed evil
Free me so far in your most generous thoughts
That I have shot mine arrow* o'er the house,   225
And hurt my brother.

LAERTES   I am satisfied in nature,*
Whose motive,* in this case, should stir me most
To my revenge. But in my terms of honour
I stand aloof, and will no* reconcilement
Till by some elder masters, of known honour,   230
I have a voice* and precedent of peace,
To keep my name ungored. But till that time
I do receive your offered love like love,
And will not wrong it.

HAMLET   I embrace* it freely,
And will this brother's wager frankly* play. –   235
Give us the foils. – Come on.

LAERTES   Come, one for me.

HAMLET   I'll be your foil,* Laertes. In mine ignorance
Your skill shall, like a star i' th' darkest night,
Stick* fiery off indeed.

LAERTES   You mock me, sir.

HAMLET   No, by this hand.   240

KING   Give them the foils, young Osric. – Cousin Hamlet,
You know the wager?

HAMLET   Very well, my lord;
Your Grace hath laid the odds o' th' weaker* side.

KING   I do not fear it; I have seen you both.
But since he is bettered,* we have therefore odds.   245

LAERTES   [Trying the foil] This is too heavy; let me see another.

HAMLET   [Trying his foil] This likes me well. These foils have* all a
length?

OSRIC   Ay, my good lord.   [They prepare to fence

KING   Set me the stoups of wine upon that table. –
If Hamlet give the first or second hit,   250
Or quit* in answer of the third exchange,
Let all the battlements their ordnance fire;
The king shall drink to Hamlet's better breath,

254   *an union:* a fine pearl – *union* giving the idea 'unique of its kind'.

257   *kettle* – i.e. kettle-drum, a drum made of metal and parchment. A great display is to be
       made as the King drinks Hamlet's health, ending in the guns being fired off
       from the battlements of the castle. Shakespeare's audience enjoyed loud noises
       and colourful display in the plays they saw.

262   *Judgement* – He wants the ruling of the judge as to whether or not it was a hit. Hamlet has
       said it was (*One*), but Laertes denies this.

269   *fat* – This is almost certainly a mistake for another word which cannot now be restored.
       Some commentators, however, think it was inserted to suit a particular actor
       who took the part of Hamlet as a man already sedentary in his habits and with
       some years behind him as a student and member of the royal household.

270   *napkin:* handkerchief – as always in Shakespeare.

271   *carouses:* drinks a toast.

278   *'gainst my conscience* – Before the play ends, Laertes will have revealed the King's treachery
       and confessed his own part in it (lines 295–302). The mention of pangs of
       conscience here may be taken as a link between Laertes' ready acceptance of
       the King's plans for the treacherous fencing match and his final confession of
       his part in it.

279   *you but dally:* you are only trifling – i.e. not fencing in earnest.

281   *make a wanton of me:* make me look like (i.e. treat me as if I were) a weakling – *wanton:*
       effeminate, inexperienced person. Laertes is not doing his best because he
       cannot forget what is at the end of his foil; Hamlet notices that he is for some
       reason holding himself back.

And in the cup an union* shall he throw,
Richer than that which four successive kings   255
In Denmark's crown have worn. Give me the cups;
And let the kettle* to the trumpet speak,
The trumpet to the cannoneer without,
The cannons to the heavens, the heaven to earth,
'Now the king drinks to Hamlet.' – Come, begin;   260
And you, the judges, bear a wary eye.

HAMLET   Come on, sir.

LAERTES   Come, my lord.   [They fence

HAMLET   One.

LAERTES   No.

HAMLET   Judgement.*

OSRIC   A hit, a very palpable hit.

LAERTES   Well – again.

KING   Stay; give me drink. – Hamlet, this pearl is thine;
                          [He puts poison in the cup
Here's to thy health.
                          [Trumpets sound, and shot goes off
                    Give him the cup.   265

HAMLET   I'll play this bout first; set it by awhile. –
Come. – [They fence] Another hit; what say you?

LAERTES   A touch, a touch, I do confess.

KING   Our son shall win.

QUEEN   He's fat,* and scant of breath.
Here, Hamlet, take my napkin,* rub they brows.   270
The queen carouses* to thy fortune, Hamlet.
                          [She takes the poisoned cup

HAMLET   Good madam!

KING   Gertrude, do not drink.

QUEEN   I will, my lord; I pray you, pardon me.   [Drinks

KING   [Aside] It is the poisoned cup; it is too late.

HAMLET   I dare not drink yet, madam; by and by.   275

QUEEN   Come, let me wipe thy face.

LAERTES   My lord, I'll hit him now.

KING   I do not think 't.

LAERTES   [Aside] And yet 'tis almost 'gainst my conscience.*

HAMLET   Come, for the third, Laertes. You but dally;*
I pray you, pass with your best violence;   280
I am afeared you make a wanton* of me.

LAERTES   Say you so? Come on.   [They fence

OSRIC   Nothing, neither way.

* *they change rapiers* – There are various ways in which this could have happened, e.g. Hamlet might have knocked Laertes' foil out of his hand and, hoping to gain some advantage, picked it up and offered Laertes his own.

  To the reader this dramatic device to bring Laertes' crime back upon himself may appear crude. But in the fast-moving scuffle on the stage such an exchange can take place without appearing very remarkable or contrived. Indeed, it was most probably a recognized ploy in fencing as practised in Shakespeare's time.

284 *incensed*: enraged (with one another) – i.e. they are now fighting in earnest and not as in a friendly match.

288 *a woodcock ... springe* – Woodcocks were used as decoys to entice other birds into traps. But sometimes the woodcock went too near the trap, and was itself trapped; *springe*: small trap made with cord.

288 *with*: by.

308 *thy union*: your fine pearl. – Evidently Hamlet suspects that what the King called *an union* was in fact poison.

310 *tempered*: mixed.

316 *chance*: (unhappy) event.

317 *mutes*: silent watchers, taking no part in the action.

318 *fell sergeant*: cruel sheriff's officer. – It was the duty of this officer to carry out arrests for the sheriff's court.

LAERTES Have at you now!

[LAERTES *wounds* HAMLET; *then, in scuffling,*
they change rapiers,* and HAMLET *wounds* LAERTES

KING   Part them; they are incensed.*

HAMLET Nay, come, again.   [*The* QUEEN *falls*

OSRIC   Look to the queen there, ho!   285

HORATIO They bleed on both sides – [*To* HAMLET] How is it, my lord?

OSRIC How is 't, Laertes?

LAERTES Why, as a woodcock* to mine own springe, Osric,
I am justly killed with* mine own treachery.

HAMLET How does the queen?

KING   She swoons to see them bleed.   290

QUEEN No, no, the drink, the drink – O my dear Hamlet –
The drink, the drink! – I am poisoned.   [*Dies*

HAMLET O villainy! – Ho! let the door be locked.
Treachery! Seek it out.   [LAERTES *falls*

LAERTES It is here, Hamlet. Hamlet, thou art slain;
No medicine in the world can do thee good,
In thee there is not half an hour of life;
The treacherous instrument is in thy hand,
Unbated and envenomed. The foul practice
Hath turned itself on me; lo, here I lie,   300
Never to rise again. Thy mother's poisoned.
I can no more – the king, the king's to blame.

HAMLET The point – envenomed too! –
Then, venom, to thy work.   [*Stabs the* KING

ALL Treason! Treason!   305

KING O, yet defend me, friends; I am but hurt.

HAMLET Here, thou incestuous, murderous, damnéd Dane,
Drink off this potion. – Is thy union* here?
Follow my mother.   [KING *dies*

LAERTES   He is justly served;
It is a poison tempered* by himself. –   310
Exchange forgiveness with me, noble Hamlet.
Mine and my father's death come not upon thee.
Nor thine on me!   [*Dies*

HAMLET Heaven make thee free of it! I follow thee. –
I am dead, Horatio. – Wretched queen, adieu! –   315
[*To all*] You that look pale and tremble at this chance,*
That are but mutes* or audience to this act,
Had I but time – as this fell sergeant,* death,
Is strict in his arrest – O, I could tell you –

323   *an antique Roman:* (like) a Roman of ancient days. – In battle a Roman might commit suicide if his senior officer was killed; this was considered more honourable than yielding to the enemy. (Shakespeare may have had in mind the parts played by Brutus and Cassius in his *Julius Caesar.* Horatio mentioned *mightiest Julius* at the beginning of the play, I.i.114.) Hamlet, however, prevents Horatio from drinking the poisoned wine.

327   *live* – The Quartos read *I leave* here, which seems to make better sense, but disturbs the rhythm of the line.

329   *felicity* – i.e. the joys of heaven. Hamlet asks him not to take his own life, but to live on, so that the truth about Hamlet will be known.

335   *o'er-crows:* overpowers – a metaphor from cock-fighting.

337   *th' election* – i.e. of the next King of Denmark.

338   *voice:* vote – given as he is dying.

339   *So tell him, with:* tell him this, together with.

339   *occurrents:* events.

340   *solicited:* moved (me to) . . . – The sentence remains unfinished, but he apparently intends to say something meaning 'to these actions'.

346   *This quarry . . . havoc:* This heap of dead bodies (*quarry*) cries out for merciless slaughter (*havoc*) – in revenge. To 'cry havoc' was to give an army the signal to break ranks and plunder what they had conquered.
       Fortinbras's entry symbolizes the outside world breaking in on the intolerable strain of a small circle of highly-placed people whose schemes have brought death to many of the protagonists.

347   *toward:* about to take place. – The *feast* spoken of here must be linked with the feasts commonly held after funerals; cf. *the funeral baked meats* which Hamlet speaks of (I.ii.179).

347   *eternal* – said of an abhorrent thing lasting for ever, 'infernal'.

But let it be. – Horatio, I am dead;   320
Thou liv'st; report me and my cause aright
To the unsatisfied.

HORATIO   Never believe it.
I am more an antique Roman* than a Dane.
Here's yet some liquor left.   [*He takes up the cup*

HAMLET   As th' art a man,
Give me the cup. Let go; by heaven, I'll have 't.   325
O God, Horatio, what a wounded name
Things standing thus unknown shall live* behind me!
If thou didst ever hold me in thy heart,
Absent thee from felicity* awhile,
And in this harsh world draw thy breath in pain,   330
To tell my story.
                     [*March afar off, and shot within*
What warlike noise is this?

OSRIC   Young Fortinbras, with conquest come from Poland,
To the ambassadors of England gives
This warlike volley.

HAMLET   O, I die, Horatio;
The potent poison quite o'er-crows* my spirit.   335
I cannot live to hear the news from England;
But I do prophesy th' election* lights
On Fortinbras. He has my dying voice;*
So tell him,* with the occurrents,* more and less,
Which have solicited* – The rest is silence.   [*Dies*   340

HORATIO   Now cracks a noble heart. – Good night, sweet prince;
And flights of angels sing thee to thy rest! –
Why does the drum come hither?   [*March within*

Enter FORTINBRAS *and the English* AMBASSADORS, *with drum,*
colours, and ATTENDANTS.

FORTINBRAS   Where is this sight?

HORATIO   What is it ye would see?
If aught of woe or wonder, cease your search.   345

FORTINBRAS   This quarry cries on havoc.* – O proud Death,
What feast is toward* in thine eternal* cell,
That thou so many princes at a shot
So bloodily hast struck?

FIRST   The sight is dismal;

AMBASSADOR   And our affairs from England come too late;   350
The ears are senseless that should give us hearing,

354   *his* – i.e. the King's.
357   *so jump . . . question:* so exactly (*jump*) at the time of this bloody encounter.
358   *Polack:* Polish – addressed to Fortinbras.
363   *carnal . . . cause* (line 365) – The *carnal, bloody, and unnatural acts* are the murder of the
         elder Hamlet by Claudius, and his subsequent marriage to the King's widow; *casual slaughters* refers to the killing of Polonius; and *deaths . . . by cunning and forced cause* are those of Rosencrantz and Guildenstern, killed by a trick of Hamlet's; *put on:* instigated. The bodies of dead rulers were displayed in this way to prove to the common people that they were truly dead, and that a new ruler was to be acknowledged; this was especially important when *men's minds are wild* (line 376).
366   *upshot:* conclusion.
371   *rights of memory:* rights which are remembered – i.e. rights to the crown of Denmark as
         well as Norway.
372   *which now . . . me:* which this favourable opportunity (*my vantage*) now invites me to
         claim.
374   *from his mouth . . . more* – (probably) '(a message) from the mouth of Hamlet, whose voice
         will bring out others to corroborate it'. Horatio evidently refers to Hamlet's last request (lines 330–1 and 338–40).
375   *presently:* immediately.
377   *On:* as a consequence of.
378   *the stage* – i.e. that spoken of at line 359.
379   *put on:* set to perform an office – i.e. inherit the throne after Claudius.
384   *Becomes the field:* suits a battlefield.

To tell him his commandment is fulfilled,
That Rosencrantz and Guildenstern are dead.
Where should we have our thanks?

HORATIO   Not from his* mouth,
Had it th' ability of life to thank you.   355
He never gave commandment for their death.
But since, so jump* upon his bloody question,
You from the Polack* wars, and you from England,
Are here arrived, give order that these bodies
High on a stage be placed to the view;   360
And let me speak to th' yet unknowing world
How these things came about. So shall you hear
Of carnal,* bloody, and unnatural acts,
Of accidental judgements, casual slaughters,
Of deaths put on by cunning and forced cause,   365
And, in this upshot,* purposes mistook
Fall'n on the inventors' heads. All this can I
Truly deliver.

FORTINBRAS   Let us haste to hear it,
And call the noblest to the audience.
For me, with sorrow I embrace my fortune.   370
I have some rights* of memory in this kingdom,
Which now to claim my vantage* doth invite me.

HORATIO Of that I shall have also cause to speak,
And from his mouth* whose voice will draw on more.
But let this same be presently* performed,   375
Even while men's minds are wild, lest more mischance,
On* plots and errors, happen.

FORTINBRAS   Let four captains
Bear Hamlet, like a soldier, to the stage;*
For he was likely, had he been put on,*
To have proved most royally. And, for his passage,   380
The soldiers' music and the rites of war
Speak loudly for him. –
Take up the bodies. – Such a sight as this
Becomes* the field, but here shows much amiss. –
Go bid the soldiers shoot.   385

[A dead march. Exeunt, bearing off the dead bodies,
          after which a peal of ordnance is shot off.

Glossary

(S.D. = Stage direction)

A

a', he IV.v.184
abate, decrease the intensity of IV.vii.115
abatement, reduction IV.vii.120
above, more than II.ii.412
about, get to work! II.ii.563
abroad, out-of doors, away from the house I.i.161
absolute, positive V.i.123
   perfect V.ii.105
abstract, summary, account II.ii.498
abuse (v), deceive II.ii.578
abuse (n.), piece of deception IV.vii.49
abused, deceived I.v.38
accord, agreement I.ii.123
addition, title, reputation I.iv.20
address, make ready I.ii.214
adieu, farewell I.v 91
admiration, astonishment I.ii.190
   bewilderment III.ii.306
advancement, advantage III.ii.53
   promotion III.ii.317
aery, brood of a bird of prey II.ii.327
affair, subject-matter, business III.ii.290
affection, affectation II.ii.419
   feeling III.i.161
affront, meet face to face III.i.31
after, according to II.ii.503
again, back III.i.101
against, *'guinst*, in expectation of (the time when) I.i.158, II.ii.458, III.iv.51
age, world IV.vii.28
aim, guess IV.v.9
alack, alas III.iv.201
allowance, admission III.ii.26
alone, only I.iii.11
altitude, height II.ii.405
amazement, worry III.ii.306
   bewilderment III.iv.113
ambition, great desires II.ii.249
amiss, disaster IV.v.18
an, if V.ii.165, p. xli
anchor, anchorite, hermit III.ii.207
angle, fish-hook V.ii.66
anon, at once S.D., in a moment II.ii.461, III.ii.p.113
answer, explain III.iv.177
   account for IV.i.16
antic, fantastic I.v.172

antique, of the old days V.ii.323
ape, monkey III.iv.195
apoplexed, paralysed III.iv.74
appliance, remedy IV.iii.10
appointment, equipment IV.vi.14
apprehension, intelligence II.ii.299
   fit of imagination IV.i.11
approve, be to one's credit V.ii.131
aptly, readily III.iv.166
argal, for Latin *ergo*, therefore V.i.11
argue, prove the existence of V.i.9
argument, plot III.ii.130, III.ii.220
arm, prepare III.iii.24
arraign, make accusations against IV.v.89
arrant, out-and-out I.v.124, III.i.129
arras, wall-hanging II.ii.164, III.iii.28
arrest, order II.ii.67
artless, unskilful IV.v.19
as, according as, whenever I.iii.2
aspect, look, the way one looks II.ii.528
assay, attempt II.i.63, III.iii.69
   attack II.ii.71
   try to persuade (someone to do something) III.i.14
   try IV vii.152
assign (n.), fitting V.ii.142
assistant, available, at hand I.iii.3
associate, companion IV.iii.44
assurance, conveyance of lands by deed V.i.105
at, up to III.iv.210
attend, accompany III.iii.22
   wait for V.ii.181
attribute, reputation I.iv.22
audience, attention I.iii.93
audit, final reckoning III.iii.82
aught, anything I.v.86, III.i.97, IV.iii.57, IV.iv.5, V.ii.205
author, agent IV.v.76
authorities, positions of authority IV.ii.15
avouch, assurance I.i.57
ay, yes, ah III.iv.53, etc., p.xli

B

back, backing IV.vii.153
ban, curse III.ii.243
bar, exclude, reject I.ii.14
Barbary, the lands along the north coast of Africa V.ii 152

bare; a bare, nothing but a . . . III.i.76
barren, unprofitable, stupid III.ii.38
baseness, sign of vulgarity V.ii.34
batten, grow fat III.iv.68
battery, physical attack V.i.93
beam, the horizontal bar in a pair of scales IV.v.154
beard, confront II.ii.402
beaver, front part of a helmet used to cover the face I.ii.228
beck, call III.i.126
become, suit, befit IV.v.168, IV.vii.78, V.ii.384
bedded, in a smooth layer III.iv.122
beetle, overhang, I.iv.71
beg, beg for V.i.78
beggared (of), lacking (in) IV.v.88
beguile, cheat, while away (the time) III.ii.214
behaved; as he is behaved, according to his behaviour III.i.35
behove, be necessary for I.iii.97
belike, perhaps III.ii.130, III.ii.277
bend, incline (reflexive: *bend you*, incline yourself, make up your mind to . . .) I.ii.115
    turn III.iv.118
bent, extent II.ii.30
berattle, fill with din II.ii.329
beshrew, a curse on II.i.112
bespeak, speak to II.ii.140
best; in the best, at best I.v.27
bestow, place in position III.i.33
    dispose of III.iv.177
bestowed, lodged II.ii.497
beteem, allow to I.ii.141
betime, early IV.v.48
betimes, in good time V.ii.206
bettered, improved V.ii.245
bevy, flock V.ii.174
bias, uneveness in the form of a bowl to give it a curved motion II.i.63
bilbo, shackle V.ii.6
bisson, blinding(?) II.ii.481
blank (v.), turn pale III.ii.208
blank (n.), white centre of a target IV.i.42
blast, destroy (with a curse) I.i.127
    corrupt III.ii.243
    turn rotten, blight III.iv.66
blastment, blight I.iii.42
blazon, proclaiming I.v.21
blench, flinch II.ii.572
blister, sign III.iv.45
bloat, soft-bodied III.iv.183
blown, in blossom III.i.158, III.iii.81
board (v.), address II.ii.171
bode, forebode I.i.69
bodkin, dagger III.i.76
bodykins, (God's) 'little body', in an oath II.ii.503
bold; make so bold, venture V.ii.16
bonds, vows I.iii.130
botch up, patch up, piece together IV.v.10
bound, ready I.v.6

bourn, boundary, confines III.i.79
brainish, headstrong IV.i.11
brave, splendid II.ii.293
bravery, showy display V.ii.79
braze, harden like brass III.iv.38
brazen, made of brass I.i.73
breach, violation (of usual practice), neglect I.iv.16
breathe, speak III.iv.199
breed, kind III.ii.295
broker, go-between, especially in love-affairs I.iii.127
brooch, precious jewel IV.vii.93
bruit again, echo I.ii.127
brute, brutal III.ii.99
bug, bug-bear, terror V.ii.22
bulk, body II.i.94
business, do business, negotiate I.ii.37
but, just III.iv.209
    only IV.iii.34
button, bud I.iii.40
buzzer, rumour-monger IV.v.86
by and by, at once III.ii.356

C

calendar, directory V.ii.108
calm, settled IV.v.114
can, be skilled IV.vii.84
canker, worm which destroys buds and leaves I.iii.39
    diseased growth V.ii.69
canonized, buried according to the rule of the Church I.iv.47
capable of, able to appreciate III.ii.11
cap-a-pe, from head to foot I.ii.198
capital, punishable by death IV.vii.7
card, guide V.ii.108; *by the card*, very precisely V.i.123
carouse, drink a toast V.ii.271
carriage, import, exact terms (of an article) I.i.94
carry it away, win the fight II.ii.344
cart, chariot III.ii.143
carve, follow desires I.iii.20
cast, scheme II.i.114
cast, tinge of colour III.i.85
cataplasm, plaster IV.vii.143
cautel, piece of trickery I.iii.15
cease, passing-away III.iii.15
cellarage; in the cellarage, underground I.v.151
censure, judgement I.iii.69, III.ii.26
    opinion (not necessarily adverse) I.iv.35, III.ii.83
cerements, grave-clothes I.iv.48
chalice, cup IV.vii.160
chance (v.), happen II.ii.318
chance (n.), event V.ii.316
changeling, see note V.ii.53
chapless, without the lower jaw V.i.80

character (v.), engrave I.iii.59
character (n.), handwriting IV.vii.50
charge (v.), call upon to answer I.i.51
   command I.iii.135
charge (n.), importance V.ii.43
charge; of charge, costly IV.iv.47
chary, modest, particular I.iii.36
check at, abandon IV.vii.61
cheer, cheerfulness III.ii.152
cheer, fare, food and drink III.ii.207
chief, principally(?); see note I.iii.74
choler, acid disorder in the stomach III.ii.285
chop-fallen, dispirited V.i.173
chopine, shoe with a high heel II.ii.405
chorus, a speaker at a play who explains or
   comments on the action III.ii.231
chough, jackdaw V.ii.88
cicatrice, scar IV.iii.59
circumstance, formality I.v.127
   detail V.ii.2
circumstances, detailed evidence II.ii.158
circumvent, outwit V.i.73
cleave/cleft, split III.iv.157
clepe, call I.iv.19
climature, region I.i.125
close (v.), fall in, agree II.i.45
close (adj.), secret II.i.117
   confined in secret IV.vii.129
closely, secretly III.i.29
closet, private apartment III.iii.27
clouds, in clouds, aloof IV.v.85
clout, piece of cloth II.ii.481
clouts, clothes II.ii.364
Cock, God IV.v.60
cockle hat, pilgrim's hat IV.v.25
coil, turmoil III.i.67
coinage, fabrication III.iv.138
cold, chaste IV.vii.172
coldly set, treat with indifference IV.iii.61
collateral, indirect IV.v.200
colleagued, linked I.ii.21
collection, deduction, putting together by
   inference IV.v.9, hence knowledge V.ii.176
colour, disguise II.ii.275
commend, give warm regards, send greetings
   I.v.184, V.ii.169
comment, observation III.ii.75
commerce, friendly contact, intercourse
   III.i.110
commission, warrant III.iii.3
common, belonging to all mankind I.ii.72
commune, share IV.v.196
commutual, given and received by two
   people to and from each other III.ii.148
companions, accompaniments II.i.23
compass, range of musical notes III.ii.343
competent, sufficient, equal I.i.90
complexion, temperament I.iv.27
   natural appearance II.ii.430
   bodily constitution V.ii.98
comply, use the formalities of courtesy
   V.ii.173

compost, decayed vegetable matter used as
   manure III.iv.152
compulsatory, that cannot be avoided I.i.103
conceit, imagination II.ii.526, III.iv.115
   thoughts IV.v.44
   design V.ii.141
concernancy, import V.ii.119
concernings, matters III.iv.192
conclude on, decide III.iv.202
conclusions; try conclusions, experiment
   III.iv.196
condolement, sorrow I.ii.93
confederate, (adj.), relating to that which
   conspires; conspiring III.ii.241
confession, admission IV.vii.95
confine, place of confinement II.ii.244
confront, oppose and overcome III.iii.47
conjoined, taken together with III.iv.127
conjunctive, closely united IV.vii.14
conjuration, appeal V.ii.38
conjure, call upon earnestly II.ii.278
   influence (by magic) V.i.237
   earnestly request(?) IV.iii.63
conscience, conscious thought, reflection
   III.i.83
consequence, effect, conclusion II.i.45
consonancy, agreement II.ii.279
contagion, evil influence III.ii.364
   contagious thing, poison IV.vii.147
containing, important IV.v.83
contend, strive (of one side against another)
   IV.i.7
content, (impersonal verb) please III.i.24
   container IV.iv.64
continent, sum V.ii.109
contraction, engagement (to be married)
   III.iv.47
conversation, dealings with other people
   III.ii.51
conveyance, safe conduct IV.iv.3
convocation, assembly IV.iii.21
convoy, transport I.iii.3
cope with, meet III.ii.51
coronet, garland IV.vii.173
corse, dead body, corpse I.ii.105
cote, overtake II.ii.306
couch, lie hidden II.ii.429, V.i.202
counsel, secret thoughts III.ii.132
   secrets, confidence IV.ii.10
count, account, reckoning, trial IV.vii.17
countenance (v.), take into account(?) IV.i.32
   favour IV.ii.14, V.i.24
countenance (n.), favour I.iv.113
counter, running backwards IV.v.106
counterfeit, in a portrait III.iv.55
couple, include I.v.93
couplet, nestling V.i.268
cousin, close relative (not necessarily the
   child of an uncle or aunt) I.ii.117
cozen, cheat III.iv.78
cozenage, trickery V.ii.67
craft; in craft, by design III.iv.189

crants, garland v.i.213
credent, believing I.iii.30
crescent, growing I.iii.11
crib, food-trough v.ii.87
crowflower, crowfoot (a flower) IV.vii.170
crowner, coroner v.i.4
cry (n.), company, pack of hounds III.ii.261
cry (v., of dogs), bark IV.v.105
cuckold, a husband whose wife is unfaithful to him IV.v.115
cunning, skill II.ii.417, II.ii.565, IV.vii.155
curiously, minutely v.i.186
currents, (perhaps) courses; see note III.iii.57
custom, familiarity III.iv.38
cutpurse, thief III.iv.150

D

dally, flirt III.ii.233
  trifle v.ii.279
Danskers, Danes II.i.7
dear, precious III.ii.59
  deeply felt III.iv.192
dearest, most grievous I.ii.181
dearly, deeply IV.iii.40
debate, settle (by fighting) IV.iv.26
debatement, deliberation v.ii.45
deceived, mistaken II.ii.357
declension, decline II.ii.149
decline, sink I.v.50
  fall II.ii.453
  lean S.D., III.ii.p.113
defeat, destruction II.ii.545
defence, skill in self-defence, fencing IV.vii.97
definement, description v.ii.110
delated, clearly stated I.ii.38
deliver, recount I.ii.191
delivered, recounted I.ii.207
delve, dig III.iv.209
delver, digger v.i.12
demand, ask (questions) IV.v.126
demanded of, questioned by IV.ii.11
desert, what is deserved II.ii.502
designed, indicated I.i.94
desires, good wishes II.ii.60
desperation, extreme thoughts, thoughts of self-destruction I.iv.75
device, scheme III.ii.200
  contrivance IV.vii.63
diadem, crown III.iv.101
difference, distinguishing feature v.ii.106
digested, arranged II.ii.416
dire, dreadful III.ii.244
disappointed, unprepared I.v.77
disclose (v.), hatch v.i.268
disclose (n.), incubation, the result of hatching III.i.165
discomfort, grieve III.ii.154
discourse, familiar contact, friendly approach III.i.109
  powers of reasoning IV.iv.36

discourse of reason, faculty of reasoning I.ii.150
discovery, disclosure of a secret II.ii.288
disjoint, disorganized I.ii.20
dismal, sinister II.ii.431
dismantle, strip, deprive III.ii.266
dispatched, deprived I.v.75
disposition, feelings I.iv.55
  manner, behaviour I.v.172
  inclination III.i.12
distemper, derangement of mind II.ii.55
  bad mood III.ii.314
distempered, out of humour III.ii.283
distilled, melted, turned I.ii.202
distract, mad IV.v.2
distraction, derangement of the mind v.ii.212
distrust, worry about III.ii.153
divulging, becoming known IV.i.22
do (auxiliary verb) see p.xli
document, piece of instruction IV.v.174
dole, sorrow I.ii.13
don, put on IV.v.51
doublet, shirt II.i.77
doubt, suspect I.ii.254, II.ii.56, II.ii.116
  fear III.i.165
dout, put out ('do out') IV.vii.192
Down a-down, a ballad refrain IV.v.167
down-gyved, drop to the ankles II.i.79
drabbing, associating with women of bad reputation II.i.26
dread, revered II.ii.28, III.iv.109
drift, aims IV.vii.151
drift of circumstances, roundabout way of getting to the point (*drift*, purpose, what one is driving at) III.i.1
drive, rush at II.ii.447
drossy, frivolous v.ii.175
ducat, a gold coin III.iv.25
dup, open IV.v.52

E

eager, biting, sharp I.iv.2, I.v.69
eale, see note I.iv.36
ease; in ease, without difficulty, abundantly I.v.33
easiness, indifference v.i.62
ecstasy, state of frenzy, madness II.i.101, III.i.159, III.iv.139
edify, instruct v.ii.147
e'en for *even*, just now IV.iii.21
effect, result II.ii.101
  general drift v.ii.37
effects, serious intentions III.iv.130
eisel, vinegar v.i.257
eldest, oldest III.iii.37
election, choice III.ii.60
else, other IV.iii.22
embrace, welcome v.ii.234

emulate, ambitious I.i.83
enacture, fulfilment III.ii.185
encompassment, talking around a subject (instead of discussing it directly) II.i.10
encumbered, folded I.v.174
ends, destiny V.ii.10
enseamed, greased III.iv.93
entertainment, welcome V.ii.109
entreatment, interview I.iii.122
envious, spiteful IV.vii.174
enviously, angrily IV.v.6
equivocation, double-meaning V.i.124
ere, before IV.vi.13, V.ii.30
erring, straying I.i.154
escot, pay a reckoning (for) II.ii.333
espial, spy III.i.32
estate, social rank III.ii.246, V.i.201
  administration of government III.iii.5
estimation, reputation II.ii.322
eternal, revealing eternity, or things which are eternal I.v.21
  infernal V.ii.347
eterne, eternal II.ii.465
even, in exact agreement I.v.49
  just II.ii.282
  fellow V.i.25
even, e'en, indeed III.ii.50
ever, before, I.ii.182; see p.xlii
the Everlasting, God I.ii.131
evidence; give in evidence act as a witness III.iii.64
exception, disapproval V.ii.213
exclaim against, abuse II.ii.337
excrement, outgrowth (of the body) III.iv.122
exercise, activity, employment II.ii.290
  religious devotion III.i.45
exeunt, (Latin) they go out; frequently, in S.D's
exit, (Latin) he, she goes out; frequently, in S.D's
expel, keep out V.i.196
expostulate, discuss II.ii.86
express, well-made II.ii.298
extolment, praise V.ii.113
extorted, taken by force I.i.137
extravagant, wandering I.i.154
eyas, young, untrained hawk II.ii.327
eye, presence IV.iv.6
eyes, presence IV.vii.45

F

faculty, active quality, ability to do things II.ii.297
fain, glad, gladly, pleased II.ii.131, III.ii.214, IV.vii.191
fair, well V.ii.32
faithful, truthful II.ii.115
fall, turn out IV.vii.70
fall a-, begin II.ii.561
fall out, take place II.ii.127

fall to, begin II.i.89
false fire, gunfire without ammunition III.ii.250
familiar, friendly I.iii.61
fantastic, extravagant IV.vii.169
fantasy, fancy, trick of the imagination I.i.23, I.i.54
  whim of fancy IV.iv.61
fardel, burden III.i.76
farm, rent IV.iv.20
fashion, passing fancy I.iv.112 (see also I.iii.6)
  customary display (?) II.ii.353
  manner III.i.174
fast, suffer torment (?) I.v.11
fat, fatten IV.iii.22
favour, face, appearance V.i.175
fay, faith II.ii.260
fear (v.), be concerned about I.iii.16
  fear for IV.v.119
fear (n.), ground of fear I.iv.64
fearful, terrible I.i.149
fee, value I.iv.65
fee; in fee, freehold IV.iv.22
feeling, understandingly V.ii.107
fell, fierce II.ii.448, V.ii.61
fellowship, partnership III.ii.261
felly, outer circle of a wheel, or a piece of this circle II.ii.470
fetch, trick II.i.38
few; in few, in brief I.iii.126
fie upon it! a curse on it! II.ii.563
fine, refined IV.v.158
fine; in fine, finally V.ii.15
finger, steal V.ii.15
fit, for *befit*, be proper for, suit I.iii.25
fitness, readiness V.ii.185
fitted, agreeing IV.v.174
flaw, gusts of wind V.i.196
flood, sea I.iv.69
flourish, loud, showy noise S.D., I.iv.p.35
  a loud trumpet call S.D., III.ii.p.111
  verbal adornment V.ii.168
flush, full of life III.iii.81
fly, flee from IV.vi.21
foil, setting of a jewel V.ii.237
fond, fatuous I.v.99
foot; at foot, close behind IV.iii.53
for, as for I.ii.112, I.iii.5, I.iii.123, III.iv.173
  as regards IV.iii.39
  instead of V.i.211
forbear, leave alone V.i.254
fordo, destroy II.i.102, V.i.201
foresaid, mentioned before I.i.103
forgeries, false attributions II.i.20
forgery, invention IV.vii.89
form, image I.v.100
  behaviour III.i.152
forward, advanced, precocious I.iii.8
  ready prepared III.i.7
fouled, dirty II.i.70
frame, order III.ii.289

frankly, without restraint v.ii.235
free, innocent II.ii.537, III.ii.228
fret, a wire to guide the fingering of a stringed instrument III.ii.346
fretful, ill-tempered I.v.20
fretted, decorated with carved ornament (e.g. of a roof) II.ii.294
friending, friendliness I.v.186
front, forehead III.iv.57
function, action II.ii.529
fust, grow mouldy IV.iv.39

G

gage, pledge I.i.91
gain-giving, misgiving v.ii.198
gait, proceeding I.ii.31
   way of walking III.ii.30
gall, damage I.iii.39
   scrape, chafe, injure lightly, IV.vii.147, v.i.127
galled, sore from rubbing I.ii.155, III.ii.228
gambol, jump away III.iv.145
garb, way, style II.ii.354
gender, kind, sort IV.vii.18
general, common people, the public II.ii.413, II.ii.536
generous, well-bred I.iii.74
gentry, courtesy II.ii.22
   gentility v.ii.108
german, appropriate v.II.150
gib, cat III.iv. 191
Gis, Jesus IV.v.57
give o'er, stop III.ii.252
go to, an expression of mistrust or suspicion of what has just been said; 'get away with you! Nonsense!' I.iii.112, III.i.145, v.i.36
gorge, the contents of the stomach v.i.169
do grace, pay respects II.ii.53
grace, gratitude (for a favour) I.ii.124
grained, ingrained III.iv.91
grapple, see note I.iii.63
grate, vex III.i.3
green, raw, immature I.iii.101
greenly, unskilfully IV.v.79
greet, address by letter IV.vi.5
grief, cause of sorrow III.i.182
grizzled, grey I.ii.238
gross, vulgar IV.vii.171
groundling, spectator standing in the pit of the theatre III.ii.10
guard, defence position (in fencing) IV.vii.101
gules, red II.ii.432
gulf, whirlpool III.iii.16
guts, inner organs of the body III.iv.213
gyves, shackles IV.vii.21

H

habit, clothes, dress I.iii.70
hams, thighs II.ii.200
hand; bear in hand, delude II.ii.67

handsome, fitting II.ii.421
hap, happen I.ii.247
haply, perhaps III.i.170
   with luck IV.i.40
happily, perhaps I.i.134, II.ii.365
haps, what may happen, chance IV.iii.67
harbinger, herald I.i.122
hard upon, very closely after I.ii.178
hatchment, coat of arms IV.v.208
haunt, society of men IV.i.18
hautboy, oboe S.D., III.ii.p.113
have after, I will follow I.iv.89
havoc, slaughter without mercy v.ii.346
   (To cry 'havoc' was to give an army permission to pillage conquered territory)
head, hostile body of men IV.v.97
health, well-being I.iv.40
heavy, sorrowful III.iii.84
hebenon, see note I.v.62
hectic, wasting fever IV.iii.65
height; at height, to the utmost I.iv.21
help; at help, favourable IV.ii.43
hem, splutter, clear the throat IV.v.5
hent, perhaps for *hint*, opportunity III.iii.88
Hercules, a hero in Greek mythology I.ii.153
Herod, a ruler of the Jews; see note III.ii.13
hey-day, state of excitement III.iv.70
Hey non nonny, a meaningless ballad refrain IV.v.162
his, (sometimes) its e.g. III.iii.62
hoar, greyish-white IV.vii.168
hoise/hoist, blow into the air III.iv.208
hold, consider, take as, regard as I.iii.6, III.i.180
hold, bear, last (until) v.i.150
hold at, consider as IV.iii.57
hold off, keep silence, reserve one's thoughts II.ii.285
hold up, carry on v.i.27
home, to the utmost III.iii.29
honesty, what is proper, seemly II.ii.202
hoodman-blind, blindman's buff III.iv.78
how . . . soe'er, however I.v.170
hugger-mugger, secret IV.v.80
husband, use economically IV.v.135
husbandry, household management, I.iii.77
hush, quiet II.ii.461
Hymen, the god of marriage III.ii.147
Hyperion, a giant in Greek mythology; a Titan I.ii.140, III.iv.57
Hyrcanian beast, tiger II.ii.425

I

idle, mad III.ii.86
if, even if III.iv.161
'ild for yield, reward IV.v.41
ill-breeding, malevolent, making trouble IV.v.15
image, representation III.ii.225
impart, tell III.ii.308
impartment, communication I.iv.59

impasted, made into a paste II.ii.434
imperious, imperial V.i.193
implorator, solicitor I.iii.129
impone, perhaps for *impawn*, wager V.ii.141
import, relate to I.ii.23
    indicate, signify III.ii.130, IV.v.27, IV.vii.01
    set out, enumerate IV.iii.62
    concern deeply V.ii.21
important, urgent III.iv.109
imposthume, abscess IV.iv.27
impress, demand of compulsory service I.i.75
imputation, reputation V.ii.135
in, in the light of V.i.275
inapproved, untried I.i.96
incapable, unaware IV.vii.179
incensed, enraged V.ii.284
inclinations, character II.i.69
incorporal, without body III.iv.119
incorpse, make into a single body IV.vii.87
index, (perhaps) prologue; (or) list of sins III.iv.53
indifferent, ordinary II.ii.226
    moderately III.i.123
indifferently, somewhat III.ii.34
individable, indivisible, preserving the unity of space(?) II.ii.378
indued, endowed (with the right qualities) IV.vii.180
inexplicable, senseless III.ii.11
inform, bring charges (as in law) IV.iv.32
infusion, qualities 'infused' in a person V.ii.114
ingenious, lively, quick V.i.229
inheritance, possessions I.i.92
inhibition, withdrawal of permission II.ii.320
innovation, change for the worse II.ii.321
inoculate, engraft, place a shoot from one plant into another to produce a new growth III.i.119
insinuation, deliberate intrusion V.ii.59
instance, cause III.ii.170
    sample IV.v.159
interpret, give the dialogue (in a puppet show) III.ii.232
intil, into (dialect form) V.i.67
investments, clothes, outward appearance I.iii.128
inurned, buried I.iv.49
issue, outcome V.ii.72

J

jealousy, suspicion II.i.112
jig, short, lively comedy in rhyme II.ii.475, III.ii.117
jointress, widow who holds her husband's entire estate after his death I.i.9
journeyman, day-labourer III.ii.32
Jove, Jupiter, lord of heaven and of destiny in Latin mythology III.iv.57
jowl, throw V.i.70

jump upon, at exactly the same time as V.ii.357

K

keen, sharp, bitter III.ii.234
keep, stay, live II.i.8
kettle, kettle-drum V.ii.257
kibe, heel V.i.127
kin, related as a family member (see note I.ii.65), IV.ii.5
kindless, unnatural II.ii.555
knave, fellow V.i.70
knavish, wicked III.ii.226, IV.ii.21
know, acknowledge IV.vii.3

L

la, indeed IV.v.56
laboursome, laborious I.ii.59
lack, to be wanting I.v.187
lapse, allow to slip away III.iv.108
lard, enrich V.ii.20
larded, decked out IV.v.37
late; of late, recently II.ii.482
lay, song IV.vii.183
lay home, deal firmly III.iv.1
lay on, lay blame on (a person) IV.i.17
lean, depend on IV.iii.56
learn, teach V.ii.9
leave, cease, stop III.ii.162, III.iv.35, III.iv.67
    lose III.iv.92
lecture, instructions II.i.65
lend, give II.ii.435
leperous, causing leprosy I.v.64
let, hinder I.iv.85
    cause; *let to know* informed IV.vi.10
Lethe, waters of forgetfulness I.v.33
level, straight IV.i.42
    plain IV.v.148
levy, troop I.ii.31
lewdness, vice I.v.54
liberal, free-spoken IV.vii.171
    tasteful V.ii.145
liberty, deliverance III.ii.315
lief; have as lief, like it just as much as if . . . III.ii.3
liege, sovereign II.ii.43
liegeman, subject I.i.15
lighted, alighted, descended III.iv.60
like, likely I.ii.235
likes, pleases II.ii.80
limed, trapped III.iii.68
list (v.), listen I.iii.30, I.v.22
list for listed, wished, chose I.v.177
list (n.), boundary IV.v.95
livery, dress I.iv.32
living, lasting V.i.278
loggats, skittles V.i.83
loose, release II.ii.163
loth, reluctant S.D., III.ii.p.113
luxury, lust I.v.83

M

machine, body, bodily frame II.ii.124
maimed, defective v.i.199
mainly, greatly IV.vii.9
make, do I.ii.164, II.ii.265
manner, custom I.iv.15
margent, margin v.ii.148
mark, take notice IV.v.28
market, marketing, putting to the greatest profit IV.iv.34
marry, an oath; see p.xlii
Mars, the Roman god of war III.iv.58
mart, buying and selling I.i.74
marvellous, extremely III.ii.283
Mass! by the Holy mass! v.i.50
massy, massive III.iii.17
matin, morning I.v.89
matron, mother III.iv.84
matter, good sense IV.v.170
mazzard, head (used jokingly) v.i.81
means, way of access, way of getting (to) IV.vi.12
meats, food I.ii.179
meditation, thought I.v.30
meed, merit v.ii.136
meet, fitting, proper I.v.107, III.iii.31
melancholy, disposition to sadness; a 'humour' III.i.164 and note
mend one's pace, go faster v.i.52
Mercury, the herald of the gods in Roman mythology III.iv.59
mercy, i.e. merciful God I.v.169
mere, only I.iii.129
   complete v.i.265
merely, entirely I.ii.137
mess, companions at a meal v.ii.88
metal, material III.ii.103
methinks, it seems to me (that) I.ii.183, I.v.58, III.ii.218
methought, it seemed to me v.i.57
mettle, courage I.i.96
miching malicho, secret mischief (?) III.ii.129
might, could I.i.56
mine, fortification defended with explosives III.iv.209
moan, grief IV.v.192
model, counterpart v.ii.50
modesty, moderation II.ii.416, III.ii.19, v.i.187
moiety, share I.i.90
moor, wasteland III.iv.68
mope, act stupidly III.iv.82
moreover, besides (the fact that) II.ii.2
mortal, of life on earth III.i.67
   subject to death IV.v.157
   deadly IV.vii.142
mote, minute particle I.i.112
motion, impulses III.iv.73
   trained movement of the body IV.vii.101
   bodily exertion IV.vii.157
motive, incitement v.ii.227
mountebank, quack doctor IV.vii.141

mouth, shout III.ii.2
   proclaim in passionate speech v.i.264
mouths; make mouths at, mock at IV.iv.50
move, cause, bring about II.i.117, III.ii.170
   urge IV.v.8, S.D., v.ii.p.211
mow, grimace II.ii.347
muddied, disturbed IV.v.77
muddy-mettled, dull-spirited II.ii.541
murdering-piece, small cannon firing multiple shot IV.v.91
mutine, rebel III.iv.84
   mutineer v.ii.6

N

naked, destitute IV.vii.43
napkin, handkerchief v.II.270
native, closely related I.ii.47
   belonging to IV.vii.180
natural, see note I.v.25
nature, life I II.73
   natural feeling I.v.81
naught, wicked III.ii.136
nave, hub II.ii.471
nay, indeed, yes – confirming what has gone before I.iv.91
needs; will needs, must IV.v.3
negligence; give to negligence, treat with contempt IV.v.131
Neptune, Roman god of the sea III.ii.144
nerve, sinews I.iv.83
neutral, one who is unattached II.ii.456
nill, literally 'not will', i.e. does not want to v.i.15
Niobe, a queen in Greek mythology I.ii.149
no, nothing III.i.61
nomination, naming v.ii.124
nonce, occasion IV.vii.160
note, draw attention to the fact I.v.178
noted, particular II.i.23
nothing, not at all I.ii.41
   nonsense IV.v.7, IV.v.170
noyance, harm III.iii.13
numbers, verses II.ii.120

O

oblivion, forgetfulness IV.iv.40
obsequious, dutiful (in showing respect for the dead) I.ii 92
occasion, opportunity, the course of events I.iii.54
   favourable opportunity II.ii.16
occulted, hidden III.ii.76
occurrent, event v.ii.339
o'ercrow, overpower v.ii.335
o'er-raught, past tense of *over-reach*, overtake III.i.17
o'er-reach, get the better of v.i.72
o'er-sized covered so as to give a glassy, polished effect II.ii.437

o'erteemed, worn out by child-bearing
II.ii.483
ominous, ill-omened II.ii.429
once, ever I.v.121
operant, active III.ii.162
opinion, estimate of one's capabilities II.i.114
opposite, opponent V.ii.62
oppression, distress II.ii.552
or e'er, even before I.ii.147
orchard, garden I.v.35, I.v.59
ordinant, controlling V.ii.48
ore, gold IV.i.25
organ, voice II.ii.569
    means IV.vii.70
orison, prayer III.i.90
ostentation, pomp IV.v.209
overpeer, rise above IV.v.95

P

packing, plotting III.iv.212
paddock, toad III.iv.191
painted, feigned III.i.53
pajock, see note III.ii.268
pale, fence, boundary I.iv.28
pall, fail V.ii.9
palmy, triumphant I.i.113
pander, help to gratify (desires, etc.) III.iv.89
parle, (form of *parley*), discussion of terms
between sides after a battle I.i.62
part, accomplishment IV.vii.76
    (good) quality V.ii.109
partisan, long-handled spear with projecting
blade I.i.140
parts, accomplishment, talents IV.vi.73
party, man II.i.42
pass, passage II.ii.77
    thrust V.ii.61
    fencing bout V.ii.156
passage, occurrence IV.vii.112
passing, extremely II.ii.386
passion, strong feelings, e.g. of sympathy
II.ii.493
    suffering IV.v.182
pat, without delay III.iii.73
pate, head V.i.71
patience, permission III.ii.101
pause; give ... pause, make ... hesitate III.i.68
    in *pause*, hesitating III.iii.42
    hesitation IV.iii.9
peak, mope about II.ii.541
peculiar, private, particular III.iii.11
perchance, perhaps I.ii.241, etc.
perdition, loss V.ii.110
perdy, 'by God' III.ii.277
periwig-pated, their heads covered with wigs
III.ii.9
perpend, consider II.ii.105
persuade, urge to do (something) IV.v.165
peruse, examine IV.vii.136
petar, bomb III.iv.208
philosophy, natural science, knowledge ob-

tained by observation and reasoning, not
revelation I.v.167
Phoebus, the Greek god of the Sun III.ii.143
phrase, expression V.i.236
physic, the art of healing III.iii.96
picked, refined V.i.125
picker, that which steals III.ii.313
pigeon-livered, gentle, like a dove II.ii.551
pioner, miner, one who digs I.v.163
pious, religious II.ii.397
pirate, pirate ship IV.vi.13
pitch, high point III.i.86
pith, most vital part IV.i.23
plausive, acceptable I.iv.30
play, fence IV.vii.105
    contest V.ii.182
plurisy, excess IV.vii.117
pocky, rotten V.i.150
point; at point, correct in every detail I.ii.198
Polacks, Poles (the oldest editions have
pollax, Pole-axe, etc.) I.i.63
Polack, Pole, Polish IV.iv.23, V.ii.358
policy, prudence in state affairs II.ii.47
politic, politically minded (?) V.iii.21
politician, intriguer V.i.71
poll, head IV.v.190
poniard, dagger V.ii.142
porpentine, porcupine I.v.20
posset, curdle I.v.68
post, hasten I.ii.156
posy, motto (in a ring) III.ii.140
pox, 'a pox on it' III.ii.238
practice, evil contrivance, plot IV.vii.66,
IV.vii.138
practices, what is done II.ii.38
precedent, former III.iv.99
precurse, omen I.i.121
pregnant, apt II.ii.208
prenominate, already named II.i.43
prescript, command II.ii.142
presence, the people present V.ii.210
present, immediate IV.iii.64, V.i.276
presently, immediately II.ii.566, III.ii.44,
V.ii.375
presentment, presentation III.iv.55
pressure, impression I.v.100, III.ii.23
prevent, anticipate II.ii.287
primal, first III.iii.37
primy, in its prime I.iii.7
be privy to, have secret knowledge of I.i.133
probation, proof I.i.156
process, story I.v.37
process, proceedings, what goes on III.iii.29
    mandate IV.iii.62
prodigal, lavishly I.iii.116
progress, state journey (of a sovereign) IV.iii.30
prologue, the person who speaks the prologue III.ii.140
pronounce, proclaim III.ii.291
proof, experience III.ii.157
    proved strength (of arms or armour)
II.ii.465

proper, own v.ii.66
property, matter v.i.62
proportions, composition of an army (forces and supplies) i.ii.32
proposer, one who puts forward something for consideration ii.ii.281
protest, promise publicly iii.ii.218
protestation, affirmation S.D., iii.ii.p.113
provide, prepare (oneself) iii.iii.7
providence, foresight iv.i.17
Provincial rose, bow for a shoe tied in imitation of a rose iii.ii.260
puffed, proud i.iii.49
purgation, cleansing iii.ii.287
purge, discharge ii.ii.199
purport, meaning ii.i.81
purpose, resolution iii.ii.176
pursy, short-winded iii.iv.154
push, trial v.i.276
put on, communicated to i.iii.94
　　instigated v.ii.365
　　set to perform an office v.ii.379

Q

quaintly, cleverly ii.i.31
quality, profession ii.ii.333, ii.ii.409
quantity, proportion iii.ii.155
quarry, heap of deer killed at a hunt v.ii.346
quest for *inquest*, v.i.20
question, cause i.i.111
　　matter, part of the plot of a play iii.ii.39
questionable, that which compels question i.iv.43
quick (n.), tenderest part (of a wound) ii.ii.572, iv.vii.123
quick (adj.), alive v.i.115, v.i.232
quiddit, subtlety v.i.90
quietus, release from life iii.i.75
quillet, over-precise dwelling on the meaning of words v.i.90
quit, take vengeance on v.ii.68
quote, observe ii.i.111

R

raced, decorated with open-work iii.ii.261
rack, mass of cloud ii.ii.459
rank, foul ii.i.20
　　evil smelling iii.ii.242
ranker, higher iv.iv.22
rapier, light, slender sword iv.vii.98
ratifier, one who confirms iv.v.101
ravel out, disentangle iii.iv.187
raw, vulgar v.ii.120
reach; of reach, of ability, able ii.i.62
receive, consider ii.ii.414
reck, heed, take notice of i.iii.51
reckon, count ii.ii.121
recognizance, bond granting bail to a prisoner v.i.95

recorder, high-pitched pipe iii.ii.275, iii.ii.322
recover the wind (of me), get (me) to run into the wind iii.ii.323
recovery, deed of recovery v.i.96
rede, advice i.iii.51
re-deliver, give back iii.i.95
reechy, dirty iii.iv.185
reels, revels i.iv.9
regards, conditions ii.ii.79
region, heavens ii.ii.462
　　air ii.ii.553
relative, conclusive, relevant ii.ii.579
relish, trace iii.iii.92
remembrance, gift as a token of love iii.i.94
remiss, off one's guard iv.vii.134
remorse, pity ii.ii.466
remove, removal iv.v.77
removed, remote i.iv.61
repair, coming v.ii.201
repast, feed iv.v.144
replication, reply iv.ii.11
requite, reward i.ii.249
　　take revenge on iv.vii.139
resolute, daring adventurer i.i.98
resolve, dissolve i.ii.130
resort, visiting ii.ii.143
respect, consideration iii.i.68
responsive to, in keeping with v.ii.144
retrograde, contrary i.ii.114
revolution, change v.i.82
re-word, repeat in words (in the form of a summary) iii.iv.144
rhapsody, string (of words) iii.iv.49
Rhenish, German wine from the Rhinelands i.iv.10, v.i.162
rheum, tears ii.ii.481
ripe, mature iv.vii.63
robustious, violent iii.ii.9
romage, turmoil, bustle of activity i.i.107
rood; the rood, the holy cross iii.iv.15
round, directly ii.ii.139
　　plain-spoken iii.i.182, iii.iv.5
rouse, full draught of drink i.ii.127, i.iv.8
　　drinking bout ii.i.56
row, verse (?) ii.ii.397
rub, difficulty iii.i.65
rude, rough v.i.91
rugged, long-haired ii.ii.427
rule, command iv.vii.68

S

sable, black i.ii.240, ii.ii.427
　　rich, dark fur iii.ii.122, iv.vii.80
sallet, tasty morsel ii.ii.417
sanctuarize, give the protection of the church (to) iv.vii.127
sans, without iii.iv.80
satyr, a mythological creature i.ii.140
say, for *say right* v.i.23
'Sblood, 'By God's blood' (an oath) ii.ii.349
scan, consider iii.iii.75

scandal, see note I.iv.36, I.iv.38
scanter, less liberal I.iv.121
scarf, throw around the shoulders v.ii.13
sconce (v.), hide III.iv.4
sconce (n.), head v.i.92
scope, end in view III.ii.207
scourge, whip, instrument of punishment III.iv.176, IV.iii.6
scrimer, fencer IV.vii.100
se offendendo for *se defendendo*, in self-defence v.i.8
seal, confirm IV.vii.1
season (v.), moderate I.ii.190
  bring to maturity I.iii.81
  confirm (as being fully developed) III.ii.197
season (n.), time, opportunity I.iv.5, III.ii.241
seasoned, quite ready, mature III.iii.86
second, supporter IV.vii.153
secure (v.), keep safe I.v.113
secure (adj.), unsuspecting I.v.61
seized of, possessed of I.i.89
select, particular I.iii.74
sense, (sexual) desire III.iv.72
  finer feeling III.iv.162
  physical perception IV.v.152
  sensibility v.i.64
  intelligence v.i.229
sense; give sense, make aware of IV.iii.58
senseless, unfeeling, inanimate II.ii.449
sensible, involving the use of the senses I.i.57
sensibly, feelingly IV.v.147
sequent, following v.ii.54
sere, catch, part of a gun-lock to keep the gun ready for firing at any time II.ii.313
sergeant, sheriff's officer v.ii.318
service, provision I.iii.13
  order of dishes at a meal IV.iii.24
set down, write out II.ii.515
  decree III.i.168
severally, separately S.D., III.iv.p.147
shadow, image II.ii.254
shape, what is being contrived, plotted IV.vii.150
shark up, pick up at random I.i.98
sheen, light III.ii.145
shent, rebuked III.ii.372
shoon, shoes IV.v.26
short; keep short, keep from roaming freely IV.i.18
should, can IV.vii.48
shrewdly, sharply I.iv.1
shriving, confession v.ii.47
shuffling, trickery III.iii.61
siege, rank IV.vii.76
sift, study closely II.ii.58
simples, (medicinal) herbs IV.vii.144
singe, scorch v.i.263
sirrah, a word used to address servants; like 'Sir' v.i.107
sith, when IV.iv.45
  since IV.vii.3

sized, of a particular size III.ii.158
skirts, outlying regions I.i.97
skyish, reaching to the sky v.i.234
slander, misuse I.iii.133
sledded, carried on a sledge I.i.63
sliver, small branch IV.vii.174
smote, past tense of *smite*, strike I.i.63
so, so long as IV.vii.59
soft, gentle, noble v.ii.106
  go softly, stop I.v.58
  gently, III.i.88
softly, slowly IV.iv.8
soil, blemish I.iii.15
solicit, move v.i.340
something, rather III.ii.70
sore, heavy I.i.75
  grievous v.ii.212
sort, fit in I.i.109
  associate, put in the same class as II.ii.262
spendthrift, wasteful IV.vii.122
spill, destroy IV.v.20
spite, worrying situation I.v.189
splenitive, hot-headed v.i.242
sport, amusement III.ii.205
  good fun III.iv.207
springe, trap I.iii.115, v.ii.288
spurn, kick out at IV.v.6
stand, stop I.i.141
stand upon, make imperative for v.ii.63
start, jump III.ii.290
station, stance, way of standing III.iv.59
statist, statesman v.ii.33
statute, bond relating to debt v.i.94
stay, wait (for) III.iii.95, v.ii.24
  restrain IV.v.133
stay for, wait for I.iii.57
stay upon, wait for III.ii.101
sterling, of full value as currency I.iii.107
stick off, stand out v.ii.239
stiffly, strongly I.v.95
still, constantly, always I.v.188, III.ii.200, IV.vii.116, v.ii.41
stir, take offence IV.iv.54
stithy, workshop, smithy III.ii.80
stomach, (opportunity for showing) courage I.i.100
stop, hole in a pipe for playing music III.ii.67
stops, finger-holes in a pipe. III.ii.341
stoup, cup v.i.55
stowed, put away IV.ii.1
straight, at once v.i.3
strewments, strewn flowers v.i.214
strike, exert evil influence I.i.162
strumpet, immoral woman II.ii.468
stuck, thrust (in fencing) IV.vii.161
study, learn (by heart) II.ii.513
subject, people (of a country) I.i.72
subscribe, sign v.ii.52
sudden, immediate IV.vii.105
suddenly, very soon II.ii.211
suffer, allow v.i.91
sully, blemish II.i.39

supervise, first glance v.ii.23
suppliance, pastime i.iii.9
supply, aid ii.ii.24
supposal, opinion i.ii.18
suspiration, breathing i.ii.79
Switzers, bodyguard (of Swiss troops) iv.v.93
swoopstake, indiscriminately, 'swooping down on the whole stake of the game at once' iv.v.139
'*Swounds*, 'by God's wounds' (an oath) ii.ii.550

T

table, tablet i.v.98
take, strike with disease i.i.163
tame, easily controlled iii.iv.70
tardy, slow-moving iii.iv.107
tardy, inadequately, incompletely iii.ii.24
target, light shield ii.ii.311
tarre, provoke ii.ii.339
tax, censure i.iv.18, iii.ii.29
tell, count i.ii.236
Tellus, goddess of the Earth in Italian mythology
temper, mix v.ii.310
tenable, kept i.ii.246
tend, attend, wait i.iii.83, iv.ii.44
tend (on), follow iii.ii.194
tender, offer i.iii.99 be concerned about, look after i.iii.107
    care for iv.iii.40
tent, tight roll of linen used to search and clean a wound ii.ii.572
terms, condition iv.vii.26
tetter, eruption of the skin i.v.71
theme, matter v.i.247
thews, bodily strength, sinews i.iii.12
thou (etc.), you (etc.); see p.xlii
though, even if i.i.127
thought, sorrow iv.v.182
thrice, three times i.ii.200, iii.ii.243
thrift, material advantage, gain iii.ii.58, iii.ii.171
throughly, thoroughly iv.v.133
time, the present time, the world iii.i.70, iii.i.115
tinct, colour iii.iv.92
'*tis*, see p.xlii
to 't, to the point, then! v.i.49
toil (v.), tax (the strength of) i.i.72
toil (n.), net iii.ii.324
top, (1) high point; (2) forelock ii.ii.450
touch, concern i.iii.89
    fingering (of a musical instrument) iii.ii.332
touched, implicated iv.v.201
touching, concerning i.v.137
toward, about to happen i.i.77, v.ii.347
toy, trifling circumstance iv.v.18
trace, follow v.ii.116
traduce, criticize i.iv.18

trespass, crime iii.iv.147
trial, examination ii.ii.158
tribute, payment to an overlord as a mark of respect ii.ii.310
tributary, subject (one paying *tribute*) v.ii.39
trick (v.), mark, delineate (arms) ii.ii.432
trick (n.), way, habit iv.vii.188
tristful, sad iii.iv.51
tropically, (speaking) figuratively iii.ii.224
true-penny, honest fellow i.v.150
try, judge ii.ii.160
turn, purpose v.ii.171
turn Turk, Take a turn for the worse iii.ii.260
twain, two iii.ii.216, iii.iv.157
twice, for the second time ii.ii.366
tyrannous, cruel ii.ii.435

U

umbrage, shadow v.ii.116
unaneled, unanointed; without the sacrament of extreme unction i.v.77
unbated, not blunted (with a button on the end) iv.vii.138
unbraced, undone ii.i.77
uncharge, not charge (anyone with) iv.vii.66
unction, ointment iii.iv.146, iv.vii.141
undo, ruin v.i.124
unfellowed, matchless v.ii.136
ungalled, uninjured iii.ii.256
ungored, uninjured v.ii.232
ungracious, profane, graceless i.iii.47
unhouseled, not having taken the sacrament in the mass i.v.77
union, pearl v.ii.254
unkennel, reveal iii.ii.77
unlimited, not limited to the unities of time and place ii.ii.379
unmannerly, unfitting, inappropriate iii.ii.325
unnerved, weak ii.ii.449
unpregnant, not stirred ii.ii.542
unproportioned, ill-considered i.iii.60
unreclaimed, untamed ii.i.34
unshaped, unformed, artless iv.v.8
unsifted, inexperienced i.iii.102
unsinewed, weak iv.vii.10
unskilful, uneducated iii.ii.25
unsmirched, clean-skinned iv.v.116
untimely, inappropriately iv.i.40
unvalued, of no importance i.iii.19
upshot, conclusion v.ii.366
upspring, wild dance (?) i.iv.9
use (v.), make a practice of doing iii.ii.5
use (n.), treat v.i.270
    custom iii.iv.169
used, treated ii.ii.498
uses, ways i.ii.134
usurp, encroach upon i.i.46
    exert an evil influence iii.ii.245

V

vacancy, empty space III.iv.118
valanced fringed (with a beard) II.ii.401
validity, strength III ii.177
vantage; *of vantage*, besides, in addition
III.III 11
vantage, favourable opportunity v.ii.372
variable, various III.i.171
ventages, holes in a musical pipe for covering
with the fingers III.ii.333
verity, truthfulness v.ii.113
Vice, a stock character in morality plays; see
note III.iv.99
virtue, essential power IV.v.152
    good quality IV.vii.144
visage, face III.iii.47, III.iv.51
voice, opinion I.iii.23, v.ii.231
    support III.ii.318
    vote v.ii.338
voucher, statement as to entitlement to the
ownership of land v.i.95
vouchsafe, be kind enough to allow . . .
III.ii.279

W

wag, move v.i.248
wait upon, accompany II.ii.261
wake, stay up late revelling I.iv.8
wan, turn pale, II.ii.527
want, lack, be without I.ii.150, III.iv.131
wanton, weakling, effeminate man v.ii.281
ward, prison cell II.ii.244
warrant; *of warrant*, permitted, warranted
II.i.38
warranty, authorization v.i.208
wassail, revelry I.iv.9
watch, state of wakefulness II.ii.148
wax, become, grow, I.iii.12, I.iv.87, III.i.102
weal, welfare III.iii.14

weed, plant I.v.32
    garment IV.vii.80
    wild flower IV.vii.173
weigh, consider, take into consideration
I.iii.17, I.iii 29, IV.iii.6
what?, how? I.ii.229
whether, *whe'r*, (a word to introduce a general
question) II.ii.494
whisper, rumour I.i.80
wholesome, healthy III.ii.245
    reasonable III.ii.301
whoreson, a swear-word, 'son of a whore'
v.i.156
windlasses, roundabout ways II.i.63
wish, hope III.i.42
wit, intelligence II.ii.90
with, by IV.vii.32
withal, with II.ii.216
wither, neck-joints (of a horse) III.ii.229
without, outside IV.iii.14, IV.iv.28, IV.v.109
woe is me, alas III.ii.151
woman, womanishness IV.vii.190
wonder, shocked surprise IV.v.85
wonder-wounded, struck with amazement
v.i.238
wont; *were wont*, used v.i.172
woo't, for *wouldst thou*, would you v.i.256
word, watch-word I.v.110
wot, knows II.ii.394
woundless, that cannot be wounded IV.i.44
wrack, destroy II.i.112
writ, piece of writing v.ii.51

Y

yaw, go along unsteadily v.ii.112
yesty, foamy, superficial v.ii.176
yet, still, see p.xliii
yield, give out IV.v.11
yielding, consent I.iii.23
yonder, that . . . over there III.ii.350